Story
of the
Century

Centennial
100
State College · Pennsylvania
1 8 9 6 ~ 1 9 9 6

Story of the Century: The Borough of State College, Pennsylvania © 1995 by The Barash Group, State College, Pennsylvania,
and The Borough of State College, Pennsylvania, publishers.

Printed in State College, Pennsylvania, USA, by Jostens Printing and Publishing,
401 Science Park Road, State College, Pennsylvania 16801.
Cover is Silver Kivar material with silver foil. Dust jacket is printed on 100# Mead Offset Enamel gloss
with 1.5 mil film lamination. Text pages are printed on 80# Mead Moistrite Matte.

Published by The Borough of State College, 118 South Fraser Street, State College, Pennsylvania 16801,
in cooperation with The Barash Group, 403 South Allen Street, State College, Pennsylvania 16801.

Library of Congress Catalog Card Number:
95-78927

ISBN number 0-9647274-3-9

Story of the Century

JO CHESWORTH

The Borough of

STATE COLLEGE • PENNSYLVANIA

1896 – 1996

Published by
The Borough of State College, Pennsylvania,
in cooperation with
The Barash Group

Preface

Had you lived in State College in 1896, the year our village became a borough, you would have been amazed by the marvelous electric stoves just introduced — but it would be years before you'd use electric washers, vacuum cleaners, and automatic toasters. There were no airplanes then, no radios, TVs, talking movies, or electric razors, no nylon stockings or helicopters, and certainly no computers.

This book chronicles the people, places, events, and milestones in our town's history in its first hundred years. But it cannot cover all inventions, innovations, and intrigues; it cannot mention all clubs, companies, or occasions; and it cannot include names of all the families this town has known. A tome such as that would be an unabridged index of just names and facts.

I've tried to make this history of State College interesting and enjoyable for you, the reader. It will show you how our town came to be and what life was like here during the past century, with some mention of what went on here before there *was* a State College.

This project, which began for me in February 1992, has been the most demanding, detailed writing I've ever done, but it has given me my greatest good feeling of accomplishment. It could not have happened without the help of the Centennial Book Committee — John Brutzman, Anita Genger, Nadine Kofman, and Carolyn Smith — and of its primary editor, Whit Yeagley, a State College native who has been improving my writing since 1969. My thanks to Carolyn and Whit for taking charge of the illustrations, to Carl von Wodtke and Nancy Folkenroth for writing the advertorials, to Chip Mock for making everything look so good, and to Lee Stout and his staff of the University Archives in Pattee Library for their invaluable assistance. I also am indebted to Mimi Fredman, who has been a friend and supporter for nearly three decades.

Story of the Century has been written for them and for everyone who has ever called State College "home" — and for posterity.

Jo Chesworth
June 1995

Table of Contents

CHAPTER ONE

Beginnings

State College officially became a borough on August 29, 1896. But if William Frear, a chemist at Penn State's Agricultural Experiment Station, had not been sick with the flu four years earlier, our town would have become a borough in 1892. And its name might have been College Park. Or even University Heights.

Petitions had been gathered in late 1891 with the intent of presenting them to the Centre County Court of Quarter Sessions when it traditionally convened in Bellefonte on the fourth Monday of January. One petition bore forty-eight signatures of property owners within the borough limits described but with the borough names of both State College and College Park scratched out; two petitions for College Park bore a total of twenty-six signatures.

However, no one filed the petitions with a notary public or the court clerk before the court convened, evidently earlier than Frear had thought. As he wrote in a letter dated January 18, 1892, the third Monday, "I had somehow gotten the idea that court would not sit until next week; the others here were waiting upon me to act. I was confined to my room by La Grippe, only getting out last Saturday. And consequently I was unable to look after the matter."

His letter, to General James A. Beaver, former governor, Penn State trustee, and partner in the Bellefonte law firm that had run the required legal notices in *The Democratic Watchman* newspaper announcing the proposal for becoming a borough, told of other problems. Professor Louis Barnard had failed to make a new survey of borough boundaries on time. And some property owners were unhappy that their land was inside the proposed borough

limits while others were unhappy that their land was not. So the whole idea rested until 1895.

Then, after several angry meetings among residents and with the officials of College Township, to whom the villagers paid taxes, the proposal came up again. And again, not everyone agreed with seceding from the township and becoming a borough, so tempers flared. But this time the petitioners did everything right.

According to law, there could be no more than ninety property owners within the proposed borough limits; four-fifths of them had to sign a petition requesting borough status before the next session of court, in this case February 5, 1896; and at least sixty signers had to be voters in the existing municipality, College Township. It was also necessary to publish legal notices for thirty days prior to the fourth Monday in August, when the court would convene for the fall, and if no exceptions to the proposal had been filed, the village would be declared a borough.

The petition was signed by seventy-five property owners — twelve of them women and the rest voters (of course, women had not been franchised yet). John N. Krumrine and Albert Emerick appeared before William S. Harter, justice of the peace, and swore that all the criteria had been met, and the court accepted the petition on April 27. T. H. Harter, editor and proprietor of the *Keystone Weekly Gazette*, swore that notices had been published in his newspaper six times between July 17 and August 21, and no one filed an exception.

Even the boundaries had caused no argument this time, as *The Democratic Watchman* reported on February 21: "The line of the proposed borough was run the early

William Frear was asked in 1891 by residents to present their petitions for designation as a borough to the January '92 Quarter Sessions Court. But Dr. Frear disappointed the signatories — George Atherton, Edwin Sparks, and "Swampy" Pond among them — by getting sick when he was to be in court.

part of the week, and it pleased most everyone."

However, nearly six months before the court decree came down, a battle did ensue, as covered by the *Watchman* of March 6: "Thinking that possibly the name of State College, under which the thrifty village had prospered ever since its size warranted a name, would not be in keeping with the new dignity of boroughhood, some of the people began talking of a new name for it. Some thought that University Heights, University Place, Barrensville, Irvinsville, or State Centre would, any one of them, be better than its present name. Accordingly a public meeting was called in the school house, last Saturday night, to discuss the matter. Most of the property holders were there or had representatives in attendance and quite a lively meeting was the result. 'The campus,'

by which the men attached to the College are familiarly known, favored a change, while most of the old residents were satisfied to leave it as it had been. A vote followed in which State College received 28; University Heights, 24; and State Centre, 1." There was no mention of College Park this time.

"Old residents" was hardly descriptive of State College people of that time, since the college and the town had been in existence only about forty years, and the first European settlers had arrived in the area barely 100 years before.

Reportedly, the first man other than a Shawanese or a Delaware to see the future home of State College was Capt. James Potter who was traveling through in 1764. He didn't stay then, but he did come back, to Penns

Valley, after the Revolutionary War, just as many people did who bought up acreage in "the West," generally in 300-acre tracts. It was also common for buyers to have second thoughts and sell their acres to more adventurous souls willing to start life anew in the wilderness of Central Pennsylvania.

Nittany Valley and its surrounding mountains then were a lush forest of hardwoods — beech, ash, maple, oak — as well as hemlocks and soft pines, inhabited by a marvelous mix of animals, including black bears, wolves, whitetail deer, mountain lions, pheasants, quail, and grouse. Crystal-clear streams abounding in trout tumbled down from the mountains.

The Valley and its most famous landmark, Mount Nittany, are named for the mythical Princess Nita-Nee, a Lenni-Lenape of the Delaware tribe who, according to legend, once lived where State College is now. The earliest record of the word Nittany is found in an Indian deed to the proprietaries of Pennsylvania dated September 5, 1768, in which "the end of Nittany Mountain" is given as a boundary point.

Actual Indians who were known to have lived nearby were Bald Eagle, a Munsee chief of the Lenni-Lenapes, and James Logan, chief of the Mingoes, of the Iroquois Nation. In State College the two have been commemorated with Waupelani Drive, a spelling variation on Bald Eagle's Indian name, and Logan Avenue.

The first European to settle in what is now the 152 square miles of the Centre Region (State College and the five surrounding townships — College, Ferguson, Halfmoon, Harris, and Patton) was Abraham Elder, who came to what is now Stormstown in 1784. In 1786, Robert Moore, adopted son of an Indian warrior, became the first permanent settler in College Township, followed by Jacob Houser (1788), David Whitehill (1789), and Christian Dale (1790). Thomas Ferguson came to Pine Grove Mills in 1791. David Boal started the Harris Township village that bears his name in 1798, although it was first called Springfield. Bellefonte was founded in 1795 and became the county seat in 1800 when Centre County was formed from parts of Huntingdon, Mifflin, and Northumberland counties. Among other towns that preceded State College, boomed for some time but later declined, were Rock, Centre Furnace, and Millbrook.

The forests were broken by only a few Indian trails that followed streams like Buffalo Run and Spring Creek, so trees had to be felled and brush cleared before houses and roads could be built and crops planted. And occasionally settlers had to contend with what they called "panthers" — mountain lions that roamed the woodlands and trails. Much later this tawny beast would come to be Penn State's athletic symbol, after the beasts themselves became extinct in this area.

One panther story told in *History of Centre and Clinton Counties, Pennsylvania* by John Blair Linn took place in 1823 in present-day College Township. Patrick Cambridge, a Bellefonte storekeeper, was riding home from "the end of the mountain" — Lemont — after an evening of drinking with friends. "Full of spirits and warmed with a beverage that puts to shame the best liquors of our day," Linn wrote in 1883, "Patrick was happy and tuneful. Suddenly, in the midst of one of his wildest snatches of song, he was startled by an unearthly scream, and before he could collect his scattered senses he imagines the hand of death is upon him. Another scream, and a heavy weight drops on the horse, but with one plunge, the panther is thrown off, but not before relieving Patrick of part of his coat and pants, and the mare of some of her flesh. The storekeeper lived long to tell admiring crowds of children the tale of his wonderful escape."

Known today as "Lion Country" because of Penn State's athletic successes, this area was literally "Iron Country" for the first fifty years of the nineteenth century. Juniata Iron, reputedly the purest in America, was made here as late as the 1920s. But the boom times were the 1790s to the late 1850s.

In 1792, the first charcoal iron furnace in Centre County was put to blast at Centre Furnace, about a mile east of what is now downtown State College, by Colonel John Patton and his partner, Colonel Samuel Miles, Patton's commanding officer during the Revolutionary War. Remaining today along East College Avenue are a stone furnace stack, a brick ironmaster's mansion just east of Porter Road, and a handful of small houses along the stream that comes from Thompson Spring near the Duck Pond.

In this once-thriving community as much as 1,300 tons of iron were produced every year from 1792 to 1809 and again from 1826 to 1858. This place was home to fifty families who worked at the furnace and shopped at the only store — the company store — although the town later acquired a bank, post office, sawmill, lime kiln, and a flour mill as well as a church.

One of Pennsylvania's richest men, Colonel Miles helped to build Fort Augusta at Sunbury in 1756 and was the first mayor of Philadelphia, when it was the nation's capital during George Washington's first year as president. Miles never lived in Centre County, but Colonel Patton, for whom the township north of State College is named, did, and was the first ironmaster of Centre Furnace.

Like the cotton plantations of the South, Centre Furnace was an "iron plantation" with life centering around the "Big House," home of the ironmaster. Here, in 1795, Colonel Patton entertained Charles Maurice de Talleyrand-Perigord during the French statesman's exile in the United States. Sixty years later, in 1855, the house was the scene of a dinner party hosted by Moses and Mary Thompson, which significantly influenced the final decision to locate The Farmers' High School in Centre County.

Patton knew that to make iron it was necessary to have vast amounts of timber, easily mined ore deposits, and a stream powerful enough to operate the furnace bellows to keep a fire burning. By 1789, when Colonel Patton arrived, he, Miles, and Miles' sons and brother had bought

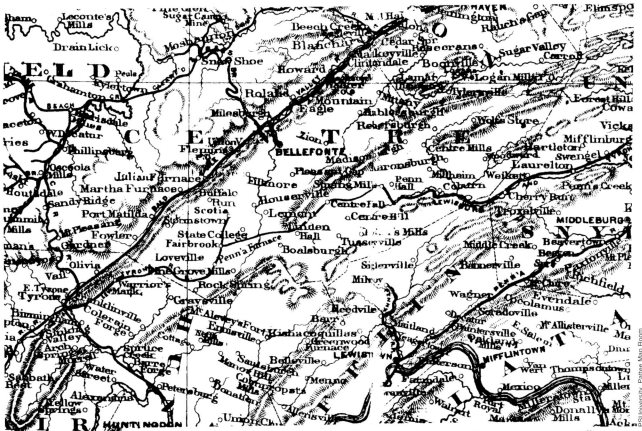

The town's post office took the name "State College" in 1874 when the Agricultural College became The Pennsylvania State College. Note, in this 1877 map, the spelling of Aaronsburgh, Boalsburgh, Hublersburgh, Madisonburgh, Milesburgh, and Rebersburgh.

Centre Furnace and its ironmaster's mansion and assorted outbuildings on either side of today's Porter Road supported a town of fifty families into the 1850s. There was a company store, a bank, post office, sawmill, brick and lime kilns, flour mill, a school, and a church.

8,000 acres of what would become "Centre Furnace lands," and within three years the mansion house was built and rude log houses for workers were erected, a company store was in operation, and the furnace was put to blast.

Tons of iron ore embedded in dirt and clay were surface-mined and hauled from Gatesburg to be washed in the stream at Centre Furnace. Acres of hardwood trees were cut and charred on Tussey Mountain and carted, often still aglow with combustion, to the furnace in mule-drawn wagons. The charcoal and ore then were fed into the top of the furnace stack and roasted for a week or two until molten iron could be tapped from the bottom and directed into sand or dirt troughs where it cooled, forming lumps resembling suckling pigs, hence "pig iron."

As was typical of these early furnaces, no facilities were available at Centre Furnace to form the pigs into bars, so the iron was carted to Gen. Philip Benner's forge at Rock where it was cast into 250-pound U-shaped bars, put over the backs of mules, and packed by Indian trail to Pittsburgh.

Rock lies between present-day Houserville and the University Park Airport, on the banks of Spring Creek where a massive limestone cliff towers above the rushing stream, near a bridge leading to Benner Springs Fish Hatchery. Nothing remains except the name of the road to give the slightest indication that in the early nineteenth century Rock was a town of more than 250 inhabitants and a leading producer of Juniata Iron ingots.

Many cold-blast furnaces — and there were about a

dozen in operation in Centre County in 1836 — required limestone as a flux to fuse the iron particles, separating them from impurities, but the local ore was of such high quality that no limestone was ever used at Centre Furnace. Even so, by 1858, new anthracite blast furnaces in other parts of Pennsylvania forced Centre Furnace to cease operations, not because an anthracite furnace could make a better product — it didn't — but because the supply of charcoal-producing timber was nearly exhausted.

It took more than three tons of ore and seven cords of wood to produce a ton of metal. To give an idea of the timber consumption, the amount of wood used at Centre Furnace in three years would "pave" Interstate-80 from the Ohio to the New Jersey border with a hardwood floor one inch thick! Because so much wood was required to produce the needed charcoal, by the mid-1800s the mountains in this area were virtually bare.

Although Patton and Miles were the first owners, the longest and most successful operation of Centre Furnace came during the tenure of General James Irvin, merchant and grain dealer of Oak Hall. Colonel Patton died in 1802, Colonel Miles in 1805, and although Miles' sons attempted to keep the furnace operating, they were forced to shut down in 1809. Then in 1826, one son, John, in partnership with his son-in-law, Joseph Green, reopened the furnace only to sell out two years later to father and son John and James Irvin and their partner, William Houston.

Houston lived in the mansion house and managed the furnace operations at a salary of $1,400 a year until 1838, when James Irvin bought his interest. Most employees earned from $18 to $30 per month — some even less since "getting the work done for the lowest wage possible" was the rule. But if laborers at Centre Furnace received a salary each month, they actually cleared only a few dollars a year because they were usually indebted to the company store for as much, if not more, than their monthly wages.

In his 1927 Penn State master's thesis, "Centre Furnace, a Chapter in the History of Juniata Iron," Sylvester K. Stevens, later to be executive director of the Pennsylvania Historical and Museum Commission, wrote that an employee could buy "100 pounds of flour for $3; butter for 12-1/2 cents a pound; beef at 5 cents a pound and pork at 7-1/2 cents." Cheese, onions, molasses, potatoes, apples, sugar, coffee, and tea were available as well as candlewicking and sperm oil, yard goods, drugs and patent medicines, eyeglasses, clocks, razors, toothbrushes, tin lamps, and palm leaf fans. The store even sold furniture, tableware, and all necessary equipment to furnish an employee's cabin home.

For the "dandies" there were such luxuries as silk handkerchiefs at $1 each — and a number of them were sold — silk hats at $5, and velvet vests at $7.50. If an employee wanted a little wine "for medicinal purposes," the store could provide that, too, selling wine at 50 cents a quart or whiskey at 75 cents a gallon. With Centre Furnace farms producing fruits, vegetables, and grain, there was little need for anyone to ever travel from this self-contained community.

In 1842, James Irvin sold a half interest in Centre Furnace to his brother-in-law, Moses Thompson. Moses had been born in 1810 in a log cabin on his father's farm "near the Presbyterian Church on Slab Cabin Branch," near the present-day Centre Hills Country Club. In 1814 his father completed "a substantial stone residence about 100 yards north of the log house by the side of the Bellefonte to Huntingdon Turnpike." The home, called "Plum Bottom," has been owned by the Gordon D. Kissinger family since 1946.

When Moses was twenty-two his father died, and he took over entire charge of the farm until his marriage in 1838 to Mary Irvin, James's sister. He and Mary lived on a farm near the Oak Hall mill, then in 1842 moved into the Centre Furnace mansion when Moses went into partnership with Irvin.

Irvin owned interests in several Centre County iron furnaces, including Hecla, Martha, and Julian, the latter named for his wife, Juliana Gregg. Because he and Moses were part owners of the Milesburg Iron Works, most pig iron made at Centre Furnace went to Milesburg. Here it was either manufactured or loaded on canal boats and sent to market as raw product. By this time there was also a casting shed at Centre Furnace where two-ton stoves and ten-pound skillets were made as well as castings "for other furnaces and sundry people."

Since transporting iron to market was a problem from remote Centre County, both Irvin and Thompson donated money for the construction of the Bald Eagle Valley Canal, the Bald Eagle Valley Railroad, and various roads and turnpikes in the vicinity. In addition, Irvin served in the U. S. Congress from 1840 to 1845 to protect his iron interests by proposing and voting for the imposition of high tariffs on iron imported from Europe.

Thompson never ran for political office but was a shrewd enough businessman to survive the Panic of 1857 that spelled financial ruin for so many people, including James Irvin, who died childless soon after in 1862. Thompson became sole owner of Centre Furnace in 1865, and in 1882 it was said of him by historian John Blair Linn: "Moses Thompson is one of the county's eminently successful businessmen, having started with only a one-seventh interest in his father's farm and without speculation, becoming the largest land owner in Centre County, owning, among other tracts, 6,000 acres of valuable farm land in the heart of the valley. He avoided disaster in 1857 by just exercising rare common sense, industry, and economy coupled with the courage to venture and the patience to wait."

Before the financial panic, however, Irvin and Thompson had attended a meeting of the Centre County Agricultural Society in January 1855, and had been asked to support the Pennsylvania Agricultural Society's proposition "That the establishment of an Agricultural High School for the education of farmers at an expense within the means of the great majority of the agricultural community is greatly to be desired . . ." This was the gleam in the eye that would become Penn State — and State College.

James A. Beaver, Bellefonte attorney, enlisted in the Union army when the Civil War began, and was discharged a Brigadier General in 1864. He was twice president of Penn State's board of trustees — 1874-82 and 1898-1914 — and was governor of Pennsylvania from 1887 to 1891. He was acting president of the college after Atherton's death and before Edwin Sparks arrived. Beaver Avenue and Beaver Stadium now honor him.

James Irvin, prosperous owner of iron works, and Moses Thompson, his brother-in-law, offered 200 acres of Centre Furnace land for the planned Farmers' High School. Years later, Thompson's granddaughter, Mary Irvin Thomas-Stahle, said State College should be named Centre Furnace. "After all," she pointed out, "Centre Furnace was here before State College, and if it hadn't been for Centre Furnace, there never would have been a State College!"

Just 22 when his father died, Moses Thompson operated the family farm until 1838 when he married James Irvin's sister Mary. The couple moved to a farm near the Oak Hall mill, then in 1842 moved into the Centre Furnace mansion when Moses became a partner with Irvin.

These Thompson family ladies enjoyed an 1890s summer day at Centre Furnace.
About 100 years later, the ironmaster's mansion became home to the Centre County Historical Society.

11

The Village Spawns a College & Vice Versa

he decline of the charcoal-iron industry in the 1850s was followed by the rise of a new, destined-to-grow venture to stoke the local economy — higher education — and, along with it, the village that became State College.

In January 1851 the new Pennsylvania State Agricultural Society held its first meeting in Harrisburg and established two major objectives: to sponsor a statewide farm fair in the capital every January and to create a state-subsidized school especially for sons of farmers. The group elected Judge Frederick Watts of Carlisle as president and charged his close friend Hugh N. McAllister, a Bellefonte attorney, to help set up a chapter in every county. Farmers could get together not only to exchange information about seeds, animal breeding, and new mechanical devices for planting, harvesting, and processing crops, but also to voice support for the farm-school idea.

Governor William Bigler gave strong endorsement for a farmers' school in 1853. The following year the general assembly passed an act establishing "The Farmers' High School" and a sixty-member board of trustees that included presidents of all county agricultural societies. They forgot only one thing — funding for it.

Just a handful of trustees came to two meetings that summer of 1854, so, in the absence of a quorum, Judge Watts formed a committee to work for a new charter that provided for state funds and a smaller board — four ex officio members and nine to be elected by the agricultural society. The committee also invited proposals for a location for the new school.

Encouraged by county societies, lawmakers passed the new charter, which Governor James Pollock signed on February 22, 1855. In a letter dated that same day General James Irvin offered to donate 200 acres of Centre Furnace farmlands for the new school. By their June meeting the trustees had received similar bids from Erie and Blair Counties, while proposals to sell 600 and 2,000 acres, respectively, came from Allegheny County and Perry County.

A review committee headed by Governor Pollock and Judge Watts, now chairman of the new board of trustees, visited each site to prepare their recommendation. They came to Centre County to inspect the land on June 26, and the more-than-500-member county agricultural society, headed by George Boal, arranged a gala welcome for them, including a sumptuous dinner for 150 people at Moses and Mary Thompson's home at Centre Furnace. The committee was impressed by the large turnout of local people and the enthusiastic support of such notables as Irvin, Thompson, Boal, McAllister, former U.S. Senator Andrew Gregg, Judge James T. Hale, Andrew Gregg Curtin — secretary of the commonwealth who would become governor in 1861 — and horticulturist and teacher William G. Waring.

At their July meeting, though, the board asked for more offers, and three more counties — Franklin, Dauphin, and Huntingdon — entered the contest. So General Irvin upped his bid, offering another 200 acres at $60 per acre, and citizens of Centre and Huntingdon Counties pledged $10,000. Blair County promptly matched both the land and money offers. The clincher came at the September meeting when Irvin, McAllister, and Curtin personally

Allen Street, looking South from Entrance to Campus, State College, Pa.

Jack's Road House in 1855 became the village Hotel by 1874, then, the College Inn, Nittany Inn, State College Hotel, and, finally, Hotel State College.

William G. Waring, first staff member of the Farmer's High School, has a State College street and a Penn State dining hall named for him.

Evan Pugh, first president of what would become Penn State, died at age 36, less than three months after marrying Bellefonte resident Rebecca Valentine.

guaranteed the $10,000 pledges. The board voted and Centre County came out on top.

The winning location for the education of farmers had many appealing features. For one, it was politically safe, being about equidistant from the voting strongholds of Philadelphia and Pittsburgh. Some twenty miles from the Pennsylvania Railroad at Spruce Creek, it also was far removed from city life and, as one man put it, "Boys had better be away from the temptations and annoyances peculiar to railroads whilst acquiring education."

The board of trustees accepted plans for a main building designed by Hugh McAllister and a barn designed by Judge Watts, and asked for a $50,000 construction appropriation from the legislature. In May 1857, lawmakers finally got around to passing the first appropriation — $25,000 outright and the promise of an equal sum if additional subscriptions were raised to

match it, a common practice in the early financing of public higher education. The campaign for matching funds was successful, and a construction contract of $55,000 was let.

But then the financial panic of 1857 and severe crop failures struck the commonwealth. When pledges went unpaid and building costs rose, the fledgling institution was kept going through the generosity of a few friends and trustees like Watts and McAllister, who made personal loans in emergencies. As it turned out, the Centre County community provided most of the school's support for the next fifty years.

William G. Waring was appointed farm superintendent to supervise construction and equipping of the building, barn, and shops; plant experimental orchards and farm plots; and make all preparations to admit students. He is remembered in town with Waring Avenue and on campus with Waring Commons.

On opening day, February 16, 1859, sixty-nine students arrived to enroll in courses of agriculture and horticulture. Made of native limestone, the imposing five-story building, where they would live and go to classes, was only one-third completed due to lack of funds, and was surrounded by piles of building materials in the well-tramped mud. But this didn't seem to discourage fifty more students or the school's first president, Dr. Evan Pugh, from joining them later that year.

A Chester County Quaker and a tall, muscular bachelor of thirty-one, Pugh had just returned from studying at some of Europe's finest universities, earning a Ph.D. at Goettingen. He gave up a promising career in agricultural chemistry to come to The Farmers' High School, where, he said, "the harvest is great and the laborers are few." He also believed that this primitive little school could eventually become one of the best agricultural schools in the world.

Dr. Pugh arrived on a gloomy, snowy day in late October in a buggy driven by trustee McAllister. Entering the wooden shanty that was the school dining hall and kitchen, he was warmly greeted by the four professors and, as he recorded it, "110 unruly, unkempt boys, some as young as fifteen."

Pugh's reputation as a scientist, combined with publicity of his curriculum improvements, attracted more and better students. But he had to turn many away for the 1860 term when a $50,000 state appropriation to complete Main Building was denied. It passed the following year.

In December 1861, eleven students earned bachelor's degrees in scientific agriculture and became the first graduates of an American agricultural college. The following year Pugh established an ambitious graduate program and, in 1863, awarded the nation's first master of scientific agriculture degree to C. Alfred Smith '61, who later served his alma mater as professor of chemistry and physics, then as trustee.

In 1862, Pugh helped organize the U.S. Department of Agriculture and twice rejected offers to become its chief chemist, saying, "I shall seek honor in the path of duty and destiny rather than at Washington." He did go to Washington, however, to lobby for the Morrill Land-Grant Bill and did the same in Harrisburg to convince legislators that his school, the only operating agricultural school in Pennsylvania, was the logical recipient of public land-sale funds. To assure its selection he got approval from the Centre County court to rename it "The Agricultural College of Pennsylvania" on May 6, 1862, just two months before Lincoln signed the land-grant act into law.

The name *high school* had originally been chosen to avoid farmers' prejudices against the word *college*, which connoted a classical education and "a place where boys only contract idle habits." Actually, the course of study always had been on a collegiate level and, Pugh said, "was more extensive than that of any European agricultural college."

This was during the Civil War, of course, and because of the war's demand for materials, Main Building was not completed until December 1863, five months after the Battle of Gettysburg, at which time it contained 165 student rooms, three chemistry labs, offices, classrooms, several faculty apartments, chapel, dining hall, kitchen, library, museum, and a bell in the tower.

To aid his teaching of regional geology, Pugh frequently consulted Abram Valentine, founder of one of Centre County's largest iron and charcoal operations and also a Chester County Quaker. It soon developed, however, that the real attraction at Willowbank, Valentine's mansion in Bellefonte, was his pretty daughter, Rebecca, who was intellectual, fluent in German, and an abolitionist like the college president.

For the first time Pugh was in love, and the school trustees approved his suggestion to build a president's home not far from Main Building. He designed it, supervised its construction, and even contributed a third of its $3,000 cost, but he never lived in it. On April 29, 1864, less than three months after marrying Rebecca and eight months before the house was finished, he died at age thirty-six.

Although his death was attributed to typhoid fever, some think he actually had worked himself to death. His arm, severely broken in a buggy accident the previous summer, had required surgery but had never healed, probably because he exhausted himself traveling often to Harrisburg, delivering speeches, writing letters to influential people, and preparing lengthy reports for the legislature, all aimed at gaining the land-grant designation for his college and dissuading legislators from dividing the fund among six colleges.

Not until 1867 was Penn State named sole recipient of the land-grant funds, which, ironically, were much less than anticipated, leaving the school deeply in debt. And not until 1882 did the college return to the course charted for it by the far-sighted Evan Pugh.

As the school had developed, so had the village across the road from it. Almost before construction had begun on campus, James Jack had arrived from Philadelphia to open the first hotel, "Jack's Road House," on what is now the southwest corner of College Avenue and Allen Street. Later renamed College Inn and then Nittany Inn, the original building is still there but was incorporated long ago into the Hotel State College, the Corner Room, and the Allen Room, now the Allen Street Grill.

Another far-sighted newcomer was David Osman, who moved his blacksmith shop from Centre Furnace to a site near the present-day University Club on West College Avenue. This, along with the roadhouse, a handful of residences, and several large farms purchased from General Irvin's Centre Furnace lands, comprised the place whose first post-office address was "Farm School." To better describe the location, some people added "Boalsburg" to the address. But as the Philadelphia *Public*

Hillcrest Ave.

Woodland Drive

N. Allen St.

The State College Times in September 1933 reported that the Krumrine barn in College Heights burned to the ground in an hour and a half. "The eighty-one-year-old barn was a landmark in this district. It was erected in 1852, three years before the official founding of Penn State . . . All the beams were hand-hewn timbers put together with wooden pins and square hand-wrought iron nails. . .For some years it was the largest structure of its kind in town and was the only place big enough for a local company to store its moving van."

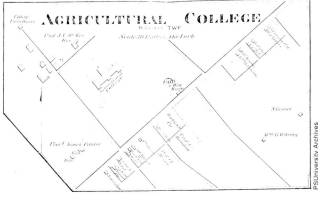

The A. Pomeroy & Co. 1874 Atlas of Centre County shows a dozen buildings on campus, plus a well house. Streets needed no names yet — the village had barely more structures than the infant college had.

Built in 1877 and enlarged and remodeled in 1887, William Buckhout's house was the subject of Dean Warnock's CDT "Half Colyum" in 1945: "When the Buckhout house at the southwest corner of Beaver and Pugh was being torn down recently, we heard a newcomer say that it was time 'that old flimsy fire-trap was being removed.' Newcomer, that was a well-built house. About the turn of the century it was one of a group of faculty homes which made up one of the residential boasts of the town . . . On the corner north of it still stands the 'Frenchy' Foster home. And on the Glennland and SAE sites were two other substantial residences."

Ledger put it, "Knowing that the school is near Boalsburg does not necessarily mean you know where Boalsburg is."

While The Farmers' High School review committee had been conducting its inspection tour, Irvin had thought about offering more land to the north, beyond the 400 acres agreed upon. But he found that his warrants to tracts north of the present Park Avenue had never been translated into patents, and Frederick Krumrine had obtained legal title to those lands years before.

The land in Irvin's final deed to The Farmers' High School was bounded on the west by present-day Atherton Street, on the north by Park Avenue, on the east by Shortlidge Road, and on the south by College Avenue. At that time Irvin still owned two-thirds of the Centre Furnace enterprise, while Moses Thompson, his brother-in-law, owned the other third.

Two farms that would make up a large portion of central State College were purchased from Irvin and Thompson by William Foster and his half-brother Robert M. Foster Sr.

William's farm stretched between South Atherton and South Pugh Streets from College to Hamilton Avenues. He had come here in 1845 and built a typical five-bay farmhouse where Paul and Peg Pierson's three-story Dutch colonial now stands at 160 West Fairmount Avenue. When Peg's father, Dean of Agriculture Stevenson Fletcher, bought the property, the Foster farmhouse was moved down the hill to 157 West Prospect Avenue and is still there today.

Robert Foster's farm lay to the west of William's, bounded east and west by South Atherton and South Patterson Streets, and north and south by the present-day Railroad

Avenue and West Hamilton Avenue. He came here in 1854 and served as the Farm School's second postmaster for two years before joining the Union Army in 1861. He was killed at Gettysburg.

Farms north of the school, in what is now College Heights, were owned by Fred Krumrine and his brother John, who together owned everything west of Allen Street, and their brother-in-law John Neidigh, who owned everything east of Allen Street, property he later willed to his son-in-law, Henry Hartswick. This line of demarcation accounts for the differences in street names in that neighborhood today: Ridge becomes Hartswick and Hillcrest becomes Adams when they cross Allen.

John Krumrine's house, now 136 Hillcrest Avenue, was built in 1852. Said to be the oldest house in the Borough (although the oldest *building*, 1836, is the former Branch Road School, now the School House Lounge), it presently belongs to Paul and Anne Bender. During the 1930s and 1940s it was home (with a North Burrowes Street address!) to the Sam Crabtree family, who rented it for $50 a month from Adam Krumrine, John's son.

The Krumrine land included the part of College Heights now west of North Atherton Street. Both farms extended north almost to the dip where the Bellefonte Central Railroad tracks and its station stop, dubbed Krumrine, used to be — in the dip today are College Village Center and Commercial Printing.

A large farm in what is now eastern State College belonged to Sam and Dan Garner, who bought it in 1868. Its boundaries were present-day Garner Street, University Drive, East College Avenue, and East Hamilton Avenue. And the land between the Garner and Foster farms belonged to William Waring until 1879, when he sold it at $100 per acre to John Hamilton, who had graduated from the College in 1868, then served as its farm superintendent, professor of agriculture, treasurer, and trustee, and as Pennsylvania's secretary of agriculture.

Hamilton and his wife, Elizabeth, daughter of Moses Thompson, lived many years in an apartment in Main Building and had three children, although only one, Anne (Henszey) lived to adulthood. In 1890, they built a large brick home, "The Highlands," which had a commanding view of campus from East Beaver Avenue. It was later sold to Delta Upsilon fraternity, which still inhabits it. Just to the west, at 234 Locust Lane, is the Hamiltons' former barn, which has long been home to Acacia fraternity.

The village's first postmaster and storekeeper was Barney McClain, who came with two other men from Bellefonte to build the first school barn, on the present site of Carnegie Building, at a cost of $3,500. He was appointed postmaster August 28, 1858, with an office in Main Building, while his combination house and general store stood near the southeast corner of College and Allen, where Moyer Jewelers and Towne Gentlemen/Towne Ladies are today. One of his building's last commercial tenants before it burned in a 1924 fire was George Graham's tobacco and confectionery shop, "Graham's on the Corner."

When Barney McClain died suddenly in 1859 at age forty, he was succeeded as storekeeper by Mifflin Snyder and as postmaster by Robert Foster Sr. Later postmasters were George B. Weaver (1861-65) and Barney's brother, Frank McClain, who served only six months before Sophie Hunter landed the postal job and held it for nearly fifteen years, until 1881.

Sophie had come to the village in 1860 with her mother and sister to run the dining room for The Farmers' High School, and built a house in 1862 on West College Avenue, just east of what is now Mellon Bank. Her home served as post office as well as a rooming house, and, in 1904, Mellon's predecessor, First National Bank of State College, rented its first office from her.

In a 1911 commencement address at Penn State, C. Alfred Smith, then a trustee, credited one of the original trustees with bringing the Hunters to town. Recalling the state of campus food service during his freshman year, 1859, Smith said that hired help did the cooking and baking, but students set, cleared, and waited on tables and washed dishes as part of their work duties. "The food and table service were good that first year, but the Irish cook and the baker were a law unto themselves, each good at his trade, but cleanliness was not one of their virtues."

Trustee A. O. Hiester, a Harrisburg judge and prosperous Dauphin County farmer, improved those conditions following the September meeting of trustees, as Smith reported. "The dinner was a good one and heartily enjoyed. At the close of the meal Judge Hiester seized my arm with the remark: 'Smithy, I want to see the kitchen where that splendid dinner was prepared.' I advised him not to, but he insisted, so we moved in upon the domain of the cook.

"The judge took a glance around and with a shudder exclaimed, 'Great God, Smith, did that dinner come out of this place?' Well, the Irish cook and the baker both disappeared at the close of the year, the student waiters disappeared, and the kitchen and dining shed passed into the care of the Misses Hunter and their assistants, and we entered upon an era of good food with good service and cleanliness."

Hiester and his son Gabriel, for whom the State College street is named — correctly pronounced HEE-ster, not HIGH-ster — served as Penn State trustees for a combined fifty-two years. Gabriel was the first elected by members of the alumni association.

Besides the Hunters, other newcomers included John Sowers (sometimes misspelled Sauers or Showers), who in 1861 opened a cobbler shop east of campus. He and his wife, Susanna, also did all the laundering at the school. Later joined by son Henry, John Sowers repaired and made shoes for an astounding sixty-six years, thirty-five of them in State College, until his death in 1896 at age eighty-six. His obituary states that he was then the town's oldest citizen, having voted for the first time when Andrew Jackson ran for President in 1832.

The town's first tailor was Billy Hoover, who walked

John Hamilton built a handsome mansion, designed by a Bellefonte architect, in 1890.
It later became Delta Upsilon fraternity, and the Acacia fraternity adopted as home the remodeled Hamilton barn.

"Thorny" Osmond's home was on the intersection Dean Warnock called "one of the residential boasts of the town" — this is the southeast corner of Beaver Avenue and Pugh Street.

Photographed from William Buckhout's yard, John Stuart's store in 1882 was one of the few downtown buildings facing Main.
In 1995, it still stood at 130 East College Avenue.

17

in from Shingletown to ply his needle in Main Building before moving to a room in Miss Hunter's house. And the first public transportation, in 1858, was a stage operated by Benjamin Beaver that traveled three times a week from Bellefonte to Pine Grove Mills via The Farmers' High School. The following year a daily stage was added between the school and Spruce Creek, closest stop of the Pennsylvania Railroad.

In 1862 one of the stagecoach drivers was fifteen-year-old Andy Lytle, who won the hearts of student passengers with his stories and friendly advice. At age eleven he had been one of 200 workmen hired to erect Main Building, proudly driving a spirited four-horse team over the fields and rough roads from his father's farm near Pine Grove Mills, hauling poles for scaffolding and cordwood for firing bricks. He also used the family mule, "Coaly," to drag stones to the building from the school quarry. Now just a small depression on Old Main lawn on the west corner of the Pugh Street entrance to campus, the old quarry site was used for many years as an amphitheatre for graduations, dance recitals, readings, and chapel services.

A farmer most of his life, Andy endeared himself to generations of Penn Staters who dubbed him "the perennial freshman" and frequently went to his house at 213 West Whitehall Road, which they called "The Refuge," when school problems became too much for them. He attended every Penn State home football game for more than forty years and, in 1924, was honored with "Andy Lytle Day" at the Penn State-North Carolina State game. There, at halftime, amid much pomp and celebration, he was paraded around the field in a sedan chair and officially inducted into the class of 1928. It was the greatest tribute ever given by students to a town resident not officially connected with the College.

As for Coaly, his hard work was so impressive that the school bought him from the Lytles for the then-high price of $190 and he became a college fixture for thirty-six years, working on the campus and surrounding farms until dying of old age in 1893. His bones were preserved at the insistence of students and can be seen today in a glass case in the Agricultural Administration Building, a symbol of the honor society that has borne his name since 1952.

In the turbulent days of the young Penn State, between the death of Evan Pugh in 1864 and the arrival of George Atherton in 1882, the College — whose isolated location was described by a trustee in 1880 as "destitute of such common aids to civilization as churches, printing presses, railroads, and telegraphs" — almost went out of existence under the tutelage of five presidents whose terms ranged from nine months to nine years.

William Allen (1864-66) proved to be popular with faculty and students, but couldn't adjust to the primitive conditions on campus. Charged with trying to pay off the College's $50,000 debt, he instead had to ask trustees to borrow an additional $80,000. Also, in July 1865, he unknowingly hired his successor when fulfilling one of the requirements of the land-grant act — to begin instruction in military tactics. Professor John Fraser, a Civil War veteran, came to teach that subject as well as mathematics and astronomy, and within a year was writing requests to the trustees to change and expand the curricula. The board accepted his comprehensive — and what turned out to be expensive — plan at the same meeting where Allen tendered his resignation. From 1866 to 1868, Fraser made radical changes in existing courses of study, substituting military drill for student labor on the farm; providing four-year programs in general science, literature, and agriculture; and proposing experimental farms and courses in engineering and mining. He also increased the size and salaries of the faculty and raised tuition to $260 a year. Student enrollment plummeted from 114 in 1866 to 30 in 1868, and no one graduated in 1867. The following year trustees accepted Fraser's resignation, discontinued the new curricula, fired faculty, lowered tuition, and called on Dr. Thomas Burrowes to help the school regain public confidence and enrollment.

Although not a college graduate, Burrowes (1868-71) was well known in Pennsylvania educational circles and was noted for his genial disposition, ready wit, and conversational powers. He had led the movement and framed the 1857 law establishing Pennsylvania's normal schools, now state universities.

He thought the Morrill Act mandated a farmers' high school, so he restored the old system of manual labor and offered one course of study. He took personal charge of the College farm, working in the fields with students. Enrollment did rise to fifty-nine during his tenure and an alumni association was optimistically formed, but trustees were still borrowing money to pay expenses when Burrowes died suddenly in February 1871.

Next came the Reverend James Calder (1871-1880), who sought to change the Agricultural College into a classical institution. In his crusade, he all but destroyed it, alienating faculty, dividing trustees, arousing harsh criticism from the press and public, and generating a legislative investigation into mismanagement.

Calder could count several accomplishments, however. The first women students were admitted in 1871, total enrollment hit a new high of 162 in 1878, and the school's name was changed to The Pennsylvania State College in 1874 to, as Calder said, "reflect its new character." He also spent money beautifying the campus grounds under the direction of William C. Patterson, who became farm superintendent at the College in 1872, when "it was a rock pile and a potato patch." Credited with laying out the original acres of campus much as they are today, Patterson became president of the First National Bank and the second State College burgess.

After Calder left, Joseph Shortlidge came in 1880 for nine stormy months, beginning with a commencement address in which he managed to offend trustees, faculty, students, and the public alike. Attempting to run the College as if it were an academy, he was described as being

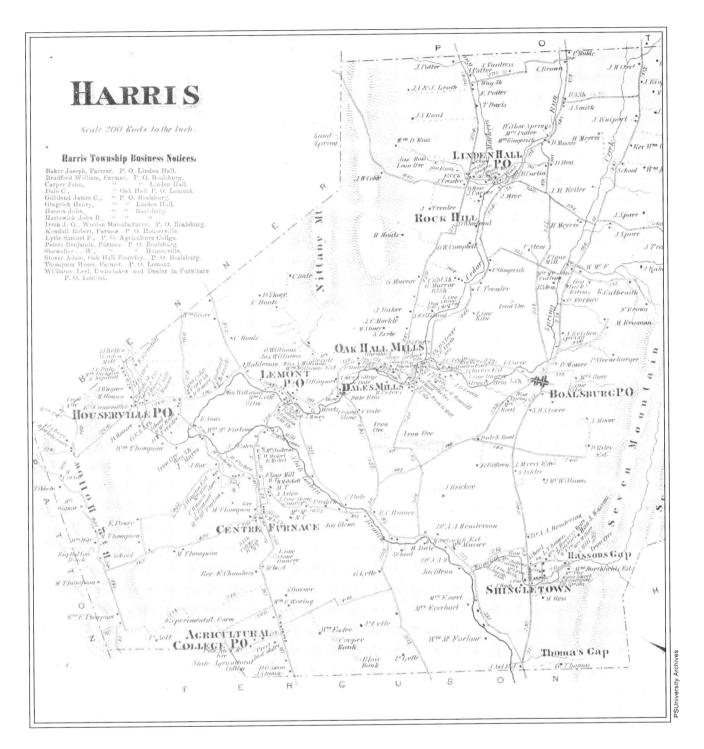

HARRIS

Scale 200 Rods to the Inch.

Harris Township Business Notices.

Baker Joseph, Farmer. P. O. Linden Hall.
Bradford William, Farmer. P. O. Boalsburg.
Carper John,   "   "   Linden Hall.
Dale C.,   "   Oak Hall P. O. Lemont.
Gilliland James C., "   P. O. Boalsburg.
Gingrich Henry,   "   "   Linden Hall.
Hazon John,   "   "   Boalsburg.
Hartswick John B., "   "   "
Irwin J. G., Woolen Manufacturer. P. O. Boalsburg.
Kendall Robert, Farmer. P. O. Houserville.
Lytle Samuel F., P. O. Agriculture College.
Peters Benjamin, Farmer. P. O. Boalsburg.
Showalter . . W., "   "   Houserville.
Stover Adam, Oak Hall Foundry. P. O. Boalsburg.
Thompson Moses, Farmer. P. O. Lemont.
Williams Levi, Undertaker and Dealer in Furniture
    P. O. Lemont.

Centre Furnace earned a listing on this map in Pomeroy's
Atlas of Centre County in 1874 —
the year the Agricultural College became
The Pennsylvania State College.

19

overbearing and uncompromising. And when he turned in his resignation in April 1881, to take effect three months later, the trustees sent him packing that very day.

One historian later lamented how ironic it was that Shortlidge should have as his namesake one of the major roads on campus, while Calder, "an infinitely more capable person," has to be content with a downtown alley. On the other hand, Fraser's legacy was misspelled Frazier Street on signs, maps, and in the media until 1963.

As always, what happened at the College affected the town. In 1875, College Township was created from parts of Harris Township — the school's original location — and Benner Township. "State College" instead of "Agricultural College" was the town's name now, and residents would fight to retain it even after Penn State became a university. And in at least two respects — population and potables — the community followed the College's lead. Except for 1860, when there were 110 students and only 25 townspeople, the growth of the town has nearly always paralleled that of the gown, with the numbers being 59 students and 50 townspeople in 1870, 157 and 150 in 1880, 209 and 200 in 1890, and 433 and 425 in 1900.

In 1883, a writer said that nearly all villages in College Township were protected from the influence of intoxicating liquor by a law that prohibited its sale or manufacture within three miles of the campus. Even after State College broke away from the township to become a borough, alcoholic beverages were banned until 1933, when beer was legalized. Liquor could not be sold, however, until a 1967 referendum by voters.

Historian John Blair Linn's description of the area at the time George Atherton became Penn State's seventh president in 1882 went like this: "Quite a little village has grown up around the college. It contains two stores and a hotel, the State College Hotel, now kept by Mr. George Hoffer, a descendant of one of the oldest of Centre County's families. There are also two or three elegant private residences." Linn added that the College building, "is beautifully located, and from the cupola one of the grandest landscape scenes is presented to view that the imagination of man can picture."

When taken to that cupola for the first time, Atherton proclaimed Nittany Valley to be "the most beautiful landscape in America." But the town must have looked pretty gloomy to the transplanted New Englander and Yale graduate who had just spent twelve years on the faculty at Rutgers. Here there were no sidewalks, no sewers, no church, no school, and no physician. Hogs had the run of the town and wallowed in muddy streets after a rain. Social life was almost nonexistent.

Dr. Atherton's youngest child, Helen Atherton Govier, age four in 1882, recalled in 1968, "We came from New Brunswick, New Jersey, to the little mining village of Scotia via the Buffalo Run, Bellefonte, and Bald Eagle Railroad and were met there by Joseph Mitchell, whose wife, Eliza, was later postmaster here. The six of us, my mother and five children, piled into his two-horse carriage and rode the several miles to our house on campus." She noted that her father must have had tremendous vision and confidence "to bring his family here to this small village and begin his arduous duties to build a large institution.

"One night during that early period, my father was very restless in bed, and when my mother asked him why he wasn't asleep, he replied, 'I'm wondering where the next freshman class is coming from!' "

Nonetheless, the forty-five-year-old Atherton proved to be just what this sinking ship needed, for during his more than twenty-four-year tenure — unmatched by any other Penn State president — the College grew into a major educational institution with 800 students, a dozen buildings, and generous state appropriations. His time as Penn State president was a turning point in the history of the town as well, for the Atherton era saw many "firsts" on both sides of College Avenue. And in the midst of it all, State College officially became a borough.

All students were eating downtown in boarding houses by then, the College having closed its dining room in 1873. Then, early 1888 saw the first Penn State fraternities, Phi Gamma Delta and Beta Theta Pi, permanently established after students pleaded with Atherton that they would not only give social advantages to members but also relieve crowded conditions in the dormitories.

"Young men," Atherton told them, "I have found that the best time to set a hen is when the hen wants to set." However, he had to convince trustees to lift a ban on fraternities in effect since 1872, when a Delta Tau Delta chapter had been started but had met with so much faculty disfavor that it was quickly disbanded. With Atherton's encouragement the trustees agreed to try fraternities again, and the Phi Gams built a spacious house downtown, on the southwest corner of Allen and Beaver, while the Betas built one on East College Avenue next to the present Faith United Church of Christ. The original (1889) Phi Gam house, now faced with stone, is still with us, although it was moved in the 1930s to the fraternity's former tennis court along Highland Alley and turned to face Allen Street where storerooms were added.

Over the years more than fifty fraternities would build houses in State College, some of which, a century or more old, still find use as residences. Six fraternities built houses on campus, Alpha Zeta, Beta Theta Pi, Phi Delta Theta, Phi Gamma Delta, Sigma Chi, and Sigma Nu.

A reincarnated Delta Tau Delta chapter first occupied a house near the southeast corner of Beaver and Allen, where Schlow Library is today. That downtown location earned them a long-standing nickname of dubious distinction, "Down Town Drunks." At the same time, Sigma Alpha Epsilon also had a nickname, "Sleep And Eat," when its members occupied a house on the northwest corner of Beaver and Allen. It was later home to the Allencrest Tea Room and then Danks, before it was razed in 1965 to make way for the present building.

Increasing enrollment at the College found many

Writing of the view from campus in 1882, Linn's History says, "Quite a little village has grown up around the college. It contains two stores and a hotel, the State College Hotel, now kept by Mr. George Hoffer, a descendant of one of the oldest of Centre County's families. There are also two or three elegant private residences."

According to Maude Grieb Mullin, daughter of innkeeper S. S. Grieb, this small hack carried overflow passengers from the Lemont train station to State College. The mail and most passengers arrived in a four-horse coach.

Part of postmistress Sophie Hunter's home was the local post office in 1866. And after the turn of the century, the new First National Bank operated in one room of the Hunter home on West College Avenue.

Until this church — the first in State College — was dedicated in February 1888, Methodists met with the congregation in Centre Furnace. And until the first full-time pastor was appointed in 1909, St. Paul's was part of the Pine Grove Mills circuit. Vivian Doty Hench, in the CDT's History of State College, 1896-1946, recalled its "precarious lighting system, consisting of kerosene lamp chandeliers pulled up and down by chains. A broken chain on several occasions almost succeeded in making it literally a 'heated sermon.'"

town residents offering room rentals in their homes for students, as they had since 1873 when students first were allowed to room and board off campus. Bellefonte's P. Gray Meek, by then a state senator and editor of the county's leading newspaper, *The Democratic Watchman*, even went so far as to buy a house on West College Avenue solely as a residence for his four daughters and one son while they attended Penn State. The son, George, was editor of the first yearbook, the 1890 *La Vie*.

As the town's population grew along with the College, so did the need for schools. Until 1889, children from age six to thirteen attended one-room schools at Centre Furnace or on Branch Road if they lived south of campus. Those living north of campus went to the Krumrine School, at Circleville Road and Corl Street on Ferguson Township land donated by John Krumrine. Now standing a few building lots west of its original location, at 1181 Circleville Road, the enlarged Krumrine School has been a private residence for many years.

Town children could also attend private schools, such as those run by Anna Cooper, near the present-day State College Presbyterian Church, and Carrie Hunter, where the Homerella Building, named for Homer and Ella Gentzel, is today at Pugh Street and Calder Way. "Campus brats," as professors' children were labeled, were tutored by Miss Mariah Penny around a table in the College library in Main Building.

In 1889, to alleviate crowding at the one-room Centre Furnace schoolhouse, the first public school within present borough limits was constructed. Since it was not quite finished when the school year began, a temporary classroom was set up in the old town band hall on the northwest corner of Garner Street and Beaver Avenue.

The town's first public-school teacher was John Laird Holmes, who earned $28 a month for instructing fifty or sixty students for six months each year. It was said that "he ruled with an iron hand and maintained order with a wooden rod that occasionally was cleverly split by a knowing pupil so that it would break when used." Evidently this didn't ruin his popularity — Holmes later served as mayor of State College.

Those desiring education beyond the eighth grade could enroll, at their communities' and families' expense, in academies then flourishing in Boalsburg, Pine Grove Mills, Bellefonte, and elsewhere. Or if college was in their future, fourteen-year-olds could attend Penn State's preparatory department.

In 1894, Will Foster, no relation to the original farming Fosters, decided to ease the faculty housing shortage a bit when he put up a three-story wooden structure at the corner of College and Pugh. It housed Will's grocery and dry-goods store along with the post office on the first floor and six six-room apartments on the upper floors, the town's first apartments not in private homes. Over the years, Foster's tenants included one of Penn State's first football coaches, William "Pop" Golden; physics professor Madison "Gravy" Garver, who later bought

the Centre Furnace mansion; and economics professor Oswald Boucke. The building now belongs to descendents of P. H. Gentzel, whose apartments now are above Spats Cafe, with the Rathskeller bar in the basement.

Also in 1894, at a cost of $26,000, a group of local businessmen including "Cal" Patterson and James Potter built the barn-like, three-story University Inn near the present College-Atherton intersection, where the University Club now stands. Dubbed "a shingle palace" by Professor A. Howry Espenshade, the inn boasted well-lighted, comfortably furnished single rooms or suites; porches on three sides; a poolroom and bowling alley in the basement; and a Bellefonte Central Railroad stop just fifty yards away. Room and board ranged from $2 to $2.50 per day and $8 to $10 a week.

From September to June, the Inn was home to some students from prosperous families and bachelor professors. But it was plagued with financial woes until 1896, when its management was turned over to Phil Foster, brother of Will, whose large brick house still stands at the southeast corner of College and Atherton. Phil opened the inn's doors to faculty and student parties, receptions, banquets, and balls, and advertised that summer visitors "may have the place to themselves, with the choicest rooms and the best board to be found in the village." The Inn burned to the ground one May morning in 1903, but its occupants — nineteen students, eight professors and their families, and twenty-five workmen employed in the building of Schwab Auditorium — escaped largely unhurt, but with only the clothes on their backs.

An earlier venture in hostelry occurred in 1884, when Johnny Corrigan, keeper of the east campus gate (near present-day McAllister Street) decided to give Jack's Road House, by then renamed the College Inn, some competition by opening the Union Hotel at 208 East College Avenue, next to the present-day Tavern Restaurant. Corrigan thought it a shame to charge a dollar a day for meals and lodgings, so he charged only fifty cents.

Many professors and their families — such as the Ponds, Armsbys, Pattees, Willards, and Ihlsengs — lived on campus in "cottages" built as faculty housing, a few of which still remain. Professors Buckhout and Osmond, on the other hand, built large homes on the south side of East Beaver Avenue, across from each other at the Pugh Street intersection. Botanist William A. Buckhout, who graduated from the College in 1868 and joined the faculty in 1871, built his in 1877, then enlarged it to seventeen rooms in 1887. Physicist I. T. "Thorny" Osmond built his about 1880. It later was moved back to Highland Avenue to make way for the present SAE fraternity house. Although Pugh Street was originally meant to be the main north-south thoroughfare, it attracted more private homes than businesses, aided no doubt by the Osmond and Buckhout beauties in the second block.

In 1882, telephone service arrived when telephones

Penn State's first permanent national-fraternity chapters — Phi Gamma Delta and Beta Theta Pi — built their first houses downtown in 1888. This Phi Gam house looked toward campus from the southwest corner of Allen and Beaver. It was later moved back to Highland Avenue, facing Allen Street, and faced in stone. It was still in use in 1995.

John Hamilton donated land for the State College Presbyterian Church at Miles Street (Locust Lane) and College Avenue. John Stuart and James McKee joined him on the building committee. The village in 1888 had 150 residents, the church had 58 members, and the new sanctuary seated 200. The Reverend Robert Hamill, first pastor, had preached 6,000 sermons in 45 years when he retired in 1890.

To alleviate crowding at the little Centre Furnace schoolhouse, the first public school within what would become the Borough limits was a tiny white-stucco building on Calder Alley, just west of Pugh Street. It was replaced soon by a large two-room school on Calder at Hiester Street.

23

were installed in President Atherton's office and seven other locations on campus, all connected to a switchboard in Bellefonte, where Mr. Bell's gadget had already been in use for two years. Then, in 1885, "townies" got service when Bell Telephone placed a toll booth in the College Inn. But calls were expensive for the time — twenty-five cents each. At first it was possible to ring up only a few dozen subscribers through the Bellefonte exchange, but by 1888 one could reach not only 166 phones on that exchange but also 1,800 others from Altoona to Wilkes-Barre. Competition arrived in 1898 in the form of the locally owned Central Pennsylvania Telephone Company, but subscribers to this service could not call those on the other. Merchants soon got wise and subscribed to both, which explains advertisements of bygone days stating "Both Phones."

Beginning in the 1890s, residents also had club meetings to keep them busy. The Independent Order of Odd Fellows was the first group to form, in 1892; the Women's Literary Club, forerunner of the State College Woman's Club, was founded in 1894 in the living room of Frances Atherton.

Woman's Club historian Winona Morgan Moore wrote that after the Borough was incorporated, the women looked around to see what they could do to improve it. "Their first project was to purchase the best encyclopedia that could be procured for the money for the town library (which the club founded) located in the Frazier Street School." They also provided public wastebaskets to keep litter off the streets and, in 1907, got approval from Borough Council to erect an iron drinking fountain on the campus side of College Avenue at its intersection with Pugh Street. Costing $152.60, it was described by Winona as "an artistic fountain which accommodated people at the top, horses in the middle, and pigs at the bottom." Rescued by Helen Atherton Govier when it was discarded in 1920, it stands today — painted silver and with a four-foot-high hitching post on top — in the yard of the house George Atherton reportedly built for his daughter and son-in-law at 518 South Atherton Street.

Although there still were no sewers and little control over wandering livestock — the College merely installed a fence all along College Avenue to keep townspeople's animals off campus — the Atherton era had brought a school, churches, and social life, as well as more hotels, houses, and stores to the growing village. Still missing were a resident physician and self-government.

Theodore Christ, son-in-law of Moses Thompson, was the first M.D. to practice in town, but he lived in Lemont and did not move into State College until his later years. The first resident physicians came in the mid-1880s in the form of William S. Glenn and his third wife, Nanny, also an M.D., who practiced for forty years from their home on Pugh Street, close to Calder Alley. Following in their footsteps were sons Grover and Billy, who together kept the town healthy for another forty years.

Self-government came when the Borough of State College was incorporated on August 29, 1896. The first signs of things to come had occurred in 1893 with the chartering of a water authority, which first bought water from the College wells, one of which was an artesian well at College Avenue and the Mall from which water was pumped to a reservoir behind Old Main. Then, in 1895, the fledgling authority laid a six-inch pipeline to the reservoir in Shingletown, and home wells and cisterns became things of the past.

Borough incorporation had not come easily. There had been sharp exchanges with College Township officials who, the State College people contended, wanted tax money from the little community without giving much in return. Townspeople wanted better schools, better streets, and better lighting, and figured the best way to get them was with their own tax dollars. So after many angry meetings and against considerable resistance, the proposition to incorporate was finally carried.

The first borough council, elected on September 29, 1896, reflects the still-evident mix of town and campus in municipal government — Ag Experiment Station horticulturist George C. Butz, president, and botany professor William A. Buckhout, hotelier S. S. Grieb, farmer and businessman James H. Holmes, cobbler Henry A. Sowers, and two men whose occupations are unknown, A. A. Miller and Frank B. Weaver. Dr. Theodore Christ was appointed the first burgess, Dr. William Glenn Sr. the first head of the board of health, and J. Laird Holmes the first tax collector.

The first ordinance Borough Council enacted, October 15, 1896, permitted the Central Pennsylvania Telephone and Supply Company to erect and maintain poles for telephone lines. Other ordinances, too, reflected the new age that was dawning by regulating sidewalks, stovepipes, streets, alleys, and peddling without a license. Still others gave an indication that this was, indeed, a college town, establishing fines ranging from $5 to $25 for vandalizing public and private street lights; prohibiting bicycle riding, coasting, skating, and driving on sidewalks; and prohibiting drunkenness and disorderly conduct, congregating on the streets, or interrupting public meetings.

But Ordinance No. 9, enacted February 23, 1897, really shows the town's emergence into civilized society — making it unlawful to let horses, cattle, mules, hogs, sheep, or goats run at large within borough limits. After much bitter debate, the council voted against it in January, 5 votes to 2, the "yeas" coming from George Butz and William Buckhout. Since passage of an ordinance requires unanimity, President Butz made a resolution, "That the question of cows running at large upon the public highways of the Borough be submitted to a vote of the citizens at the next Borough election, February 16, 1897." The people voted overwhelmingly for livestock control, 109 to 35, so council made it unanimous. State College was off and running.

When the village became a borough, livestock owned by residents were free to roam everywhere except in the fenced-in campus. An ordinance to restrict animals was enacted in 1897, but not without heated discussions. This pig is in the 100 block of East College Avenue.

George C. Butz was elected president of State College Borough Council on September 29, 1896. Physician Theodore S. Christ became the first burgess.

In 1896, Professor McKee's stone residence stood alone on east campus except for the brick kiln and drying sheds across from Sauerstown, the cluster of homes and a barn seen above Stone House. A little to the right and toward Mount Nittany, a half-dozen houses stood on "Pickle Hill." The two-room school is in front of them, behind the College Avenue homes. Then, west on College are the Presbyterian Church and the striped-steeple Methodist Church. The large house and barn back on the right are John Hamilton's.

rom agricultural college to world-class learning community, the story of The Pennsylvania State University is one of an expanding mission of teaching, research, and public service. But that mission was not so grandly conceived in 1855, when the Commonwealth chartered the school at the request of the Pennsylvania State Agricultural Society. The goal was to apply scientific principles to farming, a radical departure from the traditional curriculum grounded in mathematics, rhetoric, and classical languages.

Centre County became site of the new college in response to a gift of 200 acres from agriculturist and ironmaster James Irvin of Bellefonte. President Evan Pugh drew on the scientific education he had received in Europe to plan a broader curriculum combining classical studies with practical applications. Pugh and similar visionaries in other states won federal support for their ideas in 1862, when Congress passed the Morrill Land-Grant Act. The act enabled states to sell federal land, invest the proceeds, and use the income to support colleges "Where the leading object shall be, without excluding scientific and classical studies . . . to teach agriculture and the mechanic arts [engineering] . . . in order to promote the liberal and practical education of the industrial classes in all the pursuits and professions of life."

In 1863, the Agricultural College of Pennsylvania became the Commonwealth's land-grant institution. But Pugh died the following year, and the concept of land-grant education was so novel that over the next twenty years, his successors failed to define it. As the curriculum drifted between the purely agricultural and the classical, public confidence fell; only sixty-four undergraduates were enrolled in 1875.

In 1882, George W. Atherton, a vigorous proponent of land-grant education, became president of what had then become The Pennsylvania State College. He introduced engineering studies, and Penn State soon became one of the nation's ten largest undergraduate engineering schools. He broadened the liberal arts, and Professor of English Fred Pattee taught the nation's first course in American literature (heretofore considered an unworthy stepchild of English literature). Atherton founded the Agricultural Experiment Station as a center

for scientific research, and helped to draft the Hatch Act that gave annual federal support to such stations nationwide — thus setting the precedent of Congressional support for academic research. Impressed with Atherton's improvements, the state legislature authorized regular appropriations to the college beginning in 1887.

From Atherton's death in 1906 to mid-century, Penn State focused on undergraduate education and extension. Enrollment surpassed 5,000 in 1936, by which time the college had become the Commonwealth's largest source of baccalaureate degrees. Also in the 1930s, the administration of President Ralph Hetzel fashioned a series of branch campuses across Pennsylvania for students who, because of Depression-era economics, could not afford to leave home to attend college. The centers offered the first year or two of undergraduate studies and were predecessors of today's seventeen-campus Commonwealth Educational System, and of full-fledged colleges within the university at Erie and Harrisburg.

Extension work was primarily agricultural. Penn State pioneered in correspondence courses, disseminating scientific knowledge to farmers eager to find more efficient ways of growing crops and raising livestock. The college also worked with local and federal governments to implement a statewide system of agricultural and home economics agents who advised on issues as diverse as family life, nutrition, and food preservation. By the 1930s, Penn State had also launched outreach programs in the liberal arts, engineering, and the sciences.

Although research — the third element of Penn State's tripartite mission — developed more slowly, Penn State by 1950 had won distinction for investigations in dairy science, building insulation, diesel engines, and other specialized fields. To show that the institution had come of age, President Milton Eisenhower changed its name in 1953 to The Pennsylvania State University and established a campus post

The Pennsylvania State University

Richard Rummell created this engraving of campus in 1910. Only twelve of the buildings shown still stand today.

office designated University Park.

Research thrived under Eisenhower's successor, engineer and scientist Dr. Eric Walker, who headed Penn State from 1956 to 1970. "Space race," "brain drain," and other catch phrases reflected intense national concern for education, and public funds were plentiful. The physical plant tripled in value, and hundreds of acres of farm- and forestland were added to give the central campus room to grow (land now occupied, for example, by the Blue Golf Course, the Penn State Scanticon Hotel and Conference Center, and the Russell Larson Agricultural Research Center at Rock Springs). Total enrollment climbed from 14,000 to 40,000 during the Walker years. The Hershey Medical Center — a college of medicine and teaching hospital — was established in 1967 with a $50 million gift from the charitable trusts of chocolate magnate Milton S. Hershey.

The university's geographic isolation and conservatism held student unrest to modest proportions during the Vietnam War era, culminating in a brief occupation of Old Main in April 1970. More troubling in the long run were lagging state appropriations, which failed to keep up with inflation and the growing demand for the university's services. Finally, in 1984, President Bryce Jordan launched the six-year Campaign for Penn State, which raised $352 million in private gifts for academic programs. The campaign highlighted the fact that, despite its name and land-grant designation, Penn State was state-related, not state-owned, and would have to seek greater support from the private sector to strengthen academic quality. Dr. Jordan also pushed ahead with plans for a research park that would emphasize the economic development aspect of the university's public-service mission.

But Penn State's reputation still rests, as it has since the first graduating class of 1861, on the achievements of its alumni – 378,000 strong by mid-1995. As Milton Eisenhower observed, the alumni "are the real interpreters of the university to the people of the Commonwealth and the nation."

The Salad Days Before World War I

our weeks before the town had become a borough, a man who would greatly influence its future opened a barber shop at the corner of College Avenue and Allen Street. Twenty-three-year-old George T. Graham, with a wife and baby daughter, already had a love for canes and elegant clothing that would earn him the nickname, "The Duke of Allen Street."

Born at Fillmore and grandson of the caretaker of Centre Furnace mansion, he quit school at fourteen to become a barber's apprentice and had his own shop in Philipsburg before moving to State College. By 1916, he had changed his occupation from barber to restaurateur and finally to dispenser of newspapers, tobacco, and candy at what became a State College institution — Graham & Sons.

George also was instrumental in organizing the Alpha Fire Company, the Chamber of Commerce, Grace Lutheran Church, the local parent-teacher association, and the first American Red Cross drive in State College. He put up the town's first streetlight, bought its first commercially made radio receiver, and even installed its first pinball machine. And before he died in 1965 at age ninety-two, he saw the town and campus population grow from 600 to 50,000.

When the Grahams arrived, most State College buildings were huddled along College Avenue, and nothing but farmland could be seen north of campus, west of Frazier (Fraser) Street, or south of Beaver Avenue. There were other buildings at the east end of town, in what was called Sauerstown, but these, too, were confined to the area between College and Beaver Avenues, and none existed east of Pine (now Hetzel) Street.

"Nearly everyone kept cows, horses, pigs, et cetera," George reminisced fifty years later, "and after feeding and milking time, these animals were put out onto the fields and streets." To counter this, the College had built a fence along its side of College Avenue, sloping the top to discourage students from sitting on it. There were gates at Allen Street and present-day McAllister Street.

Campus in 1896 consisted of a handful of buildings dominated by the six-story Main Building. Others were the Armory, the president's house, a few faculty "cottages," and a smattering of barns, one of which, where Carnegie Building is today, also housed the only meat market on campus or in town.

The president's daughter, Helen Atherton Govier, recalled in 1968 that only a partition separated the meat from the livestock in that market/barn. "At four o'clock every afternoon Abram Markle, the butcher, would come to the front of his shop and blow several blasts on a small horn to let everyone know he was open for business," she said. "I've since wondered if he ever butchered any of those next-door pigs."

Abram, who spoke Pennsylvania Dutch better than English, later owned a butcher shop on College Avenue and a slaughterhouse on Pine Street, near his farm on Beaver Avenue.

"Downtown State College" in 1896 had about 300 residents, a small hotel, a post office, a laundry, two churches, some livery stables, and a few general-merchandise stores, none of which sold clothing or shoes. Consequently, most people shopped by mail in Philadelphia or traveled to Bellefonte by horse and buggy or the Bellefonte Central Railroad, which left

Albert, Nate and William Buckhout had the whole east end of town as their playground. This c1896 photograph was snapped by their father in the Buckhout yard at Beaver and Pugh. Penn State's Main Building dominated campus.

The local post office first operated in a room in the College's Main Building, then homes and stores, getting its own room when Foster's Corner was built. This building still houses businesses and apartments at East College and Pugh Street.

Helen Atherton enjoyed taking the reins of Harvey's Hack for picnic excursions. In front with her are Phil Foster and Billy Buckhout. The teenagers are Bessie Harding, Caroline Harkness, Clara Tuttle, John Andy Hunter, Nate Buckhout, Ethel Harding, Albert Buckhout, and Harriet Atherton.

Among the big first-grade class at the Frazier Street School in 1907-08 were Mary Kathryn Hoy, Addy Holmes, and Kitty Graham.

from its depot opposite Fraser Street on the present site of Hammond Building. Another rail line, the Lewisburg and Tyrone branch of the Pennsylvania Railroad, came into Lemont, two miles away. One then rode to "The College" in a horse-drawn hack for a fare of twenty-five cents. Later called Harvey's Hack, it was replaced in 1914 by Percival Rudy's automobile nicknamed "The Mountain Echo."

The first public service the new borough offered was police protection in the form of part-time constable George Taylor. He appears, though, to have spent most of his time sunning himself on a street corner because there wasn't anything else to do! No arrests were made until Phil Foster was burgess (as mayor was then called), from 1901 to 1902. He clapped a rowdy drunk, who had been standing along Allen Street threatening to knife his contemporaries, into the "hoosegow" or the "Borough Bastille." That is what many people called the 15-by-20-foot jail on the Calder Alley side of plumber Hamill Holmes' house, on the site of the present borough municipal building. The jail contained two cells, a pot-bellied stove, two tiny barred windows, and an iron bar across the door. Constable Taylor, also the street commissioner, stored his street-repair tools in there, and wasn't happy about locking up anyone since that displaced the tools.

In 1899, thirty citizens, including Phil Foster and George Graham, gathered to organize the Union Fire Company; the name was changed to Alpha the following year. George was elected its first president and was also appointed to ask President Atherton if the firemen could use the Armory to hold a fund-raising fair and festival. He admired Atherton but dreaded meeting him because of his own lack of education. However, the president soon put him at ease, granted his request, and the two became good friends. George even made regular trips to campus to trim Atherton's hair and beard.

Earning nearly $900 from that first fair in the Armory, the Alphas bought their first piece of firefighting equipment — a hand-drawn hook-and-ladder truck. They then set about to raise money for a permanent fire hall

by holding an annual Fourth of July festival, sponsoring plays, minstrels, movies, and concerts, and supporting one of the first baseball teams in Centre County, the RMFs, named for Robert M. Foster, representative to the state general assembly from State College, who supplied uniforms and equipment.

They also built up a rivalry with the area's *first* fire department, the Student Fire Company, which had been organized in 1862 and equipped with ten fire pails and a thirty-foot ladder. It is reported that by 1915, the Student Fire Company was the oldest student organization on campus; its equipment, headed by two two-wheeled hand-pulled hose carts, was stored in the lower level of Carnegie Library.

Intensely competitive, students and Alphas were not averse to turning their hoses on each other when called to fight the same fire. In 1922, the Alphas purchased their first motor vehicle, a combination pumper and chemical engine on a Reo chassis. Not to be outdone, the students acquired an Autocar motorized fire engine the next year. Finally, in 1924, in exchange for an annual contribution to the borough for fire protection, Penn State proposed that the two companies merge, house the College fire truck with the Alphas' apparatus, and allow members of the Student Fire Company to join the Alpha Fire Company.

At the turn of the century, loafing at Graham's barbershop was a favorite Penn State activity, although George said the first students to be really friendly with him were from the class of 1903 — at their fiftieth reunion, in 1953, they made him an honorary class member. But he lost points with students when he installed the town's first streetlight — a gas mantle suspended on guy wires across the College-Allen intersection — which they stoned for shedding too much light on their nighttime activities.

By the end of 1908, George Graham and his wife, Eleanora, had six more children — Randall (who acquired his lifelong nickname, "Bub," the moment older sister Ruth mispronounced "brother"), Calvin, Kathryn (Kitty Roseberry), Robert, Charles, and James. In 1911, after fifteen years of selling haircuts for fifteen cents and shaves

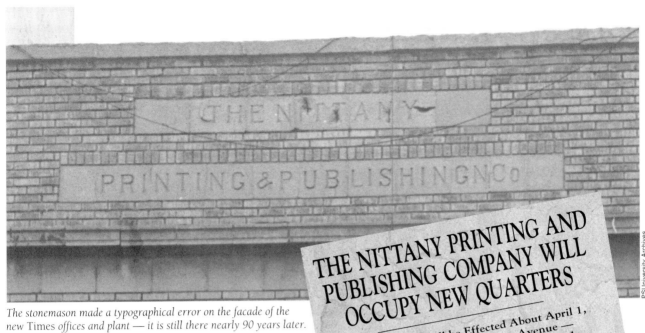

The stonemason made a typographical error on the facade of the new Times offices and plant — it is still there nearly 90 years later.

THE NITTANY PRINTING AND PUBLISHING COMPANY WILL OCCUPY NEW QUARTERS

The Change Will be Effected About April 1, New Building is on College Avenue — New Machinery Will Also be Installed

The publication office of the <u>Times</u> and The Nittany Printing and Publishing company will be moved into a new building on or about the first of next month. The new structure is on College avenue immediately adjoining the Nittany Inn property, and when fully completed will be one of, if not the largest, printing plants in Centre county.

—The Times, 3-22-07

McDowell Home First in S. C. To Receive Electricity '03

by Mary Rogers
Times Staff Writer

How a veteran of State College wishes he was through school after seeing the village from a distance when he came to enter the preparatory department of the College on April 2, 1888, was told today by M. C. McDowell.

"I remember it so distinctly," he said. "I came by horse and buggy from my home in Milroy and it took about five hours. When I saw the town from the duck pond, east of State College, I wished I were through school.

"The College football and baseball games were played on the front Campus then," he pointed out, "and many a time we used to knock flies way down on the main street."

He said his house was the first one wired for electricity and the first one to get the power. He told of a small power plant built at the rear of the present Nittany Printing plant which was to supply the power for the town. The wiring of his house was completed before the plant was in operation so the

College ran a line to the McDowell house and supplied the electricity for a few weeks.

Later, he said, the Nittany Heat and Light Company came into operation and to help use up the extra steam created, pipes were laid to furnish heat for several homes of the community, one of which was his [at 112 W. Beaver Ave.].

Mr. McDowell served as a member of the State College school board from 1905 to 1930.

"We tried to float two or three bond issues," he recalled, "but were defeated and when a law was passed about 1908 permitting the school board to assess a 25 mill tax, the State College school district was the first in the state to take advantage of it."

He recalled the last circus which came into State College. "It was in 1903", he said. "The students made it so tough for the entertainers that the 'show couldn't go on,' and there hasn't been one here since."

—Centre Daily Times, 4-11-46

A team of horses took the wedding party in the surrey to church from Russell Pearce's home with its wooden sidewalk on Allen Street at Highland Alley. Clark Herman's house was across the street, and behind it, on Pugh Street, was "Shivery's Fort."

for a dime, George decided that barbering was a tough way to make a living for a man supporting a big family. So in the same location, the southeast corner of Allen and College, he opened a short-lived restaurant called "Graham's on the Corner."

"Father kept hiring cooks from Philadelphia," Ruth said in 1974, "but they would quit and go back to the city because there was nothing to do in State College. It ended up that Mother was doing all the cooking, and Father decided it wasn't worth all the trouble."

Just before World War I, George and Bub found their business niche selling newspapers, tobacco, and candy, and Graham's became *the* hangout, especially favored by Penn State athletes and coaches who adopted the shop as their downtown athletic club, nicknaming it the "Graham A.C." Many years later, those words, carved of wood, were added to the famous and frequently stolen sidewalk bench first built in 1932 by Jacob Mattil, a Penn State carpenter, to replace candy crates George had provided for his "sidewalk philosophers." No longer owned by the Graham family or at its best-known location — 103 South Allen Street, where it operated from 1925 to 1988 — the "popsicola and peanut emporium," as one habitué called it, now shares space with Ben & Jerry's Ice Cream at 124 South Allen Street.

Only one business is older than Graham's — Hoy Transfer, started in 1885 by drayman William Alfred "Billy" Hoy. Billy was the fourth burgess of State College (1903-05) and also served on borough council and the school board. In addition to delivering such items as chicken coops and furniture from one residence to another, he hauled most materials for the many campus building projects of the Atherton era, and at the end of each semester and the beginning of the next, he saw that as many as a thousand student steamer trunks made their way to and from the train stations.

He worked six days a week and, at the insistence of his wife, Emmeline, rested on Sunday. So did their four children, William, Margaret, Charlotte, and Mary Kathryn ("Cassie"). "We just sat on the porch on Sunday," said Margaret Hoy Hoenstine, who was born in her father's

A RUNAWAY HORSE

Badly Hurts Landlord Shuman of the State College Hotel

WAGON COMPLETELY WRECKED

Horse Takes the Sidewalk and Causes Pedestrians to Flee for Their Lives —Whole Town in Excitement

Our town was thrown into a state of excitement Thursday morning caused by a runaway horse, which badly hurt J. B. Shuman.

The horse belonged to I. C. Holmes and is used in his delivery wagon driven by Russel Pearce. Russel had gone to the station for some freight which was in a car. As the car door was shoved open the horse became frightened and started down the street at a terrific speed.

Mr. Holmes' horse took the sidewalk for some distance causing pedestrians to flee for their lives and leaving fragments of the wagon in its course. The wagon was literally demolished, but the horse got through with only a few scratches.

— The Times, 3-6-03

NEW STATE COLLEGE

HOTEL IS ASSURED

A new Hotel at State College seems to be assured. The old livery barn is now being moved to its location on the alley at the rear of Wm. Hoy's residence.

The plans call for the removal of the old building about sixty feet south on Allen street. In the space thus vacated a fine new four story brick building is to be erected. The old building is to be raised up several feet; the first story is to be given a higher ceiling, the walls are to be encased with brick . . .

In such portions of the first floor as are not utilized for hotel purposes will be arranged five large, well lighted, and handsome store rooms.

It is said that the total cost of the property will be about forty thousand dollars.

—The Times, 3-31-05

first year as burgess. "We didn't dare have a Sunday newspaper and we weren't permitted to play ball." Every now and then, however, when the summer sun was bright but not too hot and there was a little bit of a breeze, Emmeline would allow Billy to make one Sunday haul. "He'd hitch up the spring wagon then," Margaret smiled, "and we'd all go for an afternoon ride around the country roads."

Billy eventually replaced the horses with trucks and continued to run the business and do much of the lifting and hauling until he was in his seventies. When he became sick and couldn't work anymore, he turned everything over to his daughter Cassie before he died in 1937. With the help of her son Dick Hoy, who worked part-time through high school and five semesters at Penn State, and drivers Ben Neff and Bill Oester, Cassie kept Hoy Transfer moving locally. Dick took it cross-country by affiliating with North American Van Lines in 1950.

In the 1890s, in order to preserve his meat, produce, and dairy products until they could be sold, butcher/farmer Abe Markle harvested ice in winter at the ore banks in Scotia and stored it in an underground cistern on his farm. The ice kept nearly all summer long, and he started peddling it to other farmers and townspeople. Soon, however, he couldn't furnish enough ice to meet the needs of the growing village, whose residents were buying gleaming new oaken iceboxes to keep food from spoiling year-round. Ice also was in demand for experiments at the College.

In December 1906, Abe and two Penn State faculty members — agricultural chemist William Frear and electrochemical engineer Ralph Myers — with financial backing from seven other businessmen and professors, including Irving L. "Frenchy" Foster, professor of romance languages, founded the Hillside Ice Company on Abe's farm. Soon they were producing distilled-water ice in a cork-insulated metal tank containing brine and ammonia-filled coils, the most up-to-date process then available. And with a horse and wagon, Harry Gill and Oscar "Orie" Barnes were delivering blocks of it at twenty-five cents a hundredweight to businesses and

Newton G. Hess built his substantial home in 1909 at 639 West College Avenue, where it stands today.

Until 1907, Lutheran women had regular meetings as the Women's Missionary Society, and were instrumental in obtaining this southwest corner of College and Atherton for the Lutheran Church built in 1909.

Principal B. H. Bottenhorn photographed the entire high school student body at the Frazier Street School in 1911. Miss Smith and Miss Martin were the teachers. Freshman class members attended their senior year in the new high school building near Fairmount Avenue.

Fraternities eventually built up the Fraternity Section in southeast State College, but often played "musical houses" on West College and Beaver Avenues. This 500 West College house was Phi Sigma Kappa fraternity in 1911 and Theta Upsilon Omega in 1931. The twin double-deck bay-window house was Pi Kappa Alpha in 1915 and Phi Lambda Theta in 1931. At the far right was Acacia in 1914.

The Krumrine School in 1911 was attended by five Hartswicks (Adam, Ethel, Fred, Herbert, Lewis), four Dreibelbises (Bruce, Dorothy, Edna, Mary), two Slagles (Dale, Winnefred), two Spottses (Ed, May), and Ruth Hoy, Ed Koch, and an unidentified pupil and teacher.

homes. "Here, sir, forty pounds, please!" and "Thirty pounds, mister!" came the cries from housewives along their route, who would then grump about what a high price that was to pay for frozen water.

In 1913, to keep up with demand, a new plant capable of producing ten tons of ice a day — more than three times as much as before — was built on land purchased from Irving Foster on North Patterson Street, next to the tracks of the Bellefonte Central, which agreed to install a coal tipple to fuel the plant's steam engine. In 1920, the company was sold to ex-plumber Forest Struble, who delivered coal as well as ice until 1939. Then, when most iceboxes had been replaced by mechanical refrigerators, motor scooter-riding Nebraska nutrition professor Rebekah Gibbons, whose father was a Penn State English professor, bought Hillside, added the newest innovations — frozen foods and lockers to store them in — and changed its name to Cold Inc. Co-owned by first Wilber Bardo and then Nevin Fisher, Cold Inc. operated until home freezers put it out of business in the 1950s. Nittany Beverage now occupies the site.

After Hoy Transfer, the oldest family-run business today is Porter Brothers, begun in 1913 as Porter and Weber, out of business for a few years in the late 1960s, and now headed by the third generation of Porters — John, who mans the paint and wallpaper store, and his brother Dave, who does the decorating. Founded by their grandfather Roy Porter and Fred Weber, the business operated out of Roy's house at 128 South Fraser Street until 1936, then moved to a building across the street. In 1953, Roy's sons — Dave, Harold "Bud", and Joe — bought out Fred Weber, changed the store name to Porter Brothers, and moved back into the family homestead, which was torn down in the 1970s to make way for the expansion of the State College Borough Municipal Building. Porter Brothers' store is now on Corl Street at West College Avenue.

Another still-operating business that began in 1913 but is no longer family-owned is Koch Funeral Home. For sixty-five years, it was a downtown

HIGH SCHOOL COMMENCEMENT

First Annual Exercises Are Held in The Methodist Church — Four Graduates Given Diplomas

In the presence of an audience that filled to over flowing the Methodist church building, the graduates of the State College High School held their graduation exercises last Friday evening . . . this is the first time any attempt has been made to mark the end of the course with any formal exercises.

The graduating class, composed of Misses Margaret Moore, Margaret Krebs, Bertha Mease and Mr. Cleveland Snyder, were placed on the right of the pulpit.

Since the establishment of the High School, four years ago, we have been striving to create a tradition of our own, a graduation exercise, a commencement.

—The Times, 5-26-05

SHALL OUR VILLAGE BE NAMED ATHERTON?

An Opportunity for Our People to Pay a Fitting and Lasting Tribute to President Atherton and the Magnificent Work he Has Done for the State of Pennsylvania.

A popular move which has been generally discussed recently has within the last couple of days taken the form of a petition, already signed by a majority of our citizens, to the Court asking that the name Atherton be bestowed upon our beautiful town.

The petition states "That we have been long under much disadvantage because the name State College is so easily and generally confused with The Pennsylvania State College."

In order to allay any fears that may arise in regards to the effect of making this change, legal advice was obtained . . . . The advice was to the effect that the expense should not exceed fifteen dollars, including all legal fees, and that the change cannot cause any legal complications or disturbance or other expense to any of the interests of the town or its residents.

—The Times, 10-26-06

business, serving the town first from a frame house at the southeast corner of College Avenue and Burrowes Street, then from a brick addition on South Burrowes added in 1935, before moving, in 1978, to its present location, 2401 South Atherton Street.

Farmer Harry Newton Koch started as a mortician by buying a thirty-five-year-old funeral business from a Pine Grove Mills man, and a team of horses, Dick and Doc, to pull the carriage and sleigh. Funeral services in those days were in family homes, with internment in nearby plots and church cemeteries, so Harry spent a lot of time traveling throughout Centre County. With the coming of motor vehicles he attached a carriage, custom-made by Boalsburg blacksmith Al Gingrich, to a stripped-down Model T in 1917. Then the two men adapted the ornate horse-drawn hearse to a Dodge chassis in 1922. By the 1930s, since many people no longer lived in homes large enough to accommodate visitors for funerals, Harry, in partnership with his son Hubert, added the funeral home behind their house. Sold by the Kochs in 1973, the business still employs Hubie's sister, Esther Koch Shaw.

One long-time family-run business that was in the same location for seventy years, 1924-94, was Crabtrees Jewelers, now site of Aurum Goldsmiths. Sam Crabtree Sr. opened a jewelry store in Tyrone in 1913, then started a second store in State College in 1920 across from where, four years later, he built the little store with the pink granite front at 132 South Allen Street. Three of Sam and Clara's four children — Becky, Sam Jr., and Allen — worked in the store after school and in summers, then in 1946, the boys joined their father in the business. Sam Sr. then could devote his time to his specialty — hand engraving everything from wedding rings and silver platters to two decades of scores on the Old Iron Kettle, the *Centre Daily Times'* trophy for the winner of the annual State College-Bellefonte High School football game. Sam Jr. later moved to Williamsport to run the jewelry store he and Al bought from their uncle, while Al, with the part-time help of his wife, Phyllis Watkins, ran the Allen Street store until selling it in 1986. The new owners kept the Crabtree name until

Billy Hoy's livery barn and transfer business had been in Calder Alley since 1905, when the hotel was enlarged into the South Allen property where his drayage operations had been. Later downtown growth saw the business move farther out.

A map from the archives of Bell Telephone's engineering office shows Atherton, Burrowes, and Highland all as Avenues. It didn't change the first two from Streets to Avenues, but may have been responsible for Highland Alley's moving up to Avenue status!

Saint Paul's M.E. Church Dedicated

Impressive Services Last Sunday by Bishop McDowell — Edifice Crowded Beyond Its Capacity Both Morning and Evening — The Church of Today is the Realization of the Dream and Vision of Yesterday — A Structure Modern in Every Detail

All Methodism rejoiced last Sunday when the beautiful and handsomely appointed new Saint Paul's church was dedicated by Bishop William Frazer McDowell of Chicago.

DEDICATORY SUNDAY

The service in the morning was attended by an audience of 1,000 and many were turned away. . . . This was also true of the services in the evening, for many came from surrounding towns to attend the dedicatory services and to hear Bishop McDowell, one of the mightiest men in the Methodist Episcopal church. The morning program opened with an organ prelude by Mrs. Helen Atherton Govier.

—*The Times, 3-3-12*

moving from Allen Street to the Nittany Mall in 1994.

Penn State students used downtown store windows as bulletin boards, pasting announcements and, on at least one occasion in 1905, protest posters on the glass. The latter concerned a history professor nicknamed "Hot Air" Ray who flunked all his students one semester and then asked President Atherton for a pay raise. The students hanged him in effigy and stoned his house.

In those days, protests were not as common as student pranks, most of which occurred in Main Building. These included dropping water or ink bombs down the five-story stairwell, sometimes hitting professors and once landing on the silk opera hat of a visiting trustee. Students also heaved books, chairs, trunks, and beds down the stairs and dragged cows, mules, horses, and other animals up, usually to the tower, sometimes painting their hairy coats with class numerals or red, white, and blue stripes.

The first recorded prank was during Evan Pugh's administration when a student hit a professor in the face with a pat of butter while grace was being said before dinner. From then on, no professor closed his eyes for prayer in the dining hall.

By 1897, the students had rolled in big guns, literally, when, angry over chemistry grades they received from Professor George G. "Swampy" Pond, they dragged a pair of Civil War cannons from the Armory lawn, loaded them with powder stolen from the College arsenal, packed them with sod, and let 'em rip. The blasts blew out every window in the front of Main Building from the third floor on down.

Another incident in the late 1890s involved a freshman who barricaded himself in Shivery's rooming house on Pugh Street, where the Days Inn is now. Refusing to submit to hazing by sophomores, he pulled out a gun and threatened to shoot. He didn't, but the sophomores did, firing a barrage of vegetables from a campus cannon that broke most of the windows.

Next-door neighbor Carolyn Buckhout Edwards, youngest of the five Buckhout children who used to play with the Shivery girls, said in 1975, "The students blew up the place and made a terrible noise. It woke everybody up. Even my father went over to see what the trouble was, and he didn't usually go out!" From then on the house was called "Shivery's Fort."

Town residents became so accustomed to hearing cannons go off that they didn't realize a crime had occurred early on the morning of October 3, 1902. "One of the most daring burglaries ever committed in Centre County," the State College *Times* called it. Thieves had broken into the post office, where Kids Clothesline is today at 138 East College Avenue, blew up the safe, and escaped with $2,320 in cash and stamps. Those who heard the explosion thought it was nothing more than the campus cannons. The only possible witness, a freshman who had seen two persons outside the building but thought they were sophomores to be avoided, had run away. He later heard the explosion, "but knowing that it was not safe for a freshman to be out, he did not venture to go and see what was going on," the newspaper said. The town constable never tracked down the thieves, but some of the stolen papers were found "along the highway."

In many ways State College was like a frontier town then. Coming here from Philadelphia, Pittsburgh, or even Bellefonte was almost like stepping into the wilderness. "We were by ourselves," one early student recalled. "We made our own fun."

ROY GENTZEL INJURED

RIGHT LEG CRUSHED, EAR PARTLY TORN LOOSE FROM HEAD

BY BEING THROWN FROM AN AUTO

A distressing accident occurred on the highway just this side of Roan's undertaking establishment last Saturday by which Roy Gentzel, an employe of the First National Bank, was the victim.

His brother, Homer, was chauffeur and had the machine under excellent control when, without a moment's warning the steering gear dropped, causing the machine to cut a few fanciful figures on the road, during which Roy Gentzel was thrown out.

—The Times, 8-16-07

"You were pretty well civilized by the time you were a junior or senior," J. Harris Olewine, professor emeritus of chemistry and longtime adviser to pre-med students, recalled in 1975. He had come to Penn State from Bellefonte as a freshman in 1911. "It was the two lower classes that raised Cain!"

Football victories were occasions for rowdyism, and town residents would frequently lose wooden fences and sidewalks, barrels, outhouses, and buggies to student bonfires. The most infamous conflagration occurred in 1914, when the football team battled unexpectedly to a 13-13 tie with powerful Harvard. Students went wild, cheering and singing all weekend and, on Monday, building what would be "the biggest bonfire ever," nearly three stories high on the parade ground where Steidle Building is today. They then doused the whole thing with five barrels of gasoline and gave the football captain, Elgie Tobin, the honor of lighting it. When he did, there was such an explosion that windows in town and on campus were shattered and Tobin and teammate Jack Saurhoff wound up in the hospital.

Prior to one victory bonfire, perhaps that one, Horton Budd Knoll, born in State College in 1906, son of Penn State Creamery superintendent Frank P. Knoll, wrote of seeing "fifteen or twenty students come down Calder Alley with a hay wagon, collecting such loose burnables as they could find. In a back yard between Atherton and Burrowes they spotted a boardwalk that extended toward the alley from the back porch of the house, but the lady of the house stood on it and defied them. If they took it, they'd have to take her, too, she said. They gave her a good-natured argument but withdrew to their wagon as if defeated. The woman remained on the boardwalk, arms folded, smiling and triumphant — till she saw three

A. Howry Espenshade organized the Episcopal congregation in 1898, meeting in Main Building on campus. John Henry Frizzell later conducted services in Schwab Auditorium, and services began in the new Parish House on Frazier Street in 1912.

The First National Bank,
the town's first bank,
and its subsidiary,
the Farmers' Trust Company,
did business side by side for
twelve years in the building
put up in 1911.

Nittany Theatre and Inn, State College, Pa.

Competition for the Pastime Theatre in 1914 was the new Nittany Theatre just across Calder on Allen Street.
Next door was Pattee's music store and the post office.

or four students, in a feinting maneuver, sneaking up on a doghouse at the side of the yard. She ran to shoo them away, like chickens from a garden, and the boardwalk was on the hay wagon and headed wildly down the alley before she realized she had been duped.

"The College had a way of atoning for such shenanigans. The owner of the boardwalk could send the College a bill and the College would pay it from damage fees collected at registration. It was then a matter of justice for the students to do enough damage to get their money's worth."

A prank that made newspapers throughout the country and even in London was a snow sculpture that six seniors built in January 1903 in front of Old Main, depicting President Atherton doffing his hat to Italian patriot Giuseppe Garibaldi mounted on a horse. The president had just returned from an extended European vacation and had told the students that he had been so moved at seeing the famous statue of Garibaldi in Rome, he had taken off his hat in reverence.

The story brought giggles from the students because a local livery stable had a horse named Garibaldi. Working five hours by lantern light, the sculptors fashioned statues from lumber, two broom sticks, a beer keg, a paint can (for the top hat), and scraps of chicken wire. In the morning the entire student body gathered to marvel at the artwork and to wait expectantly for Atherton's arrival. But when he passed them on his way to chapel, he said only, "I didn't realize we had such artistic ability at State."

Nonetheless, people came from miles around to see the snow sculpture, and pictures of it appeared in countless newspapers. The local high point of the incident came when a State College woman looked at the sculpture and said, "Well, that's Garibaldi all right, but who's that on top of him?"

In the late 1890s, bicycling was a national fad, and few local people enjoyed it more than Dr. Atherton himself. He, daughter Helen, and son Charlie often went "wheeling," as it was called, with Ladies' Cottage administrator Harriet McElwain and vice president James McKee and his family. The portly Dr. Atherton rode a sturdy Columbia "wheel," which had cost $100 from Garman's in Bellefonte, equivalent to close to $1000 in today's money. And he especially enjoyed wheeling over Centre Hall mountain. "The exercise is ever so good," said Miss McElwain, "and when we reach the top we have an excellent coast down the other side. Excellent."

According to Helen, coasting in winter was at its best on a board mounted between two sleds loaded with six or eight people. "We would start just past the Buckhout house, in front of Shivery's Fort, and slide down Pugh Street into College Avenue. And if the sliding was very good, we'd turn right and go almost as far as the Methodist Church."

She also played the organ at the Methodist Church where an admirer, Frosty Fries, would pump it for her.

In 1905, Dr. Atherton suffered a severe bronchial attack and on the advice of his physician spent the winter in California. When he returned in the spring, he was much improved but suffered a relapse after making a business trip to New York City. His last official act was to award diplomas at the 1906 commencement. Six weeks later, on July 26, he died and was buried next to Schwab Auditorium.

George Atherton had presided over astonishing progress on campus and, especially in his last two years, had seen great advances of science and technology in town, due largely to the efforts of two members of his engineering faculty, Louis E. Reber and John Price Jackson. Alumni and brothers-in-law, in fact, the two had become active business leaders in State College.

Born at Nittany in 1858, Louis became Penn State's first dean of engineering in 1885, after serving as professor of mechanical engineering. He is credited with bringing Penn State into the age of technology, creating innovative courses, buying up-to-date equipment, and, in 1898, overseeing the construction of an impressive, turreted engineering building, on the present site of Sackett.

John, whose sister Helen had married Louis in 1888, was a son of Penn State mathematics professor Josiah Jackson and organized the department of electrical engineering in 1893. He succeeded Louis as dean, but left in 1913 to become Pennsylvania's first commissioner of labor and industry.

These professorial entrepreneurs, interested in seeing the town progress along with the College, were both principals with other faculty members and businessmen in the Central Commercial Telephone Company; *State College Times* newspaper and Nittany Printing and Publishing Company; Nittany Heat, Light and Power Company; Nittany Real Estate; Nittany Inn; and the First National Bank. They also were involved, in 1904, with never-to-be-fulfilled plans for the Bellefonte Traction Company, which was to have brought trolley

---

BOOM AT STATE COLLEGE

THE TOWN IS KEEPING PACE WITH THE GREAT INSTITUTION OF LEARNING

A Great Future In Store for the People's Popular College — Real Estate Has Taken a Sudden Jump and Farm Lands Are Being Turned Into Building Sites. Town Will Soon Have a Population of 3,000

Pennsylvania Day at State College has demonstrated that the people of the state are behind it with active interest and good wishes because of its recognized value and importance to the common people.

The presence of prominent men from all parts of the state on that day added to the throb and thrill of the occasion, and gave abundant promise of State's great future.

Parties from many sections of the state who have families to rear are building with a view to living here for a few years to oversee the education of their children and then selling or renting to others who may wish to do the same thing.

—CDT 12/4/08

This 1914 post card shows that the 1899 remodeling of Meek Bros. drug store at 110 East College Avenue had served the business well.

GFWC State College Woman's Club

ounded on March 8, 1894, as the Woman's Literary Club, the State College Woman's Club is two years older than the borough it has served. Thirty-six founding members, primarily Penn State faculty wives, established the club in the parlor of the university's seventh president, George Atherton. Their original mission was "to do what is necessary to keep ourselves informed about the world around us, to be aware of special needs, whether in town, on campus, or elsewhere, and if we as members can do something to fill that need, to do so."

Members have volunteered time and financial support to hundreds of civic projects and other worthy causes — from helping establish local phone service to assisting area schools, libraries, and health-care facilities. The club has raised money for high school band uniforms, a dental hygiene clinic, the hospital building fund, a community swimming pool, the start-up grant for the Nittany Valley Symphony, an adult day activity center, the Lederer Park sign, scholarships, and Park Forest Day Nursery.

After changing its name to the State College Woman's Club in 1910, the organization was divided into departments reflecting members' individual interests. Small groups were formed to discuss gardening, bridge, literature, drama, music, art, and home-life issues. Most of the original departments continue to this day.

The Woman's Club originally met in members' parlors and living rooms, then in schools, churches, and wherever it could find space. In 1959, the club purchased a building at 902 South Allen Street for its permanent meeting place. The club's Thrift Shop, started in the 1930s, found a new home at the clubhouse. Selling donated clothing and household items, the Thrift Shop has become one of the club's primary fund-raising vehicles.

In 1994, the State College Woman's Club contributed $41,650 to community organizations supporting the arts, education, health and family services, and conservation. Members also are involved with groups such as Shaver's Creek Environmental Center, Schlow Library, Meals on Wheels, Hospital Auxiliary, and Mid-State Literacy Council. As club president Grace Bardine leads the club into its second century, more than 200 members are ready to contribute time and talents toward the good of State College and its residents.

cars right up College Avenue from Milesburg.

Professor Reber added the caveat in his memoirs, written in 1944, that "it must be remembered that the Campus members of these enterprising Companies were quite fully occupied with Campus duties." But they did have critics. One was the underground student publication *The Lemon*, short-lived predecessor to longtime humor magazine *Froth*, which nicknamed the enterprises "Not Any Heat or Light Company," "Not Any Inn," "Not Any Real Estate," "Not Any Traction," and "The Skin 'Em All Printin' Trust."

Another critic was Bell Telephone Company. In 1898, William Thompson Jr. of Centre Furnace, and Ellis Orvis, N. E. Robb, and Frank Maginney, all of Bellefonte, had teamed with Professors Reber and Jackson in founding the Central Commercial Telephone Company to compete with Bell, which by then had established an office in Dr. J. V. Foster's building on Allen Street. One report said, "So much pressure was brought to bear on President Atherton by the Bell company because of the participation of Professors Jackson and Reber in 'private business,' they were forced to resign in favor of the Rev. Aikens and John McCormick."

As for the newspaper, it had been established as a weekly on May 12, 1898, and the printing and publishing company a few years later by George Washington Burns, who because of ill health, turned the business over to his brother, Robert, in 1900. "It was not a creditable sheet for a college-dominated community," Louis wrote, so he and John with Professors Fred Foss and George Butz bought the plant in 1904. Fred's sister, Mrs. Lawrence, became editor and, as Louis said, "improved the quality of the publication. Looking back I see that more could have been made of it from every point of view, but we achieved the desired object in providing a reputable news service for town and Campus."

As more and more visitors came to the College, adequate hotel space became a concern. The Nittany Inn, where Louis had roomed as an undergraduate, had fallen into disrepair, so he and John again took the lead and with Ellis Orvis and Louis's classmate and Penn State trustee James Hamill chartered the Nittany Real Estate Company on July 1, 1904. Before the year was out, Nittany Real Estate had bought the Nittany Inn from S. S. Grieb, refurbished it and turned the street floor into a small lobby and storerooms. Louis wrote, "It then became possible to accommodate comfortably in the renovated establishment College guests whom it had previously been necessary to entertain in Campus homes. Both town and Campus made use of the greater facilities offered." The street-level rooms housed the post office for several years and the Co-operative Book Store, which students referred to as the Co-op, giving rise to the intersection's longtime

TROUSER SKIRTS FOR THE 1913 WOMAN

Fashion Has Decreed That The Spring Maid Will be Hipless and Curveless— Coats Are to be Rah- Rah Styled Affairs. Ye Gods! What Next?

The spring maid of 1913 is to be straight front, straight back, hipless and curveless. If fashionably attired, she will look like a straight line, with an oblique line at the top, said oblique line being her hat.

—*The Times, 12-6-12*

nickname, "Co-op Corner." In 1917, the property was finally sold to the Reverend Charles Aikens.

Another Reber-Jackson venture of 1904 grew out of a conversation Louis had with William "Cal" Patterson, superintendent of the College farms, who told him some out-of-towners were contemplating opening a bank. "Mr. Patterson was of the opinion that a bank in State College should be the concern of residents of the place and asked me if I would join with him in taking the necessary steps. I with a number of others agreed."

A national bank was organized, a board of directors was selected, and Cal was elected president. Other board members were: Reber, Jackson, the Reverend Mr. Aikens, Professor John McCormick, merchant and postmaster John Stuart, William Foster, and Charles Foster. "The bank paid at once and quickly became an asset to the region," Louis wrote in the 1940s, adding, "It is interesting to note that of the interests I had in the town, two of them are owned and carried on by the son of the Rev. Mr. Aikens — the hotel and the State College *Times*."

The First National Bank of State College began operations in a room in Sophie Hunter's house on West College Avenue. It then opened a subsidiary, the Farmers' Trust Company, in 1911 at 122 West College Avenue, until the trust company was absorbed by First National the same year Peoples Bank, a competitor, opened.

In 1906, Reber, Jackson, Foss, Hamill, and the Reverend Aikens pioneered yet another first for the town — their Nittany Heat, Light and Power Company built a producer gas plant in Calder Alley to generate the town's first electricity for lighting, later connecting with Penn State's steam power plant, which had been generating electricity for the campus since 1888. The commercial company later was taken over in turn by the State College Electric Company, Keystone Light Corporation, and West Penn Power.

In his memoirs, Louis said he had hoped manufactured gas would be more economical than steam for running an electrical generator. He was wrong: "We installed the producer gas plant, much to our regret. When it worked, it supplied electric current at a very low cost, but it was not possible to keep it working continuously. Professor Jackson spent many hours day and night putting it in order, trying to keep it going. After I went to Wisconsin [in 1907], a new company was organized and a steam plant installed."

Dr. Atherton's death in 1906, after twenty-four productive years for both town and campus, revived a row between the two factions that had first occurred six months before State College was incorporated — what to call the town.

The issue popped up again when a petition was circu-

The "new" Pastime Theatre on Allen Street in 1914 had rooms for Lohman's Barber Shop and Miller's Drug Store, with apartments upstairs.

The Woman's Club donated a combination drinking fountain and watering trough for livestock, installed in the 100 block of East College Avenue on the campus side of the street. In the background is the well at main campus gate.

In 1916 Lynn Platt quit his chauffeur's job with President Sparks to open this basement pool room in the Robison Building on Allen Street. He soon got a call from Dr. Sparks: "I've got to have you back — you and I never missed a train. If you'll come back, I'll have the College pay someone to manage your place." With an offer like that, Lynn resumed his duties behind the steering wheel, continuing the hectic driving pace through the First World War.

lated to rename the town Atherton in honor of "the life and labors of our most worthy citizen." Backers of the Atherton name said, "We have long been under much disadvantage because the name 'State College' is the name of the educational institution here located. Similarly, the educational institution suffers from lack of a more distinctive location than the Borough name 'State College.' " (It is interesting to note that, in 1954, when the bitterest name-change battle ensued — after College became University — Penn State's president Milton Eisenhower used that same argument.)

One of the most vigorous supporters of the Atherton name was *The Lemon*, whose editors jeeringly branded the town "State Colic." The petition attracted 150 signatures before any serious objections were raised, and when they came they were chiefly economic. The bank complained that it would cost $250 to reprint all its stationery, and other businessmen chorused, "Too much paperwork!" A counter-petition went the rounds, and the movement suddenly died, with only *The Lemon* refusing to give up, and using *Atherton, Pa.*, as its dateline from then on.

The yellow-covered, pocket-sized predecessor to *Penn State Froth* humor magazine appeared sporadically from December 1906 to June 1908, until Atherton's successor was named, published without the blessing of Penn State's administration and, therefore, anonymously. "In words of one syllable," its editors proclaimed, "*The Lemon* will direct streams of astringent juice at those things in and about our college that, in the eyes of the undergraduates, need betterment or abolishment."

One of the magazine's crusades was to effect improvement in both service and track conditions of the Bellefonte Central Railroad, whose trains made slow progress over the twisting, sometimes flooded right-of-way. Students dubbed it "Parker's Boat" following one trip when a section of track had been flooded by a nearby creek and the train stalled when it tried to go through the water, marooning passengers who then had to wade "ashore" assisted by Conductor Ross Parker. The following poem, "Short Extract from Ballads of Your Anty-Bellum," appeared in the February 9, 1907, issue:

> *Only 45 minutes from Bellefonte*
> *On the line of the A.B.C.R.R.*
> *But your life is at stake*
> *In this risk that you take*
> *As you'll find before going so far.*
> *A rap on the sconce from a fence post,*
> *A biff on the ear from a tie,*

THE COMMON TOWEL TABOOED

That Time Honored Adjunct to Factory and Office Must Go.

Must be Complied With by Corporations, Hotels, Restaurants, Offices and Factories—Public or Common Drinking Cup Also Under the Ban. Barbers Forbidden to Use General Utility Brush on Customers.

The use of the public drinking cup and the common towel has been prohibited by the advisory board of the State Department of Health. Barbers are forbidden to brush the eyes of customers with a common brush and the proprietors of public eating houses and restaurants must hereafter thoroughly cleanse all eating utensils after each individual use. Physicians are required to report two additional communicable diseases, scabies and impetigo contagions.

—The Times, 12-5-13

> *Are among the diversions*
> *On all these excursions —*
> *Only 45 minutes, Thank God!*

Soon, *The Lemon* was as avidly read by professors and townspeople as it was by the 800 students then enrolled at the College. And Parker, who absorbed good-natured ribbing from every issue, became one of its most devoted readers — and distributors! Since the editorial staff loafed there, Graham's barber shop was a principal distribution point for the magazine, which joshed George as a "hair butcher" who had "special apparatus for blowing hairs down your back."

Another who was both jeered and cheered by *The Lemon* was General James Beaver, who as trustees president served as acting president of the College for the two years between Atherton's death and the arrival of his successor, Edwin Erle Sparks. Beaver began practicing law in 1856 under Hugh McAllister, prominent Bellefonte attorney and one of Penn State's founders. After losing a leg and gaining the rank of brigadier general in the Civil War, he returned to Bellefonte to marry Hugh's daughter, Mary. When Hugh died in 1873, his son-in-law inherited his lucrative law practice as well as his seat on Penn State's board, which he held for forty-one years, including two terms as president, 1874 to 1882 and 1898 until his death in 1914, and one as governor of Pennsylvania (1887-1891). Though not as beloved by students as Atherton, he is commemorated in both town and gown with Beaver Avenue and Beaver Stadium.

To earn money for tuition and other college expenses, *Lemon* editor Harrison D. "Joe" Mason also reported Penn State fall and winter sports for big-city newspapers and is credited with giving Penn State its first football All-American, William T. "Mother" Dunn, Class of '08. While a student, "Mother" ran the campus dining room in the new McAllister Building. After graduating, he and then-student Walter H. "Babe" Wood '10, opened the Pastime, State College's first movie theatre, in 1909 in a former buggy and wagon shop at 116 South Allen Street. Admission was only a nickel, including free peanuts to throw at the villain and the piano player who accompanied the silent "flickers," but rushing the ticket-taker to get in free became a popular student activity. A new four-story Pastime was built in 1914 to seat 750 people within its luxurious walls. Also in 1914, James Aikens, brother of Charles, built the Nittany Theatre just across Calder Alley from the Pastime, and both were bought in 1916 by Maurice Baum, who, in 1926, added to his theatre holdings by building the beautiful 1,080-seat Cathaum.

Hotel State College

One of our town's oldest and most recognizable landmarks, the Hotel State College, opened in 1855 as Jack's Road House, under the proprietorship of James Jack of Philadelphia. Back then, "town" was a few houses along one or two dirt streets, at the edge of lots of open farmland. The tiny hamlet and its first "public house" grew, and changed, together.

In 1880, the property was bought by John W. Stuart, who renamed it the College Hotel, or Inn. Early on, it was a stage stop, and later, a convenient resting place for railroad passengers arriving at the train station across the street. In 1885, the town's first pay phone, and a telegraph, were installed.

Mr. S. S. Grieb owned the hotel for a time. Then, in 1904, he sold it to the Nittany Real Estate Company, which completely renovated the old "road house" — encasing the frame structure in brick, redecorating the first-floor lobby, and opening bowling alleys and a barber shop in the basement.

In 1925, the business was purchased by Claude Aikens, R. J. Kennard, and Marlin "Matty" Mateer. They further remodeled the first floor and opened, in 1926, the popular restaurant known as the Corner Room.

Through the years, the property extending along South Allen Street and West College Avenue has been home to many businesses, shops, and restaurants. The 1,000-seat Cathaum Theater once occupied space there, as did the Nittany Printing and Publishing Company. Says hotel co-owner Michael Desmond, "At one time the *Centre Daily Times*, published in the press building next to the Corner Room, was owned by Mr. Aikens. He had new menus printed every day, with information about what movies were playing in town, and a 'This Day in History' quote from the *Farmer's Almanac*. It was a nice touch."

Developer Sidney Friedman bought the property in the early 1970s. At that time it was managed by brothers Chris and Zeno Pappas. In 1986, co-owners Michael Desmond and John Cocolin took over, and do business as Hotel State College & Co.

Once having as many as seventy guest rooms, the hotel now has fourteen. The rest have been converted to apartments or shops. A highlight is the Allen Street Grill, overlooking Co-Op Corner, still the hub of downtown life.

The Hotel State College was called the Nittany Inn when it appeared on this 1914 picture postcard.

The Times' first comic strip began in May 1914

—The Times, 5/18/14

Lemon editors felt their work was finished in 1908, when forty-eight-year-old Edwin Sparks came from the University of Chicago to be Penn State's eighth president. A popular after-dinner speaker, teacher, author of eight history books, and a friend of politicians, he had administrative experience in public schools and had been principal of Penn State's preparatory department from 1890 to 1895. During those five years he and his wife, Katherine, hosted many social events that established them "as a genial force in the social life of the community," something that resumed after his return to Penn State.

Believing that the aims of the College could not be achieved by addressing the students from too lofty a plane, he allowed them to establish their own student government and opened his office door to everyone. By the end of his first year at Penn State, nearly all 1,100 students had visited his office, and he knew every student by name. In appreciation they dubbed him "Prexy."

One person who paid a visit soon after Sparks arrived — and who, by association, also got the nickname "Prexy" — was milkman Lynn Platt. Sparks had announced that in the spring of 1909 he would buy an automobile, and Platt was applying for the job of chauffeur. He won out over twenty-three other applicants because when asked what he knew about automobiles, he replied, "Nothing. There's not much to know about them, and nobody else knows either. Why don't you give me a try? If you don't like me, you can fire me." Thus began a relationship that would carry Edwin Sparks and Lynn Platt 100,000 miles in eleven years from the college in the center of the state that was, in Sparks's words, "equally inaccessible from all directions."

During his presidency, 1908-20, Sparks gave more than 6,000 speeches — an average of fifty a year! — throughout the United States, traveling to most of these engagements in the front seat of his Franklin automobile, driven by Lynn Platt. The friendship between the two men was not one of employer and employee but more like father and son. "Doctor was friendly with everybody," Lynn said, "and he treated me as well as he did his own daughter — just like I was one of the family. Yes, Doctor

and I were chums."

Dr. and Mrs. Sparks were good friends with Colonel and Mrs. Theodore "Terry" Boal of Boalsburg, and the two families led the social scene in the State College area. For instance, the Sparkses held a lavish reception at the University Club in 1915 to celebrate their silver wedding anniversary.

Revivalist Billy Sunday paid a visit and was brought from Lemont in a hack pulled by students, causing him to remark that although he had been pulled *out* of many a town, this was the first time he had ever been pulled *into* one! The president of the Pennsylvania Railroad "parked his train" at the State College depot when he came to visit the Sparkses, and ex-President William Howard Taft appreciated the Sparkses' hospitality "for this visiting circuit rider."

Lynn Platt was married in 1912, and he and his bride set up housekeeping in the Robison Building at 124 South Allen Street. Dr. Sparks always remembered the Platts at Christmas, and each of the four Platt children — Jack, Jo (Gettig), Madeline (Lynch), and Betty (Daschbach) — received annual birthday gifts from "Doctor."

Edwin and Katherine Sparks had just one child, Ethel, who graduated from Penn State in 1916 and married a man with her own surname — Carvel Sparks. In 1951, she became the first woman elected to the board of trustees by alumni, receiving the largest number of votes up to then in the history of alumni trustee elections.

Sparks's car was not the first in State College. That honor went to the mechanical engineering department's experimental machine. In 1905, the *Times* reported that the town's second and third cars, both Stanley Steamers, were purchased by Professors Fred Foss and George C. Watson. Later that same year, C. D. Fehr of the German department bought an Oldsmobile, "a red one, with seats at the sides, and shining brass lamps." The paper also said that the Fosses made a summer tour in their new auto and reported that there were twenty-six toll roads between State College and Philadelphia.

Until April 1, 1910, automobiles were bought out of town, but on that date C. E. "Peck" Snyder became State College's first auto dealer when he sold a Ford out

FYE'S STORE
1-7-'16

McDowell
Photo.

L. D. Fye bought the general store at College and Allen from Laird Holmes, his brother-in-law, in 1905. By 1916, he had his own new building at 200 West College Avenue. L. D. stands behind the counter in his complete grocery store; next door was his dry-goods and clothing store.

High-school-dropout Peck Snyder saw the future of the automobile in 1910, and by 1916 moved his new-car dealership to his own Burrowes Street building. He also sold "A complete line of Auto Supplies, Bicycles, Guns, Ammunition, Sporting Goods and Fishing Tackle." Peck kept a diary, and had written in 1914 that "I almost forgot to mention the time I was almost electrocuted in the old garage on Frazier St. one evening while working on Marion Meyer's car. I was taking up the connecting rod bearings, was down in the pit and had hold of a drag wire with a brass socket when I was shocked that I could not leave go and I holered 'turn it off' and as the current held me fast and I could not make any more noise Jim Holmes jerked the wire out of my hand and saved my life."

of the barn he had remodeled at the corner of Fraser Street and Calder Alley. A twenty-six-year-old newcomer from Tyrone, Peck had been inspired the year before by his partnership-purchase of a one-cylinder Oldsmobile with his plumber friend Forest Struble, who had preceded him from Tyrone by a month.

Peck added the Reo line to his stock in 1914, Dodge in 1915, and had just decided he needed larger quarters when a Dodge Brothers representative inspected his barn and let him know it was not a proper place to sell the company's products. Peck then built "a modern, fireproof building" at 121-123 South Burrowes Street in 1916 and went into the car business in earnest.

In 1928, ailing from diabetes and alienated from the Dodge Brothers, Peck retired and sold his garage to Goodyear Tire salesman Russ Stein, who sold Fords and later Oldsmobiles there. Although the name was changed to the R. F. Stein Garage, people continued to call it Snyder's for years after that. In the 1940s Stein sold out to Charlie Henszey and his State College Automobile Company, and in 1960, Charlie Rider, then an Oldsmobile dealer in Bellefonte, bought the building and moved his business to State College. Now run by son Chuck, Rider Auto was the last car dealership still downtown before moving in 1987 to 1701 West College Avenue. "Peck's Garage" now houses Paul and Tony's Stereo; *The Daily Collegian;* C-NET, the local government/education access channel; and some offices of Penn State's College of Communications.

Sparks's coming to Penn State set off a building boom that put State College in the news in 1910 for having completed 100 new houses and buildings in two years. One of those was built for the George Graham family at 310 South Allen Street, then only the second house south of Foster Avenue.

"Everyone thought Father was crazy to want to live 'out in the country'!" Kitty Roseberry said. "But when Stan and I built our house on Irvin Avenue in 1937, Bohn's farm was across the street and Father thought *we* were crazy to want to live in the country!"

Between 1908 and 1923, others followed the Grahams to the "Highland Park Addition to State College Borough," as that neighborhood was known. Many rented out third floors to students, even though it was considered a long walk to campus from there. But up until then the area really had been "the country" — namely the Foster farm, which also included a large sinkhole, "The Hollow," north of Nittany Avenue at Fraser Street.

To promote Highland Park, Will Foster, State College retailer and apartment owner who had bought the acreage from John Foster, son of the original Farmer Foster, ran a special train from Bellefonte for prospective buyers and treated all comers to hot-air balloon rides. Lots sold at $400 each.

His son, Russell Foster, born in 1895, also helped with the new development. "Professor Harold Shattuck was the borough surveyor then," recalled Russell in 1989. "I held the rod for him while he surveyed the lots. And my dad wrote every deed in longhand."

Russell says his mother, Mary Olds Foster, named the five avenues that crossed Allen Street in Highland Park — Foster (named for *all* the Foster families), Nittany, Fairmount, Prospect, and Hamilton. Sister of architect Frederick Olds, who designed Old Botany and Old Engineering, among other campus buildings, Mary, in 1911, became the first woman to serve on the State College School Board, which entered in its November 1913 minutes an "expression of appreciation for her helpful interest." She also helped to organize the Woman's Literary Club, the first library committee, and the parent-teachers association.

In 1920, the Fosters bought the large stone house at 425 South Allen Street, originally built in 1909 for another Mary Foster, sister of Charles Foster and no relation to the Will Fosters.

Although Will died in 1928, his widow stayed on, taking in student roomers until 1945. The house's last occupant, before it was razed to build The Towers in 1988, was the Voluntary Action Center.

Charter residents of Highland Park, who in 1908 built a house at 426 South Allen, across from the Foster home, were mechanical engineering professor A. J. Wood and his wife Helen. Their son Reginald, born in 1912, recalled a story in the *State College Times* reporting: "A big black bear shambled into town, and its presence caused quite a flutter of excitement among the nimrods, who turned out en masse with all sorts of weapons, bent on slaying his bearship. Bruin was first sighted by Hamill Holmes as it ambled across the clearing near Foster's woods. It then skirted the southern end of town until it reached Allen Street where it spent some time among the garbage cans and drove Prof. A. J. Wood to cover when he found the bear in his back yard. The animal finally escaped to Tussey Mountain."

John Henry Frizzell, who arrived in 1902 as a $15-a-week instructor in English and rhetoricals at Penn State, helped to found St. Andrew's Episcopal Church. One afternoon in 1908, he recalled, Bishop James Darlington stuck his cane into a hayfield near "The Hollow" and declared, "Here's where we'll build the church." John Henry said, "We raised $26,000 to do it, and folks hereabouts laughed at us for building it out in the country."

P. O. Site Selected

Government Finally Decides Upon the Price-Woodring Property, Corner Allen Street and Beaver Avenue, For the $50,000 Federal Building.

The department officials at Washington have at last decided upon a site for the Federal building. The purchase price was $14,000. As the plot is 100x110 it will afford ample room for the $50,000 Federal building which the department proposes to erect. The site, while not the best of those offered the government, is well situated and will have a tendency to divert the business center from the diamond to Beaver and Allen. The present properties, which are now tenanted by Miss Elizabeth D. Price and Dr. Walter J. Keith, will have to be vacated and razed.

—The Times, 1-15-15

Centre County Historical Society

It seems fitting that the Centre County Historical Society, devoted to preserving and chronicling local history, is headquartered at a site so closely associated with the county's early development. Centre Furnace gave rise to the largest local industry of the nineteenth century, charcoal iron-making, and thereby provided the incentive to create Centre County, Penn State University, and, ultimately, the borough of State College. It's clear that the face of State College would be inexorably different were it not for Centre Furnace and people such as Samuel Miles, John Patton, James Irvin, and Moses Thompson — all of whom helped make Central Pennsylvania the nation's premier iron-producing region between 1800 and 1850.

Pennsylvania Agricultural Society, setting the stage for the creation of a new school in Centre County. Documents deeding the land were signed in 1855 at Centre Furnace Mansion, and construction soon began on the Farmers' High School, forerunner of The Pennsylvania State University. Meanwhile, the town of State College, incorporated in 1896, developed on farms also originally owned by Centre Furnace Iron Company.

Today the Victorian mansion occupied by Moses Thompson's family from 1842 to 1912 has been restored and furnished with original and period antiques. Home to the Centre County Historical Society since 1978 and listed on the National Register of Historic Places, it houses a growing collection of artifacts and documents relating to the iron industry and county history. The mansion is open to the public throughout the year for tours and group gatherings.

Incorporated in 1904, the Centre County Historical Society is the oldest and largest of the county's historical organizations. The society provides assistance to individuals and organizations involved in preserving local homes or buildings of historical significance. It also conducts monthly programs and hosts annual events such as the Victorian Christmas party, Old Fashioned Fourth of July celebration, and May

Centre Furnace Mansion, home to the Centre County Historical Society, welcomes visitors year-round

Founded in 1791 by Revolutionary War officers Miles and Patton, Centre Furnace Ironworks was the region's first charcoal iron-making center. A sizable town, Centre Furnace, soon grew up around the ironworks, and in 1800 led to the creation of Centre County. More than half a century later, two prominent Centre Furnace ironmasters — Irvin and Thompson — offered 200 acres of furnace land to the

birthday party for Mary Irvin Thompson. Through a publishing fund established in 1988, the society offers a wide range of publications exploring diverse aspects of local, regional, and state history. With the help of donations and membership support, the Centre County Historical Society continues to play a pivotal role in local preservation efforts.

John Henry went on to build Penn State's speech department into one of the nation's best, was College chaplain for nearly twenty years, was a long-time Alpha fireman, and helped to establish the Alpha Ambulance Service.

Will Foster's brother Phil, whose home still stands on the southeast corner of Atherton Street and College Avenue, had his own building boom along Atherton, south of the original location of Grace Lutheran Church, at 400 West College Avenue, where Arby's is today. At the same time, houses were accumulating along Park Avenue. That neighborhood was laid out and landscaped by A. W. Cowell, and much of the construction was done by Frank Kennedy, one of the first contractors in town. His son, Dean, became a State College architect.

A pioneer real estate developer who played a large role in building up the western section of State College was John Laird Holmes. Born at Centre Furnace in 1868, Laird, as he liked to be called, was State College's first public school teacher, its first tax collector, and its first burgess to serve two terms.

He got started in the real estate business by purchasing three farms west of Atherton Street and dividing them into lots. On one of those lots, 332 South Gill Street, he built a new house in the 1920s for himself and his wife, Mittie Fye, whom he had married in 1894. Later, in 1926, he and Irving Foster, Penn State professor of romance languages, both donated land west of present-day Sparks Street for the community's first public park and playground — Holmes-Foster Park.

This wasn't all Laird did for State College before he died at age ninety in 1958. After ten years' teaching, he bought Mif Snyder's general store and its neighbor, the Condo store, and united them into one retail business in 1899. With the help of his brother-in-law, L. D. Fye, and a delivery boy, Holmes supplied shoppers in State College with groceries, dry goods, and general merchandise until 1905, when L. D. bought him out and the business became Fye's Store, operating until 1934.

Before Laird and Mittie Holmes built their new house on Gill Street, says granddaughter Virginia Keeler Smith, they had reared four children — Virginia, John L. Jr., Adelene (Mrs. William Keeler), and William F. — downtown in the house where Laird maintained an office for sixty-five years, at 206 West College Avenue, next to the Fye Building.

Laird also founded Mt. Nittany Building and Loan Company, was a charter member of the State College Presbyterian Church, was an early member of the Odd Fellows, the State College Rotary Club, and the Patriotic Order of Sons of America, and helped to organize the library association.

The town library was started by the Woman's Literary Club when they purchased a set of encyclopedias in 1898 and, as recorded by club president Mary Olds Foster, "chained them to a table in the primary room at the Frazier Street School." Mariah J. Penny, a member of the club's library committee, served as librarian, gratis, encouraging and advising children to better leisure-time reading habits. In 1911, the library committee called a public meeting with Laird Holmes presiding, and the State College Public Library Association was formed with him as president. The first paid librarians were Anna Roop and Alice Maule, who conducted their duties part-time in a room in the Frazier Street School.

House numbers were first used in 1910 to help find people in this burgeoning town, whose population grew from 1,650 in 1910 to 2,550 in 1915, and to aid in home mail delivery, which also began in 1910. For the first year or two the postman rang the doorbell, but then the law required that mailboxes be supplied to save time, so he rang only for special deliveries.

Since the College didn't have enough dormitories, most new houses in town were built to include rooms that townspeople could rent out to students. One who did beginning in 1913 was Ethel Bottorf, a widow with five children — Harold (Hobie), Helen, Kenneth, Richard, and William — and thirteen roomers at 513 West College Avenue. The rent of $3 a week, $1.50 per roomer, for a double room was the family's main source of income.

Daughter Helen, who was fifteen years old in 1913, said in 1976, "Mother did everything. She sewed, cooked, baked, did laundry, and made all the beds, even for the thirteen roomers."

Budd Knoll, whose family homestead was at the northwest corner of West Beaver and South Burrowes, half town, half country then, wrote: "Everyone then had a lot more manual work than they do today. Housewives, for example, baked the family bread in 1912. They'd mix the dough Friday night, let it rise overnight, and bake it the next morning in the oven of a coal-fired stove. There were chores for a boy to do, but chances were good on a summer morning that they wouldn't fill all or even a major part of the day. One of my chores was to sprinkle Beaver Avenue with water in front of our house. It was an 'improved' avenue, i.e., it was not flat but raised in the middle so there was a gutter on either side. But horses and Fords raised dust aplenty from it in the summer. I also got the job of feeding our chickens when I was big

TWO ALARMS OF FIRE

Elizabeth Price Property Damaged. Prompt Action Saved House From Total Destruction — Second Fire Occurred During the Early Hours Wednesday Morning.

Tuesday afternoon the Elizabeth Price dwelling at the corner of Allen and Beaver, caught fire from a defective flue. Prompt work on the part of the fire companies saved the house from total destruction.

The new chemical truck of the Student Volunteer Fire company went into service for the first time and did effective work. The building is so old that the government ought to condemn it and have it razed.'

A second alarm was sounded at 1 a.m. Wednesday. morning, the shrill blasts of the fire whistle awakening residents out of sound slumber. The fire was located in the east end and prompt action saved the surrounding property. The fire was located in the old Schilling repair shop, which has had an unsavory reputation for some time.

—The Times, 5-7-15

48

The caption reads vertically on the right: SCCentennial Collection, from Mrs. Harry Behrer/Harry B. Kropp

The Times *on October 13, 1916, announced plans for the dedication of the new I.O.O.F. hall in State College on November 24. "Uppermost in the minds of the Odd Fellows of State College and vicinity just at this time is the dedication of their new hall and building located on East College Avenue . . . The programme . . . calls for a two days' celebration, with a reception at the new hall and a dance in the evening. Friday morning there will be a parade in which visiting lodges will participate . . . The event will undoubtedly bring one of the largest crowds to State College that has ever been entertained here." Building-committee members were: E. S. Erb, Geo. T. Graham, A. H. Hartswick, W. D. Custard, Park Homan, Clark Herman, Harry Womer, Harry Lonberger, Geo. B. Jackson, and C. L. Hollabaugh. Arrangements for the dedication were made by J. Laird Holmes, the Reverend J. McK. Reiley, and J. D. White.*

SYNOPSIS

The New York police are mystified by a series of murders and other crimes. The principal clue to the criminal is the warning letter which is sent the victims, signed with a "Clutching Hand."

THIRTEENTH EPISODE

THE DEVIL WORSHIPPERS

Elaine was seated in the drawing room with Aunt Josephine one afternoon, when her lawyer, Perry Bennett, dropped in unexpectedly.

He had hardly greeted them when the butler, Jennings, in his usual impassive manner announced that Aunt Josephine was wanted on the telephone.

The Exploits of Elaine

A Detective Novel and a Motion Picture Drama

By ARTHUR B. REEVE

The Well-Known Novelist and the Creator of the "Craig Kennedy" Stories

Presented in Collaboration With the Pathe Players and the Eclectic Film Company

No sooner were Elaine and Bennett alone than Elaine, turning to him, exclaimed,

"Last night I dreamed that father came to me and told me that if I would give up Kennedy and put my trust in you, I would find the Clutching Hand. I don't know what to think of it."

Bennett, who had been listening intently, moved over nearer to Elaine and bent over her.

"Elaine," he said in a low tone, his remarkable eyes looking straight into her own, "you must know that I love you. Then give me the right to protect you. It was your father's

dearest wish, I believe, that we should marry. Let me share your dangers and I swear that sooner or later there will be an end to the Clutching Hand. Give me your answer, Elaine," he urged, "and make me the happiest man in all the world."

Elaine listened, and not unsympathetically as Bennett continued to plead for her answer.

"Wait a little while—until tomorrow," she replied, finally.

"Let it be as you wish, then," agreed Bennett quietly.

He took her hand and kissed it passionately.

—*The Times, 5-28-15*

Serialized high-suspense novels in newspapers were the original "soap operas."

enough to carry a pail of feed."

An English professor at Purdue University for more than forty years, Budd was greatly influenced by Carolyn Buckhout, his English teacher at State High, who married forestry professor W. G. "Billy" Edwards in 1919. Unlike Budd, though, she did few chores while growing up in her family's substantial house with lavish gardens at East Beaver and Pugh Street. "It seems impossible, but we almost always had a maid. I never washed dishes until I was fifteen. I was never allowed in the kitchen because I would be in the way. Mother and the cook did the meals. And my father would not have any washing or ironing done in the house. There was a woman, Mrs. Kerstetter, who came every week and got our clothes in a great big bag and brought them back in a basket, all neatly ironed."

When Carolyn was younger, she often played with the Foster children, Betsy and Russell, who then lived a block away on College Avenue, next to their father's general store. "One of the things we liked to do was to go in Old Main and climb clear to the top of the stairs and then see how fast we could come down. Russell didn't come too fast, and he'd get part way down and cry, 'Wait for me! Wait for me!' I'd go all the way down and then go back up to get him."

In the evenings, the Buckhout children would gather in the living room to listen to stories read by their mother or to play whist or backgammon while their father snapped his newspaper as he read it. "He did that, I always thought, because we were making too much noise," Carolyn said.

Mary Louisa Willard, famed forensic chemist who taught for nearly forty years at Penn State, was a "Campus Brat" who grew up in Moffatt Cottage, which was demolished in 1965 to make way for the west wing of Pattee Library. She was born there, in 1898, daughter of Joseph Willard, head of the math department, and his wife, Henrietta. "All this was country then," Mary reminisced in 1978. "It was like living on a farm. We were pretty isolated from the children in town, so we had to make up our own games and entertainments." These included playing in the apple orchard behind the house, riding on Helen Atherton's horse, and skiing down "Ag Hill" all the way from the Creamery to College Avenue.

Sometimes Mary, younger brother Ned, and next-door neighbors Dorothy Crane and Sarah Pattee put on plays written by Sarah's father. "We'd put up a curtain in the corner, and Professor [Fred Lewis] Pattee would take off his shoes, stretch out in a chair, and be our audience. Well, can you imagine! Best of all I liked to be an angel. My mother made me wings with gold on them. Sarah liked to be the one who did all the naughty things."

Norman Taylor, son of constable and street commissioner George Taylor and classmate of Budd Knoll's, lived on "Pickle Hill," at 723 East Beaver Avenue, later renumbered to 466 East Beaver after three one-block streets were eliminated. In 1993, recalling his childhood, Norman said, "Once in the teens we had a lot of snow that lasted all winter, and we would ride our sleds from Sowers Street down Beaver Avenue and down Hetzel Street to Calder Way." Another good sledding hill that both he and Budd recommended was from the Frazier Street School down into "The Hollow."

"Early on," Budd wrote, "I learned that I was not a Town Boy, a Pickle Hiller, or a Professor's Kid. My father, superintendent of the College Creamery, was a practical man and, he said, a member of what might be called the Scrub Faculty. That left me unclassified and perhaps saved from a bit of static. Town Boys and Pickle Hillers were proud to be called what they were, but a Professor's Kid, when called one, was made to feel like a pesky bug. It was feared that Professor's Kids might begin putting on airs."

He went on to say, "And always there was The Presence — Big Brother on the hill across College Avenue, Boss, Rich Uncle, Commander in Chief, Emperor of the Valley — in short, The College, a transcendent entity which townspeople loved and despised, admired and cussed, trusted and doubted, all in the same breath. The Town/Gown symbiosis had rounded corners and saw-toothed edges, Gown having the money and clout and, in some respects, dominating Town; and Town saying 'Thank you' and 'Go to.'

"Except, that is, in the matter of football, where Town loyalty to Gown was almost total. The Penn State team was to be supported, admired, maybe even revered. The days were bright when it won, dreary when it lost. A boy could sense this from what was said and how it was said, from a tone of voice, a look of wonder, from hearing names from the past that still trailed clouds of glory: Dex Very, Pete Mauthe, 'Mother' Dunn . . . and from the present: Charlie Way, Tiny McMahan, Dick Harlow, Levi Lamb. He learned it from many sorts of people: businessmen, store clerks, workmen; and wherever he went: school, church, street, barber shop, in the cheerful boisterous crowds on Saturday afternoons; and at the games themselves, where kids were admitted free till they got to be twelve or fourteen."

Laird Holmes, during his tenure as burgess (1914-1922), enforced the seven-year-old curfew ordinance, which decreed that all children under sixteen had to be off the streets by 8 p.m. from October to April, and by 9 p.m. from April to October, unless they had notes from

WELL - BROKEN HORSE IS QUITE VALUABLE

A prominent dealer once told the writer that no horse was fit for women and children to use until it was nine years old.

Now the years between five and nine are spent in work that will accustom the average horse to the sights, sounds and daily experiences incident to modern conditions.

Let us try to tell what these conditions mean. A countryman starts to town with the womenfolk; he is driving a pair of country-raised horses. They are gentle and kind when at work on the home farm — wouldn't hurt a baby.

On the outskirts of the town they meet an auto. The team is horror-struck; the ladies are in no better condition; the good man who prided himself on being a horseman for the past quarter of a century is astonished to find that his team does not respond to his commands .

—*The Times, 8-27-15*

Mellon Bank, N.A. — Central Region

With balance-sheet assets of approximately $40 billion, Mellon Bank Corporation is a financial powerhouse that conducts business throughout Pennsylvania, Delaware, Maryland, and New Jersey. With seven offices in Centre County, Mellon Bank's Central Region has come a long way since its humble origins around the turn of the century as State College's first financial institution.

Prior to the opening of First National Bank of State College, borough residents were obliged to do their banking in Bellefonte. When the new bank opened for business on December 15, 1904, it enjoyed immediate success, taking in the then-formidable sum of $6,677 in deposits by noon on its first day. Housed in a room of Miss S.S. Hunter's home three doors west of Allen Street, the bank boasted a four-and-a-half-ton burglar-proof manganese-steel safe.

From its earliest days, First National Bank remained closely tied to the community and Penn State. William C. Patterson, the bank's first president, served as the university's superintendent of college farms and buildings, and the first board of directors included several prominent local businessmen and educators. Work on what is now Mellon Bank's College Avenue office began in 1909, and in 1912 First National Bank

president John McCormick founded Farmer's Trust Company in order to offer additional financial services to residents. By 1923, the two banks were consolidated.

Successive years saw the addition of several new State College offices to the First National fold — South Hills in 1956 and North Hills and Nittany Mall branches in the '60s — and the beginnings of a series of mergers

The First National Bank in 1904.

that would eventually bring Mellon Bank into the picture. On July 1, 1971, First National Bank and Lock Haven Trust Company merged to form Central Counties Bank, serving Clinton and Centre Counties. Over the next few years, banks from Altoona, Lewistown, and Lewisburg all joined Central Counties, which in turn merged with Mellon National Corporation on September 14, 1983.

By May 1984, the Central Counties Bank subsidiary was officially renamed Mellon Bank (Central) N.A., and in September of that year the parent company became Mellon Bank Corporation. Throughout these mergers and acquisitions, Mellon Bank remained an innovator, opening, for example, Central Pennsylvania's first seven-day banking facility at the Bi-Lo office in Wal-Mart Plaza in March 1991. Now almost a century after its beginnings in State College, Mellon Bank takes pride in offering customers the best of all possible worlds — the resources and reliability of a regional financial corporation and the personalized attention of a locally managed bank.

The bank still appears as it does in this 1950s drawing.

their parents saying they were on emergencies or running errands. Adding another restriction in the spring of 1916, he ordered all businesses to close on Sundays, feeling that residents were straying too far from observing the Sabbath. Only restaurants, other places that sold food, and Graham's, which was allowed to sell only newspapers, were permitted to remain open.

According to Budd Knoll, objections to Graham's being open on Sunday were numerous: "It was argued that Sunday papers could just as well be sold and read on Monday. But enough people wanted to read their Sunday paper on Sunday, and soon a Graham boy, usually Bob, sold papers from a window about two-feet square on the Allen Street side of the store, as though he were dealing in contraband. The price was a dime, later raised to twelve cents, and the best comic by far was the Katzenjammer Kids."

The proclamation evidently worked, for the *Times* noted wryly in its April 7 edition: "The stillness of the Sabbath was broken only by the ringing of church bells last Sunday in State College. The unseemly noise of stray jitneys [nickels] dropping into the cash drawer no longer disturbs the devotions of our people. Those who not only wish to be good themselves but see that others must be good rested in peace. It was a delightful day for some."

Laird's strait-lacedness didn't seem to hurt his popularity. He was re-elected burgess for another term, then served four two-year terms in the Pennsylvania General Assembly, and was instrumental in having U.S. Route 322 pass through State College in 1930.

Six men had preceded him as burgess during the years before World War I. The first, Dr. Theodore Sterner Christ, who ran on a nonpartisan ticket, served only five months, during which time the board of health was formed to administer health ordinances, and school grounds were purchased on Fraser Street, just north of The Hollow. He also helped to draw the first boundaries of the borough — from Pine Street west to Gill Street and from Prospect Avenue north to a line south of Park Avenue. The budget-conscious borough council excluded Park Avenue to avoid having to keep up that rutted, perennially muddy street, but the core of the College campus fell within these borough limits.

Following Christ as burgess, in 1897, was William "Cal" Patterson, a staunch Democrat who said he "stood for the right principle no matter which party it favored" and had been asked several times to run for the state legislature. A director of the First National Bank of Bellefonte and first president of the First National Bank of State College, he also helped bring the first church, now St. Paul's United Methodist, to town in 1888, saving residents the trip to Centre Furnace to worship.

In Cal's three years on the job, ordinances punishing "vagrants and tramps" and establishing McAllister, Atherton, Allen and the misspelled Frazier Streets were passed. Also, in October 1897, the four-room Frazier Street Elementary School was built with a bond issue of $8,000 (it never was known as the *Fraser* Street School, because it was razed to make room for the present post office in 1961, two years before the street name's spelling was corrected). Teachers were Laird Holmes, grammar grade; Carrie Hoy, primary; Ada Hayman, junior grade; and Ella Livingston, secondary. Later, the infamous College cannons, plugged with concrete, were presented to the school where they stood on either side of the front door and became popular spots to perform gymnastic stunts or pose for photographs.

In 1901, high school courses were added and a principal and teacher for the older students, E. G. Booz, was hired at a salary of $50 a month. He was the only high school teacher until 1907, and his pupils did not get their own building until 1914, when the first unit of the school between Fairmount and Nittany Avenues was constructed. The first high school commencement, however, was held in 1905. And with the town's secondary education now in other hands, Penn State discontinued its preparatory course in 1908.

Philip DuBois Foster, a Republican, was elected State College's third burgess in 1900. An Oak Hall native, he had been assistant keeper of the state arsenal during the Spanish-American War, then returned to State College and started Foster Coal and Supply Company and became proprietor of the University Inn.

During his political tenure a battle broke out among downtown property owners over widening Pugh Street. Phil twice vetoed ordinances to change the street's boundaries and settled the dispute by turning the matter over to an impartial committee.

Louis Reber, who with Charles Foster had developed a strip of land along the east side of Pugh Street back in the 1880s, said in his memoirs, "Owners on the opposite side were unwilling to contribute. Had we widened from our side only, it would have made an undesirable jog." He likened it to an earlier dispute over the opening of Beaver Avenue "on the ridge overlooking the town. It had not been entirely easy to secure this opening.

Maps to Show State College

William Penn Highway Charts Will Give Routes To This Place—Delegation Attends Johnstown Meeting

As a result of the work done by the members of the State College branch of the William Penn Highway Association, on all the maps issued by the Association State College will be shown as located on one of the routes.

The following members of the local branch attended the meeting of the Association at Johnstown on Monday: Jas. P. Aikens, Wm. Decker, Newton Hess, Dr. Chas. Aikens, Prof. Claude Aikens, Roscoe North, David Louck, Clark Herman, Henry Myers, J. C. Smith, and John S. Dale.

Sixteen views of the road between State College and Lemont taken by Photographer Smith, historical sketches by Dr. Espenshade, and the Penn State Alumni Booster Book were presented to the Board of Governors. Different speakers urged the adoption of the Lewistown to Tyrone via State College detour route.

—The Times, 10-20-16

W. C. "Cal" Patterson
Burgess 1897-99

Irvin C. Holmes
Fire Chief 1899-1901

Philip DuBois Foster
Burgess 1901-02; Fire Chief 1909-20

Wm. A. "Billy" Hoy
Burgess 1903-05

Fred A. Robison
Burgess 1907-09

Wm. L. "Will" Foster
Burgess 1909-13

State College
Burgesses
&
Fire Chiefs
1897 to 1919

J. Laird Holmes
Burgess 1914-1919

Charlie and I would make contributions, but owners whose land lay on the opposite side were not at first willing to cooperate. They were finally persuaded, however, to do their part, and the street was opened.

"I enjoy looking back on these early developments," Louis continued, "but I must confess that my satisfaction was not due to pecuniary reward. The time had not yet arrived for money-making in real estate at State College or, perhaps, my partner and I had not sufficient foresight to realize the future value of our holdings."

In 1902, Phil Foster resigned as burgess to become county treasurer and later State College postmaster and fire marshal. Finishing his term was Billy Hoy, of whom retired attorney Gene Lederer said, "If anyone in the community died, he would take off work, put on his fine clothes, and go to the funeral. He was a very kind man." Among Billy's municipal contributions were authorizing the planting of trees and the laying out of Miles Street (now Locust Lane) and Burrowes Street before Fred Robison succeeded to the office in 1907.

Robison, a Democrat, came to Centre County in 1888 and lived in Pine Grove Mills before moving to State College. A Penn State graduate of 1897 with a dental degree from what is now the University of Pittsburgh, he held the distinction of having played football for both schools. He also played baseball for the Alphas and Robert Foster's team, the RMFs.

State College's third dentist, after Drs. William Harter and William Kelly, Fred practiced for more than fifty years. "He was a gentle man — and I mean gentle," said William Leitzell in a 1989 interview. "Any time a young person can get a good feeling from a dentist, he must be pretty gentle."

"He was quiet and gentle," agrees Fred's son, Ronnie, a retired dentist who practiced with his father for years. "When Mother used to tell him to paddle me, he would take me to another room, close the door, strike the paddle against the wall, and tell me to yell."

On one occasion the newspaper reminded the sedate burgess to enforce the ordinance prohibiting ball playing in the streets and on sidewalks. "The *Times* has enough confidence in Burgess Robison to believe that he will take the action to have the dangerous practice stopped at once. If this is not done, the names of the guilty parties will be published and the matter placed in a different shape for immediate action by the complainants."

On another occasion the paper commended Fred for laying a new tar sidewalk in front of his College Avenue residence. "There are others who should follow his example, for there are some sidewalks that are certainly in a dilapidated condition."

"There weren't so many duties for the burgess then as there are today," Fred recalled in 1946, "and not a red penny did one get for what he did. No matter what decision the burgess made, half of the people thought he did right and the other half disagreed." Fred's grandson, Dr. John F. Robison, is now the third generation to practice dentistry in State College, from an office in the former family homestead at 237 South Allen Street.

Republican William LeFevre Foster, real estate developer and brother of Phil, became burgess after Robison's term expired in 1909. Born with no left arm, Will could fish, hunt, play tennis, and hit baseballs without effort. He attended Penn State as a member of the 1874 class and taught at the Boalsburg Academy before plunging into real estate and retailing. He is also credited with laying the town's first concrete walk, in front of his store.

One ordinance Foster approved was to control the large number of dogs running at large in the borough, decreeing that all were to be licensed and tagged, and strays would be chloroformed. But he seemed to be lax on the sidewalk ordinance, according to the *Times*: "It is rather puzzling to some of the people why Burgess Foster and President McCormick of Council allow the sidewalk in front of the Hunter Estate on College Avenue to remain in such an extremely dangerous condition after their attention has been called to it. The matter is up to the gentlemen named to have the defect remedied at once, for it has been a nuisance for twelve months and there is absolutely no excuse for its continuance."

Along with matters of public safety, the issue of public health, especially on campus, drew increasing notice. Although a hospital had been opened in Bellefonte in 1902, a scarlet fever epidemic among Penn State students in 1912 showed the need for a health service closer to campus. A temporary isolation facility, called "the Pest House" by students, was set up and, in 1915, an infirmary was established in a former campus residence, Ihlseng Cottage, then called Beecher House (still standing west of Pattee Library, it now houses the Institute for the Arts and Humanistic Studies). Not until 1917 did the College employ its first regular physician, alumnus Joseph Ritenour '01.

Little Nearer A Post Office

Uncle Samuel Orders Site Cleared For the Federal Building at State College.

The people of State College have discovered, along with hundreds of other towns, that Uncle Samuel takes his sweet time about starting public buildings . . . the red tape must be unwound, some 'steen miles of it. Finally plans must be drawn, redrawn, submitted, resubmitted.

—The Times, 11-24-16

Omega Bank

or many residents, one of the most familiar landmarks in State College is the Peoples National Bank clock that has for decades stood outside the Allen Street office. When the bank decided to renovate and expand the office in 1969, plans called for a new time-and-temperature sign on the building. During demolition of the old building, Peoples board member Dr. H. Richard Ishler had the foresight to save the leaded-glass face and workings from the original clock. His prudent action proved fortuitous when, on the basis of local ordinances, State College officials rejected plans for a new sign. Long-time residents were delighted to see the old clock back where it belonged after a new post and missing pieces were manufactured with the help of Bellefonte-based Cerro Metal Products. Were it not for Dr. Ishler, the State College landmark's resurrection would never have been possible.

The Borough of State College was a young twenty-six years old in 1922 when Peoples National Bank opened at 117 South Allen Street. The bank has operated

The Peoples National Bank clock is a fixture on Allen Street.

during the Depression. Eugene Lee, who had come to the bank shortly after it was founded and would still be there nearly sixty years later, was instrumental in bringing Peoples Bank through those lean years. Today his son David is chairman and CEO of parent company Omega Financial Corporation.

In 1957, Peoples opened its Allen Street Drive-In, the first of many local offices. Soon to follow were community offices in Bellefonte, Westerly Parkway, Snow Shoe, Village Square, Hills Plaza, and Centre Hall. A 1973 merger with Rebersburg National Bank, founded in 1920, brought that office into the fold. Five additional offices — on Pugh Street and in Millheim, Port Matilda, Boalsburg, and Lemont — became Peoples Banks after a 1985 merger with Farmers Community Bank.

The 1990s brought big changes to Peoples, beginning with the 1990 opening of a limited-service branch at Foxdale Village and the relocation in 1991 of the Village Square office across the street to North Atherton Place. In 1993, Peoples' Pugh Street staff moved to a new location at 366 East College Avenue and the Milesburg office was added.

In 1995, Peoples Bank and Russell Bank joined forces as Omega Bank. With a long-standing policy of making banking convenient for account holders, Omega Bank now has five offices in State College Borough, four others in Centre Region suburbs, and seven more branches in Centre County towns — more than any other bank. While the name has recently changed, its commitment to being the people's bank remains as constant as the ticking of the trademark clock in the heart of State College.

Peoples National Bank — now Omega Bank — has been at 117 South Allen Street since 1922.

in the heart of town in that same location ever since. Now officially Omega Bank, an affiliate of Omega Financial Corporation, it combines the histories of seven regional banks dating as far back as 1872.

Peoples, like banks across the nation, fell on hard times

Prosperity Before the Crash

lthough State College had been growing ever since it was born, a real spurt came around World War I, when townspeople helped to accommodate a sudden influx of student soldiers before and during the war and unprecedented numbers of students — mostly ex-soldiers — after the war, some who had not been in college previously. Modern civic improvements, the fraternity section in the southeastern part of the Borough, and many businesses still around today also came into being during this era, when the local economy was booming right along with the stock market.

At the beginning of this time, both the College and the Borough were losing their innocence, as exemplified by two events of 1916, just a few months before America entered the Great War. A man who would forever call Penn State "a cesspool of sin" left campus to found an international evangelical crusade, and State College hired its first full-time policeman.

The night Frank Buchman arrived in 1909 as secretary of the Penn State YMCA, he claimed there were nineteen liquor parties going on in Old Main. Many years later he would say that this College "full of ruffians with low grades, lots of liquor, losing football teams, and language so foul no decent woman could walk down Allen Street" was the birthplace of his international Moral Re-Armament Movement, founded in 1928 as the Oxford Group and still in existence.

One story tells of his silently entering the Old Main office of a professor who was reading by the light of a small lamp. Staying in the shadows until he was almost face to face with the man, Frank suddenly materialized in the

halo of the reading lamp and declared, "I want you to meet Jesus!" Instead of looking into Frank's eyes, the professor merely glanced into the gloom, said, "How d'ya do, Jesus," and returned to his book.

Buchman's most noted convert in the 1920s and '30s was local hostler Bill Gilliland, an admitted alcoholic who, as principal supplier of liquor on campus, earned the nickname "Bill Pickle." Born in Oak Hall, Bill was a driver for Dr. William Glenn Sr. and also drove the hack to and from the Lemont railroad station. He lived with his wife and twelve children in the 400 block of East Beaver Avenue, still called "Pickle Hill" by longtime residents. After Buchman started his Moral Re-Armament Movement, he took Bill with him on his crusades as an example of a man who gave up drinking for Jesus. One of Bill's trips was to London to meet King George V and Queen Mary; another was to Dearborn, Michigan, to meet avid Buchman supporter Henry Ford.

"Pickle Hill" was the name, too, of a 1960 MRA stage play glorifying Frank and portraying Bill as the town drunk and an atheist to boot. But none of that was true, according to Bill's granddaughter, who claimed the MRA exploited him and upset the whole family. State College dentist Ronnie Robison — for another reason — also didn't appreciate Buchman: "When he took Bill away from here during Prohibition, we were all in trouble!"

Twenty-five-year-old Bob Mingle also was concerned about bootleggers and unruly students in 1916, when he became State College's first full-time uniformed policeman. Patrolling entirely on foot, he averaged thirty to thirty-five miles a day and earned $60 a month to start, $125 when he resigned to open a gun shop in 1925.

Students, faculty, and town residents had train service at the station on College Avenue at Fraser Street to and from Bellefonte and Red Bank (at Scotia) until 1929 when the depot was torn down.

The new officer quickly made his presence felt with a notice in *The Times* warning residents that "Policeman Mingle intends to enforce rigidly the law against carrying concealed weapons and the ordinance prohibiting shooting within the Borough limits. It is quite a common practice for young men to pull a revolver from a pocket and shoot anywhere, everywhere in State College. This is going to be stopped, and after a few fellows have paid fines, it will, no doubt, come to an end. Who will be the first?"

When students tore up wooden sidewalks, fences, and outhouses for bonfires, Bob asked the football team to help restore order. Occasionally someone would steal rugs from people's front porches and freshly baked cakes from State College kitchens. One early case, though, was more serious, involving three young men who robbed Gentzel's furniture and grocery store five times in one month, stealing $300 or $400 each time. Bob caught two of them, but the third got away to Washington, D.C., and later committed another robbery and killed three men. "I imagine they probably hung him," Bob said.

"For the boys who got in wrong, on their first offense my way of thinking was to give them a chance," he continued. "Judge Henry Quigley always told me, 'Keep the boys out of court, Bob,' and that's what I always tried to do. Most learned their lesson the first time because I'd take them into the station and let them sweat. I'd explain what the offense meant to them now and what it would mean in their future. Everyone I dealt with showed up good, so I'm glad I did it that way."

During Prohibition, many cases involved bootleggers and moonshiners. "I knocked off three stills in the county. I didn't try to keep those cases out of court. I felt that selling moonshine was like selling poison."

By September 1917, five months after America's entry into the Great War, Penn State had joined the army. Almost overnight the normally tranquil campus had metamorphosed into a virtual military camp — students doubled as soldiers, dormitories became barracks, dining facilities were called mess halls. A bugler sounded reveille and taps over campus each day, and signs were posted at main walkways and building entrances: *U.S. Military Installation — No Children Allowed.* Anyone strolling on campus, day or night, had to keep moving; the grounds were patrolled at all times by military police. An 8:30 p.m. curfew was strictly enforced. The army held rallies and parades at regular intervals to maintain patriotic sentiment among students and townspeople.

"The boys were put into khaki," said Marsh White, then

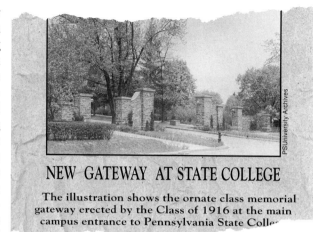

NEW GATEWAY AT STATE COLLEGE

The illustration shows the ornate class memorial gateway erected by the Class of 1916 at the main campus entrance to Pennsylvania State Colle⸱

—*The Times,* 1-5-17

a graduate student who earned Penn State's first Ph.D. in 1926 and taught physics for forty-two years. "While the war lasted, the men students not only wore uniforms, they marched to classes, drilled, and had parades and inspections. Of course, military instruction was nothing new at Penn State. Boys had to take drill and study military tactics even before the war. But in 1917 and '18 that sort of training was intensified. You might say that once the war began they were soldiers doing a bit of academic work on the side!"

At a mass induction ceremony held on front campus October 1, 1918, about 1,500 male students swore allegiance to the United States of America as members of the Penn State unit of the Student Army Training Corps. Recalled Julia Gregg Brill, class of '21, who became the first woman hired by Penn State's English department, "For some of the boys, mostly the upperclassmen, the war was a lark, an adventure. They couldn't wait to go overseas. Others didn't know what to expect; for them the SATC was an alternative to active military service. Eighteen-year-olds were subject to the draft, but if a young man were college-eligible, he could enroll in school and receive basic training in the SATC. It was understood that college students would not be called for combat duty unless the need for men became acute, so there were boys coming to college who might not have done so under normal circumstances. In 1918, freshman enrollment at Penn State was double what it had been the year before." The number of women students also rose rapidly, and total student enrollment after the war hit an all-time high in 1919 of 4,316.

Harold "Dick" Dickson, class of '22, who went on to teach the history of art and architecture at Penn State for nearly forty-one years, was eighteen in 1918: "Frankly I wasn't eager to go to war — yet. I was still a stripling teenager, weighing 119 pounds, home-tied, unathletic, bookishly bent, plagued with migraines. If I chose, I could enter The Pennsylvania State College, for free, and would be given my food, all clothing and accessories, and an unencumbered thirty dollars a month. All I had to do was sign up for Uncle Sam's new Student Army Training Corps and thus be delivered from the clutches of a draft board standing ready to collar every eighteen-year-old male in sight. I signed gladly."

Though not on active duty, SATC men were subject to rigid military routine. They bunked in commandeered dormitories, fraternity houses, and rooming houses — most of them in town. As reveille sounded each morning at seven, they turned out for setting-up exercises in the

Clark Motor Company, Inc.

The Clark Motor Company has served State College for nearly three-quarters of a century, making it the oldest continuously operated car dealership in Centre County. Founded by William Clark Sr. in 1923 as a Packard dealership, the company has been run by the Clark family ever since. Just as the Clarks have owned and operated their dealership for three generations, so, too, have many State College families remained loyal customers from one generation to the next. By providing efficient, professional service with a personal touch, the Clark Motor Company has successfully endured the ups and downs of America's automotive industry and emerged a winner in the competitive arena of car sales.

Originally the Clark dealership was downtown at the present site of the Pugh Street parking garage. William Clark Jr. took over full-time operations from his father in 1950 and soon brought in the popular Jeep franchise. Over the years, the Clarks also sold Maxwell, Jaguar, and Austin-Healey vehicles, though all were eventually dropped. With the demise of Packard in the mid-'50s, the company took on the lucrative Chrysler line of cars.

William Clark Sr. ran a Packard dealership at 120 South Pugh Street before the business moved to 1080 East College Avenue.

Today Chrysler/Plymouth and Jeep/Eagle form the core of Clark's car inventory, supplemented by a variety of previously owned vehicles. As the most-awarded car company over the past decade, Chrysler has enjoyed an unprecedented rebirth, the fruits of which still fuel the Clark dealership's growth. Moved to 1080 East College Avenue on December 1, 1965, the dealership underwent a 1989 expansion that doubled its size.

Rob Clark, William Jr.'s son, has run the company since his father's fatal P-51 airplane crash in 1988 (the World War II fighter plane was part of William Jr.'s nationally recognized vintage aircraft collection). He is assisted by his brother Dave and mother Julia. Rob got his start at the dealership as a youngster sweeping floors on weekends and learning the business. He and his wife Becki have three children, who they hope will eventually carry on the family's longstanding tradition of serving State College's automotive needs.

In 1973, Clark Motor Company was half a century old.

street in front of their respective "barracks." They marched to meals, to and from classes, and back and forth on the drill field. They devoted sixty percent of their on-duty hours to infantry training, including bayonet and grenade practice, and forty percent to academic studies. And all students had to take a course called "War Aims," designed to improve campus morale by outlining the causes and purposes of the war.

"Those morale-boosting lectures never impressed me much," said Julia. "I had to sit through them three mornings a week, and I always found it difficult to stay awake."

Retreat and flag lowering took place at 4:30 p.m., and then came dinner, after which the men were at liberty until 8:30 p.m. "Then," said Dick Dickson, whose barracks was the house at 120 South Burrowes Street, "we hit the books — all the while on the alert for surprise visits from nosy MPs — until taps and lights out at eleven p.m."

Peck Snyder, State College's first car dealer, taught many women to repair autos during World War I. "He taught classes at night," his daughter Polly Rutter said, "and the women would come in coveralls to learn how to change oil, change tires, and do all manner of repairs. Two of his pupils, Alice and Hilda Thompson, became ambulance drivers during the war."

State College area men who served in the military included Claude Aikens, Billy Edwards, Grover Glenn, Wilbur Leitzell, and "Jut" Neidigh, who said he enlisted in the National Guard of Pennsylvania and spent several months under continuous shellfire in France's Argonne Forest. "That's a long time under shellfire," Jut recalled in 1993 at age 100.

As the war went on, some food items became scarce for civilians. "State College was pretty well isolated from regular commercial traffic," said Marsh, "and the war made it even more difficult to get supplies. Some things just couldn't be had. Butter, for instance. We had other dairy products, like milk and ice cream, but there was no butter. And no vegetables. Once in a while, one of the stores in town might have some fresh carrots, but most of the time all we could get was canned peas or corn or beets. We had apples. You could buy those quite cheaply from the College. On the whole, though, there were many things we simply did without."

Dewey Krumrine, grandson of original College Heights settlers John C. and Christina Decker Krumrine, also

FALL IN LINE AND SHOW YOUR COLORS

Big Demonstrations To Be Held In State College On Saturday Afternoon, May 5th, At 2 O'clock

Everybody out!
Fall in line and show your patriotism!
Don't be a mouse — be a man; a patriotic man!
The flag raising will be at 2 o'clock — be there.
The parade starts at 3 o'clock — be in line!
The date — Satufday, May 5, at State College — Turn out!
If you have a place of business, close it from 2 until 4 Saturday afternoon — close it tight!
There will be four bands — four!

Formation of Parade

1 Marshal — L. D. Fye
2 Escort — Boal Machine Gun Troop
3 "Spirit of '76"
4 Position of Honor — Veterans of the War
5 Cadet Band of Pennsylvania State College
6 Cadet Battalion of Pennsylvania State College
8 Ferguson Township Band
9 City Officials
10 Fraternal Orders
11 Patriotic Order Sons of America
12 Odd Fellows and Rebeccas
13 Woodmen and Royal Neighbors
14 Red Men of the World
15 Fraternal Order of Eagles
16 Boalsburg Band
17 Boy Scouts
18 Camp Fire Girls
19 Red Cross
20 High School Students
21 Patriotic Citizens

— The Times, 5-14-17

remembered not having butter — or sugar. "The only things you could get then were Karo syrup and oleomargarine, which was something like lard."

Area farmers could not supply what the town needed, either, since most were in the business of raising dairy cows and large crops of grain. They, like many area families, grew vegetables for their own use in what the government termed "Victory Gardens," a practice that would be revived during World War II.

Students, faculty, staff, and townspeople made sacrifices large and small without complaint. One man who worked tirelessly for his school and his country, particularly during those war years, was President Sparks. Though he was relieved of many administrative chores while the army was in charge in 1917 and '18, Sparks was actually busier then than at any other time during his term of office. It was important to him that Penn State do her part for the nation as efficiently and effectively as possible, so he worked to coordinate the school's wartime policies with those of other colleges around the country. At the same time, he refused to lower entrance requirements as the army wished, and he encouraged young people still in school to remain there and work hard. "If the educated man or woman is valuable in the ordinary times of peace, he or she will be of even greater value in the extraordinary times of war," he said.

By the first of November 1918, approximately 2,000 Penn State students had entered active military service, with more signing up every day despite rumors that the end of the war was imminent. "Then, on Monday, November 11, came the blast-off, the steady blowing of the fire whistle at the Engineering Building signaling the end of hostilities and the birth of Armistice Day," said Dick Dickson. "Julia Brill told me that the girls who were dormitoried at the University Club all joyously snake-danced that day a full kilometer along College Avenue to McAllister Hall and breakfast.

"In addition to everyone's whooping it up," Dick continued, "there were speeches, cheers, tears, and that afternoon by far the biggest parade the county had ever witnessed. People from the entire area, individually and in organizations, converged on State College, the town that had what even the county seat lacked, a ready-made marching phalanx in the SATC."

Frank Buchman

Walter O'Bryon

Russell Foster

Earl Bool

Jake Jackson

Earl Kline

Herbert Cole

William Foster

Jim Kerstetter

Marshall Foster

In 1915, Frank Buchman was joined by state YMCA Secretary Hugh McAllister Beaver '91 and his brother Albert in spreading his Bible-study work. The Beaver Club met in a rented room downtown, helped by "contributions" from dean of faculties Arthur Holmes and Professor T. I. Mairs, but the club broke up when the furniture was sold to pay the rent.

PSUniversity Archives

George Graham's family outgrew the ability of his barber shop to support them, and after a short-lived restaurant venture, he succeeded with a newsstand combined with tobacco and candy.

PSUniversity Archives

Helen Atherton, Dr. Atherton's daughter, was active in the suffrage movement. Helen, with the drum, later remembered, "We figured we needed uniforms for our parades — the hats we borrowed from soldiers on campus. I'm not sure where we dug up the rest."

PSUniversity Archives

Altogether, 2,200 Penn Staters and State College residents served in the war, with seventy-five losing their lives. In addition, countless students and townspeople served on the home front doing farm, conservation, Red Cross, and YMCA work.

But danger lurked even for those who saw no war service — a deadly influenza epidemic began sweeping the nation in September of 1918. Within two weeks, symptoms started showing up locally: a sore throat, a nosebleed, fever, deliriousness, pneumonia. Death, where it came, came swiftly. There were stories of pine boxes ranked ten high at railroad stations in central Pennsylvania. Physicians went without sleep for days, treating flu victims in their homes or in makeshift hospitals, such as one that was set up in Old Main. There was no miraculous vaccine and no palliative but aspirin or whiskey. The best medical advice was to let the disease run its course and pray that the patient was strong enough to pull through.

The death toll mounted through October and into November. Many communities fared worse than State College, where an estimated six Borough residents and six Penn State students died, but worldwide the flu is said to have killed 20 million people and in the U.S. the figure was 548,000, nearly five times the number who died in the war.

Those who caught the flu and survived felt lucky to be alive. One was Maude Krumrine Hussey, grand-daughter of John Krumrine, cousin of Dewey, and daughter of Penn State's superintendent of grounds and buildings, Jacob Krumrine, and his wife, Margaret Dreibelbis. A 1917 Penn State graduate, Maude was teaching at Osceola Mills High School that fall of 1918 and her parents were still living in State College, at the corner of Atherton and College, next to the University Club.

"In the first part of November, I decided I'd go home over the weekend," she recalled. "Then my mother called me on the phone and said, 'Don't come down here now because State College is just filled with flu.' And I said, 'Mama, you know I never get sick.' She told me it was dangerous, but I went anyway."

On Sunday after church, Maude got a phone call from one of her teacher friends in Osceola Mills telling her not to bother coming back for Monday because the schools were all closed and the high school was being used for a

flu hospital. Also, one of her students who went home sick on Friday had died, the friend told her.

By Monday afternoon Maude had the chills, and her mother sent for Dr. Glenn. "That was around lunchtime, but he didn't get there until almost midnight. In the meantime my mother had packed me into bed and tried to get me to perspire. And she gave me whiskey. You wouldn't hear a doctor say it today, but the doctors back then said whiskey was the best thing in the world for the treatment of flu!"

Although Dr. Glenn thought she was dying and rumors spread that she *had* died, Maude recovered and lived to tell her flu story in 1977, when she was eighty years old. "There weren't so many people who died from the flu here. I had a cousin and an uncle who did. They both lived in State College. My cousin was a big, healthy, strong girl, almost the strongest looking girl you ever saw. She got pneumonia from it. That's what caused most of the deaths. I remember my uncle was very ill with it, and my aunt was worried. Dr. Glenn said to her, 'You don't need to worry. He isn't half as sick as Maude.' And yet my uncle died and I didn't. It seemed it was just whoever got taken, that's all."

Mickey McDowell Jr. recalled in 1992, "None of my friends got the flu, but my dad was awful sick with it — we thought he was going to die — but he lived until 1958, just thirteen days shy of his eighty-seventh birthday."

Mickey Jr. was on the State High football team at the time of the flu epidemic and said, "We played only the first two games of a ten-game season, then all athletic events, movies, church services, and so on were shut down all across the state because you weren't allowed to congregate and possibly spread the flu." Penn State's 1918 football team, under its new coach, Hugo Bezdek, played just four games that fall. But in 1919, the flu was evidently not a problem any longer — the Nittany Lions had a 7-1 season.

November 25, 1918, two weeks after the Armistice, became a memorable date in State College history when the Engineering Building, where Sackett and part of Hammond Buildings are today, burned down in a spectacular fire that lasted all night. When the fire whistle blew and a hubbub began on College Avenue, seventeen-year-old Mickey McDowell was at Dr. Fred Robison's office in the Leitzell Building, catty-cornered across from Engineering, for an after-supper dental appointment. "Dr.

Fire Rages in Center of Town's Business Section

Snyder Building in Ruins But Fire Laddies Keep the Flames From Spreading to Other Buildings; Several Overcome By Smoke

Tuesday morning just before daylight, fire was discovered in the Snyder building, near the corner of Allen street and West College avenue . . . At one time the entire building from the cellar to the garret was a raging furnace of fire . . . While it was realized that it would be impossible to prevent the Snyder building from being ruined, it was also well known that if the flames reached any of the other buildings, especially the nest of wooden structures in the rear, State College would have the most disastrous fire in its history. But the volunteer firemen worked like Trojans and kept the fire confined to the one building and finally succeeded in extinguishing the flames. . . . The fixtures in the C. A. Meyers barber ship . . . were ruined . . . The same is true of the fixtures in the A. C. Longee restaurant . . . The paraphernalia of the Red Men, on the third floor, was destroyed.

Mr. Snyder was out with a fishing party at the time of the fire. A farm house was reached by telephone and word of the fire was taken to the camp where the men were sleeping. They made record time in their car coming to town.

— *The Times, 8-3-17*

The Elder Agency

Mary Dunkel, owner of The Elder Agency at 215 East Beaver Avenue, believes there's always room in the insurance business for someone who treats clients as individuals. For almost twenty years now, she has put her belief into practice, successfully carving out a niche for her company in a highly competitive marketplace.

Elinor Eckert, shown here in 1962, worked at the business for five decades.

Elinor Eckert braved a 1961 snowstorm to pose for this photo outside the Henry S. Elder Agency.

The Elder Agency grew out of a firm established by Preston A. "Jack" Frost on South Allen Street in 1925. By 1926, Frost was joined by John R. Doty, and in 1928 Henry S. Elder came on board to form the Frost, Doty and Elder Agency. At that time, a standard fire insurance policy, which covered most State College dwellings, cost as little as $3 per year.

Frost moved on in 1940 to form his own agency, and Doty followed suit in 1953, leaving Elder in business for himself. A lifelong Pine Grove Mills resident described as very compassionate and attuned to the community, Elder remained actively involved in the agency until his death in May 1973, at which time Elinor Eckert, an employee since 1938, became owner. At the same time, The Elder Agency became the first all-woman agency in Central Pennsylvania. Four years later, in 1977, Mary Dunkel, who had been employed by the agency since 1971, purchased the business.

Today The Elder Agency offers a full range of insurance options for individuals and businesses. As a fully licensed independent agency, it represents a variety of clients. And as a small, locally run firm with a long-standing reputation in State College, The Elder Agency takes special pride in serving clients with a personal touch.

The Elder Agency still serves the community from this house on East Beaver Avenue.

Robison wouldn't let me out of his chair until he was finished with my tooth!" Mickey remembered.

Flames leaped high into the night sky as the Alphas and the Student Fire Company fought to save what was then the jewel in the crown of campus buildings, built with thick walls of brick and stone in 1892 at a cost of $100,000. With more than two acres of floor space, Engineering accommodated hundreds of students in its classrooms and much sophisticated equipment in its laboratories.

"The College power plant was attached to the Engineering Building," Mickey said, "and heat and light for the campus were generated by steam boilers, which also activated the fire whistle on top of one of them. Well, some smart man tied the fire whistle open and turned on the water full blast so the boilers wouldn't explode. If they had, they probably would have taken the town with them. So the fire whistle blew all night, gurgling with water and making such a weird noise, you couldn't get any sleep!"

When the enormous slate roof collapsed, firemen gave up and turned their hoses on the hotel and other wooden buildings across College Avenue where live embers were blowing onto rooftops. Lynn Platt, Babe Wood, and

War Crops At State College

Ten thousand bushels of potatoes will be produced this season in State College community! Almost eight thousand dollars worth of crops have been raised this year on lots not previously used for garden crops [pictured above]. The people of State College are richer by just that amount and the Nation is just that much better prepared to wage a victorious war.

—*The Times, 8-24-17*

others wet down the roofs of the Pastime Theatre and the neighboring Robison Building, where the Platt family lived. Mickey McDowell recalled that embers and charred wood were found as far away as the Branch Cemetery near Lemont, two miles away.

Esther Koch Shaw, then eight years old, remembered visiting the fire site with her friends the next day and taking away a charred brick as a souvenir. Dick Dickson recalled that a section of brick wall from the building remained standing along College Avenue for years: "In time it was grown over with ivy that each autumn turned glowing red as though in recollection of the great holocaust."

College students were dismissed early for Thanksgiving that year for what was a welcome eight-day furlough. But Robert Sigworth '19, a senior in mechanical engineering who worked for his alma mater as supervisor of utilities from 1920 to 1955, figured eight days would not apply to engineers. "I took a job installing a heating system in a greenhouse in my hometown, Tionesta, and did not return to school until after Christmas," he said in 1993. "Then, when I walked into a labor history class taught by State College lawyer John Taylor, he told me, 'Sigworth, you're kicked out of school. You've missed too many classes.' So I

Roman Catholic services were first conducted by the Reverend Byron A. O'Hanlon in the foyer of Schwab Auditorium. This Church of Our Lady of Victory at 200 West Fairmount Avenue, first used in 1914 and completed in 1917, had a carved-timber front wall designed for future expansion.

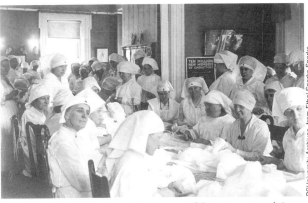

Katherine Sparks organized a local chapter of the American Red Cross. With the help of Dr. C. E. Kennedy and nurses of the College Health Service, the group conducted classes in first aid and field nursing, made soldiers' comfort kits, and prepared magazines and newspapers for shipment to troops. Ladies from town met regularly in the Penn State president's residence to make Red Cross bandages during World War One. Dust raised from handling so much gauze clogged and stopped the grandfather clock in the front hallway.

Allen Street of 1920 evoked a promise of wonderful times ahead for the town in its twenty-fifth anniversary year.

In the 1920s, motor cars, motor buses, and train service helped to make State College less "inaccessible from all directions." This view is from the corner of College and Fraser.

State College had a "Big Building Boom" in 1921, with thirty houses under construction, but The Times reported that "Scarcity Still Exists." Ten of the thirty were "being erected on Gill Street by the housing committee of the Chamber of Commerce," and were already "purchased by E. N. Sullivan, R. B. Nesbitt, G. W. Sullivan, R. E. Minshall, Dr. J. P. Kelly, W. H. Pielemeier, Dr. Jacob Tanger, P. M. Iloff, M. W. White and Lillian Lehenthaler."

had to get a letter of apology from Dean Sackett."

Edwin Sparks, who suffered a nervous breakdown in 1919, retired from the presidency the following year but remained on the faculty as a history lecturer until he died of a heart attack in June 1924, one month before his sixty-fourth birthday. Said Julia Brill, "I can't help feeling he was a casualty of the war, as surely as any of the young boys who lost their lives overseas."

Another casualty of that time was Dr. George G. "Swampy" Pond, dean of the School of Natural Science, who was appointed acting president during Sparks's illness but refused to accept the position on a permanent basis. Instead, he made numerous trips in search of a suitable candidate, wore himself out with traveling and teaching, and died of pneumonia while on a trip to Yale in 1920.

Sparks's chauffeur, Lynn Platt, returned to his Allen Street poolroom — "Prexy's Place"— in the basement of the Robison Building until 1938, when he moved it to Boalsburg.

After the war, Dr. Glenn, who had presided over many a State College bedside from the 1890s through the flu epidemic and until his death in 1931, was known as "old Doc Glenn" to distinguish him from his two sons, "Billy" (William Jr.) and Grover, who also became physicians in State College. Their stepmother, Nannie, was a doctor, too — the town's first woman physician, treating mainly women. "Nobody ever worried about the women before Nannie came to town," said Virginia Dale Ricker, who grew up on a farm just south of State College.

All four Glenns practiced eclectic medicine — using what they considered the best method, whatever it might be, to cure a disease. Sometimes Billy, who specialized in eye ailments, could be induced, with the help of $2 in cash, to write an excuse for a student who had slept through a class, perhaps feeling that this was the best method to cure that particular disease!

Following service in the medical corps in World War I, Grover Glenn returned to State College, firmly convinced that what this growing town needed was a hospital. The Bellefonte Hospital had been in full operation since 1904, when 101 patients were treated, but even in the best of weather the drive to Bellefonte, via Pleasant Gap, took thirty minutes or more. In winter it was often necessary to drive down the railroad tracks

PENN STATE MAY BE ENLARGED

Legislature Considers Merging University of Pennsylvania With Pitt and State

Negotiations are under way by which the state may take over the University of Pennsylvania and combine it with the Pennsylvania State College and the University of Pittsburgh. In such a case, it is likely that the Liberal Arts School of the college would be greatly enlarged while the U. of Pa. medical school would be transferred to Pitt.

—The Times, 2-15-18

when the highway was buried in snow. So in 1919, Grover and Billy opened their private Glenn Sanitarium at 701 West College Avenue, former home of First National Bank cashier David Kapp. From then until 1922, they delivered 103 babies and cared for 282 medical and surgical patients.

Bess Hoy Horton came to work at Glenn Sanitarium as a nurse in the fall of 1919, having just come out of military service: "Billy and Grover's sister, Anna Glenn, was the dietitian and there were three other nurses besides me. We worked very hard in those days. If we were needed twenty-four hours a day, we worked twenty-four hours a day, and we didn't get paid for overtime. I remember one time a patient was brought in with a ruptured appendix. Ordinarily, Dr. Melvin Locke would come from Bellefonte to perform surgery, but this time he couldn't get to State College because of a snowstorm, so Dr. Grover performed the appendectomy while another nurse and I assisted. I know I'd never do that again — give a patient anesthesia — but I was young and didn't know any better."

At that time, anesthesia was commonly given by dripping ether onto a cone or a wad of cotton placed over the patient's nose and mouth. Occasionally, in maternity cases when a nurse was unavailable, the patient's husband became the anesthesiologist, pouring ether when Dr. Glenn said, "Pour," and stopping when he said, "Stop."

It soon became obvious, though, that the two doctors could not simultaneously manage the hospital and care for their patients, so in 1922 they sold the building to Pi Kappa Alpha fraternity. The *State College Times* reported that the Glenn brothers had first offered to sell the hospital and its equipment to the people of State College. The price was reasonable, but the townspeople were not interested. Reported *The Times*, "Of 400 questionnaires sent out to residents by the Chamber of Commerce, only 25 came back."

Many town residents felt that the Glenn Sanitarium and Penn State's Health Service, which had opened in 1915 in what is now Ihlseng Cottage, were a duplication of services. Certainly, they reasoned, they could use the Health Service if they had to, but the College didn't agree to that, and the town was left with no hospital.

Not for long, however. By 1925, Grover Glenn had opened the State College Private Hospital at 249 South

REMEMBER THE DAYS

SUNDAY◆◆◆◆◆	ONE MEAL WHEATLESS	THURSDAY◆◆	ONE MEAL WHEATLESS
MONDAY◆◆◆◆	ALL MEALS WHEATLESS	FRIDAY◆◆◆◆◆	ONE MEAL WHEATLESS
TUESDAY◆◆◆	ONE MEAL WHEATLESS	SATURDAY◆◆	ONE MEAL WHEATLESS
WEDNESDAY◆◆	ALL MEALS WHEATLESS		

—The Times, 4-19-18

66

Frost & Conn, Inc.

*I*n the early 1920s, P. A. Frost was a student at Penn State who hoped to become a surgeon. Then he lost a hand in a hunting accident. Forced to modify his career goals, he bought a small insurance agency and later became a state legislator.

In the mid-1960s, Burton Conn, then employed by Metropolitan Life, decided to open his own insurance agency. His first office was a cubbyhole on the third floor of an old house at 403 South Allen Street. He recalls, "I had a desk, a phone, and one file cabinet."

The companies once owned by these enterprising gentlemen today remain in sure hands. Owned and operated by Frost's son-in-law, Casey Cummings,

P.A. Frost (1887-1975)

Burt Conn (1927-1995)

from 1949 to 1984, the Frost Agency was bought by Rod Fletcher, Cummings' son-in-law. In 1994, Burt Conn retired, and turned his enterprise over to long-time partner Bob Medsger.

Later that year the two companies merged to become the largest insurance agency in State College, offering a complete array of insurance and financial planning options and services. Still, it has kept its "hometown" way of doing business. Says Bob Medsger, "We like to deal with our customers one-on-one, and not just over the phone."

Rod agrees. "P. A. Frost had a motto: 'Our product is service.' That's still the way we do business."

Garden House Realty

*G*arden House Realty, formed in 1969, grew out of several earlier businesses launched by one of State College's most noted citizens — Charles Schlow. In 1919, Charles, a former teacher, and his wife Bella opened a women's clothing store, Schlow's Quality Shop, in Bellefonte. Six years later they moved their store to the first floor of a new building they'd erected in State College at 106 East College Avenue. Above the store were twelve rental units they named Campus View Apartments.

The Schlows ran their dress shop, and a furniture store, managed by their son Frank, for many years, but since the late 1960s their main business has been apartments. They built the Georgian at West College and Burrowes in 1939, Garden House at East College and Hetzel in 1958, and the Crestmont in 1962. To manage their properties, the Schlow family formed Garden House Realty, Inc., a corporation now in the hands of the Schlows' daughter, Irma Schlow Zipser; her husband, Harold Zipser; their daughters, Ruth

Zipser and Judith Zipser Lang; and Judith's husband, Peter Lang.

The family still manages most of the properties it built — about 100 units in all — including Campus View. "They're fine folks," says area resident Russell Hartman. "They give good value, and they treat tenants and workers fairly." He should know. When Russell retired on January 1, 1995, he had been a Schlow-Zipser employee for nearly seventy years.

The Schlows and Zipsers in 1949: (top row) Frank Schlow and Harold Zipser. Middle row: Marthamae Schlow, Bella Schlow, Charles Schlow with baby Judy Zipser, and Irma Schlow-Zipser. Front row: Stephen Schlow, Ruth Zipser, and David Schlow.

Pugh Street. It was more like a modern-day birthing center, with two nurses managing it for Grover while he divided his time between it and his office in the new Glenn Building at 120 East College Avenue. Two years later, in response to the population boom, the Bellefonte Hospital, which had been renamed Centre County Hospital in 1924, was enlarged to accommodate forty-eight adult patients and fifteen newborns.

Both Grover and Billy had their offices on the second floor of the Glenn Building, while Wilbur "Pete" Hoy's drugstore, where most of their prescriptions were filled, was at street level. Pete and his sister Bess were natives of Waddle, where their father had run the general store and Bellefonte Central Railroad stop. Pete washed dishes as a teenager at Rea & Derick's Rexall Drugstore at 121 South Allen Street before graduating from pharmacy school in Philadelphia in 1919. He returned to State College to open his own store in 1925, then sold it to Paul Griggs in the 1950s, and became a pharmacist at Penn State's health center.

During the 1920s, Pete Hoy's wife Catherine had a baby at the Pugh Street hospital; so did Sarah Bissey, Mary Dengler, Frances Forbes, Cassie Hoy, Mary Mead, Maizie Rowland, Helen Stavely, Mary Bottorf Stearns, Ruth Watkins, and Blanche Yeagley. The fee for a week's stay and delivery charge for Blanche Yeagley and her second son, Whit, in 1926 was $40.

In the spring of 1929, four babies were born at the State College Private Hospital in the space of one week: Ernest "Chickie" Callenbach, Clarke Young, Pat Roseberry (Myers), and Nancy Neusbaum (Dolbeare). According to Nancy's father, Frank Neusbaum, the hospital was a highly personal place. "When Louetta was in labor, I was given a gown to put on and was allowed to sit with her. Then Dr. Glenn sent one of the nurses on an errand and I ended up being the anesthetist! But the women were well cared for. Why, after my wife and baby came home, the baby cried so much that Dr. Glenn took her back to the hospital for a week so we could get some rest!"

A combination of the stock-market crash and an auto accident that took the life of one of his nurses led Grover

'Twas a Grand, Glorious Day; a Real Big Day

Largest Crowd Here the Town Has Ever Entertained

Two Big Parades Were the Features

The Fourth of July of the year nineteen-eighteen will be a day ever remembered in the annals of State College. The weather was perfect and the town was filled by a crowd the like of which has never before been seen within its borders.

It was war time, but the people endeavored to cover up the grief of the heart and show a radiant countenance at the thought that it was the nation's birthday and deserving of one's cheers rather than one's tears.

. . . If there had ever been a question of the patriotism of our borough, a ride through it on that day would have dispelled every doubt. If His Imperial Majesty, the Emperor of Germany, could have looked in on us in our festive array, he would have realized at once the futility of further effort.

—The Times, 7-12-18

CHURCHES, SCHOOLS AND MOVIES CLOSED

Following Instructions From State Board of Health, Local Board Closes Public Gathering Places

In the most drastic step ever taken to fight an epidemic in this state, Dr. B. F. Royer, the acting State Commissioner of Health, last night from Harrisburg, ordered every place of amusement and every saloon in Pennsylvania to be closed, as a measure of warfare against the further spread of influenza.

—The Times, 10-4-18

to close his hospital doors forever. "I know it was no longer in existence in June 1930," said Frank Neusbaum, "because Louetta had our daughter Helen [Goodwin] then and she was born at the hospital in Bellefonte, even though Grover Glenn was still our doctor." The State College area would not have another hospital for more than four decades, when Centre Community Hospital opened its doors in College Township in 1971.

Another World War I veteran, Pine Grove Mills native Claude Aikens, returned in 1919 to take over operation of the *State College Times* and Nittany Printing and Publishing Company. He handled business and editorial duties as well as the commercial printing part of the operation, even running a linotype machine when necessary.

Also in 1919, Robert Breon Sr. renamed the photography studio he and his brother-in-law, Guy Stover, had purchased two years earlier from his former boss, W. W. Smith. With that, Bob and the Penn State Photo Shop at 212 East College Avenue were on their way to being State College institutions for the next fifty-four years.

A Millheim native, Bob began work as Smith's assistant in 1909, earning $2.25 per week plus room and board. His first assignment was to photograph the Penn State class of 1910 standing on the steps of Schwab Auditorium. From then on he personally took more than 100,000 photographs of town and campus events, places, and people, including student pranks, downtown stores, State High and Penn State athletic teams and clubs and seniors, thousands of State College children, and Bill Pickle, who refused to take off his hat. "It wouldn't be me without my hat," Bill said.

A photographer, too, of Penn State presidents, Bob said, "Dr. Sparks would call the studio to talk 'to that fellow who always has a cigar in his mouth' — that was me — and if he knew he was going to have his picture taken, not a hair in his moustache would be out of place." Sparks's successor, John Thomas, became a good friend of Bob's, and in 1925 the two joined the new State College Rotary Club as charter members.

The Times *of May 29 with the Class Roll of seniors, announced that "The 1920 Class, the Largest in History of State College School, to Hold Exercises in Presbyterian Church." Top: Isabell Boyd, Harold Alexander, Fred Wagner, Harry Rountree, Herb Glenn (secy), Tom Mairs Jr., Ruth Watt, Liz Shawley. 3rd: Beckie Close, Grace Watts, Florence Weaver, Jim Hoy (treas), Mildred Williams, Franklin Heckman, Pauline Way, Mary Louise Boyd, Mary Reno Frear. 2nd: Sara Lenker, Cliff Pearce, Emma Elwell, Lee Robb, Alice Gernerd, Russell Tressler (pres), Ruth Martin, Henry Clay Musser, Elva Yocum, Maxwell Young Markle. 1st: Clayton Ripka, Dean Kennedy, Edna Shirk, Hutchison Mitchell, Margaret Williams, Jim Rupp, Adelene Holmes, Jim Homan (vp), Maude Evey, Mary Grace Hazel.*

Boy Scout Troop 2 sat for a portrait, June 2, 1922, on the steps of the Presbyterian Church. 1st row: John Henszey, Charlie Stoddart, Reg Wood, Jim Graham, Ed Mairs, Bill Henszey, Skib Glenn, Junior Thompson. 2nd row: Dick Smith, Claude Meyer, Clarence Meyer, Steve Fletcher, Bill Hodgkiss, David Ailman, Bill Frear. 3rd row: Hayes Keller, Ned Willard, Paul VanSant, Logan Martin, George Pearce, Curt Mairs, William Biddle. Top row: Bob Fletcher, George Haller, Dick Fletcher, Sherwood Hollobaugh, Charley Graham, Hank Sauer.

On a sunny day in 1922, 31 Centre Hills Country Club charter members posed for charter-member Bob Breon's camera. 1st row: Jimmy Aikens, Adams Dutcher, Earl Wilde, J. Ben Hill, E. W. Runkle, Bill Edwards, John Taylor, Andy Hurrell, Harry Parkinson, and club steward Mr. Porter. 2nd row: Bob Hafer, C. W. Stoddart, Pete Stuart, Joe Ritenour, A. E. "Ace" Martin, Sam Hostetter, R. I. Webber, Frank Kern, "Mike" Sullivan, Dick Grant, and Park Homan. 3rd row: Golf pro Tony Walker, Ray Smith, Fred Robison, Claude Aikens, William Rothrock, D. A. Anderson, Ray Warnock, Howry Espenshade, Dave Kapp, Fred Disque, E. C. Woodruff, and Edwin Sparks.

The Photo Shop also gave jobs and rooms to numerous students and townspeople. One was Fred Waring, who worked there for three years but was happier using the studio as a rehearsal hall for his four-piece banjo band, which played at College events and fraternity dances and eventually grew into the famous Pennsylvanians. Other tenants were: 1920s' Nittany Lion football standout Jay "Tiny" McMahan; Breon employee (1921-44) Gilbert "Gib" Haupt and his wife, Naomi; newlyweds Shirley and Bob Bernreuter in 1931; Betty Welch (Bice) and sons Bill Jr. and Jim, during World War II while Dr. Bill Welch Sr. was in the service; and the Breons themselves in the late 1940s and early '50s.

In 1914, Bob and his wife, Myra Stover, also of Millheim, had built the first house in the new development of College Heights, at 511 North Burrowes Street, now the residence and office of Dr. Edward West. Their first child, Harold, was born that year, followed by Bill, Bob Jr., and Helen, now Mrs. Carl Volz Jr. In 1929, because she had difficulty finding suitable clothes for her boys, Myra opened State College's first clothing store devoted exclusively to children — The Children's Shop at 138 East College Avenue — and ran it for two years before selling it to longtime owners Verda and Ross Edmiston.

The Breons had one serious setback — the photo shop burned down in 1926 and every negative in the files was destroyed. But they built a new three-story stucco building in its place, and through generous loans of Smith and Breon prints owned by area residents and Penn State alumni, they were able to make new negatives, partially restoring the vast collection. Many prints of these historic photographs now hang in The Tavern Restaurant, next door to the former studio.

When Bob Sr. retired in 1952, Bob Jr. took over the business and ran it until 1973, when he sold the complete files — an estimated 50,000 negatives — to Infinity Photography, which later donated them to the University Archives.

The first wireless radio in State College was built in 1920 by George Haller, later to be one of the founders of HRB Systems, whose family lived at 518 South Allen Street. "On Thanksgiving night," his friend of two blocks away, Charlie Graham, said, "I came home from George's

THOMAS J. BAUDIS KILLED IN ACTION

First State College Boy in American Army To Meet Death in France

The first death among the State College boys on the battle front in France to be reported since America entered the war is that of Thomas J. Baudis, his sister, Mrs. David Slagle, having received the following telegram on Friday noon of last week, from the Navy department, and a like one from the Adjutant-General's office about the same time.

"Washington, D.C. Sept. 12, '18
"Florence Slagle,
"State College, Pa.

"Deeply regret to inform you cablegram from abroad advises that Private Thomas James Baudis, Marine Corps, was killed in action July nineteenth. Body will be interred abroad until end of war. Please accept my heartfelt sympathy in your great loss. Your brother nobly gave his life in the service of his country."

Baudis had been in France but about a month when the great battle at Chateau-Thierry occurred and the following letter was the only one received by his sister after landing in that country:

June 14, 1918

Dear Sister Florence:
This is a beautiful country and is very interesting to travel through. A few of the people can speak English. I have learned a few French words . . . as we have not been paid for nearly two months we can't buy anything.

Everybody over here has on a uniform and the women do most of the work. The people of the United States have not the least idea of what war is. They kick about one meatless day a week, but they do not realize that they are all meatless over here.

Well, Florence, if I ever get back to the States, I will know how to appreciate it and will be able to stand almost anything.

With love to all,

Tom B.

— *The Times, 9-20-18*

and told the family, 'I just heard Marshal Foch speaking from Pittsburgh!' They said I was crazy, but Dad was really interested and made arrangements to have a man in Pittsburgh build me a radio for Christmas. It was a dilly — had two variocouplers and a variometer!"

Later, George Graham bought the first commercially made radio in town and took it to his store, where townspeople, faculty, and students could listen to KDKA with earphones. At World Series time, fans would take turns listening and reporting the action to others crowded around the radio. Meanwhile, George would chalk inning-by-inning results on a big scoreboard at the rear of the store, a practice that was continued into the 1960s.

Three events occurred in 1920 that showed how much State College was maturing as a town: George Graham organized a 165-member chamber of commerce, "because it was a good thing to have," and was elected its first president; Houts Lumber Company was founded by twenty-two-year-old Orlando Wilbert Houts, who sold paint, hardware, and building supplies beside the railroad siding in Lemont; and College Avenue was paved with bricks, making it the first State College street "to come out of the mud."

The chamber's first act was to alleviate the post-World War I housing shortage by building a row of ten small family homes on the west side of Gill Street between West Beaver and Foster Avenues in 1921. Local builder Park Homan was awarded the contract and promised to have the project completed by September 15. Shortly thereafter, Delbert Myers built the Borough's first "townhouses" in the 100 block of South Sparks Street, and O.W. Houts built every house except one on both sides of East Foster Avenue between Garner and Hetzel Streets. His wife, Mary Barnes, whom he had met at Penn State and wed in 1923, drew many of the house plans. O. W. also built many houses in College Heights on McKee, Holmes, and other streets, including one at 705 McKee for Penn State football coach Bob Higgins.

"In those days you could build a house that included the lot, a garage, driveway, and cesspool for $3,700 or

70

Kranich's

For fine jewelry and watches and crystal, it's tough to beat Kranich's.

Founded in York by the Kranich family in 1903, Kranich Brothers jewelry shop opened an Altoona location in 1923 by Charles and Mildred Kranich. In 1976, the Kranichs opened a State College store at 216 East College Avenue, and subsequently turned over control to their son Michael. Now operated by his son Charles, Kranich's boasts such prestigious lines as Rolex, Gucci, Waterford, Tiffany, and Orrefors. The recently renovated store caters not only to upscale shoppers but also to students looking for a special engagement ring or gift.

Jack Harper for Men & Women

Jack Harper's name has been associated with quality men's apparel for seventy years. The Penn State alumnus, diehard Nittany Lion football fan, and impeccable dresser operated his men's shop at 114 West College Avenue for nearly half a century before selling it in 1973 to Ron Tirabassi. Expanded to double its former size by Ron in 1976, the store retains its original threshold and classic interior appointments. With the 1993 addition of a women's department and more emphasis on sportswear, current owners Charles Kranich and Chris Kopac have updated the venerable clothing store without sacrificing the traditional style and service on which it was built.

Gordon D. Kissinger

He was a spry, courtly gentleman and a familiar figure in town. Gordon D. Kissinger, born in Tioga County in 1908 and raised in Williamsport, graduated from the Pennsylvania State College in 1931 in architectural engineering. Two years later he launched his own real estate firm, and today the agency now known as Kissinger Bigatel & Brower still thrives.

Gordon's career spanned sixty years, and to the community that nurtured him and his family for so long, he gave back a lot. He served on the planning commissions of College Township, State College, and Centre County, chairing the latter two. He was on the school board, and the boards of directors of the State College/Bellefonte Industrial Development Corporation, C-COR Electronics, Centre Video, Peoples National Bank, and Omega Financial Corporation. He was a charter member of the State College Elks Club, and served as president of the chamber of commerce, the Kiwanis Club, and the Centre County Board of Realtors, which named him Realtor of the Year in 1975.

Gordon, who died in 1994, spent many happy hours at Plum Bottom Farm, the home he renovated for his family in 1958. Ten acres of this land, and the two-story fieldstone house, originally built in 1813 by the Moses Thompson family, are listed on the state and national historic registers.

The fellow who played golf for a nickel a hole gave $100,000 to the university to establish a fellowship in architectural engineering. In memory of his son Jack, killed in 1993, Gordon and his wife Alice donated $100,000 to the Centre County Community Foundation for the benefit of the Association for Retarded Citizens, a fitting gesture for a man who cared about the community — and all its citizens.

Gordon D. Kissinger

"$3,800," O. W. said. "We even graded the yard, seeded it, and put in shrubbery. It took eight to twelve weeks to finish each house, and we were finishing one every six days."

In 1929, O. W. moved his business to its present location on West College Avenue at North Buckhout Street and added a sawmill and a batch plant to make cement block and ready-mixed concrete. "Everyone but Dave Kapp told me I was making a mistake moving 'so far out of town.' For years there was a farmhouse in front of the store and an apple orchard behind it. But the town didn't stop growing — it just moved on past us."

For his most ambitious construction projects, O. W. teamed up with Dr. Grover Glenn and built the Orlando Apartments, at 221 South Barnard Street, and the Glennland Building, at East Beaver Avenue and Pugh Street. Later the pair developed a portion of College Heights west of Atherton Street where three streets are named for them — Orlando Avenue, Glenn Road, and Glenn Circle.

The four-story Orlando Apartments, built in 1930, many with sun rooms and fireplaces, were considered lavish for their day. Mickey McDowell, who from 1928 to 1962 had the Penn Dairy diagonally across the street, recalled, "I was glad to see the Orlando built. I sold a whole lot of ice cream cones to those construction guys!" The five-story Glennland, built in 1933 with forty apart-

THOUSANDS GATHER FOR BIG PEACE CELEBRATION

Day of Jollification Opened With Ringing of Church Bells and Blowing of Fire Whistles

LARGEST PARADE EVER HELD IN STATE COLLEGE

The populace awakened early Monday morning by the ringing of the church bells and blowing of the fire whistle, announcing the fact that at last the world was to be at peace.

Shortly after daybreak the college and military heads met on the Nittany Inn balcony and after a brief consultation, the Mayor announced that all business, school work and military duties were suspended for the day.

The official parade was scheduled for 2 but was delayed for more than one hour, awaiting the arrival of the Bellefonte contingent, which was held up by a lot of railroad red tape . . . .

Burgess Holmes asked whether it was the wish of the ten thousand people gathered on the campus that the following cablegram be sent the local company at the front:

Capt. Theo. Davis Boal A. D. C.
Keystone Division A. E. F.
A. P. O. -- 744
Ten thousand people in State College celebrating our boys' part in victory. Notify the boys.

JOHN L. HOLMES
Nov. 11, 1918   Burgess

—The Times, 11-15-18

ments and offices, was for forty years the tallest building in State College.

Another longtime businessman who provided State College with much-needed housing as well as a library building and a Jewish Community Center was Charles Schlow, who, in 1922, opened a women's dress shop at 123 South Allen Street in the Gregory Building. "In that store you had to walk sideways," the wisecracking Charlie said. "It was one-hundred-ten feet long and about six feet wide, so the size fifty-two's couldn't get in. Why, before a woman could come in the store, I had to go outside and measure her beam!"

In 1925, both "broad beams" and narrow ones got a break when Schlow's Quality Shop moved to larger quarters, sharing with the Blue Moon Restaurant the first floor of Charlie's own newly constructed building at 106-108 East College Avenue. The two upper floors were and still are apartments. Morris Fromm did likewise in his new building next door, putting his men's clothing store on the ground floor and eighteen apartments on the upper floors.

A former schoolteacher from Philadelphia, Charlie Schlow and his wife, Bella, had owned and operated a dress shop in Bellefonte since 1919 and continued to do so until 1934. "We closed it after we discovered most of the customers were coming from State College," he said. With their children, Frank and Irma

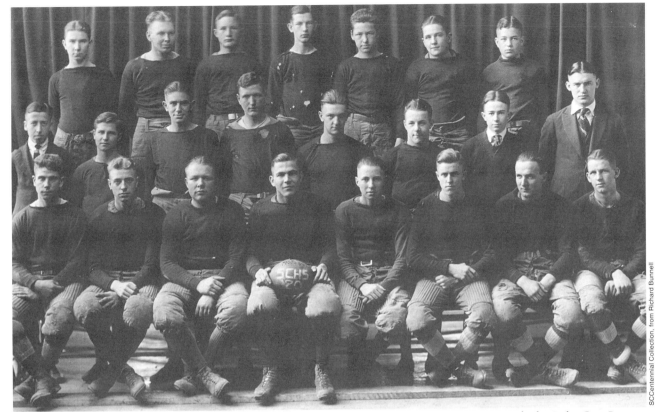

1920 produced State High's first unbeaten football team. 1st row: Joe Campbell, Harold Witmer, "Fats" Winters, Charley Light, Gene Pearce, "Jerry" Koch, Otto Scott, Bob Graham. 2nd row: Manager Herbie Glenn, Frank Resides, Glenn Edmiston, Miles Hubler, Forrest Homan, "Dude" Stephens, Manager Bill Slagle, Coach Frank Wolfe. 3rd row: Dan Lonberger, Roy Searson, Dick Fletcher, John Erb, Sherwood Hollobaugh, John Holmes, "Turk" Shirk. Captain Light would be the first SCHS player to letter on the Penn State varsity.

Ernest and Carrie Gernerd bought a 1910 farmhouse at 138 South Allen Street, where "Pappy" Gernerd, shown here waiting on a customer, opened a tailor shop and clothing store in the 1920s.

State High fielded its first basketball team, with the minimum five players, in 1922-23. In front are Hubert Koch, Richard Fletcher, and Theodore Rush; standing are Hugo Bezdek Jr. and Sherwood Hollobaugh.

(Mrs. Harold Zipser), they lived in the county seat until 1929, when they bought a large Dutch Colonial home in State College at 505 East Fairmount Avenue, at what is still the end of that street. The Schlow house and two others across Fairmount Avenue — long occupied by Ted Gates, head of Penn State's English department, and Robert "Pop" Rutherford Sr., Penn State golf pro — were built by contractor John Hamilton Henszey.

When the Schlows first moved to Fairmount Avenue, there were only six Jewish families in State College. But they had no trouble assembling a *minyan*, the ten men required by Jewish law to hold religious services. "We just held them at a Jewish fraternity," Charlie said. "Any boy over thirteen who has been bar mitzvahed is considered to be a man. So we had plenty of them at the fraternities." Charlie brought rabbis to State College for the High Holidays — Yom Kippur and Rosh Hashonah — and later was instrumental in establishing the Hillel Foundation and the Jewish Community Center. And from 1920 until the late 1970s he was the sole provider of Judaism to inmates at Rockview.

In the mid-1930s, when the Blue Moon went out of business, Charlie expanded the dress shop over the entire first floor and added a gift shop in the basement. Until it closed in 1968, Schlow's was the only women's shop in the area to carry sizes as large as fifty-two, something that once earned it a dubious honor. "I caught a man who had been shoplifting for quite some time," Charlie said, "and he told me 'Yours is the only store I ever steal from, Mister Schlow. Nobody else has dresses big enough for my wife!'"

Virginia Ricker appreciated the "lovely Fenway Tea Room — a real *tea* tearoom, if you know what I mean," at about 126 East College Avenue, run by Ruth Young Boucke, wife of economics and sociology professor Oswald Boucke. Considered to be the most widely read man on campus, the German-born Boucke once berated a student for saying hello to him: "You have just interrupted my thinking and have cost the country thousands of dollars!" Boucke also had no time for women in the classroom, intimating that they were more useful in the kitchen or as mothers. "He used to make us all sit in the back of the room," chuckled Virginia. "So did Dr. Tschan, Peg Riley's father, in the English department."

A bachelor of forty-six, Oswald met Ruth when he came to eat in her tearoom, or "kitchen," so to speak, and shocked the whole community when he married her in 1927. Despite her

deference to his intellect, Ruth did disagree with Oswald at least once — she ran for Centre County Register on the Socialist ticket, even though he had told her socialism would never work. They had only a few years together — in 1930 he had a kidney operation and never fully recovered, dying in 1935, but not until after he had published two of his best-known books, *Laissez Faire and After* and *Europe and the American Tariff*, which he wrote while he was dying.

In 1922, one of State College's first neighborhood groceries, the Highland Market and Grocery, opened at 118 East Nittany Avenue, and in 1925 the first building designed for apartments only, the Heatherbloom, went up next door. Both were creations of John Haugh, who had come from Scotland to work in the Scotia iron mines and later ran the company store there.

As was common with grocery stores then, the Highland had two entrances — one to the grocery, the other to the meat market — and in the middle, a third door leading to two large apartments upstairs. Another apartment, where the Haughs lived, was at the rear of the store. As was also common with grocers then, customers could call in orders by phone and have them delivered to their homes later that day. This went on until 1965, when owner Budd Hoy, who had started there as a clerk in 1946, sold the business to go to work for the State College post office.

Referring to his and other food stores in town, such as the Shaffer Store at 308 West Beaver Avenue, Struble's (later a Clover Farm Store) at 111-115 South Fraser Street, J. J. Meyers Food Store at 431-437 West College Avenue, and McKee's Market (later Temple Market) at 131 West Beaver Avenue, Budd said, "Each store had its own delivery truck. I had a Studebaker station wagon, then hired Handy Delivery in later years."

An A & P grocery store came to town in 1923, to 134 South Allen Street, but did not deliver. However, delivery is obviously a service shoppers like, for the Giant Food Store successfully revived it in 1992, urging customers to phone or fax orders and have them delivered for a nominal fee.

Next owner of the Highland Grocery after Budd Hoy was Joe Curilla Jr., who until 1975 used half the first floor for offices while his father ran the market in the other half. Last occupied by architect Jack Risheberger, who used the entire first floor for offices, the building was torn down in 1987 to make way for The Towers condominium at 403 South Allen Street.

The three-story Heatherbloom, at 126

W. R. Hickey Beer Distributor

R. Hickey Beer Distributor was founded in 1933 by William Ralph Hickey, a former iron worker and World War I veteran who moved to State College in 1930 and was employed as manager of Wards Restaurant.

The beer distributor was remodeled in 1994, and now has a staff of twenty-five.

Soon after Prohibition ended, W. R. purchased the license of the Hillside Ice Co., owned by Forest Struble. He moved the business to the site of the Old Mill on the Benner Pike, east of the present Clasters.

Through the lean years of the Depression and a devastating fire in 1939, W. R., with hard work and determination, kept the business afloat. After the fire, W. R. Hickey Beer Distributor moved to its current location at 1321 East College Avenue.

In 1947, W. R. formed a partnership with Charles Abramson, who had served as a company driver. A State College native since 1928, Charlie had enlisted in the Army Air Corps in 1941, and, by the time of his discharge, had attained the rank of master sergeant.

During the 1950s, Hickey's continued to grow, despite the Benner Pike being closed for two years as it was widened. In 1961, W. R.'s health started to decline, and he asked his son, William H. Hickey, to join the business as president. Bill had served in the Army Air Corps during World War Two. After graduating from Penn State in 1951 and marrying Beverly Corman from Pleasant Gap the same year,

W. R. Hickey founded the beer distributor in 1933.

he moved to Washington, D. C., as a Special Agent for the FBI. During the 1970s, their children — Jon, Chris, and Molly — joined the beer distributor full-time. After working all job responsibilities, Jon and Chris are currently vice presidents, and Molly is responsible for office administration. In 1973, Gary Bollinger joined the corporation, and is now general manager.

Hickey's enjoyed a renaissance of sorts over the ensuing years as the company obtained an Anheuser-Busch franchise. Between 1963 and 1975, the distributorship was enlarged and remodeled three times before the tiny "gas station" sales room was finally torn down and replaced. In 1980, a fire destroyed the warehouse and stock, but Hickey's was soon back in business.

By 1984, Charlie decided to retire and asked his son Ellis to return to State College. Ellis had graduated from Penn State 1970 and moved to New York City to begin a career in accounting and finance. After marrying his wife Lynn in 1980, he came back to State College to replace his dad as secretary/treasurer and partner.

The W. R. Hickey staff in 1995: (seated) retired partner Charlie Abramson and president William H. Hickey. Standing: vice president Jon Hickey, secretary/treasurer Ellis Abramson, office administrator Molly Hickey Hartman, and vice president Chris Hickey.

Today, Hickey's handles wholesale and retail sales, and offers fast in-car service or showroom browsing. Hickey's — a master distributor for Anheuser-Busch, Heineken, Labatts, Becks, Yuengling, and Gallo — thanks the community for its loyal patronage, and will continue to offer the best products and service.

East Nittany, is still standing and is still apartments. John Haugh's son and daughter-in-law, C. Hubert and Blanche, lived in the Heatherbloom, and their son, Hubie, was born there in 1927. After John died in 1931, the younger Haughs moved into the apartment behind the store, where Hubie's sister Helen was born. "Dad and my Uncle Tom ran the grocery business after my grandfather died," Hubie said. "Then Dad built a building on North Barnard Street by the railroad siding and ran our wholesale grocery business there from the mid-1930s until 1949, when he died."

Boyd Kapp, a practicing architect and professor of engineering mechanics at Penn State, was the architect for the Heatherbloom. "Legend has it," continued Hubie, "that when my grandfather went to the First National Bank to borrow money for the project, David Kapp, who had been a minister at Scotia before he went to work for the bank, told him, 'I'll lend you the money, but you have to use my son as the architect!' "

The Heatherbloom's resident of longest standing was Julia Gregg Brill, distinguished professor of English. She moved in with her parents the day the place opened in 1925 and made it her home until the early 1980s, when she moved to a retirement community in Mechanicsburg.

The growth of State College in the 1920s brought new and better public services, beginning in 1920, when College Avenue was bricked. In 1924, Allen Street, which then traversed campus through what is now the Mall, was paved with concrete from College Avenue south to Irvin Avenue, and about a mile of macadam with curbing was laid on Hartswick and Ridge Avenues north of campus.

In 1916, a "wide awake citizen," perhaps newly transplanted from Cornell, had proposed the paving of College Avenue in a *State College Times* article entitled, "The College City Beautiful." Citing Ithaca, New York, as a role model, the writer said, "State College resembles Ithaca in fundamental things. It is a college town with no manufactories to dirty the air, no traffic to wear out the street, and with a topography sufficiently varied to prevent monotony in treatment." Admitting that Ithaca has a beautiful lake, which State College lacks, the writer said, "Nature and location cannot make 'the city beautiful'; the inhabitants must, by wise judgment, by activity, by liberality and by exercising good taste. Especially must they look to the appearance of that part of the city which the stranger first enters. First impressions are always the strongest."

ERA OF PROSPERITY FOR STATE COLLEGE

With 850 freshmen enrolled, and 500 refused admittance on account of the lack of accomodations, the local institution of learning will exceed all previous years in the number of students and in the wide scope of educational work being propagated.

With a strong, vigorous college; a splendid student body; a magnificent campus and fine buildings; attractive homes and up to date business places managed by honest dealers; elegant water, sparkling and pure; air that is sweet with the breath of mountain pine and hemlock; a class of people famous for their integrity, thrift and hospitality, State College stands second to none among the towns of Pennsylvania.

BE A BOOSTER.

—The Times, 9-5-19

STATE COLLEGE MAN HAS RECORD EGG LAYING HENS

Mr. E. F. Grundheoffer, who resides at 412 West Foster Avenue, and who is in charge of research testing at the Eng. Exp. station at the college, has the champion egg-producing machine in the shape of a barred plymouth hen, which made the exceptional record of 313 eggs during her first year's laying period.

—The Times, 1-3-20

The writer went on to say that College Avenue, as the main artery of State College, should have more attention than any other street. "At present no citizen can be proud of its appearance or point it out with pride to a stranger. It has rare opportunities because it is faced on one side for many squares by the campus, which will probably never be built up. Consequently, it lends itself to a treatment different from that given to a street having closely built business blocks on each side.

"The avenue should be given a park treatment. It should be widened, paved and have a planting down its center. This would regulate traffic and make easy the handling of vast crowds which mark special occasions. The college should be asked to give the ground necessary to widen the street. The improved appearance will help the college as well as the town. Professor Cowell and the department of landscape gardening have drawn a sketch showing the results of such a treatment, including the enlarging of the paved 'diamond.' The proposed plan gives a driveway of 20 feet on the business side and 16 feet on the campus side."

In a *Penn State Alumni News* article of 1926, updating alumni on the quickly changing town, the editors reported that the two main arteries of traffic had been paved "in the most modern way," the state and county assisting the Borough in the financing of both; the abutting property owners paid for the Hartswick and Ridge Avenue improvements. "Most of the remaining streets have a foundation of crushed stone and they were improved in 1925, when Tarvia B and crushed rock was applied and the whole rolled. At present the Borough is spending about $15,000 a year on its streets." The magazine also noted that "there is a five-year oiling and curbing program that will bring about traffic channels comparable with those of the best of small towns" and that practically all streets had cement sidewalks, totaling some twenty miles in length. "The students now look elsewhere for their bonfire material as the old wooden sidewalks have long passed out of existence."

Other civic improvements included: a large water storage tank built in February 1926 at the western end of Foster Avenue; a complete sewerage system — some fourteen miles of mains — built in 1924 and 1925 and connected to the disposal plant the College had built east of town "for which Council pays proportionately for its use"; and ornamental lamps, designed for service as well as beauty, along the entire length of Allen Street and part of College Av-

Watchmaker Ben Hann stands between Beryl and Louis Riddles in the jewelry store at 124 South Allen Street in 1922. Lou and Sam Crabtree, who are cousins, were partners in the business in its early years.

Arthur "Ray" Warnock, well-liked dean of men on campus, wrote "The Half Colyum" in the weekly Times; it became the "Daily Half Colyum" when the paper became a daily.

George Smith's new — and different — barbershop building replaced his little old frame structure lost in the fire that destroyed the Leitzell building on the corner of Allen and College.

Residents and college students enjoyed skating on the frozen Duck Pond at Thompson's Spring, with Mount Nittany as a backdrop.

77

Alpha firemen with their Reo pumper and newly acquired Penn State Autocar in 1925. Chief Harry Resides, at the wheel of the Reo, is surrounded by (from left) Poppy Williams, Lynn Woomer, John Gilliland, Diemer Pearce, Phil Foster, Bob Graham, and Fred Weber. Beside Autocar driver Dan Krumrine is Harris Holmes, on the bumper are Riggs Mingle and Frank Holmes, and standing front to back are Bill Dunkel, Irv Holmes, and Jiggs Struble. Before joining forces, the Alphas and the student fire company were not averse to turning their hoses on each other when fighting the same fires. In 1924, in exchange for an annual contribution to the borough for fire protection, Penn State proposed a merger of the two companies, so the students and their fire truck moved to the town's fire hall.

enue, while the rest of the town was lighted by large corner lamps.

By 1923, there were 1,006 telephones in State College, and on January 1, 1926, Bell Telephone became a monopoly in the area when it took over Commercial Telephone. What began with eight telephones on campus in 1882, all connected to a switchboard in Bellefonte, became two phone systems by 1898. Still, not many families felt they needed phones. A long-distance call for someone without a phone was held at the switchboard while a messenger dashed through the village looking for the recipient. And since subscribers of one system could not talk to subscribers of the other, the more progressive merchants installed both Commercial and Bell systems in their stores. But by offering six months of free service and extolling the virtues of private lines and extension phones, Bell finally achieved its goal of absorbing the Commercial system.

In the early 1920s, showing there was sufficient business in State College to sustain a second bank, Peoples National Bank (now Omega Bank) opened its doors at 117 South Allen Street. E. J. Williams was president; Harry J. Behrer, Marion B. Meyer, A. H. Yocum, W. D. Custard, B. P. Homan, Frank P. Knoll, E. S. Erb, and A. J. Hazel made

STATE COLLEGE HAS BIG GROWTH

The announcement of census figures for the various boroughs and townships of Centre county, made this week, shows that State College has made the most rapid growth of any borough and that Rush and Snow Shoe townships have a nice increase.

	1920	1910	1900
Centre County	44,301	43,424	42,894
Rush township	4,645	3,763	2,430
Snow Shoe township	2,825	2,786	2,166
State College boro	2,405	1,425	851

—The Times, 8-21-20

up the board of directors. By 1930, when future president and chairman of the board Eugene Lee started working there as a twenty-three-year-old bookkeeper, Peoples was capitalized at $125,000 with total deposits on hand of $428,000 and resources of $762,000. First National Bank, by that time in business for nineteen years, was capitalized at $200,000 with $1.5 million in total deposits and $2.4 million in total resources. Both contributed mightily to the growth of the town.

Late in 1924, a new, much-needed post office building opened at the corner of Beaver Avenue and Allen Street, largely through the efforts of former state representative and former postmaster (1914-21) Robert M. Foster Jr., Congressman William Swoope of Clearfield, and other citizens. The one-story building with its "generous basement" that now houses Schlow Library cost $60,000 to build and held a staff of twenty-four men headed by postmaster George Glenn. A first-class post office since 1921 and the only one of that rating in the county, it handled a daily average of approximately 40,000 letters and 800 parcel post packages. "The amount of mail handled in State College is comparable to a city of approximately seventy-five thousand people, and the old quarters were completely inadequate," wrote

McLanahan's

cLanahan's got its start in 1903 as a Tyrone pharmacy founded by William H. McLanahan, who successfully ran it until his death in 1932. His son Bob, who helped manage the store with his mother Ivaloo after his father passed away, saw a bright future for State College, so in 1933 he opened a drug store at the northeast corner of Beaver Avenue and South Allen Street, quickly gaining a reputation for friendly service and cut-rate prices (soap was 5 cents a bar, shaving cream was 21 cents a tube). By 1937, Bob moved his store to more spacious quarters at 124 South Allen Street.

In 1948, with business booming, Bob McLanahan moved his store to the former site of the A&P grocery store at 134-136 South Allen Street. Six months later, on December 8, the newly remodeled store, boasting an eighty-foot lunch counter with state-of-the-art soda-fountain equipment and air conditioning (unusual in businesses *or* homes in '48), opened with unprecedented fanfare. The grand-opening celebration attracted more than 10,000 customers, with the first 1,000 ladies receiving free roses. The new store employed forty-five people, including part-time dishwasher Hubie Shirk, who, with the exception of four years during the Korean War, spent his working life at McLanahan's. Hubie was later named manager of a new self-service McLanahan's opened on East College Avenue in 1959.

In 1961, Ray Agostinelli joined McLanahan's as comptroller after graduation from Penn State. By 1969, at Bob's retirement, Ray and Hubie purchased the then-two stores from Bob and LaRue McLanahan and opted to keep the McLanahan name. By 1976, the local chain included five stores: Allen Street (1937), East College Avenue (1959), Village Square (1969), Centre Hall

When McLanahan's opened in 1948 at 134-136 South Allen Street, it was flanked by Centre Hardware and Crabtrees Jewelers.

(1973), and 611 University Drive (1976). At the death of Hubie Shirk in 1977, Ray and his wife Rose purchased the remaining portion of McLanahan's.

By the late '70s, McLanahan's had more than 200 full- and part-time employees. In 1986, Ray rewarded five of his pharmacists by franchising three stores: Allen Street to Phil McIntyre and Neil Foster, Village Square to Bruce Johnston and Wayne Foster, and Centre Hall to Mark Doyle. In 1989, the Allen Street store was destroyed by fire and was relocated to 116-118 West College Avenue.

Over the years, McLanahan's has built its reputation on the dedication of employees like Jack Archer, Jerry Chambers, Dick Davidson, and Milly Henry, just to name a few. In 1971, Jerry Chambers had the honor of filling the store's one-millionth prescription, a formidable achievement for an independent pharmacy. Today the McLanahan's Student Store at 414 East College Avenue is managed by Ray's two sons, Ray Jr. and Ronald. Like all of the company's employees, both are devoted to assisting townspeople and students in the McLanahan's tradition of service.

The busy soda fountain at McLanahan's last Allen Street location seated thirty-one people, with waiting lines at lunch time.

alumni association editors on campus. The old post office, in rented space belonging to Robert Foster, across East Beaver Avenue from the new facility since 1917, had burned and flooded but when refurbished became home to five businesses — a music store, meat market, print shop, photo shop, and the Western Union Telegraph Company.

Telegrams were as common in those days as faxes and overnight letters are today. When Western Union established an office in State College in 1902, there were about 1,200 townspeople and students and between thirty and forty telegrams sent and received each day. By 1932, the number of residents had increased nearly seven times while telegrams had increased nearly tenfold to about 300 per day. The first manager was jeweler Clyde Shuey, who hired operators to transmit and receive, in addition to individual telegrams, press material from the College, dispatches for *The Times*, and information concerning baseball, football, basketball, and other collegiate sports.

As for Borough schools, "there is need for more buildings to care for the large number of pupils enrolled," reported *The Alumni News*. In 1897, when Frazier Street School opened, there were 120 pupils and three teachers who each were paid $35 a month. By 1924, enrollment had jumped to 888, 100 of whom came from outside the Borough, and teachers numbered twenty-eight, each making at least $100 a month.

With automobiles also on the increase in 1924, twenty-five-year-old Dewey Krumrine, in partnership with his father, John N., started what is now State Gas & Oil by opening a gasoline station on Old Boalsburg Road. The single pump was gravity-fed from a 10,000-gallon tank up the hill on Pugh Street and dispensed gas at fifteen cents a gallon. Fuel oil, in little demand in those days of coal-fired furnaces, sold for just five cents a gallon. Over his lifetime Dewey opened seventeen gas stations in the Centre Region, including those in College Heights, Boalsburg, Millbrook, at Carson's Corners, and the one long operated by his nephew John "Buffer" Krumrine, at 815 South Allen Street, across from Dewey's original location. First affiliated with Tydol and then Shell, State Gas & Oil became a Standard Oil wholesale distributor in 1938 and moved to 1217 North Atherton Street, where fuel could be more easily received from the Bellefonte Central Railroad at its old

Krumrine stop.

One of the worst fires in State College history ushered out 1924. On New Year's Eve, all stores, offices, and apartments in the Leitzell Building, at the southeast corner of College and Allen, and the buildings adjoining it in the heart of the downtown were completely gutted. According to the *Collegian*, published January 9 after vacationing Penn Staters had returned to school, the blaze was discovered about 2:30 a.m. on December 31 and was not extinguished until nearly noon, with damages estimated at $125,000 — a huge loss.

Charlie Graham vividly remembered that fire, which destroyed his father's store and a dozen others, because he was one of the Alphas who turned out in the bitter cold to fight it. "But there was nothing we could do," he said. "The hydrants were frozen." Much time was wasted dragging hoses first to Pugh Street in a futile search for water, and then to Beaver Avenue, where a usable hydrant was found.

Every structure from 112 East College Avenue around the corner to 109 South Allen Street was destroyed. *Collegian* reported that the businesses affected included Wilbur Leitzell's Varsity Store and restaurant, Calvin Kline's shoe shop, Walter Hoy's grocery store, George Smith's barbershop, Graham & Sons tobacco and confectionery, Montgomery's clothing store, and the offices of Dr. Fred Robison, dentist, and Dr. R. H. Fox, chiropractor.

Ronnie Robison said his father had him run to the office from the family home at 237 South Allen Street to save patients' records and his dental school diploma. But Ronnie forgot the key, ran home to get it, then came back again. "The fire was a whole lot worse when I got back, and I nearly got burned getting the stuff my dad wanted," he said.

Barber Smith also lost his apartment on the third floor of the Leitzell Building, along with his business at 107 South Allen Street. "All carried insurance except Mr. Kline, who suffered heavy loss, having recently installed new machinery and a large stock of leather," reported *Collegian*, adding that for a time L. K. Metzger's book and school supply store at 115 South Allen was in danger. But a metal partition, installed between it and Montgomery's when the Metzger Building was put up in 1917, saved it. "At the present time no definite arrangements have been made for the rebuilding of the structures," the newspaper went on,

A Bigger and Better State College On the Way - - - Chamber of Commerce Organized

A larger and serious minded citizenship gathered together Tuesday night for the purpose of forming an organization to place State College in a progressive class.

THOSE WHO HAVE ENROLLED TO WORK FOR A BETTER TOWN

Edwin E. Sparks	C. E. Snyder
John L. Holmes	F. P. Resides
R. L. Sackett	J. T. Rogers, of
H. P. Armsby	Pittsburgh
P. H. Dale	R. H. Breon
R. L. Watts	G. Z. Stover
W. R. Woods	T. I. Mairs
C. B. Struble	Morris Fromm
L. D. Fye	F. H. Koons
C. W. Hockman	Robert J. Miller
J. H. Musser	C. E. Goddard
H. W. Sauers	Louis J. Riddles
G. E. MacMillan	A. J. Wood
W. K. Corl	R. H. Smith
James J. Markle	Hugo Bezdek
William Frear	Harry N. Koch
E. S. Erb	R. I. Webber
Jas. I. Thompson	M. S. McDowell
John W. Long	Jas. P. Aikens
David O. Etters	Arthur W. Cowell
P. B. Brenneman	H. B. Shattuck
Jas. M. Williams	A. H. Hartswick
P. J. Gregory	E. H. Dusham
G. C. Gregory	A. H. Yocum
Maurice Baum	W. L. Foster
E. N. Sullivan	F. A. Robison
D. M. Cresswell	E. J. Williams
C. I. Goodling	N. N. Hartswick
J. P. Ritenour	F. A. Forman
J. Fred Harvey	Grover C. Glenn
C. R. Orton	David F. Kapp
C. E. Marquardt	Eugene H. Lederer
Harry K. Metzger	W. G. Murtorff
A. L. Warnock	A. J. Zimmerman
W. R. Gentzel	

—The Times, 9-4-20

Ready for dinner are Rotarians and sons (from left, standing): Maurice Baum, Harry Koch, Dr. Grover Glenn, Rev. John Harkins, Ray H. Smith, Harry Sauers, Lynn Daugherty, David F. Kapp, John L. Holmes, Joseph W. Henszey, Penn State President John M. Thomas, Harry Behrer, Ed Hibshman, C. E. Snyder, Ray Warnock, Edward N. Sullivan, Claude G. Aikens, R. W. Grant, S. K. Hostetter, Dr. W. S. Glenn, Dr. Joseph P. Ritenour, Harry Leitzell, Stephen Fletcher, Charles L. Kinsloe, Robert Hafer, Neil Fleming. Sons kneeling: Bob Fletcher, John Henszey, Hubert Koch, Kenneth Sauers, Richard Smith, John Thomas, Steve Fletcher. Seated front row: William Henszey, Jack Fletcher, Richmond Ritenour, William Leitzell, Harry Leitzell Jr., Richard Hostetter, Jack Sauers, Web Grant, Phil Grant, Pete Fletcher, Sam Hostetter. This was in 1925.

A lady customer became a part of history as Kenneth Ishler, Andrew Struble, and Kenneth's father, Harry Ishler, looked into a 1925 camera in Struble's grocery store at 111 South Fraser Street. Butcher Harry Ishler's department was next door at 115 South Fraser, accessible through a connecting doorway in the wall and its own door to the street.

"but it is likely that they will be replaced by modern buildings as soon as plans are completed."

Wilbur Leitzell and his brother Harry, proprietor of the Co-op Book Store in the hotel across the street, owned the old wooden building at 100 East College that was lost in the fire. Both they and George Smith, whose small wooden building had adjoined it on Allen Street, engaged architect Boyd Kapp to design new buildings for them, and from the ashes a year later rose two handsome brick structures.

George's narrow but distinctive Italianate building, with arches, twirled columns, and a green tile roof, was specifically designed for a barbershop and for The Powder Puff, the beauty parlor his wife, Frieda, ran on the second floor. Now State College's oldest continuing barbershop, it still sports the same mosaic tile floor, mirrors, sinks, and cash register, as well as most of the barber chairs it had when it opened in December 1925. But it has been Rinaldo's Barber Shop since 1953, when Dick DiRinaldo, who had come to work for George in the mid-1930s, bought the business. Wayne Britten owns it today, having been passed the "tonsorial torch," as he called it, by Dick in 1987. One thing is different today, though — most of the barbers are women.

Wayne said the historic cash register draws more comments from customers than anything else in the shop. "When George first installed it, some regular customers were alarmed because the register could record sums up to $9.99. Because they'd been paying fifteen cents for a haircut and two bits for a shave and a haircut, they thought prices were about to soar. Several quit the shop for a while because they thought George had got 'uppity.' "

After the new Leitzell Builing was completed, with its arched leaded-glass windows above rectangular plate glass, Harry Leitzell moved his bookstore into George Graham's former corner location at 100 East College Avenue and renamed it The Athletic Store, or, as people came to know it, "The A Store." Run for many years by Harry, sons Bill and Harry Jr., and son-in-law Ed Brown, the store was closed in 1971.

Early in 1926, Graham & Sons moved into 103 South Allen, and in Leitzell's former storeroom across Allen Street, Claude Aikens, Dick Kennard, and M. C. "Matty" Mateer opened a new restaurant they dubbed The Corner Room. It became popular almost from opening day with townspeople, faculty, and students. In the 1930s, from faithful customer Arthur Warnock, Penn State's dean of men, it got the motto it still uses: *Haec olim meminisse juvabit*, "it will be a pleasure to recall memories of time spent here in times to come."

Claude and Dick had purchased the hotel in 1923 and hired Matty, a 1922 Penn State graduate, as hotel manager. In 1930, they became Aikens, Kennard, and Mateer, Inc. Three of their earliest employees and the year each started working are: Martha Hoover Conway (1931), Ruth Ritchey Houston (1936), and Matt Hayes (1939). They are among about twenty Mateer employees of fifty or more years ago still living in State College and nearby towns.

The Alumni News reported that the preferred business locations in 1926 were on Allen Street between College and Beaver Avenues, and on College between McAllister and Fraser Streets, a fact that was making rents prohibitive to many merchants. "When State College was chartered in 1896," the editors wrote, "a hundred houses had been built, the population was 300, and 337 students were attending the College. At that time the assessed valuation was about $217,000 and lots on College and Allen, in proximity to the Allen Street entrance, were selling for $500, or $10 per front foot. At the present time, there are 850 houses with a population of 3,600, and 3,714 students. The assessed valuation is $2,500,000 and the lots referred to above sell for $25,000, or $500 per front foot, some having sold for $1,000 per front foot in extreme cases. In order to secure a $500 lot today, it would be necessary to venture nearly a mile from College Avenue and Allen Street."

The town cop at this time was Albert E. Yougel, who had

Miller, Kistler, Campbell, Miller & Williams

The firm began as a one-man practice nearly a century ago, and today Miller, Kistler, Campbell, Miller & Williams, Inc., remains firmly established and continues to grow. The practice was established by Newton B. Spangler, the first male stenographer in the Centre County courts. He passed the bar in 1898 and immediately opened an office in downtown Bellefonte. In 1913, he hired Ivan Walker, and the firm name was changed to Spangler & Walker. The two enjoyed a thriving practice and in 1935 welcomed a third associate, State College native R. Paul Campbell.

In 1937, Ivan Walker left the firm to become Judge of the county's Court of Common Pleas, and Newton Spangler passed away one year later. For the next decade, R. Paul Campbell maintained the office as a sole practitioner. Following World War II, Paul was joined in 1948 by John R. Miller, Jr., with the firm name being

changed to Campbell & Miller. Robert K. Kistler came aboard in June 1957, opening a second office on Beaver Avenue in State College under the firm name Campbell, Miller & Kistler.

In 1962, the State College office was moved to its present location at 1500 South Atherton Street. For years the firm's Bellefonte quarters were in the Crider

The firm has been at its present State College location for more than twenty years.

Exchange Building, and in the 1980s were relocated to 124 North Allegheny Street.

In 1958, R. Paul Campbell began his twenty-year tenure as Judge of the Centre County Court of Common Pleas. His son, Richard L. Campbell, joined the firm in 1966, and the firm was incorporated four years later as Miller, Kistler & Campbell, Inc.

Following the addition of John's son, John R. Miller, III, and Terry J. Williams in 1973, the firm name was changed to Miller, Kistler, Campbell, Miller & Williams, Inc. Robert Kistler's son, Thomas King Kistler, and Tracey G. Benson also have joined as members, and the firm has added associates James L. Green, Stephanie L. Cooper, and Scott C. Etter.

Staff and attorneys enjoy a "family" atmosphere at the firm. Says John Miller, Jr., "Everybody knows everybody and we can rely on each other. That's one of the advantages of working in a town such as State College."

The firm assumed the position of State College Borough Solicitors in 1922 and has since continued in that post. Like State College, the firm's first century is drawing to a close, and it looks forward to a second century of service to residents of State College and Centre County.

The firm's Bellefonte office is on North Allegheny Street.

replaced Bob Mingle in 1925 and, with the help of a dozen Penn State students who were first hired by the Borough in 1927 as special patrolmen at forty cents an hour, maintained law and order up to 1936. A Brooklyn native, Yougel was fresh from the Pennsylvania State Constabulary and had been one of General John Pershing's "hell-for-leather boys" of the Sixth Cavalry who had chased Mexican revolutionary Francisco "Pancho" Villa.

"To me as a child, he personified a policeman — the law," said retired attorney Eugene W. Lederer, whose father was burgess, 1930-32. "Yougel seemed to exude a certain amount of confidence and gave the appearance of being fearless."

He once unsuccessfully tried to catch a speeder with his slower Ford coupe, which Borough Council quickly replaced with an Indian motorcycle and later a Harley-Davidson. In 1927, he made 419 arrests for crimes that included adultery, window-peeping, child abuse, army desertion, and "using a car without owner's permission." That winter he also went on a fining spree, collecting $4.50 from "every other landlord" for not clearing icy sidewalks. "Last year not one fraternity was among the victims," *The Collegian* complained. "This year you can't count 'em — almost all the lodgers except the DUs, and the only reason they didn't get a summons is because Yougel couldn't spell Upsilon." Al himself complained about pool halls, where students were encouraged to gamble until three or four o'clock in the morning. "This is when the rot-gut moonshine is distributed," he said. "The poolroom is the rendezvous for bootleggers and gamblers. Something should be done."

A major event of 1926 was the opening on April 8 of Maurice Baum's elegant Cathaum Theatre, named for his wife *Cathe*rine *B*aum. Just west of Co-op Corner on College Avenue, it was described by *Collegian* as "the last word in modern entertainment houses," having taken more than eight months and "at least eighteen firms" to handle the difficult excavating project and to build and outfit the theatre. Of brick and steel fireproof construction, it had a spacious lobby with alcoves and nearly eleven hundred seats on the main floor and balcony.

"As early as five o'clock anxious movie fans began to line up for the scheduled first show at six-thirty," reported *Collegian*. "Gasps of surprise were audible as the first entrants viewed the

25th Anniversary Celebration Keynoted 'Phenomenal Growth'

Keynote of the 25th Anniversary celebration in State College was the description of the "phenomenal growth" of the town during the 25-year period after the charter was granted.

The anniversary was marked by a special edition of the Times. . . .

Here's how one of the lead stories in the Times carried the news of town progress:

"It has often been said that the growth of the boro of State College has been greater in recent years than any other town in Pennsylvania . . ."

—The Times, 8-28-46

STATE COLLEGE RATS MUST GO

The Edict Has Gone Forth And Committee Will Shortly Begin Raid on Rodents

Within the next two weeks the rat extermination committee of the Chamber of Commerce expects to have its campaign started in the borough and in the college buildings. Three difference samples have been tested out by Dr. I. D. Wilson, chairman of the committee, on rats around the college farm building.

Assisting Dr. Wilson on the Chamber committee are George Graham, H. C. Knandel and H. N. Koch.

—The Times, 1-14-22

splendor of the interior." The gold and cream walls and ceiling, enhanced by decorative plaster, were lit by 225 electric lights in three colors controlled by twenty-four switches and four rheostats. Seats were heavily cushioned; artistically concealed vents regulated the temperature-controlled air flow; the curtain covering the silver screen was electrically operated from the orchestra pit; and two of the most modern projectors flashed the pictures on the screen. Two more accouterments were not ready in time for the grand opening — a pipe organ and a large electric outside sign.

A dedication ceremony emceed by the Honorable J. Laird Holmes featured remarks by Ralph Watts, Borough Council president; Burgess William Rothrock, who in the name of the people of State College accepted the theatre "as a place devoted to wholesome shows"; and G. L. Setman, class of '27, speaking for the student body, who declared, "We don't accept it, we take it!" Dean Watts was more subdued, saying, "I have watched with keen interest the progress of this theatre from the hole in the ground to the magnificent structure it is now. A town is judged by its people and their attainments and by the structures they rear. Mr. Baum is to be congratulated for his achievement as well as are the people of State College in being so fortunate as to have recourse to such an educational center as this." Everyone then settled back to watch the first Pennsylvania and New York showing of *Beverly of Graustark* starring Marion Davies and Antonio Moreno, followed by *Monkey Business*, a Paul Terry animated cartoon based on Aesop's fables. Both were silent movies, but in 1928, soon after the first "talkie" was released, Baum equipped the Cathaum and Nittany theatres with Vitaphone sound systems.

Also in 1928, the famous Paul Whiteman band came to the Cathaum for a stage show billed as "the highest priced feature ever offered in a theatre." (Admission was $1.10 per person, whereas "the prevailing rate" for movies was fifty cents.) Frank "Duke" Morris, class of '31, who in 1929 formed his own band, the Varsity Ten, patterned after Whiteman's, recalled, "There were so many good musicians with Whiteman then: Tommy and Jimmy Dorsey, Bix Beiderbecke, Henry Busse, Bing Crosby, and as chief arranger, Ferde Grofé. That was the type entertainment we were getting then — really top quality."

In the Cathaum building were two stores "facing the sidewalk on either

84

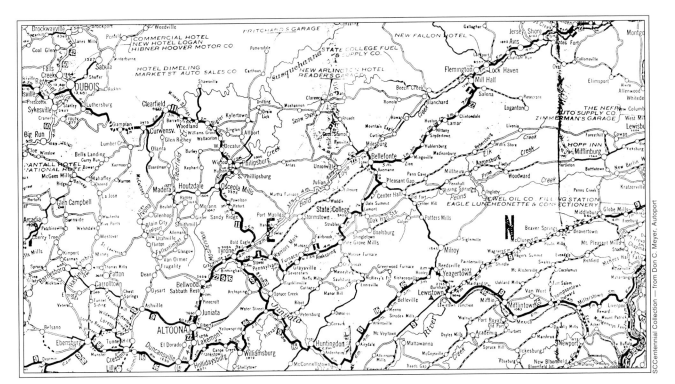

Marion Meyer's State College Fuel & Supply
Company was one of the sponsors of a Rand
McNally "Auto Trails Map of Penna." in 1924.
There was not yet a Lakes to Sea Highway
(U.S. Route 322) or a Benner Pike.

The Penn State Alumni News of April 1926
reported that there were 52 fraternities housing
3,350 men, compared with two fraternities and
165 students in 1888. Dean of Men Warnock
mentioned that most of the land shown in
Eugene Lederer's drawing was farm land five
years before.

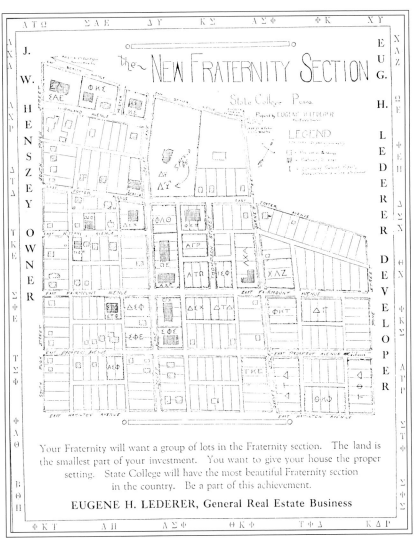

the NEW FRATERNITY SECTION

State College, Penna.

LEGEND

Your Fraternity will want a group of lots in the Fraternity section. The land is
the smallest part of your investment. You want to give your house the proper
setting. State College will have the most beautiful Fraternity section
in the country. Be a part of this achievement.

EUGENE H. LEDERER, General Real Estate Business

A 1926 student "pajama parade" left movable property of town residents piled on the "diamond" in the morning after. Had it been a celebration of a football victory, this paraphernalia could have fed a bonfire — and wrecked the brick street pavers.

side of the lobby." They also made their debuts in 1926 — Keeler's book store at 116 West College, and Stark Brothers and Harper's men's shop at 114.

Bill Keeler, a Purple Heart veteran of World War I and Penn State class of '23, had worked for Harry Leitzell while a student, said his daughter Ginny in 1993, and opened his own book and stationery store when he was twenty-five. He married Adelene Holmes, daughter of J. Laird, in 1925 and had two children, Ginny and Janet (Palermo), before he died unexpectedly at age fifty-five in 1956.

Before becoming one of the best known clothiers in the East, Jack Harper, a 1922 Penn State graduate, was a traveling haberdasher, selling fine clothes out of a suitcase to fraternity men at fifteen colleges and prep schools, among them Penn State, Rutgers, Colgate, West Virginia, Bucknell, and Mercersburg Academy. The store he represented was in Camp Hill and belonged to two brothers he had met in college, George and Ken Stark, who after four years decided to take Jack in as a partner and put him

FRAZIER or FRASER

EDITOR THE TIMES:
    Answering the criticism of the spelling of this name: —
Ordinance No. 11 ....Page 27
"An Ordinance, accepting, defining, laying out and opening FRAZIER STREET in the Borough of State College."
    Enacted Sept. 23, 1897.
    GEORGE C. BUTZ,
        President of Council
Approved Oct. 21, 1897.
    W. C. PATTERSON,
        Burgess.
    Here we have the official seal on the name and spelling of this street and both the President of Council and Burgess were then members of the College Faculty. So for all official business of the borough it is Frazier Street.
    E. J. WILLIAMS,
        Secretary Boro. Council

—The Times, 1-21-22

in a permanent location in State College.

"When I started this business, Manhattan shirts sold for $2.95 and Palm Beach suits were $19.50," Jack said in 1978. "Now we take in as much in one day as we did in one month in 1926. But in those days this town was so dead at Christmas time, I'd go down to Stark's in Harrisburg to work and leave Norm Corl in charge here. And in August we'd just close up for two weeks and go out and play golf."

In 1929, nine years before Jack bought out the Stark brothers and changed its name to Jack Harper Custom Shop for Men, he initiated the annual Dollar Days in State College. An avid football fan and longtime recruiter for the Nittany Lions, he employed many Penn State athletes in his store, and in 1959, with Ridge Riley, class of '32, then executive director of the alumni association, Jack designed a haberdashery best seller — the "original" Nittany Lion necktie.

By 1926, Penn State had seen another president, John Thomas, come and go and was waiting for his succes-

The Autoport Motel & Restaurant

Then, gas at the Autoport service station cost 8 cents a gallon, cabins, each with a private bath — unheard of in those days — were 50 cents a night, and 20 cents bought a hearty breakfast. Now, some sixty years and several additions later, State College's *and* Pennsylvania's first motel continues to serve travelers with a style and tradition all its own.

M.B. Meyer first conceived of his roadside motel while visiting Florida, where auto courts were popular with vacationers. A local businessman who owned a car agency and fuel company, M.B. felt State College could use an inexpensive rest stop where travelers could spend the night, enjoy a good meal, and have their car looked after. In 1935, he bought a twelve-acre plot out of town, formerly part of the Dale farm, and began construction of his motel. M.B. personally oversaw all aspects of the project and insisted on the best materials, including hand-selected pine wall paneling, maple flooring, and top-quality furnishings. To attract motorists, he incorporated a service station into the main building and installed gas pumps out front.

During the 1940s, the Autoport became the gathering spot for State High and Penn State students and military trainees on campus. Young people packed the Pine Room dance floor every weekend, jitterbugging and slow-dancing to live music and jukebox tunes. The Autoport's ten-stool soda fountain, serving fresh homemade ice cream, did a brisk business. M.B.'s son, Don, helped out behind the counter as a teenager, cooking hamburgers and making sodas and milkshakes. Motel business boomed throughout World War II as the Autoport cabins became a home away from home for military

faculty at Penn State, and afterward, for young couples unable to find housing in town.

Don took over the Autoport's restaurant business in 1950, shortly after graduating from Penn State. He soon built up a loyal local following by serving old-fashioned fare such as homemade pies, soups, and fresh-baked bread. Today, the restaurant remains an important part of the Autoport's business, and pies and bread are still made fresh daily.

The Autoport was in the middle of windswept farmland when it opened in 1935.

In 1953, the first motel building with eight units was constructed, as the gas pumps were converted to a motel lobby, now the Cadillac Room dining area. Later, construction of another building added eighteen more rooms to the Autoport. Through the years, Don also added a swimming pool, dining decks, bar and lounge, and two more buildings. With the recent restoration and conversion of an 1840 farmhouse behind the Autoport into a rental duplex, the motel now counts eighty-eight rooms in its inventory.

Don took over the business from M. B. in 1962, and is now passing the torch to another generation, represented by his son, Jim, and son-in-law, Mike Ferringer, both business partners. The Autoport remains a popular gathering spot for reunions, cocktail parties, and delicious dinners in a casual setting. The days of nickel Cokes and dime cheeseburgers are gone, but the dedication to traditional hospitality remains intact.

Don Meyer with his father, M.B., shortly after Don took over the Autoport's food service.

The Autoport's soda fountain occupied the area of the present-day front desk until the early 1960s.

Maurice Baum brought a "major event" to town with his Cathaum Theatre's Eastern premiere showing of "Beverly of Graustark," a comedy-drama, in April '26. Two retail stores, one on each side of the theatre, began long runs — Jack Harper's haberdashery, selling Palm Beach suits for $19.50, and Bill Keeler's bookstore. The new theatre filled the space between Nittany Printing & Publishing and the First National/Farmers Trust Banks.

sor, Ralph Dorn Hetzel, to arrive. Dr. Thomas's three-day inauguration in October 1921 had been the most elaborate ceremony in the College's history, with speeches and conferences, a massive pep rally and fireworks display, a two-hour float parade, a football game, and an alumni cider-and-pretzel smoker in the Armory. But it was on the second day that Thomas dropped the bombshell that would spell his doom four years later.

A crowd that included representatives of 120 colleges and universities gathered in Schwab Auditorium to hear the new president outline his goals for the "cow college," saying it was time to become a university.

"This college has grown rapidly in recent years and needs only the change of one word in its name to take its place with the most noble product of American democracy." He envisioned it as the capstone of the Pennsylvania public school system, with a main-campus enrollment of ten thousand and with affiliated professional and technical schools throughout the Commonwealth. He said Pennsylvania was financially able to support a great state university, and denounced public funding of private schools.

Thomas's frankness — some called it tactlessness — got him off to a bad start. Legislators fought his every budget request, and economy-minded Gifford Pinchot, who became governor in 1923, sliced every appropri-

FUNDS MAY COME FOR POSTOFFICE

The building of a new post office at State College has been brought one step nearer by the recent introduction into Congress of a bill increasing the money appropriated for this purpose from $75,000 to $110,000.

Should it be approved by this committee and passed in this present Congress, the indications would be that the new post office building would be constructed during the year 1923.

—The Times, 7-15-22

ation. In 1925, after four years of frustration, Thomas gave up the battle and accepted the presidency of Rutgers. It wasn't until many years later, as is often the case with prophets, that most of his dreams for Penn State were realized and people admitted he had been right.

His tenure had seen the beginning of sororities at Penn State, the first comprehensive athletic program for women, and the first long-range development plan for campus landscaping and future building sites.

Dr. Thomas had arrived in the midst of "the golden age of football" at Penn State, when Coach Hugo Bezdek's players, many of them war veterans, included All-Americans Bob Higgins, Charlie Way, Glenn Killinger, Joe Bedenk, and "Light Horse" Harry Wilson. Higgins later coached Nittany Lion football, 1930-48; Bedenk was baseball coach, 1931-62.

Bezdek's teams lost only one game in the three seasons of 1919, 1920, and 1921, compiling a thirty-game winning streak. The '22 team went on to play in Penn State's first post-season bowl game, January 1, 1923, losing 3-14 to Southern California in the still-under-construction Rose Bowl but bringing home a share of gate receipts of more than $21,000, a substantial sum then.

Notorious for working his gridders hard and making them stay in games when injured unless they had broken bones, Bez also had a fiery temper with downtown mer-

This football summary is offered by the 1928 high school yearbook: "The 1927 football team has been an indication of the growth of a better school spirit at State High. The development of an undefeated team has been made possible by the remarkable interest shown in football this year. Our boys played a season of nine games, winning each one." In the team photo, 1st row: Gilliland, Neff, Gravatt, Captain C. Meyer, Thompson, Hodgkiss, Tomlinson. 2nd row: Manager Stoddart, Horner, Barnes, McQuigg, Glenn, R. Meyer, Coach Zerbe.

The Times, in its thorough report on the opening of the Cathaum Theatre, said "The spaciousness of the theatre is most noticeable from downstairs. Whereas many motion-picture houses are long and narrow, the Cathaum is wide and commodious . . . . Leather cushioned seats will add to the comfort of the patrons . . . . In addition, more than the usual amount of space has been left between rows to permit plenty of leg room to avoid cramping."

Three years after fielding its first basketball team, State High had a coach, uniforms, and a manager. 1st row: Dick Smith, Hayes "Mose" Keller, Capt. Paul Krumrine, Harold "Skib" Glenn, Charley Stoddart. Standing: Coach Alex Wieland, Joe Miller, Cal Shawley, John Kessinger, Mgr. Frank Glenn.

Carrying on the Christmas candlelight service tradition in the Presbyterian Church in 1930, 1st row: Edith Meyer, Sara Jeffries, Frances Forbes, director Harriet Holben, Mary Mead, Dorothy Jones, Clara Calvert, and Nora Noll. 2nd row: Fred Pierce, Ed Keller, Charles Graff, Eugene Bish, Jaman Strong, and J. O. Keller. Max Krumrine was organist; decorations were provided by Hilda and Alice Thompson.

Their record was 2 wins, 4 losses, but the 1926 girls' basketball team was outscored by opponents an average of less than four points per game. 1st row: Kunes, Smith, Capt. Mitchell, Slagle, Wieland. 2nd row: Mgr. Behrer, McMahon, Meek, Mallory, Winter, Snyder, and Coach Long.

In 1926, the Schlow apartments and storerooms stood east of the Leitzell Building. Going down Allen Street were Smith's Barber Shop, the Montgomery & Co. store and apartments, and the Metzger Building. Across Calder Alley were Peoples Bank and Gregory's Candyland.

chants. Prexy Platt was once chewed out vigorously for kicking Bezdek's preteen son out of his poolroom, and Walter Hosterman, service manager at Peck Snyder's garage, remembered the time Bezdek stormed in, grabbed John Glenn by the shirt collar, lifted him off the ground so his feet were dangling, and banged him against the wall, growling, "Now get my damned battery fixed or else!"

After making his Lions a national football power, the athletic director/ coach, an ardent golfer, next set a goal of building an eighteen-hole golf course at State. Bez invited Robert Burns "Pop" Rutherford, a mild-mannered golf professional and former accountant from Connecticut, "to look at the place and give me some advice" in 1921. "Looking" turned into a twenty-eight-year career for Pop as golf coach and supervisor of all athletic fields.

Another golf course began materializing in December 1921, when fourteen men who were leaders in State College or at Penn State applied for a charter to incorporate as Centre Hills Country Club. Signing the application were Robert H. Breon, A. W. Cowell, Ray Gilliland, Grover C. Glenn, William S. Glenn Jr., S. K. Hostetter, Park Homan, David Kapp, Frank D. Kern, A. L. Kocher, C. W. Stoddart, Guy Z. Stover, John Taylor, and

GIRLS WORK WAY THROUGH COLLEGE

30 Penn State Girls Throw Aside Idea That None But Rich Can Be College Girls

There are at least thirty girls now attending the Pennsylvania State College who have thrown aside the old-fashioned idea that it takes a great deal of money for girls to get a college education which none but those from very wealthy families can afford. There are several hundred young men students who earn most of their way there during the entire four years, and more girl students are looking to odd jobs every year for the payment of the bulk of educational costs.

One out of every ten girls at State College earn most of their expenses, and the percentage for men is even greater.

—The Times, 2-10-23

A. R. Warnock. Grover Glenn became first president of the board of directors, followed by S. K. Hostetter for the years 1922-24.

The first official meeting of general membership was held in January 1922, attended by sixty "eager and enthusiastic supporters of a project which represents an investment of $60,000." The money gained them title to eighty-five acres and an eighty-year-old barn overlooking Slab Cabin Creek and the Branch Road near Lemont. By 1924, the barn had been converted into a clubhouse and the hillocks, patches of wild woodland, and other natural hazards into a nine-hole golf course planned by two Philadelphia golf designers. A second nine holes, designed by Robert Trent Jones, was added in 1967 on the other side of Branch Road on land purchased from Gordon Kissinger. And a third nine, opened in 1993, stretches beyond that to border the Mount Nittany Expressway and Canterbury Crossing development.

During the Thomas years, freshman customs, suspended by the military commandant in 1917, were reinstated, requiring the wearing of green dinks by men, wide green hair bows by women, and name tags by all freshman. Frosh also were not allowed to walk on the grass or enter

90

Mondell Butterfield, left front, directed State High's two-year-old marching and concert band. Under this 1928 yearbook photograph, it says, "Its enrollment now numbers forty-two uniformed members, of whom about one-third are in the Junior High School. We here extend our appreciation to the Rotary Club for its kindness in furnishing uniforms."

Second-grade girls braided the Maypole in the school yard at the Frazier Street School — this would become Central Parklet in fifty years. The Hollow is in the right background.

One of the biggest fires fought by the Alphas in the 1930s was the one that destroyed Penn State's Chemistry Annex - the "Bull Pen." Bill Secklinger, Earl Flick, and "Brownie" Dippery were there with the Buffalo pumper.

According to Virginia Ricker, the Blue Moon was one of the first restaurants in town. Another was the Club Diner, which in 1926 had been squeezed between the Schlow and Fromm Buildings. Renamed Boots' Diner, for Rufus "Boots" Ripka, who began managing it for owner Russ Adamitz in 1930, it moved in 1941 to the northeast corner of West Beaver and Atherton Street and was renamed again, this time Electric Diner — for being the first all-electric restaurant in State College.

By 1929, last year of the train station at the head of Fraser Street, four private residences remained in the 100 block of West College Avenue —Billy Hoy's was one. Theta Kappa Phi fraternity on Hamilton Avenue is the State College building closest to Mount Nittany.

a building by its main entrance, and they had to carry matches at all times. The last invariably led to a freshman's arrest by Bob Mingle following each of the many football-victory bonfires at Co-op Corner.

All coeds lived on campus, in McAllister Hall or Woman's Building, signing out before leaving and signing in before 10 p.m., when doors were locked. Only seniors could attend nighttime athletic events with men or walk unchaperoned with men by day. After special College dances, girls were allowed to go to approved downtown restaurants but had to be back in their dorms thirty minutes after the dances were over!

Although some male students lived in Old Main, most lived in fraternities or in the many rooming houses President Sparks had encouraged towns-people to build to relieve the campus housing shortage. A room in State College in the 1920s rented for $3 or $4 a week, a one-bedroom apartment for $25 a month.

Dean of Men Arthur Warnock reported that in spring 1925 better than 45 percent of the men students were members of fraternities — thirty-eight national chapters and fourteen locals. "In 1920 only seven chapters owned their chapter homes," he wrote in *The Alumni News* of April 1926. "The other chapters lived in rented houses of the conventional lodging house type.

AS TO NEW POST OFFICE BUILDING

Communications From Those In Authority Would Lead One To Believe It's Not Coming Yet

Since the proposed new post office building is at the present time agitating some of our people, it might be well to let the general public know just how the matter stands . . .

Senator Pepper: "I understand the situation at State College thoroughly, and you may rest assured I will do everything I can to help in this matter. Of course you understand that it is difficult to get any legislation through so late in the session

—The Times, 3-10-23

During the next five years sixteen chapters built new, good-looking homes, with several other chapters engaged in financial preparation for building." He went on to say that except for the six chapter houses on campus and a scattering of three or four remaining in the older part of town west of Pugh Street, the fraternity house area was becoming centralized in the district east of Pugh Street and south of Beaver Avenue. "Most of this area was farm land five years ago," he wrote, referring to a map prepared by Eugene Lederer showing thirty properties with Greek letters on either finished houses or lots waiting to be developed. "The houses built in these last five years are excellent examples of fraternity house architecture. They are distinctive in style and design, well arranged and not unduly pretentious."

"The financing of these houses has been pretty well reduced to a formula," he continued, citing one method adopted by contractor H. O. Smith '20 in building the Sigma Phi Sigma (now Theta Delta Chi) house at 305 East Prospect Avenue, one of several fraternities his firm constructed. With less than $500 in cash, Smith and a small group of alumni members took an option on a building site, then authorized the issue of $15,000 in second mortgage bonds, and collected $5,000 from alumni and friends before the bonds were delivered. They then

Laying of the cornerstone of the new Episcopal Church, across Fraser Street from The Hollow, took place February 1, 1928. After an address by Bishop Ward of Erie, The Times *reported that "the congregation marched to the site of the new building for the cornerstone ceremonies. The services were attended by virtually the entire parish membership . . ."*

Falk Realty

n 1938, Chris Falk and his two sons, Harry and Bob, built a small two-story apartment building on the corner of South Atherton Street and Nittany Avenue, beginning a tradition of serving the borough's rental housing needs that continues to this day. The Falks had hauled coal from mines near their Houtzdale hometown to State College, where they learned of the growing need for rental units to house Penn State faculty. As demand for rental housing increased after World War II and peaked during the 1950s, the Falks continued to build apartments and other rental properties throughout the area. Today, through Falk Realty Management Company, the family owns and manages more than 330 rental units in sixteen apartment buildings.

The father-and-son trio, with the help of laborers from Houtzdale, performed all their own construction work, from excavation to the placement of furniture. Over the ensuing years, they built apartments at the corner of Foster Avenue and Fraser Street, West College Avenue and Gill Street, and on South Sparks Street, to name a few, plus numerous single-family custom homes and duplexes. Their biggest single-building project, completed in the early '60s at 532 East College Avenue, was the five-story Colony Apartments. With the completion of their Corl Street apartment project in 1977, the Falks left the building business and concentrated on managing their existing properties.

These days, Falk Realty is run by Harry Jr., whose father passed away in 1983, and his uncle Jack, the third of Chris Falk's sons.

Apartment-building has been a family affair for the Falks. Pictured above are Lovenia, Christian, Jack, Harry, Betty, and Bob.

Bob remained active in the business until he suffered a stroke a few years ago. He still lives in a house he helped build, one of many the Falk family can take credit for in State College.

entered into a contract for a house to cost approximately $33,000, but before it was finished, they sold a first mortgage on it for $18,000 and sold the rest of the second mortgage bonds principally to parents of the active members. "Not the least of the contributions of fraternities to Penn State life," Warnock continued, "is the part they take in furnishing comfortable, home-like living conditions and places for social diversion in a community notably lacking in such facilities of a public kind."

For other entertainment, students went to the movies at the Pastime or the Nittany, where admission was a nickel and peanuts were sold at the door only to be thrown at chandeliers, freshmen, or the piano player who accompanied the silent "flickers." One such pianist was Hummel Fishburn, class of '22, who played at the Pastime for two or three years and even managed to study while he played. "And I always collected the peanuts for my dinner," he quipped.

Destined to direct the Blue Band and most other campus musical groups and to teach at Penn State for forty years, Hum also was a volunteer in first the Student Fire Company and then the Alphas. The first fire he fought was the Engineering Building blaze, in his freshman year, when the fire chief was H. O. Smith.

In the '20s, Hum and State College native Charlie Light, played one or two summers with the Seven Singing Seamen in The Evergreens dance pavilion at Centre Furnace. Next door was a public swimming pool. "Don't ask me how we got the name," Hum laughed, "because we didn't sing and we'd never been to sea. We just played music. Didn't make much money, but at intermission we could go swimming free." Both the pool and the dance hall, later to become a rollerskating rink, were run by David Garver, class of '12, whose father, physics professor Madison "Gravy" Garver, had bought the Centre Furnace Mansion in 1920 for Dave and his wife, milliner Anita Imboden.

Another longtime State College musician, as well as physician, was Dr. Ernest Coleman. When he came as a student to Penn State from Johnstown in 1923, he played piano with Hap Walters' band, in which were two State College boys, Budd Knoll and Ken Bottorf. By 1926, he was starring with Joe Machlan and

His Orchestra; with Hum Fishburn and Lew Fisher in a three-piano act in a Thespians show; and with six other Penn State musicians on Cunard's *Franconia* and *Caronia* cruise ships to Europe and back.

In 1928, Bud Wills, a young saxophonist from Tyrone, moved to State College and formed the nine-piece Blue and Gold Orchestra, whose members included vocalist and front man Bud Frizzell, son of Penn State chaplain John Henry Frizzell; saxophonist Bob Kirby, a State College native who became president of Westinghouse Corporation; and two State College High School students, trumpeter Harold Breon and bassist Olin Butt.

Bud, who also directed the Lemont Marching Band, 1929-32, said, "Fraternity parties were the sustenance of the Blue and Gold, although we did play at various dance halls, such as Hecla Park or the Triangle Ballroom at Bald Eagle. I even took the band to Savannah and later to New York City, figuring we'd make it in the big time, but from both places I had to write home for money!"

One local group that *did* make the big time was the State College High School basketball team, which won the District Six championship for the first time in State High history by defeating a mighty Altoona team in March 1926. Many years later, Jo Hays, who had taught most of the players that year in his classroom, wrote about this big event of his teaching days:

"In the 1920s State High teams were known simply as the 'Maroon and Gray.' The 'Little Lion' appellation had not yet appeared on the scene. Paul Krumrine was captain and leading scorer of that championship team of 1925-26 and had also quarterbacked the football team that provided the highest score in State High's football history, defeating Petersburg 96-0. He later was the first local boy ever to make the Penn State basketball team.

"For the climax of the 1925-26 season the District Six Committee chose State College, Altoona, Portage, and Mt. Union to play in the two-day tournament at Tyrone. State High had been defeated earlier in the season by both Mt. Union and Altoona, but drew Portage for Friday night and defeated them 34-22 in an unimpressive showing, while Altoona really trounced Mt.

McQuaide, Blasko, Schwartz, Fleming & Faulkner, Inc.

cQuaide, Blasko, Schwartz, Fleming & Faulkner, Inc., is a distinguished State College law firm with a century of evolution behind it. Today twenty-one attorneys and thirty-one support staff are based at McQuaide Blasko's spacious office complex on University Drive. As did many thriving modern businesses, this one began on a much smaller scale.

Charles Brown, Jr. (now President Judge of Bellefonte's Court of Common Pleas), senior partner Delbert McQuaide, the late Roy Wilkinson, Jr., and senior partner John Blasko.

Just over 100 years ago, John Blanchard, reputed by some to be the best lawyer in Central Pennsylvania, opened a law office in downtown Bellefonte. When he retired in the mid-1920s, his practice was taken over by John Love, a Bellefonte native who had graduated with honors from the Bellefonte Academy, Haverford College, and the University of Pennsylvania Law School.

John enjoyed his solo practice and had no plans to take on an associate. He changed his mind as he watched, through the late 1930s, the progress of a talented law student named Roy Wilkinson, Jr.

Roy, too, had grown up in Bellefonte. He graduated from Penn State in 1936 and entered law school at the University of Pennsylvania. There he served as an editor of the *Law Review* and earned his degree, cum laude, in 1939. After a year's clerkship in Philadelphia with Pennsylvania Supreme Court Justice Horace Stern, Roy

returned to Bellefonte and practiced law in the office of John Love.

Just a few months later, Roy interrupted his career; one day after the bombing of Pearl Harbor, he enlisted in the Army, and served until 1946. He then rejoined the firm, which soon became known as Love & Wilkinson.

In the mid-'60s, after the retirement of John Love, Roy hired three new attorneys: Charles Brown, Jr., John Blasko, and Del McQuaide.

The firm established its principal location in State College in 1970 when Roy left the practice to be a Judge on the newly created Commonwealth Court. He later served as a Justice on the Pennsylvania Supreme Court. In 1980, Charles Brown departed when he became a Judge of Centre County's Court of Common Pleas. He now serves that court as President Judge. Roy Wilkinson retired from the bench in 1982, and was active "of counsel" to the firm until his death in 1995.

The growth of the firm has paralleled the growth of the State College community and, in particular, the growth of Penn State, which has been a client since the firm's beginnings. Since 1970, Del McQuaide and John Blasko, along with several other principal attorneys, have guided its growth into the largest firm between Harrisburg and Pittsburgh. Although best known for its representation of Penn State, the firm also has developed a substantial and growing practice throughout Central Pennsylvania in the areas of defense litigation, estate planning, and business and corporate law.

The firm moved to State College in 1970, and occupies this modern office complex at 811 University Drive.

McLanahan's Cut Rate Drugs opened at Beaver and Allen in 1933. A few years later they moved around to Allen Street, as did Frost, Doty & Elder Insurance (above McLanahan's here) and Western Union (far right in this photo).

Union. Altoona fans now had reason to be overconfident. In contrast to their presence in huge numbers for the Friday game with Mt. Union, they stayed away in droves for the final contest on Saturday night. State College fans, apparently sensing an outside chance of victory, stormed the Tyrone Y that night to experience the most thrilling, spine-tingling forty-eight minutes of their lives as State High emerged victorious, 36-33. The fans' excitement erupted into the streets of Tyrone with a snake dance led by none other than C. W. Stoddart, Penn State's dean of Liberal Arts, and John Henry Frizzell, later to become College chaplain."

In addition to Captain Krumrine, other members of that championship team were Harold "Skib" Glenn, Hayes "Mose" Keller, John Kessinger, Joe Miller, Cal Shawley, Dick Smith, and Charley Stoddart Jr. Manager was Frank Glenn, and coach was D. Alex Wieland, a State High alum just graduated from Penn State. "Alex had coached basically these same boys in football that fall," Jo said, "and they were basically the same basketball team as the previous year's when the seeds for the championship were sown by Coach Hugh Johnston."

Jo Hays was a York County native who got his teaching certificate from Shippensburg Normal School, then earned a bachelor's degree from State in 1923 in the John Thomas era, and started teaching that fall at State College High School. One of his first students was R. Paul Campbell, who became an attorney and a Centre County judge.

"Jo Hays put up with no horseplay in his class," Judge Campbell recalled, "and he insisted that his students be attentive. If it looked like you were ignoring him, he might pick up an eraser and wham it at you. When he caught you in class without a pad or pencil, he would say, 'What kind of capenter do you think you can be without a hatchet and a saw?'"

Occasionally the young teacher might give a student a good shaking, but he soon ruled out severe corporal punishment. "My favorite trick was to tell a kid, 'Look, I'm gonna whale you. You get down there to the basement and ask the janitor for whatever piece of wood you want, and I'll be down later.' In about twenty minutes I'd go down and tell him he could come back up. The waiting and wondering did more for that kid than any whipping."

Jo's days in the classroom didn't last long. In the spring of 1927, Eugene Weik resigned as supervising principal and the school board chose Jo to take his place. He held the job for the next

ERNEST SAUERS IS ELECTROCUTED

A few minutes after seven o'clock this morning, just as he had started his day's work at the college power plant, Ernest Sauers, the college electrician, took hold of a live wire and was electrocuted. 2,200 volts passed through his body and death was instantaneous.

A connecting link between the lines of the Keystone Power Company and the College plant had been installed, but had not been fully taped when work for the day was suspended last evening. The current was turned on during the night for the purpose of testing out the connection . . . . It is supposed that Mr. Sauers was of the impression that the current had been turned off when he attempted to resume the taping this morning.

—*The Times, 5-8-25*

Henry Myers built a bowling alley upstairs and rented out the ground floor at 616 West College Avenue. Star Cars owner Mr. Snyder stands by the brick column, and the three people to his right are his secretary, Ron Johnson, and Chet Poorman. Sales manager Boyd Miller is at far left. In front of "Speed" Bradford's car are customers for the free "Candy for the Kids."

Harry W. Sauers
Burgess 1922-25

W. P. Rothrock
Burgess 1926-1929

Robert Mingle
Police Chief 1916-25

Harry Resides
Fire Chief 1921-30

State College Burgesses and Fire & Police Chiefs
1916 to 1930

Traffic was not quite a problem in Allen Street in the early 1930s — but commercial development had taken the trees.

twenty-nine years, after which he was elected state senator from this district and then mayor of State College.

A few months before Jo was appointed supervising principal of the State College schools, forty-four-year-old Ralph Dorn Hetzel had come to be Penn State's tenth president, in December 1926. He soon discovered that the athletic director and football coach, Hugo Bezdek, was earning $14,500 annually, more than the president's salary! He also found a college so financially ignored by the state that Old Main Building was a shambles and faculty salaries were so meager that professors were leaving for more lucrative jobs. Research was practically non-existent, and football was the be-all and end-all in the eyes of many powerful alumni.

Although warned that he would lose his job if he meddled with the athletic program, Dr. Hetzel made sweeping changes shortly after his arrival, believing that athletics should be available to all students and not to just a few heavily subsidized football players. He cut the salaries of the football coaching staff; formed the School of Physical Education and Athletics and appointed Bezdek director, charged with overseeing the College Health Service and a program of physical education and intramural sports for *all* students; and named Bob Higgins the new football coach. At the same time, Hetzel abolished athletic scholarships, making it so tough for

NITTANY SOON TO OPEN WITH SOUND

Allen Street Theatre Receiving Movietone and Vitaphone Equipment

Workmen have been busily engaged at the Nittany Theatre, on Allen Street, for the past several weeks, preparing the theatre for the installation of sound equipment. The projection booth has been considerably enlarged to provide for the vast amount of equipment necessary and an extension to the rear of the theatre is necessitated to accommodate the horns which are placed behind the screen.

—The Times, 11-22-29

Penn State to compete with other schools that he, Bezdek, and Higgins came under fire for many years by alumni outraged at having losing football teams.

But Hetzel knew how to handle legislators, win appropriations, and gain recognition for the school. Beginning in 1928, fifteen major buildings were constructed. Decreed unfit for human habitation, Old Main was razed in 1929 and rebuilt with the same stones but with a different exterior look, this time just four stories high with pillars and a tall central tower. Its formal rededication came in 1930, the seventy-fifth anniversary of Penn State's chartering.

Also in 1930, ground was broken at the northwest corner of campus for the Nittany Lion Inn, which, College officials hoped, would help to attract conference and convention groups to campus and also benefit the community by bringing more people into the area. The site was just about ideal. Rec Hall was only a hundred yards to the south, Beaver Field stood just to the east, and the College golf course was just a chip shot to the west. In addition, the new "Lakes to Sea Highway" (U.S. Route 322), which would soon separate the inn from the golf course, promised to make State College less inaccessible from all directions than Edwin Sparks had found it to be in 1908.

In 1917 the small church east of the Methodist church housed the Reformed congregation. The new building on campus, just east of Pugh Street, is the new Mining Building, which later was remembered as Pauline Beery Mack's Textile Chemistry Institute, where Mary Louisa Willard found her first job.

Alpha Community Ambulance Service, Inc.

Alpha ambulances have served the Centre Region for more than half of State College's 100 years. Founded May 5, 1941, by members of the borough's volunteer fire company, the Alpha Ambulance Club addressed a growing need for a full-time ambulance service. Prior to the organization's formation, the only ambulance in State College belonged to Koch Funeral Home. With borrowed money and donated equipment, the club outfitted its first ambulance and sold memberships door-to-door to cover expenses.

Today the Alpha Community Ambulance Service functions as a nonprofit business independent of the Alpha Fire Company. From its quarters at the corner of West College Avenue and Osmond Street, the service maintains four fully equipped ambulances and a staff of eighty-five volunteer and paid attendants. Alpha ambulances handle more than 4,000 calls per year, and attendants take pride in providing high-quality care twenty-four hours a day.

As a state-licensed basic life-support unit, the Alpha Community Ambulance Service requires paid and volunteer staff members to participate in a comprehensive training program. Requirements include CPR, emergency-medical-technician, hazardous-material, blood-borne pathogen, and emergency-vehicle training. Ambulance attendants also are trained to operate special equipment such as the automatic external defibrillators recently added to all Alpha ambulances.

Since the ambulance service receives no tax dollars, it continues to rely on member subscriptions for the bulk of its funding. Numbering close to 8,000 subscribers, Alpha Community Ambulance Service's membership helps it meet the community's need for quality pre-hospital and interfacility patient care and transportation, which the ambulance service has provided for fifty-five years.

Hard Times
Through
Wartime

he coming of U. S. Route 322 on Atherton Street brought many changes to the look, the lifestyle, and even the shape of State College beginning in the 1930s.

In 1929, before the two-lane highway cut a swath through the countryside and town, Atherton Street ended at Fairmount Avenue, and the Borough was about half the size it is today. Borough limits then were what is now Adams Avenue on the north, Irvin Avenue on the south, High Street and Bigler Road on the east, and Buckhout Street and the Bellefonte Central Railroad track, skirting the Penn State golf course, on the west. Changes to the original (1904) boundaries of Park, Foster, High, and Gill had been made with the additions of Highland Park and the Markle Farm in 1909; Hamilton Addition in 1912; Krumrine Addition in 1915; Southside Addition, between Burrowes and Gill south of Foster, in 1917; an L-shaped piece from College and Ferguson Townships, on the north to Hillcrest and on the west to Buckhout, in 1922; and the Henszey tract, "the fraternity section," from Locust Lane to High between Foster and Irvin, in 1923.

Then, in 1930, a large V-shaped chunk of College Township was annexed on the east and south, extending Borough lines along the eastern edge of the dam forming the Duck Pond, south to present-day Ellen Avenue, and west as far as Old Boalsburg Road. Included was Manor Hills, a development of Eugene H. and Lucy Kemmerer Lederer's that stretched from Garner Street to Centre Hills Country Club.

Brooklyn-born Eugene, a real estate developer, was State College burgess from 1930 to 1932, noted for punishing offenders not by fining or jailing them but by having them, for example, write the Pennsylvania motor vehicle code five times in longhand or write out parts of the Bible or attend Sunday school. Students called him "Modern King Solomon" and "Bible-Slinging Burgess," but, said the *Philadelphia Public Ledger*, "Violations diminished rapidly under these penalties, [which] apparently were far more effective than the paying of a ten-dollar fine." A veteran of both World Wars, Eugene eventually attained the rank of lieutenant colonel and, after an unsuccessful bid for U.S. Congress, served as justice of the peace.

Lucy, whose grandparents were John and Christina Krumrine, one of State College's founding families, had trained in art and architecture. She drew up plans for some of the houses being constructed in Manor Hills and later sold or rented some of the properties. "She was a darn smart cookie," said Paul Foreman, her neighbor for more than twenty years. "She could define a deal as good as anyone." A 1914 graduate of Penn State, Lucy also was one of the first State College women to drive, cruising the streets in a big green Packard, for which she was dubbed "The Green Hornet" by Henry Rudy, a mechanic at Clark Motor Company, which began operations in 1923. Before she died at age ninety-nine in 1992, Lucy was honored with a Borough park named for her, her husband, and their son Eugene W. on land donated by the Lederers off University Drive.

In 1931, another chunk of land was annexed from College and Ferguson Townships which included the northwestern portions of College Heights on both sides of Atherton. And then, in 1932, Lytle Addition, a small

Preschoolers ages two to five attended private kindergarten in the 100-east block of Fairmount Avenue in 1930. 1st row: Charles Smith, Ernest Noel, Fred Metzger, Ginny Keeler, Mary Jane Keller, Virginia Parkinson, and Sonny Stein. 2nd row: Bill Garrison, Mary Louise Davey, Anna Hope Parkinson, Tom Egolf, Phyllis Deal, and Harold Tarpley. 3rd row: Barbara Kinley, Tim Baker, Virginia Spannuth, Bill Graffius, Chester Rupp, and Paul Margolf. 4th row: Nancy Stein, Nancy Ruef, Betty Trainer, Jack Storch, Chuck Noel, Jean Thurston, and Malcolm White.

College Heights mothers made "Four and Twenty Blackbirds" costumes for a May Day program in the second year of the Depression for these third and fourth graders. 1st row: Betty Hartswick, Faye White, Robert Scheirer, Miriam Lisse, Jean Hartswick, Allen Crabtree, Eddie Lower. 2nd row: Eugene Rhinebaugh, Pete Mckenzie, Martin Knudsen, Ruth Popp, Anne Carruthers, Dean Breon. 3rd row: Tom Starr, Peggy McKenzie, Edna Suydam, Katie Popp, Henry Yeagley. 4th row: Norma Eisenhuth, Gilbert Olewine, Guthrie Patrick, Bill Minshall, Dave Arnold. Dorothy Baum is looking out the window.

The American Legion and Auxiliary Junior Drum and Bugle Corps earned state championships in 1936, '37, '38, '39, and '41, and a national championship in 1941. Members from 1935 to 1942 were William Adams, Richard Aurand, John Aurand, Sheldon Baird, David Ballenger, Leland Baughman, Wayne Bechdel, J. Bechtol Jr., Robert Bence, Donald Benner, Charles Bubb, Kenneth Bunn, Virginia Lou Burney, Catherine Burns, Pauline Burns, Hubert Corl, Isabel Craig, Harry Daily, David Dawson, Russell Dickerson, Gerald Dietrich, Melvin Dietrich, David Doan, Ann Donahoe, James Donahoe, Duane Doty, Alice Dunkel, Betty Fletcher, Miriam Fortney, Rachel Fulton, James Fulton, William Garrison, Blanche Gearhart, Ella Mae Gearhart, William Graffius, Ann Grazier, Miriam Green, Harold Green, Gerald Green, Wendell Green, Daniel Grove, Paul Grove, Robert Hamilton, Robert Hoenstine, Emily Jean Holmes, Ronald Houck, Barbara Houtz, Ruth Hutchison, Donald Hutchison, Jennie Intorre, William Intorre, William Ishler, Patricia Johnston, Robert Johnston, Lettie Knutsen, Martin Knutsen, Lois Kreamer, Patricia Kribs, Kenneth Kunes, Charles Kunes, Jane Lindsey, Donald Lindsey, Richard Livingston, John Malloy, Joseph Malloy, Margaret Markle, William Marshall, Richard McNaul, Frederick Metzger, Richard Mitchell, David Mitchell, Richard Morrell, Dean Moyer, Harold Neff, Robert Park, Joseph Porter, Bonnie Powell, Glenn Reed, Jean Reed, James Reid, Myrrell Rewbridge, Helen Reish, Joyce Ripka, Dean Ripka, Alexander Rupp, Marian Schrack, Calvin Shawley, Ann Sheehe, Bernard Sheehe, Edward Sheehe, David Slagle, Susan Smith, Marian Smith, Betty Jane Smith, Gloria Snyder, Jane Snyder, Barbara Snyder, William Snyder, Daniel Stearns, John Storch, Betty Lou Stover, Charlotte Taylor, Barbara Ulmer, Mary Lee Ulmer, Ethel VanTine, Ann Wahl, Clarence Warner, Richard Weber, Martin Whitmire, Ruth Wilde, Robert Williams, Richard Young, William Zellers, Robert Zellers. Among local parents who trained and drilled the corps were "Bucky" Taylor, John Doty, Guy Stearns, Bill Marshall and Earl Wilde.

square bounded by Old Boalsburg Road, Cross Avenue, South Atherton Street, and the Neidigh Brothers limestone quarry, part of which is now behind Hamilton Square Shopping Plaza, was made a part of the Borough.

The annexation of Lytle Addition caused one of the biggest controversies in State College since the name-change battle of 1896. It seems that what had been part of the Andy Lytle farm in College Township had become home to many Depression-poor families, a number of whom had neither the means nor the inclination to keep their small, overcrowded homes and yards in good condition. Consequently, many State College residents had no inclination to accept Lytle Addition into the Borough, but it was added, nonetheless, by court decree, and its street names eventually were changed from Lytle Street and First, Second, and Third Avenues to Walnut Street, Crestmont Road, Logan Avenue, and Sunrise Terrace.

Also because of Route 322, two popular places to stay and eat — the first large hotel and the first *motel* in the State College area and probably the first in Pennsylvania —came into being in the '30s. On May 5, 1931, the new seventy-five-room Nittany Lion Inn marked its grand opening with a gala dinner-dance for 125 invited guests who were quite literally treated to everything from soup (essence of chicken *en tasse*) to nuts (toasted, salted). In between they dined on fresh crabmeat cocktail, filet mignon with mushrooms, and a Nittany Lion sculpted from Penn State ice cream.

Some people thought the inn's prices were high. A Sunday breakfast for the Penn State Alumnae Club, for example, cost one dollar a person. Making arrangements in March, before the inn had opened for business, an assistant to dean of women Charlotte Ray said that the management offered a pleasant dining room and perfect service. "That was their inducement when I said of course we could get just as good a meal elsewhere for sixty or seventy-five cents," she told Dean Ray.

Inn manager John Lee with Ed Keller, then head of what is now continuing and distance education, traveled through the state encouraging groups to hold meetings and conferences in State College. And to induce the community to use the inn, John worked with civic leaders and volunteers to organize the first Charity Ball and helped the Red Cross raise money by offering elegant but inexpensive arrangements for the organization's affairs.

In 1936, before "motel" was a word, Marion B. Meyer built nine tourist cabins, comprising twenty-five rooms, with private bathrooms behind his gas station and small restaurant, "one mile south of State College in the farmfields," according to an early post card. Having discovered such "auto courts" on a trip to Florida, M.B. wanted to offer overnight guests private accommodations, room-side parking, and inexpensive suppers and breakfasts all in the same location. He held a contest to name the place, and engineering professor Eugene Woodruff won the grand prize, a $25 savings bond, for his suggestion: "There are *air*ports and *sea*ports, so there ought to be an *auto*port."

In those days, The Autoport charged fifty cents a night for a room, twenty cents for a hearty breakfast, and eight cents a gallon for gasoline. One of the founders of Peoples Bank, M. B. also owned State College Fuel and Supply, which provided coal and fuel oil to many area homes, and had opened one of the first local gas stations, at 601 West College Avenue. He also sold and always drove the car he considered the top of the line — Cadillac — and his son, Don, named a private dining room at The Autoport for it. Today, the Cadillac Room is on the spot where customers used to pull in under the canopy by the four gas pumps to "fill 'er up." The Coffee Shop was once a car-repair shop with a grease rack and mechanic's bay, and cars were washed in what is now the kitchen.

With its popular ten-stool soda fountain, homemade ice cream, a jukebox that gave four plays for a dime, and a large dance floor ringed by booths, The Autoport was *the* weekend hangout in the 1940s for high school kids, college students, and servicemen on leave, who went there to jitterbug and to dance cheek-to-cheek. "This was the only place to go and dance then," said Don Meyer, who put his Penn State hotel-administration degree to work there in 1950. "Sometimes it would be so crowded it seemed the walls would be pushed out! The Nittany Nine, directed by Olin Butt, played here every Friday night, and we also hosted 'Square Dance Night.' Newt Neidigh, the greatest square dancer Centre County ever had, danced every dance."

Newt was the father of Jut and veterinarian Maurice "Doc" Neidigh, whose Hamilton Avenue limestone quarry, according to Jut, supplied much of the stone for construction of Route 322, for many Borough homes and

Park Forest Enterprises

(formerly J. Alvin Hawbaker, Realtor)

The man whose vision created Park Forest Village always had a talent for real estate development, but then so did many builders who came to the Centre Region after World War II. What really separated J. Alvin Hawbaker from the pack was his love of the land and a desire to serve the community — a combination that helped turn an area known as the Barrens into one of Pennsylvania's most successful planned communities.

In 1944, Al came to State College to meet with then Pennsylvania State College President Dr. Ralph Dorn Hetzel, who was searching for a contractor to build homes here for newly arriving employees of the Navy Ordinance Research Lab (now Applied Research Lab). Al brought his family and crew, and they stayed in rooming and boarding houses that were plentiful in town.

J. Alvin Hawbaker

The first homes built were on Mitchell Avenue and North Atherton Street in the College Heights section at a cost of $8,000, followed by single-family homes on Westerly Parkway, Waupelani Drive, and South Hills and Panorama Village. By the time his building projects were finished, he had decided there was so much natural beauty and unlimited development potential in this still-small town that he decided to stay.

To help the community keep up with postwar mortgage financing demand, he assisted his friend John Madore with the start of State College Federal Savings and Loan Association, later United Federal Bank and now PNC Bank. Also, he was president and one of the chief organizers of the State College Flying Service (now University Park Airport).

Al's biggest and best-known project began with an idea he had in the early 1950s for development of a Patton Township area known as the Barrens. Many local residents thought he was crazy to sink capital into the 1,000-acre project, but time bore out his wisdom, and today Park Forest Village is considered a model family community. Park Forest Village saw State College's first condominium project, Georgetown.

Al received numerous awards recognizing Park Forest's innovative design and features. Though there was almost no regulation of the building business at that time, and features such as sidewalks, curbs, and wide streets were not required, Al included these things at Park Forest. He paid for water lines and a pumping station and installed his own temporary sewage-treatment plants — one of the first outside State College.

The early 1960s found Al expanding his business interests from builder and realtor to the multi-family market, and he was a forerunner of property management services for the more than 3,000 apartments built in outlying areas. All were major apartment complexes built before downtown high-rises.

Today property management is the Hawbaker family's main interest. Since 1981, his son Sam and daughter Joan Hawbaker Brower run Park Forest Enterprises, Inc., which manages Park Forest Villas and apartments and homes in State College and surrounding areas. The company also is developing Valley Vista Park, another new concept with affordable homes and smaller lots suited to first-time home buyers and retirees.

Al Hawbaker, builder-developer-realtor, who always believed in leaving the land better than he found it, has indeed left his mark on State College.

Sy Barash and Al Hawbaker admire a late-1950s Nittany Advertiser billboard promoting the up-and-coming Park Forest project.

some for the rebuilding of Old Main. Operated by the Neidigh brothers from 1923, the quarry's days were numbered as the town grew around it — people built houses nearby and then complained about noise from the dynamite used to loosen stone. Members of Our Lady of Victory Catholic Church, then on the corner of Fairmount and Fraser, complained that the dynamiting was jiggling their pews. The Neidighs finally bought out their competitor in Oak Hall and moved there to quarry and crush limestone until 1985, when they sold out to Herbert R. Imbt.

One of the houses that literally had dishes falling from the cupboards during blastings at the Hamilton Avenue quarry was "Camelot," David and Madeline Campbell's English Wayside cottage at 520 South Fraser Street. The first residence in the Borough on the National Register of Historic Places (because of its unique architecture), it was designed by David, who taught engineering drawing at Penn State for forty years. It also was named by him as both their dream house and a play on their last name.

Begun in 1922, it was not finished until 1937. "The design was so radical, we couldn't get any contractors to bid on it," Madeline said in 1992, citing the five pointed gables, sagging roof with wooden shingles that made it look thatched, woven gutters, and rounded windows. "We couldn't get a mortgage for the same reason, so we built whenever we had some money saved."

Builder John Hoy finally agreed to build it on condition that the Campbells not tell anyone. "But after it began to get compliments, John started bragging about being the builder," she said.

To help pay for their unmortgaged house, Madeline got a job in 1928 as Borough secretary, first woman to hold that position. Over the next five years she did just about everything for the two burgesses she worked for — Colonels Rothrock and Lederer. Harry Leitzell, then Borough council president, had encouraged her to apply for the job. "I attended council meetings, made up the agenda, took minutes, bought supplies for the fire company, was secretary to the board of health, issued permits, recorded

Cathaum Theatre Makes Initial Move in Raising Fund For Aid of Unemployed

After a brief but intensive selling campaign, in which all of the various town organizations took an active part, a large quota of tickets for the Special Benefit show at the Cathaum Theatre, at 10:45 o'clock tonight, has been sold...through the generous offer of Warner Brothers, every cent derived from this special show will go directly to local relief.

—The Times, 11-20-31

all property deeds, and, believe it or not, even did housing inspections!" she said.

After David's death in 1962, Madeline groomed French poodles for eighteen years and continued to live in Camelot until 1989, when she sold it to realtor Jack Heckendorn and moved to Brookline Village.

Penn State's leader during the Depression days of the 1930s and through World War II was Ralph Dorn Hetzel, whose presidency spanned nearly twenty-one years, second only to George W. Atherton's tenure. The Hetzel era saw the value of the physical plant increase from $3.7 million to more than $26 million and a growth in student enrollment from 3,800 to nearly 11,000.

During those troubled, wonderful growing-up years, fraternities dominated the headlines of *Collegian*. It was a time of house parties, proms, swing bands, saddle shoes, and hell weeks . . . a time when students battled police, complained about prices in local stores, marched on Washington, DC, and preached pacifism through anti-war articles in campus publications . . . a time also when about 4,000 men and women students, 150 faculty and staff, and hundreds more townspeople marched off to war, and more than 400 never returned. But 7,000 ex-GIs did return to finish or start degrees — swelling the 1946 enrollment to 10,600 — and question everything professors said and everything the administration did.

A shy, gentle man, Dr. Hetzel had tremendous foresight and ability, along with an intense conviction — almost an obsession — that land-grant institutions were just as important and just as good as traditional Ivy League universities. He was always thinking at least five years in advance, envisioning a Penn State enrollment of fifteen thousand students by the mid-1950s.

In 1917, thirty-five-year-old Hetzel had become one of the country's youngest college presidents, of the New Hampshire College of Agriculture and Mechanic Arts, and a trustee grumped that he was "too darn young." But Ralph replied with a twinkle in his eye, "Time will take care of that." His success in nine years there — during which time it became the University of New

—The Times, 9-23-32

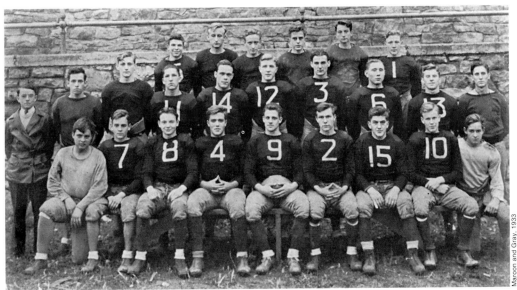

Five years after a State High football squad went undefeated, this team ran into a "disappointing season" — losing all nine games. Highlights of the season were scoreless ties with Cooper Township and Bellefonte, and the Maroon's only score of the year in losing 6-7 to Clearfield. Six other teams scored 118 points against State College. 1st row: J. Krumrine, R. Warnock, M. Zorella, D. Merritt, Capt. E. Martz, B. Moore, E. Hess, C. Bell, and J. Ritenour. 2nd row: Mgr. H. Snyder, G. Krumrine, R. Ammerman, C. Mothersbaugh, J. Zonge, R. Eisenman, R. Sproat, R. Koon, M. Henninger, and Coach H. L. Glenn. 3rd row: W. Mitchell, R. Herman, J. Crissman, K. Steele, D. Aldinger, and R. Burgin.

Many two- and three-sport athletes were on State High's '32 track team. 1st row: Jim Reed, Stanley Myers, Ralph Weaver, Gregg Thompson, "Slim" Fortney, "Bud" Zonge, and "Ox" Corl. 2nd row: "Flash" Light, Joe Myers, Tom Moore, "Whirlwind" Packard, Ken Turner, Elwood Strouse, "Junior" Green, and Coach Dick Detwiler. "Whirlwind" is Vance Packard, who became famous for his best-selling books on American sociological change — the first, The Hidden Persuaders.

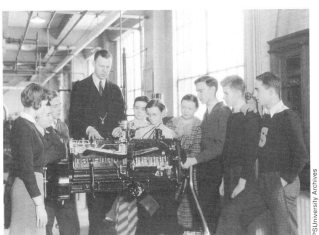

Penn State professor Amos Neyhart explains the workings of an automobile engine to members of the world's first driver-education class at State College High in 1933. Left to right are Jean Taylor, Harlan Hostetter, John Harkins, Professor Neyhart, Miriam Zeigler, Ann Marshall, Betty Murtorff, Willard Robinson, Jim Shigley, and Bill Reish.

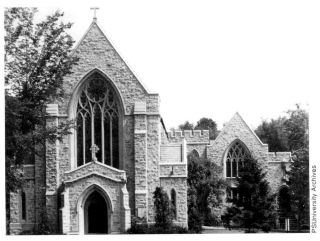

New Faith Reformed Church, seen by the pastor, the Rev. A. S. Asendorf, as "a dream of more than ten years ago finally realized in stone," and what The Times called "In all respects . . . a model in modern church architecture," was dedicated May 29, 1932 at 300 East College Avenue.

105

Hampshire — and his experience with two other land-grant colleges — Wisconsin and Oregon State — prepared him for the presidency of Penn State, which he accepted in December 1926.

During the early Hetzel years here, Prohibition was still in effect, and while meeting the demand in town and on campus, bootleggers such as the infamous Prince Farrington of Lock Haven, were frequently arrested by State College police. But those looking to quench alcoholic thirsts also drove to Goldie's in Snow Shoe and other speakeasies in the area.

Then, with the nationwide legalization of beer in 1933, traveling, at least for a big ten-cent draft, became a thing of the past. The first tavern license in State College Borough was issued to "Pop" Flood and his wife, owners of the Green Room Restaurant at 142 East College Avenue. After renovating the former barbershop under their restaurant, the Floods ushered in fall House Party weekend by officially opening "The Green Room Rathskeller and Gardens" on November 9, 1933, giving it a proper debut by sending printed invitations to friends and hiring Bud Wills's Blue and Gold Orchestra. With the added attraction of dancing every Wednesday and Friday night to such groups as the Blue and Gold, Harold Breon and Olie Butt's Campus Owls, and Duke Morris's Varsity Ten Orchestra, the Green Room Gardens soon became "the talk of the College" and the place was considered to be "the only really *nice* bar in town."

Within six months of opening their basement taproom, however, the Floods sold it to C. C. "Doggie" Alexander, who changed its name to The All-American Rathskeller, implying its popularity with Nittany Lion athletes. These have included Sever "Tor" Toretti '39, who checked I.D. cards at the door in exchange for meals; Rosey Grier '55, who tippled Cokes and played a mean game of pool; and Mike Reid '69, who loved to bang out songs on the upright piano.

In the Hetzel days of no athletic scholarships,

"Doggie's Place," as it was frequently called, used to feed athletes for free. "And some of them could really pack away the food," said bartender Fritz McGrail, who worked there from 1935 until the beginning of World War II. "Why, I remember Ferky Frketich would eat six eggs and a half-pound of bacon every breakfast! One time I slipped an athlete a draft beer with his lunch, and Doggie got mad. 'Don't do that again!' he told me. 'He's got to *buy* beer — that's where I make the money to pay for his food!'"

Fritz recalled, too, that when he first tended bar at the 'Skeller, there was no closing time. "Some so-called intellectuals would be there drinking and arguing until four o'clock in the morning. But then Doggie started closing at midnight, mainly to keep peace with the neighbors because beer was almost voted out twice in State College *after* it became legal."

Born Carey Collins Alexander at Julian in 1896, Doggie attended Bellefonte Academy, Penn State, and, as Tor Toretti put it, "more prep schools and colleges than anybody in the world but didn't graduate from any of them." He also served in the navy and the army and worked as a railroad fireman, a tire salesman, and a high school football coach before going into partnership with Jim "The Greek" Harris, owner of a combination billiard hall, gambling parlor, shoeshine stand, and hat-cleaning establishment at 147 South Allen Street. An avid sports fan and golfer, Doggie used his own car to chauffeur the Penn State golf team to out-of-town matches. "Even after he retired in 1957 and until he died in 1961, Doggie would spend his winters in Florida and his summers at Penn State's pro shop," said Dean Smith, who became the 'Skeller's manager in 1950 and its co-owner in 1958.

Doggie's Place reached the height of its renown during World War II, when, in a broadcast "from the front," a correspondent asked a GI, "Where would you rather be right now, soldier?" Radio listeners in all parts of the world

Glenn O. Hawbaker, Inc.

If any family can claim to know State College from the ground up, it's the Hawbakers. Between Glenn O.'s excavation and paving company and J. Alvin's contracting business, the Hawbakers had a hand in dozens of local construction projects. From Panorama Village to Park Forest, Glenn and Al left an indelible mark on State College.

Glenn came to State College in 1945 from Mercersburg to work with his brother Al, who at the time was building homes on Mitchell and Ridge Avenues. The two worked closely for several years on various excavation and site-preparation projects before Glenn purchased some equipment from Al in 1952 and formed his own excavating and grading company. Glenn then began working with other housing contractors in State College on developments such as Toftrees and downtown apartments like Parkway Plaza. He soon branched out into more heavy commercial work, opening a Pleasant Gap asphalt plant in 1974 and an aggregate-crushing operation in 1983. His company's facilities and equipment made it the natural choice for many local paving projects and curb, sidewalk, driveway, roadbed, and bridge construction work.

Glenn and Thelma Hawbaker are proud of all the company has done in State College.

Today Glenn O. Hawbaker, Inc. offers a full range of heavy-construction services — asphalt production, quarrying, concrete construction, utilities work, and heavy-equipment rentals. The company serves most of north-central Pennsylvania from its locations in Pleasant Gap, DuBois, Turtlepoint, and its State College headquarters on West Aaron Drive. Recent projects include new tarmacs and taxiways at University Park Airport, Weis Market on Martin Street, and Tioga County

The headquarters of Glenn O. Hawbaker is filled with awards and commendations.

Airport near Wellsboro, plus infrastructure development at Gray's Woods. The company also played a major role in laying the groundwork for Penn State's Research Park and supplied construction materials for the university's new Bryce Jordan Center. PennDOT is one of its biggest customers, primarily on road resurfacing and widening projects.

Under the direction of Glenn's son Dan, who is now president and CEO, the company remains a family affair. Dan's brothers, Alan and Glenn O. Jr., are actively involved with the business. Glenn Sr. and his wife Thelma spend half the year in Texas, where they operate a seventy-five-acre citrus grove.

With yearly sales exceeding $40 million and more than 450 workers during peak construction season, the company is one of the Centre Region's largest employers. Its corporate mission reads, in part, "We will meet the challenge to grow and increase our skills, leadership, and self-worth, personally and professionally." To that end, employees are encouraged to participate in basic- and continuing-education training programs offered at the company's headquarters. By fostering personal and professional growth within its work force, Glenn O. Hawbaker, Inc. is helping build a better community — in more ways than one.

heard the young man reply, "I'd rather be in State College, Pennsylvania, at the All-American Rathskeller."

Collegians of the 1930s were fashion-conscious to a fault, probably as a result of the growing co-ed population. Men's and women's clothing shops, barber and beauty shops, and dry cleaners and laundries all benefited from the boys' desire to impress the girls, and vice versa. A comparison of downtown businesses of 1932 with those of 1900 reveals the economic impact of the students in twelve clothing stores — five specializing in women's clothes, six in men's, and one in children's — as opposed to just one, for men, in 1900. Also in 1900, shoes could not be bought or repaired locally; in 1932 there were four shoe stores, four shoe-repair shops, and five shoe-shine parlors. In 1932 there were five beauty parlors, eight barber shops, two florists, and three jewelers; in 1900 there had been one barber and none of the other shops. Perhaps most telling of the student influence was the growth from one restaurant in 1900 to eleven in 1932, plus four hotel dining rooms and innumerable boarding houses. Bellefonte, on the other hand, largest town in the county, had only four restaurants.

Even in the 1940s male students almost always wore shirts and ties with sport coats or sweaters, and women could wear slacks only in dormitories. State College optometrist Dr. Gerald Stein '43 said, "My wife, Sylvia, was one of the Curtiss-Wright Cadettes, who were being trained at State to work at aircraft plants during the war. The girls had to take a welding course, so they wore blue jeans to class, but for that they were hauled into the dean of women's office!"

During the early years of the Depression, as biennial state appropriations dropped from $6.3 million in 1929 to $3.7 million in 1934, job vacancies on campus were not filled and salaries were cut. Hetzel made up for that by increasing fringe benefits, such as enrolling Penn State faculty and staff members in the State Employees' Retirement System. He also established Penn State Centers (forerunners of Commonwealth Campuses) around the state so students could save money by commuting close to home. But a few students, whose families seemed unaffected by

"hard times," complained that it was unfair to cancel a dance or an activity just "because of the Depression."

State College schoolteachers also saw their salaries reduced by anywhere from one to ten percent, and sometimes unmarried women teachers were forced to skip a pay day, preference being given to married male teachers with families to support. But with 1,241 residents, about 28 percent of the population, employed by Penn State and 160 families keeping student roomers and boarders, hard times were not as lean here in the thirties as they were in more urban areas.

In the fall of 1934, students had a rude introduction to the new State College burgess, Wilbur Leitzell, who warned them, via *Collegian*, to obey Borough ordinances and declared that "the destruction of a traffic sign carries with it a penalty of $25." Wilbur was quoted by *Collegian* editor John Brutzman '35 as saying that he could have any student arrested for disorderly conduct, even if that student were merely leaning against a post at Co-op Corner. "And when the person's arrested, he's guilty!"

That in itself was an invitation for the November riot, in which 1,500 students tangled with Borough and state police at a gigantic bonfire at Co-op Corner on the eve of the Homecoming football game. Alumni, townspeople, and Alpha volunteers were also on the scene when chief of police Albert Yougel arrested a freshman for lighting the first match. A huge, milling crowd followed the chief and "his fugitive" to Borough Hall. In the melee, the sleeve of a state policeman's uniform was ripped off and, according to *Collegian*, Wilbur told Al, "Break out the rifles!" The riot was finally quelled when President Hetzel came downtown and persuaded the students to leave.

But that wasn't the end of it. When debris from the bonfire was cleared away, there was no longer any road underneath — the bricks had disintegrated. This started a chain of meetings and letters, beginning with a paving bill sent from Borough secretary C. Edgar Book to Penn State Alumni Association secretary Ed Hibshman, who forwarded it to President Hetzel, who gave it to student council president Paul Hirsch, it being a tradition that class funds be used to pay for off-campus damage from student celebrations.

Student council offered to pay half the bill, claiming the bricks had had fourteen

WPA laborers worked for 15 cents an hour in mid-Depression — and were happy to be working at all. Mrs. Charles J. Graham, who gave this photograph to The Tavern, identified her husband, a foreman, as the man with his foot on the wheelbarrow. Trucks from Swartz Hauling and O. W. Houts distributed the last of the topsoil to complete the athletic field in The Hollow. Stone walls around the stadium represent less than 20 per cent of the rock removed from the town sinkhole to finish the project.

May Day celebrations had had regal overtones for decades at Penn State, and State College continued its own traditions in 1939. Mary Glenn and Albert Daugherty are King and Queen of the May; Rietta Conger and Tom Smith are "mock" monarchs. Two seated attendants at left are Bob Bence and Randy Rice; on right are Sally Duffy, Robins Young, and Jack Nesbitt. Attendants not in photo are Mary Jane Doerner, Ann Grazier, Margaret Hussey, Charlotte Taylor, and Elizabeth Yeagley.

years of wear and tear. Borough council demanded full restitution. The state highway department jumped into the dispute, saying that because the Borough and the fire department had not exercised proper authority, responsibility for repairing the street belonged to the local bodies, not the highway department.

A small band of students, apparently irritated at being sent the repair bill, stole the flags of the Alpha Fire Company. The Alphas thereupon presented a bill to the student body for $189, the estimated replacement cost. Dean of Men Arthur Warnock wrote to Borough council, explaining why the students had offered to pay only half the cost of repairing the street — they had found that bricks in 1934 were cheaper than in 1920, when College Avenue was paved. As for the Alpha's flags, Warnock wrote, "The student board then inquired of a local purchasing company and found that they could buy the flags for approximately $47, four times *less* than the original estimated cost. This discrepancy, of course, aroused student resentment, not against the fire company but against the merchants who quoted the higher price for the flags. This unfortunate occurrence only served to confirm most students' mistaken belief that the townspeople are not averse to hiking the prices when dealing with students."

And what, finally, was the cost of repairing almost the entire intersection, after College leaders, the burgess, engineers, and highway personnel spent six months attending meetings and writing letters? It was $200.

Burgess Leitzell came to the fore again in 1935, when he sent Chief Yougel to arrest a Clearfield County coal company for "peddling without a license" by attempting to deliver coal to Delta Upsilon fraternity. The campus literary magazine *Old Main Bell* declared, "This time Leitzell has gone too far! He's obviously trying to protect State College merchants!"

Nevertheless, Wilbur was reelected in 1937, only the second man after Burgess Holmes to hold the office for two consecutive terms. Al Yougel succeeded him as burgess in 1942 and also won reelection.

In 1938, State College set a Borough construction record of $543,202, including fifty-five houses costing

2 ARRESTED FOR HAULING STUDENTS

Charged with transporting passengers in motor vehicles without bus registration, two persons were arrested by members of the Highway Motor Patrol last Friday, as they were about to leave for Philadelphia with a cargo of students . . . Each was fined $10 and costs.

Green had published an advertisement in the columns of the Collegian advertising for passengers to Philadelphia, for $4.50 round trip, and it was through this lead that the Motor Patrol made the subsequent arrest.

—*Centre Daily Times, 11-13-34*

Visit the Automobile Show

You Will Enjoy These Newly-Created Automobile Designs for 1935 at the First State College Exhibition

With the swiftness of wings and the quick poise of birds, the designs of all the ages have eclipsed themselves in the conception of automobiles — for 1935. Streamlining attains new dignity, colors are radiantly rich, and from every point of criticism only the most enthusiastic praise is merited by these automotive creations.

The Cars and Their Dealers

Clark Motor Co	Dodge, Packard, Plymouth
Hafer's Garage	Buick and Pontiac
McClellan Chevrolet Co	Chevrolet
Nittany Motor Co	Ford
Smith Brothers	Chrysler and Plymouth
R. F. Stein Motor Co.	Oldsmobile
Storch Motor Co.	Plymouth and DeSoto

—*Centre Daily Times, 2-12-35*

$401,190; the State Theatre, built for an estimated $70,000; and additions of about $25,000 to Grace Lutheran Church at College and Atherton. Residential construction reached another new high in 1939 — $404,940 for fifty-one houses. Total construction that year, however, was less than in 1938, just $533,820, but more than twice what it had been in 1936. While most Pennsylvania communities had peaked and then receded in building activities by the late 1920s and early 1930s, State College, enjoying the economic stability of a college town, never seemed to stop building. Architect-designed, pattern-book, and even mail-order houses were filling Borough lots with what historic preservationists have described as laboratory examples of fine twentieth-century styles.

H. O. Smith, Dean Kennedy, Boyd Kapp, Clarence Bauschspies, John Henszey, and O. W. Houts were just some of the architects and contractors responsible for the Borough's rich collection. And several of the town's early architects and landscape architects gained statewide and national reputations. For example, A. Lawrence Kocher, head of Penn State's architecture department, 1912-26, supervised the 1921 addition to State College High and built a house at 357 East Prospect Avenue for electrical engineering professor Leonard Dogget which included parts of old Bellefonte, Milton, and Lancaster houses. Kocher was noted for his restoration work at Colonial Williamsburg and Washington Irving's home in Tarrytown, NY. Raymond A. Hall, who in 1939 designed a home for English professor Philip A. Shelley at 114 East Whitehall Road, had been a student of Frank Lloyd Wright. Walter W. Trainer, Penn State's supervisor of landscape planning, not only designed his own home at 714 McKee Street but also developed a detailed garden plan for it. And Arthur Cowell, a landscape architect involved in projects across Pennsylvania, chose to build a Sears mail-order house at 144 Ridge Avenue but lowered the front windows so his children could better see the gardens.

Sears, Roebuck & Co., the Aladdin Co., the Gordon-Van Tine Co., and other mail-order suppliers were ready to offer would-be home owners the latest in style choices to meet their space needs and pocketbooks with total

110

HRB Systems

When two Penn State faculty members and a graduate student founded an electronics company just after World War II in a graduate student trailer at Windcrest (present site of South Halls), they scarcely could have imagined that it would grow to become one of the region's largest employers. Dr. George Haller, Dr. Richard Raymond, and Walter Brown met during the war and discovered they shared a connection with Penn State. After the war they started Haller, Raymond & Brown, Inc. — later shortened to HRB — as a part-time business. Before long, the company had expanded to Raymond's basement and garage, and in 1947 moved to a house at 401 Clay Alley.

From its earliest days, HRB relied on ideas to fuel its growth. One such idea, conceived by Haller and Raymond, resulted in a piece of equipment that eventually became one of the company's biggest sellers. Called RECONOFAX, the device produced photo-like images of objects or substances from the heat that they radiated. The device was used for airborne surveillance during the Vietnam War and later to detect water pollution and underground mine fires. Another HRB idea first brought television to State College in 1953 via a special antenna. Spun off the following year, the TV business provided the seed for Centre Video and C-COR Electronics. HRB was also among the first companies to use a digital computer, a novelty described in 1954 as "the magic brain."

With the purchase in 1958 of HRB by The Singer Company, Haller and Raymond departed to join General Electric as executives. By that time the rapidly growing company had moved to the Smithfield Building on Atherton Street and to two other locations. By 1960, HRB-Singer boasted sales in excess of $7.2 million, primarily to the Department of Defense. From a handful of workers in 1947, the firm had grown to more than 700 by 1960.

Dr. George Haller

Additional offices opened in Ohio, New York, Texas, and Washington, D.C., and a new State College headquarters site was constructed on Science Park Road. In 1965, the company was awarded its largest contract to date, $15 million for airborne infrared-surveillance equipment. By 1968, HRB-Singer had 1,456 employees on its payroll.

During the height of the Vietnam War, defense spending on strategic electronic systems decreased sharply, and HRB-Singer was forced to downsize. The company hit a low point of 439 employees in 1971. Following the cessation of hostilities in Vietnam, HRB-Singer's business improved and, in 1983, the company was awarded a contract for $150 million. By 1985, employment was again nearly 1,500.

Dr. Richard Raymond

In the 1990s, HRB was again required to change, this time in response to the end of the Cold War. The company responded by branching out into three major areas: mobile data communications, language training, and automated information processing.

A subsidiary of E-Systems, a $2 billion defense and electronics firm in Texas, HRB Systems, as it is now called, employs approximately 1,000 workers at three locations: State College; Linthicum, Maryland; and McLean, Virginia. At one time considered primarily a defense contractor dealing in classified equipment, HRB Systems is now calling itself the best company you never heard of. Expect to hear a lot more from the firm that started out in a Penn State trailer and built its reputation on innovative ideas.

Walter Brown

HRB Systems' facilities today on Science Park Road are a far cry from a trailer on the Penn State campus.

In the 1930's Sherm Lutz was flying photographers over town and campus for aerial views. This one shows just a few homes west of Sunset Road (right forground); Adams and Hillcrest Avenues (left and center foreground) were just beginning to see development on the north edge of College Heights; and the town's main residential areas ended at Fairmount Avenue on the south.

house packages and, in the case of Sears, mortgages and money-back guarantees. The package prices included plans, most materials (even nails), and overall cost estimates on labor and excavations. All building parts arrived in State College, pre-cut and numbered, on the Bellefonte Central Railroad, and shipping dates were staggered to allow materials to arrive when they were needed. Once lots were selected and foundations completed, these homes were ready for assembly by local builders or even by the purchasers themselves.

Early examples of four-square and bungalow mail-order houses can be seen on many Borough streets within three or four blocks of Col-

lege and Allen, while later models, many of stone, are found in abundance in the College Heights, Holmes-Foster, and Highlands neighborhoods. The Historic Resources Study Committee, established by Borough Council in 1991 and headed by Jackie Melander, inventoried, photographed, and gathered architectural and historical information on homes fifty years or older in these neighborhoods. In 1995 the neighborhoods were included in the National Register of Historic Places, the nation's official list of cultural resources worthy of preservation.

President Roosevelt's Works Progress Administration (WPA) funds cer-

'Little Orphan Annie' Is Coming To Town In the Centre Daily!

This friendly little waif, whose adventures are followed by millions, will come to readers of the Centre Daily Times each night, beginning Monday. Several months ago, the Centre Daily Times decided to add another comic strip to complete its already popular page of well-known features, including Joe Palooka, Alley Oop, the Bungle Family, and Out Our Way with Worry Wart and his friends.

We know that it won't be long until both Annie and Sandy, her dog, will have won their way into your heart.

—Centre Daily Times, 3-19-35

112

Roy Jamison, a new State High teacher in 1936, was told by Supervising Principal Jo Hays that the school board had authorized fielding a wrestling team. "Great," said "Jammie," "but what's it got to do with me?" Jo said, "I've told them you'll serve as coach." This was the first SCHS team — 1st row: Mark Gilligan, Claude Homan, Al Crabtree, Tony Droege, George Zins, and Bob Blair. 2nd row: Coach Jamison, Assistant Coach Howard "Red" Johnston (who was Penn State's first national champion wrestler), Charles Ridenour, Jack Henry, Elwood Horner, Elmer Etters, Sam Crabtree, and Manager Eddie Coombs.

A wagonload of swimmers on their way to Centre Hills Country Club in the summer of 1938 — in foreground: Jill Brown, Pat Gilbert, Becky and Hum Fishburn, David Fishburn, Dick Boerlin, and Dick Pearce. In back: Gene Pearce, Joyce Gilbert, and Anna Keller. Chauffeur is John Stoner.

Joyce Gilbert Sipple

SCCentennial Collection

Burrowes Street, looking from Beaver to College Avenue, kept its village-quiet, tree-lined look through the 1930s.

113

Bob Wetterau enjoyed his work in Bill Keeler's book store at 116 West College Avenue.

Long a fixture downtown, Rea & Derick Drug Store wrapped around Peoples Bank, with a door on Allen Street and a door on Calder Alley into the lunch counter/soda fountain — a preferred hangout for high school kids.

tainly helped with civic improvements in the Depression era, especially in the final transformation of The Hollow into State College High School's Memorial Field. For years the huge sinkhole at Fraser Street and Nittany Avenue, just south of the Frazier Street School, had been used as a dump that smelled even worse after filling with water from a thunderstorm. This natural amphitheatre had been purchased by the school board from owner John Noll in 1914 for $3,042 at the suggestion of Arthur Cowell, who envisioned it as a school playground. The first effort toward that goal came in 1916 when ground was leveled for a baseball field. Nothing else happened for ten years until the Rotary Club paid for an outdoor running track. Then in the summer of 1930, Lowe Construction Company did the wall, steps, and landscaping at the south end at cost plus 10 percent, and that fall the field was first used for State High football games. Four years later, for $200, H. O. Smith installed the first permanent seating, on the Fraser Street side — wooden bleachers he had salvaged from refurbished Beaver Field.

Finally, at the behest of new school board president Stevenson Fletcher, supervising principal Jo Hays suggested applying for federal aid, and the project won

LEITZELL BALKS SCENERY MOVING

State College Burgess Refuses To Allow Student Dramatists To Haul Sets Sunday

The Penn State Thespians, student dramatics group at the College, ran afoul of a snag in Burgess Wilbur F. Leitzell when they asked permission to transport scenery for a forthcoming Thespian show from the basement of the Cathaum Theatre across the main street of State College to the campus on Sunday afternoon.

Burgess Leitzell refused the students permission to transport the sets . . . . the students waited until after midnight, when a State College drayman, refused a permit to do the hauling as originally intended, took the settings to Schwab auditorium in the early morning hours, where students spent the rest of the night erecting them.

—Centre Daily Times, 4-2-35

approval in 1935. The board guaranteed to pay up to $5,000 while federal WPA funds would provide the rest of the nearly $43,000 cost. Calvin Graham, whose family home bordered on The Hollow, was appointed general foreman, supervising 15-cent-an-hour laborers with picks, shovels, and wheelbarrows who, aided by a few trucks and drivers from local contractors like Houts, Lowe, and Swartz, graded and enlarged the depression and built more stone retaining walls to provide a beautiful and full-sized venue for football and track. John Bracken, a Penn State landscape architecture professor, designed and supervised the planting of trees and shrubs. Permanent bleachers and floodlights for night games were installed all around, and the completed stadium was inaugurated on October 1, 1937, as State High gridders beat Osceola Mills. Its present name, Memorial Field, came about in 1946 when it was dedicated to the State College High School dead of both world wars. In 1993, it was dedicated again, this time to the dead of all wars, including the Persian Gulf War of 1991.

In summer 1937, at a cost of $5,000, the school board bought more "play ground" — an eight-and-one-half-

The Tavern Restaurant

erhaps no other establishment better typifies the town-and-gown character of State College than The Tavern Restaurant. Opened in May 1948 by Penn State graduates John "Jace" O'Connor and Ralph Yeager, the restaurant has catered to residents and students for nearly half a century. Although it has grown several times over the years and Jace and Ralph have retired, the Tavern remains a popular spot for dinners and drinks in a tradition-steeped setting.

The Tavern saw early success as returning World War II veterans intent on pursuing their educations jammed State College. Most of the restaurant's waiters were vets, and all were Penn State men over age twenty-one. A camaraderie soon developed among waiters that often became the basis for lifelong friendships.

With ex-GIs from the Korean War also returning, the Tavern continued to employ many veterans through the 1950s. Jace and Ralph worked in the kitchen nearly every night. Waiters doubled as bartenders, serving beer from behind the restaurant's beautiful hand-carved mahogany bar, imported from Caruso's in New York City. Several prominent Tavern alumni started as waiters during the '50s, including Walter Conti, who joined the staff in 1951 and later became president of Penn State's board of trustees and president of the National Restaurant Association. The famed Tavern twins, hosts Andy and Joe Besket, began working at the restaurant in 1958, and today still greet returning Penn State alumni and friends.

Pat Daugherty and Bill Tucker, two waiters who joined the Tavern staff in 1967, bought the business in 1979

from Jace and Ralph. The new owners soon began work on a dining-room extension into an adjacent space that had housed a travel agency. The Adam's Apple, a cozy place to enjoy a fireside drink, resulted from another expansion. Designed by former waiter/bartender Csaba Balazs and his wife Ann, a Tavern regular, the lounge opened with a ribbon-cutting ceremony officiated by Walter Conti.

The Tavern first opened its doors in May 1948, and within a few months its busy proprietors had moved the bar — and a wall or two — to expand the original dining area.

Although one Tavern tradition fell by the wayside in the mid-'70s — that of an all-male wait staff — most others have remained unchanged. Rare prints and photographs, artwork, and memorabilia from Penn State's and Pennsylvania's past, a collection started by Jace and Ralph, still grace the Tavern walls. And some of the same menu specialties that tempted patrons decades ago are today prepared by kitchen manager/chef Al Clymire, who has been with the Tavern for over twelve years, and chef Dave Judice, a fourteen-year Tavern veteran. Desserts like the Tavern's delicious cheesecake, originally made by Ralph's mother, have been baked fresh daily by Pat Krezo for over a dozen years. The restaurant is managed with the considerable help of partner John Leedy, who has been with the Tavern for more than twenty years.

If you stop by the Tavern today, you won't find Jace and Ralph in the kitchen, but you just might see them enjoying the tradition they started forty-seven years ago — dinner at the Tavern.

Tavern troops over the years have served under the most genial of taskmasters: (seated) founding owners Ralph Yeager and Jace O'Connor, and restauranteurs Pat Daugherty and the late Bill Tucker.

A thirty-year institution, the Sewing Club, let these wives and mothers keep up with latest events in town and on campus — and they did bring darning and sewing to every meeting. Standing: Ruth Watkins, Ethel Pielemeier, Mabel Gearhart, Anne Margolf, Clara Crabtree, Norma Currier, Betty Glenn, Stella White, and Faye Beam. Sitting: Nina Minshall, Harriet Nesbitt, and Blanche Yeagley.

The Alpha Fire Company's Fourth of July carnival on Allen Street was, for 33 years, a week for family fun and hometown reunions. Firemen built and operated all the games and booths, even constructing the street-wide canopy to weatherproof most of the midway. The carnival went a long way toward financing fire company requirements.

Greyhound bought property from the Foster Coal company on North Atherton to build a Post House — necessitated, as the CDT reported on Monday, February 17, 1941, "by action of State College borough council which ordered the busses off College Avenue . . . by this Thursday." With elegant touches like the bay windows and a copper-capped cupola, H. O. Smith put up the building for $26,000.

52 Tubercular Cases Were Given Treatment in S. C. Area This Year

Of the 52 tubercular cases given attention in the State College area during the past year under the supervision of the State College Tuberculosis Society, the vast majority were children 14 years and under.

The improvement shown in all cases with the exception of the one, was made possible by the funds received through the sale of Tuberculosis Christmas Seals last year.

One of the most significant allotments made from the seal proceeds is the maintenance of a State College Milk Fund. With this money, milk, which is distributed through the public schools, is provided for children who cannot afford it and for whom its consumption is necessary.

The State College Tuberculosis Society is composed of the following persons: E. A. Dambly, chairman; Mrs. C. O. Jensen, Jo Hays, Miss Laura Jones, Curtis Watts, Miss Grace Smith, Ernest Johnson, Miss Ida S. Segner, A. L. Burwell, Miss Margaret Kane, Mrs. J. R. Miller, Miss Clara McClellan, Dr. C. A. Morgan, Mrs. H. N. Worthley, R. J. Miller, Mrs. W. M. Lepley, Mrs. R. D. Williamson, Mrs. F. L. Bentley, secretary; and E. F. Lee, treasurer.

—Centre Daily Times, 12-7-35

State College Welfare Fund Campaign To Raise $6,000 To Get Under Way Monday

State College's first Welfare Fund campaign will get under way Monday morning . . . in an effort to . . . meet the financial needs of seven and probably eight welfare and social service agencies . . . .

The team captains: John R. Doty, Jo Hays, Rev. E. H. Jones, Mrs. F. W. Owens, William Marshall, R. Y. Edwards, Howard E. Hopkins, Frank Reed, E. I. Wilde, Earl Stavely, Earl Myers, Paul Campbell, Charles Wagner, William Seckinger, Mrs. C. M. Bauchspies, H. P. Griffith, C. A. Eder, L. D. Fye, A. R. Warnock.

The seven organizations definitely aligned with the fund are the Centre County Hospital, Crippled Children's Society, Boy Scouts, Legion Junior Drum and Bugle Corps, Emergency Nursery School and Associated Charities.

—Centre Daily Times, 10-17-36

Clyde Fishburn, Ted Watson Among 8 Dead When Fishing Boat Sinks; 2 S.C. Men Saved

Clyde W. Fishburn, prominent State College merchant, and T. J. "Ted" Watson, State College insurance agent, were drowned off Bowers Beach, Delaware, after the cabin cruiser in which they and eight other men were fishing foundered and sank at 4 o'clock yesterday afternoon.

Charles W. Stoddart, Jr., and Edward McKee, also of State College, are . . . recovering after 14 hours exposure in the storm-tossed waters. . . .

Five of the six Altoona men in the party also drowned . . . .

A State College resident unable to go on the trip was "Boots" Ripka, who decided to stay home at the last minute.

—Centre Daily Times, 6-15-37

The State College yearbook says, "One of those new teachers got the swell idea of organizing a school swing band, and before the year was over they were giving out with some pretty solid stuff." Seated: Mary Eldred Anderson, Paul Grove, Bob Korman, Don Krebs, Dave Hess, George Cohen, and Joan Bissey. Standing: Emily Jean Holmes, new teacher Carl Sassaman, Owen Ridenour, Bill Graffius, Randy Rice, Marie Thompson, Blanche Gearhart, Jack Meyers, Marcia Gauger, Alex Gregory, Charlie Swartz, and Ann Grazier.

A 3 a.m. fire on April 1, 1941, discovered by Matt Hayes, left 25 roomers homeless and closed the Allencrest Restaurant and the Dairy Store on the northwest corner of Allen and Beaver. Three other stores — Paul Mitten's men's shop, Kalin's ladies' wear, and the Blair Shop of gifts, sustained water damage. Alphas fought the fire for four hours.

State College Boys Sentenced by Burgess

State College boys were recently given sentences following a hearing before Burgess Wilbur F. Leitzell . . . for watching a high school football game from a tree.

Adrian L. Pace and J. Burton Peasles were fined $2 each for watching the State High-Jersey Shore football game from a tree on Frazier Street.

It is understood that borough police will continue to enforce this law at all future high school games.

—Centre Daily Times, 10-23-37

Two S. C. Streets Are Closed for Coasting

Closing of Gill street between Nittany and Beaver avenues and East Foster avenue between Garner and Pine streets for coasting was announced by State College Burgess Wilbur F. Leitzell today.

Parents are warned that they will be fined if their children are caught coasting on any other than Gill street or East Foster avenue.

—Centre Daily Times, 12-8-37

Will Dedicate State High Athletic Field

Formal dedication of the new State College high school athletic field will take place tomorrow night with a brief ceremony to be presented in the ten-minute interval between the halves of the game between State College High and Claysburg.

Among those who have been invited to speak briefly at the ceremony are . . . Thomas G. Haugh, president of the school board; Burgess Wilbur F. Leitzell; and the Rev. John F. Harkins, president of the Board of Athletic Control.

The State High band will also take part in the dedicatory ceremony.

—Centre Daily Times, 10-7-37

Installation of State College Parking Meters Begun Today

The installation of 32 parking meters on South Allen street, State College, between College avenue and Highland alley, began this morning.

The meters will be on trial 60 days, and one hour parking will cost five cents.

—Centre Daily Times, 7-31-38

Some of the older boys in this Lutheran Sunday School class would be in military service before too long.
1st row: Al Wisner, Tony Corman, Anselm Wurfl, Eugene Maelhorn, Dean Spayd, Jim Pease, "Tuffy" Krumrine, Clarke Young, Bev Edmiston.
2nd row: Hubert Shirk, Bob Shirk, Chuck Weber, John Weber, Ken Hosterman, Don Krumrine, Bob Park, Ralph Hosterman, Byron Hoy.
3rd row: "Doc" Lonberger, Ken Shope, Bob Myers, Bill Ishler, Dick Houtz, Dick Miller, John Neff, Jim Neff, Russ Spayd, Pastor John Harkins.
4th row: Bill Corman, Sam Marquebreck, Mel Rockey, Chuck Noel, Joe Ammerman, Luther Maelhorn, Jack Reen, Norm Hartman, Max Ross, and Bob Bunnell.

acre tract along South Atherton, bounded partially by West Prospect Avenue and South Gill Street. Also WPA-approved, it was converted into Community Field, whose main attractions are tennis courts, a baseball diamond, and a football practice field. Until the soccer fields were built behind Welch Pool in the 1960s, varsity soccer games were played on Community Field below the tennis courts.

As early as 1908, high school boys had club teams to compete with other schools in basketball and football, but coaches such as John F. Harkins, football, and Charlie Morrill, track, were unpaid volunteers, until physical education was required of all boys (1929) and girls (1931). Girls also participated in intramural and interscholastic athletics, under the guidance of Evelyn Kirtland, first full-time phys-ed teacher. Like the boys, the girls practiced in rented facilities of the Methodist Church and the Modern Woodmen of America, whose hall was on West Hamilton Avenue near South Allen Street, now site of an apartment building.

In the 1930s, with help from the Borough, Penn State, and the WPA, State College became the first public school system in the nation to offer driver training. Amos E. Neyhart, an industrial engineering professor, first offered the course as a non-credit elec-

S.C. Boy's Bike Found for Him

Paul Bender, son of Mr. and Mrs. Fred Bender of 532 West College Avenue, is one of the happiest kids in State College today. A bicycle he won in a contest was stolen from the front porch of his house in April, and yesterday it was recovered by Chief of Police "Marty" Kauffman and some of Paul's friends.

Although repainted and with most of the accessories missing, Paul decided to check the serial number. The numbers corresponded and Paul immediately took steps to recover his once beautiful and prized possession. Today Paul is looking forward to the time when the thief will make restitution in the form of a new, shiny bicycle with all the "trimmings."

—*Centre Daily Times, 7-22-38*

tive after school hours in spring 1933. It was added to the high school curriculum in 1940 and led Penn State to establish an Institute of Public Safety. It also led the American Automobile Association to have Neyhart arrange national driver-training programs under its auspices.

Keeping up with the growing school population — 1,021 pupils and 37 teachers in all grades in 1930, compared with 612 and 19 in 1920 — was difficult. For years, parents in rapidly expanding College Heights had been asking for a school in their neighborhood, so in 1931, one was built on the east side of North Atherton Street on a triangular piece of land donated by Adam Krumrine, following the example of his father, John, who had given land for the one-room Krumrine Schoolhouse near the present site of Radio Park Elementary School. Designed by Jo Hays for expansion, the College Heights School started with two rooms and grades one through four — and the Krumrine farm dinner bell in the school belfry, found by Sam Crabtree, who then lived in the original Krumrine farmhouse and whose son Allen was a fourthgrader. In 1938, two more rooms were added to accommodate fifth and sixth grades.

The high school, built in 1914 at 411 South Fraser Street, received many

Moyer Jewelers

For three generations and counting, the Moyer family has served jewelry, watch-repair, and engraving needs from downtown State College. While the shop's location has changed over the years, the family's commitment to providing personalized service and one-of-a-kind merchandise remains unchanged.

Founded by Belty "Ben" Moyer and his wife Jane in the fall of 1949, Moyer Jewelers originally occupied a second-floor shop on the corner of Allen Street and Beaver Avenue, above what was then called College Sportswear. Ben subsequently moved his business to a ground-floor location in the 100 block of South Pugh Street, but it was destroyed in 1951, when a nearby furniture store and several adjoining small businesses were hit by fire. Moyer Jewelers then took up residence in a College Avenue storeroom in The Tavern Restaurant building, where it remained until Ben passed away in 1965, at which time his son Gary assumed responsibility for the management of the family business.

Barry, Gary, and (front) Don Moyer, the three sons of Belty and Jane Moyer, outside the Moyer Watch Shop on South Pugh Street before it was destroyed by fire in November of 1951.

A recent Penn State graduate, Gary had started working in the jewelry store as a teen and learned the art of engraving from his father. With the help of his mother Jane and master watchmaker George Jones (still an integral part of the service department), the store continued to grow. In the fall of 1965, Gary's wife Judy graduated from Penn State and began working in the store. About the same time, the shop moved from The Tavern building to a larger space in the building next

From 1952 to '65, Moyer Jewelers was housed in a storeroom in The Tavern Restaurant building.

door. In 1975, Gary and Judy arranged for a move to the Leitzell Building at the corner of College and Allen. Since then, Moyer Jewelers has been a fixture at 100 East College Avenue for more than two decades.

Today Gary and Judy's daughter Lori, also a Penn State graduate and a Graduate Gemologist of the Gemological Institute of America, manages the store. She is assisted by her mother Judy, who also operates The Animal Kingdom next door. In the shop, two watchmakers and two jewelers create original pieces, which account for about half the jewelry sold. Still very much a family affair, Moyer Jewelers has been synonymous with quality merchandise and service now for almost half a century.

The present store has attractive window displays on both College Avenue and Allen Street.

additions. The first, in 1921, was five classrooms and an auditorium/study hall. In 1931 came a wing on the Nittany Avenue side, featuring a well-equipped gymnasium whose bleachers could seat 700, a home economics lab, and a manual-arts shop. This marked the beginning of the junior-senior high school, both under one principal, Walter H. Passmore, and an ending, temporarily at least, to renting facilities for athletics, instruction, and graduation exercises, previously held in the Presbyterian Church and the Cathaum Theatre. But growth continued, so in 1936, a wing containing a boys' locker room and five new classrooms was added to the alley behind the school, and in 1940 construction began on the Fairmount Avenue addition, which included a new auditorium to replace the old one, and a new library.

On the other end of the grade spectrum, the first public kindergarten was begun in 1939 at the Frazier Street Elementary School, with N. Isabell Boyd assigned as teacher. Miss Boyd, who had taught first grade and special grade since 1923, would continue to teach kindergarten at Frazier Street and then Easterly Parkway Elementary until 1965, when she retired. A strict disciplinarian, she nonetheless was respected and fondly remembered by most of the 2,200 students she taught during her forty-two years with the school district.

One of those ex-pupils, who would later become school board president, was Duane Doty, a career marine officer who retired in 1964 to join his brother-in-law, Frank Hench, in the State College insurance agency founded by his father, John Doty, and Henry Elder in 1925. "Sure, I had Miss Boyd for first grade," Duane chuckled, recalling that she spanked him on his birthday. "I don't know to this day whether she spanked me for a punishment or because it was my birthday. But when she said, 'Sit down!' you'd better do it. When other teachers said, 'Sit down,' you sort of slid into your seat. Apparently, however, Miss Boyd was good for me."

In the 1930s, changes for State College were coming fast and furiously: dial telephones arrived in 1936, a new

County's Residents Join in Hysteria At Fantasy Broadcast

People in this district shared with others the hysteria which accompanied a radio broadcast last night in which New Jersey was reported attacked by a strange horde, a U. S. army battalion destroyed, and bombing planes flew high over New York City.

The Centre Daily Times offices in State College and Bellefonte were deluged with 'phone calls asking if any information had been received from the United Press.

A number of co-eds fainted in the dormitories, it is understood, while in the men's fraternity houses automobiles were being loaded, some to go to the "front," others to go just anywhere.

—The Centre Daily Times, 10-31-38

sewage-disposal plant was built in 1937 (and almost immediately drew complaints from nearby residents about its odor), parking meters were placed on Allen Street and College Avenue in 1938, daylight-saving time was ordained in 1939, and a third set of traffic signals was installed in 1940. Fast-changing red and green (no amber) lights at Burrowes Street and West College Avenue followed earlier installations at Beaver and Allen and at College and Atherton. Police Chief John Juba said they would be a big help at morning, noon, and evening rush hours and following campus athletic events.

Medical service also increased as a surgeon and four general practitioners opened practices within months of each other in 1937 and '38. Surgeon Esker "Bucky" Cullen treated patients at 212 South Allen, on the second floor of what is now the Allen Square building; H. Thompson Dale joined his father, Dr. Peter Hoffer Dale, in their office-residence at the corner of Fraser and College; H. Richard Ishler opened an office in his family's home at 229 West Beaver Avenue; and Eugene Mateer practiced above the Cathaum Theatre. Dr. Harriet Harry (Henning) also started in 1937, but at Penn State as the first woman doctor hired by Ritenour Infirmary; in 1941 she opened a private practice downtown at 322 West College. Other doctors already practicing at that time included Billy, Grover, and Nannie Glenn and J. V. Foster, who was known to take tonsils out in his office at 141 South Allen Street.

Dr. Ishler, who practiced until 1993 and for more than fifty years gave Alpha firemen their annual physicals, said, "When we all first started, there was no ambulance except for Hubie Koch's hearse. And when you ordered it, you had to go along with it — there were no medics like there are today."

In response to this — and because the hearse was available only when there was no funeral in progress — the Alphas started their ambulance club in 1941, naming Hubert Koch president for what would be a ten-year term. "We borrowed money to buy our first ambulance — a 1941 Cadillac — and equipped it with linens and other supplies donated by State College busi-

Chief of Police Albert Yougel issued police badges to physicians during World War II to give them instant access to emergency vehicles and accident sites.

The 1942 SCHS Red Cross Council members were, 1st row: Miss Ruth Smith, vice president Marjorie Triebold, president Ruth McCord, treasurer Susan Bissey, secretary Nancy Ruef, and Mary Lawther. 2nd row: Charles Margolf, Jane Watson, Mary Armes, Barbara Kinley, Jean Moyer, and Ted Crow. 3rd row: Pauline Williams, Maralyn Davis, Betty Lou Stover, Evelyn Sweeney, and Algie Smith. Absent were Emily Jean Holmes, Richard Nicholas, and Russella Adamitz.

State High's 1943 880-yard relay team was undefeated in dual competition: "Nick" Nicholas, Bill Keller, Bill Hickey, Chuck Noel, and Jim Holtzinger.

College scheduling officer Ray Watkins had one of wartime's most difficult home-front jobs in town as chairman of the State College War Price and Rationing Board. He was also a school board member, and succeeded John Henry Frizzell as "chief barker" at the Alpha carnival's bingo stand.

121

Salvage drives were important to the local war effort, putting usable rubber, metal, and paper to work for the Allies. During September and October, 1942, in a drive headed by Dick Kennard and John Henszey, Centre County was eighth among Pennsylvania counties in total scrap collected — 220 pounds per capita!

nessmen," said Hubie. "Then, every man in the fire company went door-to-door selling memberships in the club to local residents."

One of the Alphas' biggest fires occurred in 1937, when Penn State's Chemistry Annex, the so-called Bull Pen, was destroyed on December 29. Erected in 1907 as "temporary," the cinder-block building on the present site of Whitmore Laboratory housed offices, laboratories, and the five-hundred-seat amphitheatre where the "Bull," chemistry professor Swampy Pond, lectured.

Fueled by oiled wooden floors and exploding cylinders of compressed gases, the white-hot fire, which melted steel and glass, lasted only a short time. But it took with it some of the country's best-known laboratory setups, including Dr. R. B. Dow's high-pressure lab, second only to Harvard's, and Dr. Wheeler P. Davey's x-ray equipment.

Physics professor David C. Duncan, who, like Dr. Davey, had an office in the Bull Pen, said, "For years we all had complained about the building. Wheeler and I continually said we wished it would burn down, and when it did, Wheeler said, 'They're going to think we did it, Dave!' But

he lost all his x-ray equipment and files, and several graduate students saw their research projects go up in smoke."

One of the biggest news years in State College history was 1940. In the headlines were two murders, an airplane crash, the building of "Benner Pike" between Bellefonte and State College, and the beginning of a longtime rivalry for a football trophy.

The top local news story of the year was the murder of Penn State freshman Rachel Taylor whose nude, bludgeoned body was found in front of the new elementary school in Lemont on the rainy morning of March 28. It was the first homicide in recorded history in the State College-Lemont area and the first ever linked to Penn State, reported the *CDT.*

The inquest the next night at the school drew a capacity crowd of residents, students, and "the biggest collection of newspapermen ever to be attracted to the usually peaceful Centre County town." School janitor Harold Leightley had discovered the body of the seventeen-year-old when he came to work at 6:30 a.m. Neighbors testified to hear-

Lutz, Fellow Pilot Badly Hurt in Plane Crash

Sherm Lutz

BULLETIN
Physicians at the Centre County Hospital at 1 o'clock this afternoon said that Pilot Lutz was critically injured, suffering from severe head and chest injuries, a fractured right thigh and left arm. Charles Neyhart suffered a fracture of the leg and other minor injuries.

—Centre Daily Times, 8-7-40

PNC Bank Corp.

On April 13, 1949, State College Federal Savings and Loan Association was established by a determined State College resident who went door to door to secure the necessary $100,000 in deposits. Less than fifty years later, through a succession of mergers, acquisitions, and name changes, the association, PNC Bank Corp., has become one of the nation's largest and strongest financial institutions.

From modest beginnings at 209 East Beaver Avenue, the State College Federal Savings and Loan Association eventually became United Federal Bancorp, a formidable financial force that boasted nearly $1 billion in assets by the beginning of 1994 when it was acquired by PNC Bank Corp., then the nation's tenth-largest banking institution.

John Madore founded State College Federal more out of necessity than

John and Mary Madore

a desire to operate a bank. A home builder at the outset of the World War II housing boom, he found he was spending more time arranging financing than constructing homes. The most practical solution seemed to be the organization of his own savings and loan institution. With deposits he had secured, his own savings, and the help of founding directors Harold Albright, R. Paul Campbell, C. R. Carpenter, John Dreibelbis, Wayland Dunaway, Henry Elder, J. Alvin Hawbaker, O. W. Houts, M. C. Mateer, Charles Rowland, and Charles Schlow, Madore succeeded in securing a charter for the new association.

Rapid expansion and the doubling of deposits to

$2 million necessitated a move to newly renovated quarters at 122 East College Avenue in 1957. Over the years, branches opened in Bellefonte (1962), Philipsburg ('64), Clearfield ('69), Huntingdon ('73), Nittany Mall ('75), North Atherton Street ('77), and South Atherton Street ('81).

On February 1, 1983, under bank president Jack Falk, State College Federal merged with Mt. Nittany Savings and Loan, which had previously merged with Centre Building and Loan of Bellefonte, to form United Federal Savings in 1961.

In 1984, the year Madore retired as chairman emeritus, United Federal Savings converted to a federal mutual savings bank charter as United Federal Savings Bank. In 1988, Charles C. Pearson Jr. was appointed CEO. One year later, in February 1989, the bank issued $42 million in stock to become a publicly held corporation. Seven additional offices — in Williamsport, Mifflintown, Shippensburg, Newport, and Chambersburg — were added through acquisitions in 1990. As its branch system grew, United Federal became the largest residential and commercial real estate lender in Centre County. By 1993, the bank had grown to nearly $1 billion in total assets.

In January 1994, United Federal was acquired by PNC Bank Corp., the largest banking organization in Pennsylvania. With over $64 billion in assets and more than 500 community banking offices in seven states, PNC Bank is the tenth-largest bank in the United States. Through PNC's enhanced serves such as investment, management, and trust, customers now enjoy additional

The original board of directors included (seated) Harold Albright, M.C. Mateer, John Madore, Wayland Dunaway, Charles Rowland, (standing) O.W. Houts, J. Alvin Hawbaker, Charles Schlow, Henry Elder, John Dreibelbis, R. Paul Campbell, and C.R. Carpenter.

benefits when doing business with a bank that traces its local roots back to the borough's first savings and loan institution.

ing a car drive up to the school around 2 a.m. Police found Rachel's shoes, handbag, and textbooks at the Shiloh Church, three miles away. But there were no suspects.

Then, on May 5, another young woman, Faye Gates of Mt. Eagle, close to Howard, was murdered. Her killer, Richard Millinder, who lived near Faye in Spook Hollow, was caught in June, and though he confessed to killing Faye, he contended that he did not kill Rachel. The police concurred. Not until 1954, after some 3,000 people had been questioned by police, did Jack Ray, a thirty-four-year-old convict serving a life term in an Oklahoma state prison for another murder, confess to killing Rachel. "Ray made the mistake of telling about his crime years ago in Dallas," said the deputy sheriff who had worked on the case day and night for six months after receiving a tip from another inmate.

The August plane crash, the third big headline of the year, involved Centre County's pioneer pilot Sherm Lutz and one of his students, sixteen-year-old Charles Neyhart. Not far from Lutz's Boalsburg airport, the controls locked and the new airplane crashed in an apple orchard on the John Stoner farm, now part of Brookline Village, near Centre Hills Country Club. Sherm lay near death for a week but then started the long, slow process of recovery, while Charlie, younger and with fewer injuries, was nonetheless in the hospital for several months until he was back to normal. Sherm, whose first airport was by the Indian Pine on the "Hill" in Boalsburg, built the State College Air Depot, near what is now CATO Industrial Park, in 1945.

In November 1940, two Penn State students, exploring fields that had been the estate of General Philip Benner at Rock, unearthed an old cast-iron kettle, believed to have belonged to the pioneer ironmaster himself. The *Times* told about the find in a front-page story, and the next day Louis H. Bell, then an instructor but later to be director of public information at Penn State, wrote to Bob Wilson, sports editor, saying, "Since it was found halfway between Bellefonte and State College, the thought struck me that this little curio might make an interesting trophy for the winner of the Bellefonte-State College football game".

The idea caught on immediately. Jo Hays said it would "enrich the tradi-

County Registers 7,647 Men for Draft

Lottery to Determine Order of Selective Service; State College Lists 839, College 1,554.

A total of 7,647 men between the ages of 21 and 36 were registered for selective service military service in Centre County . . . .

The lottery will determine the order in which men who registered for the draft will be called to be classified and possibly inducted into the armed services for a year's compulsory military training.

—Centre Daily Times, 10-17-40

Sunday Movie Vote Is 'No' in State College

By a vote of slightly less than two to one, State College citizens voted "no" yesterday on whether to have Sunday movies. The vote was 1,772 against to 893 for.

—Centre Daily Times, 10-31-40

2 S.C. Men Ready For First Draft

Allen Melville Green of 225 S. Burrowes street, State College, and Richard William Hoffman of the Nittany Lion Inn, State College, will be the first two men inducted into the army under the Selective Service Act on Wednesday, November 27, at Altoona.

The State College Rotary Club will honor the two draftees at the weekly dinner to be held at the State College Hotel Tuesday evening.

—The Centre Daily Times, 11-19-40

tion-soaked football rivalry that already exists." So the kettle was sandblasted to rid it of rust, and Titan Metal Company (now Cerro) of Bellefonte made two handsome brass bands and a nameplate for it. Everything was ready for the first game in 1940, but it was canceled due to a snowstorm. An extra game was scheduled to open the following season, and they continued to play each other twice each year until 1946, when they reverted to their prewar, once-a-year-on-Armistice-Day schedule. Bellefonte won both games in 1941 and the first one in '42, but State High took the Kettle back up the Benner Pike eight straight times after that through 1946. Though interrupted for several years, the annual rivalry still continues, and in 1993 the Red Raiders triumphantly took the Kettle back to Bellefonte for the first time in twenty-five years. The Little Lions won it back, however, in 1994.

Fueling the long-standing rivalry was the 1940 census, showing that for the first time State College was bigger than Bellefonte. Although both went over the 5,000 mark, State College, with 6,400 people, was now the largest municipality in Centre County.

That summer and fall of 1940 saw the building of the two-lane Benner Pike, the gently curving road between State College and Bellefonte that shortened traveling time and distance between the two towns and eliminated several hazardous turns. Prior to the Pike, travelers went through Lemont and Pleasant Gap to what is now Route 144, and from there to Bellefonte through Axemann.

Nineteen-forty also saw construction of one of the Borough's biggest apartment projects, the twenty-four unit, ninety-room Locust Lane Apartments, at Locust Lane and East Foster Avenue. This partial solution to the perennial housing problem was built for the Lowden Corporation (J. J. and Pauline Lowden and Gertrude Hoffman) at a cost of $100,000 by John Hamilton Henszey, who had built the State Theatre, the new Schlow Apartments at 230 West College Avenue, and a new cell block at the Pennsylvania Correctional Institution at Rockview.

A leading builder in State College, Henszey was one of the reasons Gordon Kissinger settled here after earning a degree in architectural engineering from Penn State in 1931 and working a few months in his native

Sunset Park was a new place to play — and with supervised activities — in 1943, when this College Heights gang posed there. 1st row: Patsy Marble, Roscele Nelson, Ann Farrell, Bobby Murphy, Jackie Guerrant, and Pat Farrell. 2nd row: Jean Marble, Gay Brunner, Marilyn Guillet, Scott Frear, Robin Brunner, and Martha Guerrant.

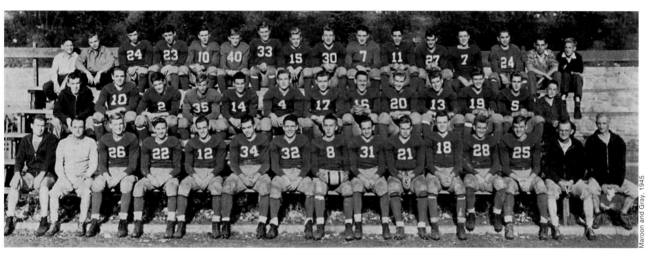

For the first time in history, the Little Lion football team won the Western Conference title in 1944, going undefeated in eight games. 1st row: Ass't. Coach Weir, Head Coach Kemmerer, W. Garrison, R. Harter, C. Brouse, J. Shilling, W. Rogers, K. Bunn, D. Corman, J. Griffith, R. Rice, R. Artz, J. Porter, and Ass't. Coaches Jamison and Dale. 2nd row: Mgr. D. Randolph, R. Kidwell, W. Ishler, K. Meckley, D. Watkins, C. Weaver, G. Neff, M. Ross, C. Shawley, R. Keller, R. Hoy, J. Neff, and Mgr. T. Kemmerer. 3rd row: Mgrs. L. Ross and J. Neff, E. Ellis, R. Spearly, E. Noel, W. Dux, A. Wisner, R. Bunnell, C. Young, S. Baird, J. Gulton, D. Lambert, J. Smith, D. Harpster, and Mgrs. W. Leonard and R. Bunnell. Coach Kemmerer's 1945 team extended the unbeaten streak to 18, going 8-0-1 and sharing the Big Twelve Conference title with Huntingdon.

With the best offensive and defensive records, the 1945 SCHS soccer team was unbeaten and untied, and won the league championship. Seven players made the County All-Star team (*). 1st row: W. Ream, J. Beede*, E. Watson*, D. Dawson*, Capt. W. McKenzie*, D. Storch*, K. Cloetingh, B. Gordon, N. Hartman*, and E. Armstrong. 2nd row: Coach Serff, D. Vonada, S. Tussey, D. Bischoff, P. Friese, G. Hartman, C. Schilling, R. Boerlin, N. Minshall, C. Burrell, and D. Stavely*. 3rd row: Mgr. B. Rimmey, A. Bascope, F. Bascope, D. Zong, D. Miller, and Mgr. W. Wilkins.

Williamsport. "I came back for spring House Party with a fraternity brother," Gordon said, "and I was impressed with the amount of construction going on — more than in Williamsport. Competition was keen, and people were begging to work. Why, you could get all the 'saw-and-hatchet men' you needed for twenty-five cents an hour and finish carpenters for seventy-five cents an hour."

He got a job as estimator for Henszey, who that year was building fifteen residential buildings in State College, a huge number for the time, as well as the cell block at Rockview. It was in Henszey's real estate office that Gordon found his niche in life — he started his own business in January 1933, sharing an office in the State College Hotel with "Pop" Garrison, a former Penn State wrestler who was selling life insurance. Gordon eventually became a major developer in and around State College, and his firm, renamed Kissinger, Bigatel & Brower in 1993, with three offices and nearly fifty agents and employees, is State College's oldest real estate firm. The partners today are his son Fred, Mark Bigatel, and Ralph Brower; former longtime partner Bill Leonard has retired.

When Gordon was young and courting Alice Reidy, whom he married in 1936, he hitchhiked to Williamsport each weekend. This is how he met John Glatz, who became a business partner and lifelong friend. "I'm from Williamsport, too," John said, "where I worked at Vanderlin Dry Cleaners. In 1933, Mr. Vanderlin and I bought Mr. Balfurd's tailor shop and dry cleaners under the Corner Room in State College, and I came here to operate it. One day I was driving to Williamsport and I picked up this hitchhiker. Turned out it was Gordon Kissinger."

The next year Gordon and John pooled resources to buy the twelve-unit Nor-Lea Apartments at 315 West Beaver Avenue, built in 1929. In 1935, the two, along with *CDT* editor Bill Ulerich, collaborated again to help charter State College Elks Lodge 1600.

Newlyweds Gordon and Alice made their home for five years at the Nor-Lea Apartments, where John and Myra Glatz lived for many years in Apartment 1, with Balfurd's

Dry Cleaners at the rear of the building next door to the east. Then in 1941, the Kissingers built a house bordering Holmes-Foster Park, at 740 West Fairmount Avenue, one of several that Gordon built or sold lots for in Fairview Heights, an area developed by theatre owner Maurice Baum. Baum created the park-like divider in that block that earned it the nickname "Baum Boulevard," and had a stately brick Georgian home built for himself atop a hill near the intersection of Fairmount and Buckhout Street. It later was home to attorney William Litke.

By the mid-1930s, State College was getting so metropolitan, a weekly newspaper did not do it justice, so publisher Claude Aikens turned the State College *Times* into a daily and renamed it *Centre Daily Times* in 1934. Six years later, he contracted with John Henszey to build a new, much larger printing plant for the *CDT* and Nittany Printing and Publishing Company on Fraser Street, facing borough hall. When Aikens took over the *Times* in 1919, it had a circulation of less than 2,000 and a weekly output of four to six pages; by the time of his death in 1966, the *CDT* had gone county-wide with a circulation of more than 15,000 and a daily average of more than twenty-four pages.

Another Aikens, Kennard, and Mateer enterprise was the Allencrest Tea Room, which the trio opened in 1932 in the former Sigma Alpha Epsilon (later, Sigma Pi) fraternity house, at the corner of Beaver and Allen. Noted for its good home-cooked food and run by Matty Mateer in conjunction with the Corner Room, the popular and well-appointed Allencrest faced Beaver Avenue while a dairy store faced Allen Street.

Ken Hall, who made more than two million sandwiches for both enterprises until his death in 1990, worked at the Allencrest from 1936 until World War II, while waitress Ruth Houston started in 1936, met her dishwasher-husband there in 1937, and was still working part-time for the Corner Room in 1992. Like all hotel and restaurant employees then, each received a salary (in Ruthie's case, a dollar a day) plus room and board, the room being above the Allencrest. But on April 1, 1941, a fire destroyed the building. Although no one was hurt except Alpha firemen

126

Ruetgers-Nease Corporation

hances are good you used a Ruetgers-Nease product today without knowing it. The company manufactures specialty chemicals employed extensively by the detergent industry to formulate dish-washing and laundry detergents plus other common household and industrial cleansers. Known collectively as hydrotropes and surfactants, these chemicals are essential ingredients in many brand-name products taken for granted every day. By supplying them to detergent-industry giants, and by earning a reputation for quality chemical synthesis, Ruetgers-Nease Corporation has built a sound business base during its forty-five years of operations.

Founded in 1951 by Dr. Aubrey Nease and Dr. Wes Pedlow, the Pedlow-Nease Chemical Company originally produced custom chemicals from a manufacturing plant in Lock Haven. In 1956, the firm was renamed Nease Chemical Company. With the opening of a new plant in State College the following year, Nease established its headquarters in the heart of Happy Valley. New offices and research-and-development labs followed at the State College site in 1959. Today Ruetgers-Nease employs more than 200 workers at its three U.S. sites, including over 135 in State College and the remainder at plants in Augusta, Georgia, and Cincinnati, Ohio.

Since 1977, the company has been a subsidiary of Rütgerswerke AG, a global organization operating more than thirty-five plants in Europe and North America. With about 15,000 employees worldwide, Rütgerswerke AG is a stable, well-financed corporation that stresses managed growth and long-term planning. Since its

More than 135 employees work at the State College plant.

affiliation with Rütgerswerke, Ruetgers-Nease has seen annual sales grow nearly tenfold from $5.5 million in 1977 to almost $50 million today.

Keenly aware of its responsibilities to the Centre Region as a corporate citizen and good neighbor, the company takes special pride in its thorough and precise attention to employee health and safety, and to the maintenance of proper environmental safeguards during all phases of production. As a member of the Chemical Manufacturers Association (CMA), Ruetgers-Nease supports the continuing effort to improve the industry's responsible management of chemicals. Under the "Responsible Care"® program, each CMA member pledges to rigorously pursue environmental excellence. Nowhere is this more important than in an industry where reputations are earned through safe manufacturing practices and full compliance with environmental regulations. As it prepares to meet the challenges of tomorrow, Ruetgers-Nease Corporation is working hard to ensure that future generations enjoy the same quality of life so highly prized by Centre Region residents today.

Ruetgers-Nease products are essential ingredients in many detergents and household cleaners used every day by consumers.

State College Burgesses
1930 - 1950

Eugene H. Lederer
Burgess 1930-32

C. E. Snyder
Burgess 1932-33

Wilbur F. Leitzell
Burgess 1934-41

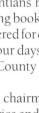

Albert E. Yougel
Chief of Police 1925-36
Burgess 1942-50

Don Jones and Tom Sauers, who sustained minor injuries, most of the employees lost their belongings.

Within days the Allencrest was back in business in the Corner Room's large second-floor banquet room, and by September a new building had been erected on the site of the old one, this time with four retail stores on the Allen Street side. The Tea Room continued to operate until the mid-1950s and gave Dick Benefield, who managed it from 1948 to 1954, his start in the restaurant business. Dick subsequently gained culinary fame with the four-star Hotel Magee in Bloomsburg and then the Nittany Lion Inn.

A longtime Allen Street neighbor of the Allencrest that also suffered a devastating fire was McLanahan's Drug Store, one of State College's oldest still-operating businesses. Originally opened in 1933 across the street at the northeast corner of Allen and Beaver, it moved to the Robison Building at 124 South Allen in 1937, and then to the Gernerd Building at 134-136 South Allen, former location of the A&P food store, in 1948, where it remained for the next forty-one years.

The A&P was not the only food store in town, nor was it the first of the new-style "super markets." Acme Super Market, at the southeast corner of Beaver and Atherton, claimed that distinction, always tagging its ads with "State College's first and finest self serve store." Another market of the '30s and '40s was McKee's, at 131 West Beaver, where Temple Market would succeed it. "If It Is To Be Had, We Have It. Three Phones, Free Delivery," declared

McKee's in ads during World War II.

The Second World War brought many changes to State College and Penn State, as the campus became a training ground for 10,000 military men billeted in fraternity houses on and off campus, and the extension service trained nearly 150,000 people to work in new war industries. Also at that time Henry Varnum Poor, assisted by his daughter Ann, was painting the land-grant frescoes in Old Main, and Heinz Warneke was attracting crowds while carving the Nittany Lion statue from a thirteen-ton block of Indiana limestone on site close to Rec Hall, New Beaver Field, and the Nittany Lion Inn.

For State College residents, wartime meant tending Victory Gardens; buying meat, sugar, cigarettes, gasoline, and other commodities in short supply with ration books; car-pooling to save gasoline; and buying War Bonds. It also meant blackouts, air-raid drills, and salvage drives for paper, scrap metal, rubber, and rags.

In May 1942, it was reported that 14,433 Centre Countians had signed up for sugar-rationing books. In June, 1,600 families registered for extra sugar for canning in just four days, standing four deep at the County Home in Bellefonte to apply.

Ray V. Watkins, chairman of the State College War Price and Rationing Board, curtailed pleasure driving and recommended that shoppers help merchants conserve paper bags and wrapping paper by taking their own containers with them to the stores. "Too few people are taking the critical

State College Over Quota in National War Fund Campaign

State College borough today had gone away over the top in the National War Fund campaign with a total of $8106.70, Chairman Jack Harper announced this morning. The quota was $4500.

The initial gifts committee headed by Russell Adamitz raised $2380.50. Of this amount $260 was contributed by fraternal organizations and service clubs and $2120.50 by businessmen, banks, corporations and partnerships. Assisting Mr. Adamitz . . . were G. R. Hershberger, Ford B. Cole, Earl Houts, and C. R. Stitzer.

The State College block leader organization raised $5421.60 in the house-to-house canvass. Captain of the blockleaders is Mrs. E. M. Grove. Her lieutenants are Mrs. C. W. Taylor, Mrs. F. M. Torrence, Mrs. M. T. Bunnell, Mrs. H. I. Tarpley, Mrs. Roy Decker, Mrs. Fred Bender, Mrs. Ray Baker, Miss Theresa Smith, Mrs. H. K. Kistler, Mrs. Kathleen Taylor, Mrs. H. W. Loman, Mrs. P. R. Hall, and Mrs. H. H. Arnold.

—Centre Daily Times, 11-29-43

Martin L. Kauffman
Chief of Police 1936-39

1930 to 1970
State College
Fire & Police Chiefs

Edwin Moore
Fire Chief 1930-31

Daniel Krumrine
Fire Chief 1932-42; 1948

John J. Juba, Chief of Police 1939-70, had weekly meetings with
Penn State student leaders in the Corner Room.

Albert Kerstetter
Fire Chief 1943-47

paper shortage seriously," officials pointed out. However, some people must have been serious about it, for the *Times* happily reported that State College Boy Scout Troops 31, 32, and 33 collected 14,000 pounds of waste paper one Saturday in 1945.

On another occasion during the war, principal Jo Hays donated some Frazier Street School landmarks to the scrap-metal drive — the two cannons donated by Penn State that had stood on either side of the front door for years, serving as favorite sites for teachers to be photographed and for children to climb. According to teacher Isabell Boyd, "George Graham never forgave Jo Hays for giving those cannons away. He said they were part of the town's history and Jo had no right to dispose of them."

When the war in Europe was nearly over, Titan Metal in Bellefonte began advertising, "Don't WAIT for Victory — WORK for it at Titan!" But the war in the Pacific was still going strong, and the company was losing fifty or more part-time workers to the draft at a time when production of ammunition was to be doubled.

The end of the war came officially at 7 p.m. on Tuesday, August 14, 1945, when President Harry Truman made the announcement on nationwide radio. The next day's Victory Edition of the *CDT*, under editor Bill Ulerich, bore a four-inch-high headline, "PEACE!" and reported how the news had been received in State College. "There was

Fire Sweeps Through L. K. Metzger Store And Building in S. C.

The L. K. Metzger building which housed the State College landmark known to thousands of Penn State Alumni all over the world for its slogan, "You Can Get It At Metzger's," was gutted by fire yesterday afternoon.

Hundreds of onlookers stood in the small area near the building. Soldiers, sailors, X-GI's, and civilians formed a line and assisted in carrying supplies from the Metzger store and beauty equipment from the Rand Salon.

—Centre Daily Times, 6-6-45

V-J Day Plans For State College

State College business places will close and College classes will be dismissed immediately following the official announcement from the White House that hostilities with Japan have ceased. This action was announced today in separate statements by Albert E. Yougel, burgess of State College, who also issued a V-J Proclamation, and by Dr. Ralph D. Hetzel, president of the College.

The signal that official word has been received will be the ringing of the Old Main bell, the blowing of the whistle at the College power plant in a manner unlike that in case of fire, and the ringing of the church bells in the community, the officials said.

—Centre Daily Times, 8-11-45

a split second of stunned silence, as if the unbelieving populace awaited some other official sign. Then the fire whistle at the College power plant burst suddenly wide open and moaned the happy news for nearly an hour."

People jumped with joy, kissed one another, shook hands, smiled, wept. The entire fleet of Alpha Fire Company trucks took to the streets, with firemen waving, shouting, and ringing bells. Residents took to their autos, honking horns incessantly, shouting, cheering. Students rushed downtown, making V-signs with their fingers and forming impromptu snake dances. People handed out newspapers to tear up, and soon the town streets were white with "victory snow." Soldiers, sailors, and civilians jammed into the fire trucks. Others joined the impromptu parade ringing cowbells. Even children did their part with parades of bikes, trikes, wagons, scooters, and hikers.

Truman also reported that from 5 to 5.5 million men and women then in the military services could be returned to civilian life within the next twelve to eighteen months. This statement would have a major impact on what happened next to Penn State and State College. Things would never be the same.

C-COR Electronics

he future is now at C-COR Electronics, where forward-thinking design engineers already have developed products to tap into America's growing "information superhighway." An example of the Centre Region's burgeoning high-tech industry, the company has been an innovator since its founding in State College by Penn State Ph.D.s George Haller, Walter Brown ("H" and "B" of HRB Systems), and John McLucas. Now a major manufacturer of broadband cable-TV amplifiers and fiber optic components, C-COR has experienced a recent growth spurt that prompted a $10 million expansion at its Decibel Road facility and increased its total work force to approximately 1,500 employees worldwide.

The company currently operates in seven locations, the largest being its headquarters. Also located in Pennsylvania are the Tipton and Reedsville plants, both devoted solely to manufacturing. Elsewhere in the United States, C-COR has a Denver office — where sales, network design, and training activities are conducted — and a Fremont, California, facility — where digital fiber optic product development and manufacture takes place. In addition, C-COR employees staff offices in Ontario, Canada, and Almere, the Netherlands. Worldwide, C-COR has approximately 270,000 square feet in facilities, where sales, marketing, and technical support services are performed.

Maintaining the highest level of quality and service, C-COR has recently achieved the ISO9001 registration, in recognition of quality assurance in design, development, production, installation, and servicing. ISO, which stands for the International Organization of Standardization, currently comprises the national standards bodies of ninety-one nations. Its function is to develop global standards to improve the international exchange of goods and services.

Now looking toward the twenty-first century, C-COR Electronics remains on the cutting edge of cable technology. For consumers, new technological breakthroughs translate to enhanced services such as video on demand, home ordering of movies, and significant educational opportunities. With the continued convergence of the telephone, computer, and cable industries, C-COR is poised to provide components for the networks of the future — today.

Coldwell Banker University Realty

ounded by a Penn State University professor, the late Charles "Chuck" Woodring, and incorporated in 1954, University Realty grew along with Centre County during the prosperous development and expanding economic cycles of the 1960s and '70s. In 1983, the firm became affiliated with the Coldwell Banker Corporation, a realty sales network that has had record growth in the 1990s and has maintained a position as one of the nation's largest and most respected real estate companies. Historically, one in nine homes sold in America involves a Coldwell Banker associate.

Upon Chuck's death in 1969, Anita N. Coombs, the number-one sales agent at University Realty, took over as owner. She remained active in the business through the 1970s, while her son Tom managed the company. He engineered the Coldwell Banker affiliation, a move that provided University Realty with national name recognition, educational programs that support recruiting and training of new associates, a progressive office environment, and advertising that penetrates the local and national real estate markets.

A part of the Coldwell Banker University Realty building is occupied by Mortgage Placement Services, Inc., which was incorporated in 1976 by a group of local businessmen as a successor to a mortgage business begun by Claude Decker in the 1950s. Now owned by Tom Coombs and its president, Sally Lenker, the company secures financing for the purchase of homes and refinancing of existing mortgages. The company brokers mortgages for eight to ten national lenders, allowing customers to shop smart for interest rates.

From appraisals to listings, homes sales to mortgage financing, Coldwell Banker University Realty and Mortgage Placement Services, Inc., provide convenient one-stop shopping to area residents.

131

Boom Times on
Both Sides of
College Avenue

*A*fter the war came peace, prosperity, and problems for State College and Penn State. As President Truman had reported in his victory speech, more than 5 million GIs were returning to civilian life to compete for jobs that didn't exist yet. They also would get married, start the baby boom, and 600,000 of them would begin or return to college on the GI Bill of Rights.

Penn State did its part by giving enrollment priority to nearly 7,000 veterans for the fall of '46 in addition to admitting about 4,000 of the regular crop of high school graduates. Before this, regular resident enrollment had dropped from a prewar high of 7,300 to only 3,300 in the 1943-44 academic year. "With all-out cooperation of the staff and from public and private agencies," President Hetzel said, "we were able to enroll almost 11,000 of the 22,853 well-qualified students who wanted to come to Penn State that fall."

State College residents comprised one group whose "all-out cooperation" enabled a large portion of those students to be housed and fed. Nearly everyone helped in one way or another — by renting out one or two rooms in private homes, operating full-fledged rooming houses that accommodated as many as forty students, or offering inexpensive meals in boarding houses and restaurants. Yet it was still a case of "more bodies than rooms," and a common question, as it had been after World War I, was, "Whose attic are you living in?"

Before the war Penn State had dorm rooms for only three hundred men — in Irvin (Varsity), Jordan, and Watts Halls — and there were no campus dining halls for them. But during and for a few years after the war, all

College-owned housing was reserved for women only. To help out, the fifty-some fraternity chapters in town, whose members had finally reclaimed their houses from wartime military occupation, agreed to reopen their doors to ex-servicemen and rent rooms, preferably to alumni. This was how John C. "Jace" O'Connor '38, who had spent the war in the Corps of Engineers, and Ralph M. Yeager '42, an ex-Army Air Corps meteorologist, met for the first time — heading up the sidewalk of Kappa Delta Rho where each had lived as an undergraduate.

Remembering how much they had liked living in State College and having no definite career plans, both men returned to Penn State to give graduate school a whirl. They wound up as roommates and soon discovered something else they had in common — a long-standing desire to open a restaurant.

"We scouted around and found an empty storeroom where the Harvey Brothers bakery had been, between Lew McGill's Sandwich Shop on College Avenue and Centre Beverage on Calder Alley," Jace said. The property, bordered on the east by McAllister Alley, was owned by P. H. Gentzel and consisted of what had been a private home built in 1893, a barn and carriage house adjoining it, and a large brick building at the rear where the Harvey Brothers had manufactured ice cream.

After the lease-signing came months of remodeling as the new restaurateurs paneled walls, laid a flagstone floor, built sawbuck tables, and rebuilt the brick bakery ovens into a handsome fireplace. "But we weren't finished with the floor or the tables, and the chairs we had ordered hadn't arrived yet when it was time to take a picture to apply for a beer license," Ralph said. "So we borrowed

Forty duplex residences went up on South Atherton Street to ease the postwar housing shortage — and Easterly Parkway and Centre Lane came into existence. Everything south of Irvin Avenue and East of Old Boalsburg Road was still farmland.

Hal Byers was the popular Troop 3 scoutmaster for years. Seated from left: Frank Reed, the Rev. John Harkins, Hal Byers, Bob James, and John Harry. Ed Crossley and Buzz Triebold hold the BSA and USA flags. 2nd row: Howard Kerstetter, Albert Cooper, Mel Rockey, Dick Lutz, Russell Dickerson, Stan Segner, Jack Beerman, David Kapel, and Ray Johnson. 3rd row: Don Slavin, Jack Hartman, Alan Warefield, Eugene Slavin, Paul Friese, Arlan Peters, Joe Hartman, Dick Goheen, and Jim Stevens. 4th row: Dave Lockard, Bill Hyslop, Norbert Ott, Bob Bunnell, Don Kerstetter, Bev Edmiston, Don Krumrine, Ted Kemmerer, and Dick Bunnell.

The A&P market, shown here at 134 South Allen Street, moved in 1948 to Beaver at Atherton and eventually to the Westerly Parkway Shopping Center.

KDR's dining room furniture and that's what the Liquor Control Board saw."

It was raining that night of May 12, 1948, when Jace and Ralph, who also did the cooking, first opened their fifty-seat restaurant to the public. They worried that no one would come, but in no time at all, whether out of curiosity or to seek shelter from the downpour, customers had filled every table in the cozy pine-paneled room. They could choose from only two entrees — steak at $1.50 and spaghetti at 85 cents — but they could wash it down with twenty-seven different brands of beer. And when the roof began to leak, causing it to rain almost as hard inside as out, people were in such good spirits they just raised umbrellas over their dinner plates. By midnight the student waiters were exhausted, the food was all gone, and the Tavern Restaurant was on its way to becoming a State College and Penn State tradition. Bought in 1980 by former waiters Pat Daugherty and Bill Tucker, the Tavern has been expanded six times into neighboring buildings and can boast of having employed over 4,000 Penn State students since that rainy opening night.

Of the seventeen hundred coeds — as women students were known then — at Penn State in 1946, nine hundred lived on campus in the three formerly (and again-to-be) male dorms, plus Woman's Building, McAllister Hall, Atherton Hall, and sorority houses — the latter originally built to house faculty members and their families. The other eight hundred coeds lived downtown in houses approved by the dean of women and supervised by full-time chaperons.

In the summer of '46, before the avalanche of newcomers began, State College celebrated its fiftieth anniversary as a borough. The three-month-long party kicked off with the annual State High senior-class pageant during commencement exercises in early June, this one featuring the class of '46 reenacting the history of the town. One of the narrators, Marnie Forbes Hoy, said that, as was usual for the annual class pageant, everyone in the class had a part, and she named such current residents as Elliott Armstrong, Phyllis Lutz Barr, Katie Poorman Blair, Billie Elder Hosterman, Shirley Long Keller, Jim Smith, and Keith Udine, all of whom lived in the State College area following graduation from high school.

Also commemorating the golden anniversary of State

College was the traditional Alpha Fire Company Fourth of July parade, chaired that year by Hal Byers and featuring more than a hundred floats in a two-mile-long procession. Dr. James Shigley, the popular veterinarian, was grand marshal, as he was every year, leading the parade on Lindy Lou, his prancing, dappled bay hunter. But instead of his usual jodhpurs, boots, and riding crop, "Doc" wore the garb of an early resident of the Nittany Valley, an Indian. "Pioneer" Guy Stearns of Lemont, with his hand-built covered wagon drawn by two oxen brought in from Clearfield County, won first prize of $100 in the historic division. The thousands of State College residents, Centre Countians, and visitors lining College and Beaver Avenues termed it "the best parade ever."

State College Golden Jubilee Viewed as 'Best Parade Ever'

The "best parade I ever saw."

That was the consensus of residents of State College and other Centre Countians and visitors who witnessed yesterday's Golden Jubilee parade of the Alpha Fire Company.

From the time the huge line-up got underway promptly at 6 p.m., until the last exhibit passed through the double-lined throng nearly an hour later, precision marked the gala event.

The parade chairman said his greatest laugh during the three-day event came from a remark made at the parade by a child when he saw Lady Godiva advancing on his horse:

"Look Mummy, here comes the snow man."

—Centre Daily Times, 7-5-46

Closing the festivities on the evening of August 29, the actual Borough birthday, was a special ceremony in the high school Hollow, emceed by John Henry Frizzell and broadcast by the new radio station, WMAJ. Featured were a drill by the prize-winning State College American Legion Junior Drum and Bugle Corps and speeches by representatives of town, college, and county — ex-burgess and State Assemblyman J. Laird Holmes, who had helped lead the fight to secede from College Township in 1896; Penn State Prexy Ralph Dorn Hetzel; Judge Ivan Walker of Bellefonte; and Harry Adamitz of the junior class, president of the high school student council. It was almost like giving a last hurrah to the small town it would no longer be.

Borough limits existing at the beginning of 1946 had not changed since Lytle's Addition was annexed by court decree in 1932. Pugh and Garner Streets ended at Irvin Avenue, where one had a panoramic view south across the Bohn, Henszey, Homan, and Dale farms toward Tussey Mountain and Boalsburg. More farm land and forest stood less than a mile east, west, and north of town, while on the northernmost part of campus — inside borough limits — still stood Hort Woods and an apple orchard where football players on their way to practice on New Beaver Field could pick a snack right off the tree.

Scheduled airline service was inaugurated at the State College Air Depot in June 1949. Adelene Keeler cuts the ribbon held by Chamber of Commerce representative Louetta Neusbaum; others, from left, are Bellefonte Chamber secretary John Tiley, Burgess Albert Yougel, W. B. Keeler, air pioneer Sherm Lutz, HRB's George Haller, express agents George Eminhizer and Miles Rachau, and air-mail dispatcher Lloyd Minnich.

Nittany Office Equipment, Inc.

Nittany Office Equipment has served Central Pennsylvania businesses and residents for forty of State College's 100 years. Founded by Clarion natives Tom and Jean Kerr on October 1, 1956, the company originally sold typewriters, adding machines, and a few office supplies from its 400-square-foot store at 231 South Allen Street. Today Nittany Office Equipment provides customers in four counties with everything necessary to outfit an office — from furniture and

Tom and Jean Kerr with their first employee, Robert Marshall (center), and a shipment of typewriters.

copying machines to business supplies and equipment.

In 1964, the Kerrs purchased property at 1207 South Atherton Street and built a new sales office and warehouse. During three expansions — in 1968, 1973, and 1978 — the facility grew to its present size of approximately 42,000 square feet. Stacked to the rafters with copy machines, office chairs, desks, and the like, the Nittany Office Equipment warehouse is periodically purged during an annual Porch Sale instituted in 1980. The August event, featuring overstocked and floor-model furniture at discounted prices, always attracts large crowds.

Still under the guidance of Tom and Jean, Nittany Office Equipment is run with the help of their sons Mike and Paul, both of whom joined the business after graduating from Penn State. From humble beginnings as a "mom-and-pop" business, the company now employs about thirty-five workers, including seven service technicians. As Nittany Office Equipment enters its fifth decade of serving Central Pennsylvania, it remains committed to the same high standards of service that marked its first forty years.

Borough population was about 6,400, and it seemed that everyone knew everyone else — and everyone else's business. Almost no one locked doors, neighbors regularly visited each other, and radio was king of the family living room. Movies were popular, too, with the Cathaum, State, and Nittany Theatres open every evening but Sunday, and with Saturday matinees for the kids. Clubs were well attended, including I.0.O.F., Kiwanis, Masons, Rotary, American Association of University Women, Eastern Star, and Rebekah Lodge. The Woman's Club, founded two years before the Borough, had 273 members; also popular were the Elks, with 400 members; Nittany Post 245 American Legion, with 750; the newly chartered Lions Club, headed by young home-builder J. Alvin Hawbaker; and, for the younger set, Boy Scouts, Cub Scouts, Girl Scouts, and Brownies. Church membership was also high in 1946 — for example, 1,976 people were on the rolls of the Presbyterian Church, while 900 worshiped at St. Paul's Methodist, 525 at Grace Lutheran, and 300 at Faith United Church of Christ.

The State College Commerce Club, led by president Dewey Krumrine, had 367 businesses enrolled, more than double its number when it was chartered in 1920. Claude Aikens's *Centre Daily Times*, headed by editor Jerome Weinstein and business manager Eugene Reilly — a duo that would continue for another thirty-five years — boasted fifty full-time employees, twenty-six county correspondents, and seventy-five carriers. Staff member Vivian Doty Hench compiled columns by herself and others into a lively fifty-year history of State College, 1896-1946, but due to the paper shortage that lasted well beyond V-J Day, the ninety-four-page booklet was not published until 1948, coinciding with the *CDT*'s fiftieth birthday.

To help accommodate the sudden influx of people in 1946 and '47, the federal government gave the College 41,000 square feet of surplus buildings to serve as emergency classrooms; 350 trailers that housed seven hundred married students and their families in what the residents dubbed Windcrest, along College Avenue where South Halls are today; and thirty-nine prefabricated army barracks north of Windcrest housing nearly 2,400 unmarried men. These last — "semipermanent" buildings, in Pollock Circle and Nittany Dorms — were not replaced by their modern namesakes until 1958 and 1988, respectively. Still standing are similar buildings put up east of

1,000 Join in Celebrating 50th Birthday of Charter For State College Borough

State College officially celebrated its 50th birthday last night with an impressive ceremony at High School Hollow.

They heard fine talks from representatives of the town, College and County as well as the youth of the borough.

Asserting that "history doesn't happen, it is made," President Hetzel traced the growth of the College and the borough, outlined the trials and tribulations of the founders, and predicted still greater expansion.

"The future, particularly the next few years, may be our most crucial period," the College president added. "They will determine if the College is to become a great state university. We need supreme effort to accomplish our common cause so that we shall prevail to the best interests of the state, nation, and of the world."

Harry Adamitz, president of the State College High School student council who represented the town's youth, declared the occasion not only the end of the first 50 years but also the beginning of the next 50.

Former councilmen on the stand were Harry Leitzell, Diemer Pearce, Al Bowersox, Russ Clark, Earl Houtz, Bob Miller, L. D. Fye, Roy Porter, Harold Alderfer, L. E. Doggett, Sam Crabtree, and Russ Adamitz.

And present councilmen there were President E. L. Keller, H. G. Reed, Fred Spannuth, H. L. Stuart, and L. K. Metzger.

And Laird Holmes and Harry Sauers represented the ex-burgesses on hand.

The committee of Councilmen J. E. Kaulfus and H. L. Stuart who handled the affair is to be congratulated on a fine job.

—*Centre Daily Times, 8-30-46*

Windcrest as a stopgap measure in the summer of 1947 to house seventy-six faculty families. After the emergency had passed, Eastview Terrace was turned over to married graduate students.

To gain some breathing room Penn State also "farmed out" its freshmen class for the next three years to off-campus schools, including its five existing undergraduate Centers (predecessors to Commonwealth Campuses), thirteen state teachers colleges, and four private colleges. Enrolled as Penn State freshmen at the cooperating schools, they had the privilege of transferring to main campus at the start of their sophomore year. This policy upset many Centre County residents who did not like the prospect of students leaving home for a year, often at considerable expense, to attend an institution that had always been in their own backyard. So emergency centers were opened in State College, Bellefonte, Philipsburg, and Lewistown, in addition to those in Sayre, Shamokin, and Somerset, and enrolled about nine hundred students until the plan was discontinued in 1949.

Even so, it was an enormous task finding classroom space and housing on the State College campus. "Every useful nook and cranny has been utilized," Hetzel wrote in a report. "We've even pushed a research laboratory into an old coal bunker to provide one more classroom for veterans."

Wilber and Reba Files lived at Windcrest for almost two years, until he earned an electrical engineering degree in 1948 and was hired as the first full-time engineer at what is now HRB Systems. "We had a seven-month-old daughter, so we qualified for one of the larger trailers, which were fifteen by twenty feet," Reba said. "But we had to carry water for home use, we had an icebox — not a refrigerator — and we had community bathrooms and laundries. Also, we had a gasoline cooking stove that had to have air pumped into it like a camp stove. But we were young, so it was fun!"

There were so many children in Windcrest that ex-resident Jack MacMillan said, "The village was called 'Rabbit Row.' And we all dressed in Army surplus clothes like they did in the '60s and '70s, only in the '40s we were worried about eating!"

The GI Bill paid for books and tuition plus a small monthly allotment, so most of the women worked and the men often had part-time jobs, in some instances shoveling snow for fifty cents just to earn enough for a loaf of bread and a jar of peanut butter. But as one ex-GI said, "In

Galen Dreibelbis

n the State College phone book, the name "Dreibelbis" fills nearly a full column, testament to the family's longevity in the area. One of them is an eighth-generation Pennsylvanian and a lifetime local resident.

Galen Dreibelbis, over years of hard work, has been busy with varied business interests ranging from land development to cattle ranching, and with many charitable efforts. His business and civic accomplishments have been recognized with his honoring at the 1993 Renaissance Dinner and his naming as a 1994 Penn State Honorary Alumnus.

Galen was born on January 3, 1935, in a Ferguson Township farmhouse that still stands near his current home. One brother, Don, lives in the farmhouse, the third-generation family member to do so. The middle of five children born to Bruce and Ruth Herman Dreibelbis, Galen spent his youth working on the family's 200-acre dairy farm and dreaming of ways to earn extra money. His enterprising nature became evident early. At ten, he raised and sold rabbits and turkeys. At seventeen, he launched State College's first fast-food-on-wheels business, selling to fraternities from a converted bread truck. And at twenty-two, with a wife and two children to support, he borrowed $1,000 from his father and bought the fledgling Nittany Gas and Oil Company, turning it into a highly successful business.

Focusing primarily on real estate development, the sixty-plus Galen shows no signs of slowing down. Since 1981, when he sold most of his fuel-oil interests, Galen has been responsible for several major local real estate projects, including Teaberry Ridge, Edwards Industrial Park, Windmere Office Park, Ridgeway condominiums, and Pennwood North apartments. After completing the second stage of Teaberry Ridge adjacent to Penn State's Blue Golf Course, he launched a fifty-eight-acre project off Science Park Road.

In between business enterprises, Galen found time in 1970 to run for office in the Pennsylvania General Assembly. After serving three terms as a legislator he

From farm boy to developer, Galen Dreibelbis has devoted his life to the land. Time spent on his Nittany Farm "is my highest source of therapy," he says.

decided not to seek re-election, preferring instead to concentrate on projects that offered tangible results more quickly. His local volunteer efforts have found him serving as board member, president, or campaign chairman of such diverse organizations as the Juniata Council of Boy Scouts, Centre County United Way, Centre Community Hospital, Mellon Bank, Pennsylvania Agriculture Advisory Council, Pennsylvania Economic Development Partnership, and Central Pennsylvania Homebuilders Association. He was also an Alpha fireman for more than twenty-three years.

Each year, Galen attends the Dreibelbis family reunion on a Berks County farm originally owned by German immigrant John Jacob Dreibelbis in the mid-1700s. There he can proudly point to his grandchildren who will be among those representing the next generation of Dreibelbises in Pennsylvania.

Windcrest we were like one big happy family with everyone looking after everyone else."

Townspeople helped them, too, by establishing the Ex-GI Nursery School in 1947 in the Presbyterian Church. Parents paid twenty-five cents a week to cover the cost of cod-liver oil, fruit juice, and crackers three mornings a week for children aged three to five years old. Mrs. Donald Carruthers, wife of the student minister at the church, and the AAUW organized the school, and Dr. Winona Morgan Moore, associate professor of home economics and head of the College nursery school, advised the staff, headed by Mrs. Walter Troll, wife of a graduate student. She was assisted by coeds, faculty wives, and mothers of some of the children. Five years later, in 1952, the AAUW sponsored another preschool that is still in existence, the Friendly Playschool Cooperative, now called Cooperative Playschool, held at the Friends Meeting House.

Keeping its agreement with the government to prevent slums by not selling the well-used trailers after they were no longer needed, Penn State stopped accepting new tenants in Windcrest after June 1950. As families moved out, trailers were demolished, and by mid-1955 the campus trailer town was history.

Rooming, however, was still going strong. For fifty years or longer, renting rooms to students had been commonplace for State College families — and the livelihood of numerous widows, typically nicknamed "Ma" or "Mom." One such was Inez "Ma" Fletcher, who until she died in 1973 operated a large rooming and boarding house at 234 South Allen Street. One of "Ma's Boys" was Mike Lynch, who later became director of staff development for the Cooperative Extension Service, compiled a popular slide show on Penn State history, and, as a Lion's Paw alumnus, founded the Mt. Nittany Conservancy. He lived at Ma Fletcher's with about nineteen other men for three-and-a-half years in the 1940s. Twenty more men lived in the house next door, many taking their meals at Ma's, the others eating in downtown restaurants. "She was a mother to hundreds and hundreds of students," Mike said in 1973, shortly after "Ma" died, "and her passing was symbolic of what's happened here in town. Taking roomers used to be a business, and most landladies were like mothers. Nowadays kids want to live in apartments."

Proof of that is the former College Arms, a long-time thirty-man rooming house and former fraternity at the southeast corner of West Foster Avenue and South Atherton Street. In 1993, it was remodeled into six one-bedroom apartments — two on each floor — and four efficiencies in the basement.

Ex-GI and graduate student Milton "Mickey" Bergstein, who joined State College's first radio station, WMAJ, as a student announcer in 1946 and became its general manager in 1951, roomed in what he called "Homer's House" in the 200 block of Pugh Street, two doors south of Highland Alley. The girl he later married, Betty Reed, lived with about thirty other freshman women in Cody Manor, at 301 South Allen Street.

"Our house was full of single grad students, all ex-GIs," Mickey said, "and we each paid four dollars a week for half a double room. We paid by the week because no one had enough money to pay by the month or the semester! Also, we had no kitchen privileges, so most guys worked for their meals as waiters. One of my roommates, who became an M.D. on Fifth Avenue in New York, was a dishwasher at the New College Diner."

Betty Reed Bergstein spent only her first year at State in Cody Manor but vividly remembers being "campused" (confined to quarters except during classtime) for signing in a few minutes late one night. "Freshman girls had to be in at nine-fifteen on weeknights," she said. "This one night I stopped at Kaye's Korner on my way home and was appalled to see the clock reading nine-fifteen. I rushed back to the Manor but, of course, I was late." Upperclass women also had curfews, but male students did not.

During the '40s, Charles Hosler, now dean emeritus of Penn State's Graduate School, rented a room for $2.25 per week in a house next to Mickey Bergstein's rooming house and got meals for seventy cents a day at the Allen Street Co-op, at Allen and Fairmount. "About twenty women students lived on the second and third floors of the Co-op," he said. "We boys just ate there, but everyone had to cook or wash dishes or wait tables in addition to paying board." He added that to hold down costs, both the Allen Street and Nittany Avenue Co-ops bought groceries in large quantities from wholesaler Hubert Haugh. "Although cooperatives were criticized as being socialistic at that time, they were a great arrangement for extremely poor kids like I was then," Charlie said.

A popular eating place for College Heights roomers was a large house at 207 East Park Avenue that had been offering rooms to sixteen students and meals to 110 boarders since World War I days. Originally owned by Annie Klinger Hartswick, it was operated as Billett's Board and Room from 1936 to 1945 by Bertha Billett

Nearly 500 Employers in State College

There are nearly 500 employers in State College.

That information was given State College Borough Council at its meeting last night by Borough Treasurer R. Y. Edwards.

He reported completion of a survey which turned up 485 employers in town.

—Centre Daily Times, 8-17-48

1-Way Streets Recommended

ONE-WAY STREETS

S. Burrowes St., north-south, College to Fairmount
S. Pugh St., north to south, College to Fairmount
McAllister St., north to south, College to Beaver
Frazier St., south to north, Fairmount to College
Locust Lane, S. Miles, south to north, Hamilton to Coll.
Calder Alley, east to west, McAllister to S. Burrowes
Highland, west to east, S. Burrowes street to Miles.

—Centre Daily Times, 10-19-48

138

For twenty years, Bill Whitehill was the only sign painter in State College. Here he installs new signs for the Chamber of Commerce at 100 West College Avenue in 1952.

In 1948, State College residents (and Penn State students, too) believed that Crabtree's, Kalin's, and Fred's would go on forever in the 100 block of South Allen Street. Fred's would be first to go, in 1953.

Santa's first arrival by air in State College was in 1950 — O. W. Houts & Son was the sponsor, sales manager Bob Ishler was the pilot, and plumbing department manager Les Weaver was in the red-and-white suit.

At 324 West College Avenue, Hoy Brothers was a store gaining legendary stature. Times staff writer W. L. (Bill) Welch Jr. recalled years later that "When syrup was drawn from the soda fountain, a music box in the pump played the Pepsi jingle." At one time, Dick and Jim Hoy had the only stock in town of "those small, four-wheeled dollies which restaurants put their garbage cans on so they can be rolled, not lugged, from place to place . . . One man . . .approached Dick about buying a dozen more . . .'We quit carrying them,' Dick said, 'There got to be too many people in here bothering us for them.'"

139

(later Mrs. Walter Storch). In 1945, John and Mary Madore from Uniontown bought the house and gave it the name by which it was known for nearly fifteen years — the Ag Hill Dining Room.

"Most of our boys were ex-GIs, mainly ag majors, who lived around the neighborhood and in the college barns," said Mary. "They were all good workers, too. Many of them worked as waiters or dishwashers in exchange for meals, and one boy fired the furnace to pay for his room and waited tables to pay for his board."

Meals were served at Madore's every day but Sunday at a weekly rate of $9, and ex-boarder Virge Neilly said the food was excellent. "You could have seconds, too," he said. Two breakfasts were served every morning, one at 7 and the other around 7:45. "The ag boys came to late breakfast," Mary said, "because no one wanted to eat with them — they smelled like the barns!"

For three years the Madores lived on the second floor, then built a house of their own on Adams Avenue in 1948. Taking their place as live-in chaperon to the male roomers was Viola Redman, whom the boys nicknamed "The Great White Mother."

Viola and the Madores cooked for ten other dining rooms, feeding nearly four hundred men in addition to their Ag Hill regulars. "Many returning GIs had houses to live in but no cooks," Mary recalled. "We didn't really plan to run a catering service — it just sprang upon us — but we did it for a year."

The women would prepare food for other dining rooms in large kettles; then John would deliver them in a truck. Viola said, "Mary and I got up every morning at three o'clock and started baking pies. We made all our own cakes, cookies, cupcakes, too, and the boys especially liked Mary's homemade rolls and cinnamon buns."

Mary's pies were also popular at the Milky Way, a small hamburger and milkshake restaurant at 147 South Allen Street that the Madores bought in 1947. Regular customers there were Al and Vera Hawbaker and their daughter Joan, who lived across the street in the Gernerd Apartments, above McLanahan's Drug Store.

One of the area's most prolific builders, Al Hawbaker came here from Mercersburg in 1944 at the behest of President Hetzel and Dean of Engineering Harry Hammond to build houses for the people being relocated from Harvard to Penn State with the navy's Ordnance Research Laboratory (now Applied Research Lab). Lab director was Eric Walker, who would succeed Hammond as dean in 1951 and become Penn State's president in 1956. "We got priority from the navy to build housing for eighty families," Eric said, "and we found this young man whose construction company was just completing a government housing project in Chambersburg." That young man was Al, who said, "They needed a builder to come to State College as soon as possible, someone who was familiar with building under difficult wartime conditions and who had a crew ready to work. I was interested."

Since 1945, Al has built some one thousand houses in the State College area, and the first was for Eric and Jo Walker, at 628 Fairway Road. He then built a dozen more "H-8's" (navy terminology for $8,000 houses) in College Heights, all very similar to the Walkers'.

Al intended to go home after that one job but, like so many who fall in love with this area, he never got around to it. Besides, the Hawbakers had had another child, Sam, now a partner with his sister, Joan Brower, in Park Forest Enterprises. "When Walker arrived with the ORL," Al continued, "development really took off in this town. We had customers standing in line — we simply couldn't build houses fast enough. So the College invited another developer with a larger crew, Shapiro Construction of White Plains, New York, to work here, too. And still there was more than enough work to go around."

Shapiro built the forty brick duplexes along South Atherton Street, Westerly Parkway, and Centre Lane, an area soon nicknamed "Shapiroville." Al, whose partner in Cumberland Valley Construction did go home, dissolved that company and went into business for himself, building more than eighty homes in the South Allen Street and South Hills and Lytle Avenues area, which was annexed by the borough as South Hills in 1946. He also started developing Panorama Village, near Boalsburg, where he put up about thirty homes. Then he bought fifty acres in Patton Township, part of what locals call "the Barrens," where poor soil supported just scrub trees and weeds. In the first nine months of 1954, he built ninety houses there in his Park Forest Village development, and eventually bought more than a thousand neighboring acres, building more houses to meet demand. By 1966, Park Forest had 450 homes and 1,700 residents.

Overlook Heights, another development outside Borough limits, was begun in 1955 with 145 houses built by Homer Grubb. Some of the land was owned by Clinton

State College Studies Recreational Lake Project

PROPOSED LAKE PLAN

RECREATION LAKE: Still in the planning stage is a large Recreation Lake for the State College area. Current plans place the body of water in the Millbrook-Houserville-Puddintown area. Map above shows one version with the dotted lines above Millbrook outlining an area which could be added.

—*Centre Daily Times, 5-16-50*

Bostonian Ltd.

ostonian Ltd.'s early history is closely intertwined with that of Jack Harper's clothing store, where Bostonian shoe shop founder Guy Kresge first came to work in 1951. At the time, Jack had been looking for someone to take over his Bostonian Shoe Company lease account, so he asked the Bostonian salesman to recommend someone for the job. That someone turned out to be Guy, who was working in Wilkes-Barre at a clothing store called The Hub. Guy agreed to move to State College, and from 1951 to 1957 — except while serving in the Korean War — he sold shoes and clothing for Jack, who he remembered as a demanding but fair employer.

Shortly after Guy returned from Korea, Jack agreed to help him open his own store if shoe business increased to the point where it needed more room than Jack's shop could give it. By 1957, with business booming, Guy opened Bostonian Ltd. a few doors east on West College Avenue, selling shoes and leather goods. Nine months later he moved to more spacious quarters at 106 South Allen Street, where it remains to this day. Later expanded into the room that had long been the Penn State Barber Shop next door, Bostonian Ltd. now sells men's and women's clothing in addition to quality footwear and leatherware.

The Bostonian Ltd. business is a family affair. Guy passed away in 1991, leaving his oldest son Scott in charge as president. Scott's wife Jill and his three brothers — Jeff, Ron, and Todd — are all involved in the business, as is his mother Catherine. Scott started working with his father in 1973 during summers while still in high school. After graduating from Penn State with a business degree in 1978, he went to work full-time at the store.

Although the shop has remained basically the same size since its last expansion, its supply of clothing, shoes, and leatherware is constantly changing and expanding. Customers appreciate the service from a hospitable and knowledgeable staff. Bostonian's traditional atmosphere, enhanced by its old-fashioned architecture and elegant decor, makes the shop a meeting place for old friends and acquaintances.

One of State College's most attractive stores, Bostonian Ltd. has beautiful window displays along South Allen Street.

Otis Cromer, professor of farm crops, who named Clinton Avenue and Cromer Drive after himself, Denton Avenue after a son-in-law, and Abby Place after his wife, long-time curator of the Penn State Archives, who actually spelled her name Abbie. Other lots in Overlook Heights were developed by the Kofman brothers of Bellefonte, who named Harris, Linn, and Curtin Streets after those in their hometown.

One of the first residents of Overlook Heights was Rufus "Boots" Ripka, who said, "When I bought my house at 208 West Aaron Drive in the mid-fifties, there was only one other house below me in this development." Boots was in the diner business from 1926 until 1959 when he opened one of the first convenience stores in State College, Boots Dairyette, at the corner of Beaver and Atherton, across from his Electric Diner.

John Madore also was building houses in "the suburbs" (Boalsburg) as well as in the Borough after the war — prefabricated Gunnison Homes that he had first built in the late 1930s in southern Pennsylvania and northern West Virginia, until they went off the market "for the duration." But he, like Al Hawbaker, found that getting local financing was tough, so the two often made weekly trips together to Philadelphia in search of mortgage money. By 1948, John found he was spending more time arranging financing than building homes, so he decided to organize the second savings and loan association in State College — the first was Laird Holmes's Mt. Nittany Savings and Loan.

Going door-to-door seeking depositors, John convinced enough people so that State College Federal Savings and Loan (now PNC Bank) was chartered on April 13, 1949. Two months later the first mortgage was granted to Frank and Ruby Cone for a home at 632 Fairway Road. Founding directors were attorneys Wayland Dunaway and R. Paul Campbell, and businessmen O.W. Houts, Charles Schlow, and Harold Albright, manager of Shoemaker Brothers trucking. Federal Savings had a series of offices — one so narrow John had to turn sideways to get past his desk — until settling into its long-time main office at 122 East College Avenue in 1957 (PNC's present headquarters office is at 1631 South Atherton Street). John took no salary until 1952 ($25 a week), and only because Mary continued to operate the boarding house were the Madores able to support the business. But it did succeed.

In 1956, the Madores sold the Ag Hill Dining Room to Charles Rallis, who sold it to James Beamer in 1959. Jim's sister, Ann Beamer, lived in the house, which she renamed the Park Avenue Club, and rented rooms to twelve

Fluorination for Water Given Approval by CDC

The executive committee of the Community Development Committee of State College approved fluorination of the State College water supply at its February meeting yesterday.

The motions were approved by the CDC executive group following a discussion of the project by Dr. Charles G. Stewart and Dr. L. William Nieman, State College dentists, and R. R. Kountz, sanitary engineer who is serving as consultant to the dental society.

—Centre Daily Times, 2-21-51

2-Way Radio Added To Alpha Truck

Alpha firemen have joined the police on the borough's two-way radio station in State College and there are signs that it is only the beginning of a convenient communication network for emergency use.

—Centre Daily Times, 4-7-51

students into the 1970s, but she stopped serving meals in 1971. As for the Madore's live-in chaperon, Vi Redman, she worked briefly at the Dutch Pantry restaurant before finding the job she held for nearly thirty years, until 1986 — chief cook at Beta Theta Pi fraternity.

As the building boom took hold, new developments sprang up almost overnight. One that was annexed by the Borough in 1947 was White Oaks, on the eighty-three-acre Homan Tract, bordered roughly by South Atherton Street, Old Boalsburg Road, Ellen Avenue, and the future Penfield Road. The story goes that dairy farmer and World War I navy veteran Merle Homan named the streets in White Oaks after his three favorite military heroes of World War II — Admiral Chester Nimitz, General Douglas MacArthur, and General Omar Bradley. But he became disenchanted with MacArthur and renamed that street Homan, after his own family. A map of State College published as late as 1954 still shows the street name as MacArthur.

Merle's widow, the former Frances Harpster of Rock Spring, said in 1993 that from the time they were married in 1920 until 1950, they lived in the 1830-vintage plank farmhouse that still stands behind the Autoport. In 1950, they built a stone house at 221 Nimitz Avenue. Merle's brother Forrest Homan built the house next door, at Pugh and Nimitz, and Delbert Myers, who added many apartment buildings to State College, built the first house — his own — in the development, at 1219 Old Boalsburg Road.

"Our farm had been part of Andy Lytle's farm," Frances said. "My father-in-law, Franklin Homan, who owned a farm in Oak Hall, bought the land from Andy but let it sit idle until Merle came back from the war and started farming it. We were married January 20, 1920, by Reverend John Harkins [of Grace Lutheran Church] in his dining room with no witnesses, and I wore a dress a lady made for me out of fabric that cost me ten cents a yard." The couple had four children: Ralph, Louise (Horner), Frank, and Claude, and were married sixty-three years, until Merle's death in 1983.

Their first home, originally on the Township Road — later named East Whitehall Road — was rented in the 1950s to neighboring dairy farmers Joe and Carolyn Meyer, then sold to engineer Fred Nicholas, and then to photographer Harry Shadle. In 1991, he sold it to The Autoport, which refurbished it into a guest house.

In early October 1947, students, faculty, and townspeople were stunned by the sudden death of

Even with traffic lights added each year, traffic in 1954 was becoming a problem for the Borough — particularly at Allen and Beaver, where the town's first signals had been installed in the 1930s.

In 1954, Pete Hoy (brother of Dick and Jim) had sold his pharmacy (left) at 120 East College Avenue to long-time resident Paul Griggs.

Metzger's, "The store with the black granite front," had replaced the fire-destroyed "You Can Get It at Metzger's" store remembered by students and townspeople.

State College Borough entered a float in the 1955 Alpha's Fourth of July parade commemorating Penn State's centennial. The Dutch Pantry was in the Odd Fellow's building, and Storch Motor Company was next door at 224 East College Avenue.

Painted pedestrian crosswalks came to town in 1954 — and Kaye and Betty Vinson's popular Kaye's Korner was a harbinger of the convenience stores to come.

President Ralph Hetzel, who suffered a cerebral hemorrhage while talking on the phone to his secretary, Virginia Hartman. "I thought he'd hung up on me, and I was puzzled because he'd never done that before," Virginia said. Worn out by the stress of his job, the sixty-four-year-old Hetzel nonetheless had wanted to stay on until at least 1949 to finish his plans for Penn State. However, in summer 1947, he ruptured a spinal disc while playing golf and underwent two back operations. At the beginning of October, though still constantly in pain, he told his wife he probably would go to the Bucknell football game on Saturday. A pep rally was scheduled the night before on the steps of Old Main, and to boost his spirits, *The Daily Collegian* said, part of it would be conducted in front of Prexy's house since he had attended and enjoyed so many rallies in the past. But the pep rally never took place, for he died on Friday morning.

Letters of sympathy came to Estelle Hetzel from thousands of friends and alumni. Her husband had led the College for twenty-one years, during which enrollment quadrupled, faculty size doubled, the value of the physical plant increased more than nine times, and expenditures for instruction and research had similarly multiplied. He also had conferred 23,753 degrees, while the nine presidents who preceded him had conferred a total of just 9,026. But rapid growth would continue, and five years later, in 1952, Penn State would award its 50,000th degree and in 1965, its 100,000th.

The football team that played its second game of the 1947 season on the day following Hetzel's death had a preponderance of GIs and went on to play in the Cotton Bowl on January 1, 1948, tying Southern Methodist 13-13. It was the first undefeated team Bob Higgins coached, and the bowl game was Penn State's first since 1923. The team was noted for setting three Penn State and three NCAA records that season, yielding only seventeen yards per game and holding five teams to minus yardage. They also were noted for being the first team in Cotton Bowl history to field black players, and for unanimously deciding to stay at a military base outside Dallas after discovering that the bowl hotel would not allow their black teammates to register.

Former Penn State athletic director Ed Czekaj, a member of that team, organizes frequent reunions at The Autoport for his teammates and coaches. That group included others who lived many years in State College,

Sunday Movies Lose In State College, College Township

The margin was 107 votes in State College and 36 ballots in College Township.

It was the second time in four years State College turned back Sunday movies. In 1947, the unofficial margin was 85 votes. This was later reduced to 68 by the official count. At that time, two of the three precincts voted in favor of Sunday movies but a vast majority in the West against the issue decided it.

—Centre Daily Times, 11-7-51

10 NEW NAMES FOR 4 STREETS

More than ten names have been suggested as new tags on four State College streets. . . . the planning Commission recommended to Borough Council that Lytle street be called Walnut street, that First avenue become Andrew Place, Second avenue Russell place and Third avenue James place. Twelve of 16 people living on Third avenue . . . suggested that the new name be "Sunrise Terrace."

—Centre Daily Times, 12-4-51

such as All-American Steve Suhey, who provided State High and Penn State with three more standout football players, sons Paul, Larry, and Matt; former State High football coach Bill Luther; and ex-Penn State assistant coaches John Chuckran, Ray Ulinski, Earl Bruce, and Jim O'Hora.

When the team returned from Dallas, a welcome-home party complete with reception committee was waiting for them at the Corner Room. But when they got off the bus, the boys piled into Graham's store instead. "We had no student union then, so the big hang-out was Graham's," said Ed. "I once won a pinball tournament there, and Old Mr. Graham in his fancy vest presented me with a trophy!"

Leo Houck, Penn State's cigar-smoking boxing coach, was also a frequenter of Graham's, as were football coach Bob Higgins, wrestling coach Charlie Speidel, and other coaches and athletes. State College had no Catholic school then, so Leo's wife and children remained in Lancaster, where he visited them on weekends. The rest of the time, "he virtually *lived* at Graham's," Ed said. "Leo often helped out behind the counter when the store was busy, and was always helping himself to beer pretzels. He could never remember people's names, either, so he called everyone 'Fred,' while Charlie Speidel, who actually had a phenomenal memory for names, called everyone 'Doc.'"

In the fall of 1949, after Leo underwent an operation in Lancaster and was dying of cancer, George Graham wrote a get-well letter that some *ten thousand* people signed at stations in Graham's AC, the Cathaum Theatre, the Student Union at Old Main, and the Corner Room. It was the largest letter ever mailed in State College, and special precautions were taken by the post offices here and in Lancaster so that Leo would receive it intact. It read:

"Dear Leo: Greetings from your army of Penn State and State College friends who love you and admire you very much!

"Salutations from all the boys who come into Graham's every day and who miss seeing you on the Bench or in front of the candy counter or on the chair in front of the radio or maybe back of the cash register with your hand in the pretzel barrel.

"Felicitations from all the Freds who greeted you every day; from all the people you knew and many, many more who knew you as Leo or Lem or Professor or Doctor — terms of friendliness and genuine affection.

Atotech USA, Inc.

appy Valley meets the Silicon Valley at Chemcut Equipment Group, a division of Atotech USA. An example of Centre County's burgeoning hi-tech industry, Chemcut supplies well-known electronics firms with spray-etching equipment for the production of printed-circuit boards. The company owns about 80 percent of the North American market, and is the number-one supplier worldwide of in-line wet processing equipment for the printed-circuit manufacturing industry.

Chemcut's roots in State College go back to 1957, when the company was first incorporated as Centre Circuits. Founding partners Harold O'Connor and Rufus Benton, both Penn State engineering graduates, set up shop in a two-story Pine Grove Mills house and developed their first product, the Mark II spray etcher. The name Chemcut was originally a trademark used to describe the process whereby a pattern is chemically etched or cut into the surface of a metal-plated circuit board.

Increased sales prompted the company to move in 1960 to a 12,000-square-foot building in State College. By then, a network of seventeen independent distributors was in place for sales throughout North America. In 1963, Chemcut established a European distribution system based in West Germany, and the following year sales topped $1 million for the first time.

With more than 100 employees and yearly sales exceeding $2 million in 1965, the company changed its name to Chemcut Corporation and embarked on an ambitious expansion program. At a thirty-four-acre site on Science Park Road, it began construction of a new office building to house administration, sales, and laboratory space. An adjacent 45,000-square-foot manufacturing facility was completed in 1968. Additional expansions begun in 1979 have since more than doubled the plant's size. The company also has increased its presence worldwide with additional sales and service facilities.

In 1980, Chemcut merged with Schering AG as part of the West German chemical conglomerate's Electroplating Division. The merger signaled Chemcut's evolution from a primarily equipment-oriented company to one offering a package approach consisting of quality manufacturing, custom processes, and superior service.

With the August 1993 sale of Chemcut to a French chemical corporation, ELF Atochem, the company is now part of Atotech USA, a supplier of equipment, chemistry, and services to the worldwide electronics and metal-finishing industries. About 220 employees staff the State College plant, which turned out its 10,000th system in 1991 and now boasts annual sales in the neighborhood of $25 million. Chemcut's success, however, also is measured by the significant contributions its employees have made to the community. In the final analysis, they represent the company's most lasting legacy.

On February 29, 1972, Rodney Hockenberry, Clifton Treaster, Harold O'Connor, Les Moyer, Mike Wills, and Charles Lynn posed with Chemcut's 5,000th "547" unit, a wet processing system for printed circuit boards.

Rodney Hockenberry, Clifton Treaster, Mike Wills, and Charles Lynn saw production of Atotech's 10,000th system in 1991.

"Best wishes from our community's leading citizens and the College's highest officials to the smallest urchin whose illegal entrance to Recreation Hall you aided and abetted.

"Hurry back, Leo. State College hasn't been the same this fall; Penn State just can't get along without you."

The "doctor of hard knocks," as he liked to call himself, died two months later, but State College didn't forget him. Students and townspeople collected nearly $4,000 as a gift for Leo's widow.

Heading Penn State at that time as interim president was Judge James Milholland Sr. who had become president of the board of trustees in 1946. During Milholland's tenure as Hetzel's successor, 1947-50, enrollment of veterans reached its peak, and large men's and women's residence halls — Simmons and McElwain for one thousand women; McKee, Hamilton, and Thompson for fifteen hundred men — were constructed to accommodate regular resident undergraduates as the "farming out" program ended. But since there were fourteen thousand students at the College in 1949, overcrowding was still a problem that spilled over into the Borough.

In June 1948, Milholland was approached by State College school board representative Ray Watkins with a proposal to build a high school on the campus, with the College financing part of its construction. This would kill three birds with one stone, Watkins suggested, taking the strain off the burgeoning school system, giving Penn State's School of Education a convenient place for teacher training, and making up some of the money the Borough felt it was denied by Penn State's tax-exempt status. Milholland said the College would consider the proposal. But in December 1949 he turned the high school idea down with no explanation.

In 1947, State College and Halfmoon Township formed a joint school board, first of its kind in central Pennsylvania. Prior to that, each township ran its own school system, and if students from outside the Borough wanted to attend State College High School, they paid tuition. By 1950, the other four neighboring townships — College, Ferguson, Harris, and Patton — had come into the fold to form the College Area Joint School District, which, in 1964, was reorganized under a state mandate and renamed the State College Area School District. This change also reduced the

school board to nine members elected at large, replacing the board made up of five members from each township and seven from the Borough. Even though the old thirty-two-member board might have made for some confusion, supervising principal Jo Hays told the *Centre Daily Times* he saw at least one benefit: "The rural people were often quite suspicious of the 'city slickers' of State College," he said. "I always felt more comfortable with at least five people from each of the outlying townships to go back and interpret our actions to the residents."

Also, until 1935 the school board was not allowed to borrow money unless the electorate approved it. "In order to build buildings, we had to precede the project with a publicity campaign," Jo said. No campaign was necessary to enlarge the College Heights School in 1946 or to build the Corl Street Elementary School for $197,000 in 1952 and follow it in 1953 with the Matternville School, based on the same floor plan. After those came the Easterly Parkway Elementary School in 1955, a new senior high school on Westerly Parkway in 1957, the Houserville and Panorama Elementary Schools in 1959, Westerly Parkway Junior High (now the High School South Building) in 1962, and Radio Park Elementary School in 1963. The last took its name from its proximity to WMAJ's antenna tower, which was later moved to a hilltop behind Centre Furnace Mansion.

The announcement in 1953 that the high school would be moved from Nittany and Fairmount Avenues caused a dilemma concerning the "public library." Housed in the basement of the Frazier Street School from 1898 to 1923, it was run by the State College Library Association, whose board members had tried unsuccessfully to get funding for a building. They then gave up and turned over the assets — three thousand books, $212 in cash, and one share of Pennsylvania Railroad stock — to the high school library, which agreed to stay open two hours on Monday nights for public use.

Penn State librarian Ralph McComb and his wife, Lois, also a trained librarian, began speaking to local civic organizations as often as five times a week, maintaining that a library other than Pattee or the high school's was necessary. It would supply a selection of current fiction and non-fiction, they said, as well as books for preschool and elementary children, who at that time

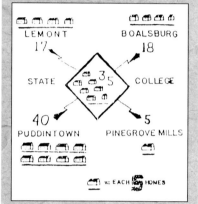

Suburbs in Major Home-Building Boom
Survey Shows 84 New Homes

HOME BUILDING was down in State College borough during 1951 but, as shown in the drawing above, the industry boomed in the smaller communities surrounding the borough. The Puddintown-Houserville area, rising with the development of Spring View, led with 40 new homes.

—*Centre Daily Times*, 1-5-52

University Title Ok'd For College

The College, which in 1955 will observe the 100th anniversary of its founding, today was formally renamed The Pennsylvania State University.

President Milton S. Eisenhower, informed of the court's action . . . expressed his pleasure and pride in "a new name that reflects more appropriately the stature, function and character of the institution."

—*The Centre Daily Times*, 11-13-53

Electric Supply was a long-time tenant of the Pastime Theatre room. In 1957, the staff had its picture taken: Marvin Swatsworth, Jay Bathgate, Ray Rewbridge, Marcile Tressler, Russell Fisher, and Bernard Sheehe.

Back in the 1930s, employees of Electric Supply were Vilas Wise, Ray Rewbridge, Bern Sheehe, Ethel Burwell, and Russell Fisher.

Jim and Jane and the Western Vagabonds brought live country music to town every day on radio WMAJ. Their Sunday broadcast originated at Radio Corral on West Aaron Drive. From left are Peewee, Jane, Jim, Texas Lil, Ken Montana, and Smokey.

The first Schlow Library, on West College Avenue, was a gift to townspeople from Charles Schlow, as a memorial to his wife, Bella S. Schlow.

From the Times *caption in 1957: Proceeds of $550 from the concert benefit featured in State College recently by wives of members of the Lions Club were turned over to Dr. M. A. Farrell, chairman of the Centre County Hospital Board, to be used in helping to furnish a room in the new wing. Mrs. Quinton Dabbs, center, co-chairman of the project, made the presentation. Looking on from left are Robert McLanahan, a member of the board, Mrs. William Whitehill, wife of a Lions Club member, and Col. Lucien E. Bolduc, a Lion.*

Graduate Nurses Study Club members in the Penn State Centennial parade were Blanche Stitzer, Gertrude Stevens, Ila Burns, Stella McClintic, Hilda Synder (in Army uniform), Helen McCord, and Polly Yerg.

147

were served only by the Centre County Bookmobile.

Many people scoffed: "There's no real need." "We've got books at our house, but we like TV better." "I don't have time to read." But a committee representing the League of Women Voters, the Woman's Club, AAUW, Centre County Library, the high school library, State College businesses, and Penn State helped organize a library board and promoted a town library until the school board in 1955 finally passed a resolution "welcoming the establishment of a public library in State College." This took the schools out of the melee but there was still no suitable building for a library.

Then, at the October 1956 library board meeting, State College businessman Charles Schlow surprised everyone by announcing that he would donate two rooms in a house he owned at 222 West College Avenue, rent-free and utilities paid for eighteen months, because "this town really needs a public library." Response from the community was immediate — a check for $100 arrived the next day from an anonymous donor. A woman offered thirty years' worth of *National Geographic* magazines. Others gave subscriptions to a host of periodicals and paid for a year's telephone service.

William Werner, in his *Centre Daily Times* "Book-worm" column, remarked that it would be nice if some "rich" interested person gave the library the one hundred best books for children chosen by *McCall's* magazine. That evening an anonymous couple made the gift! Charlie Schlow also contacted his high school classmate, Book-of-the-Month Club founder Harry Schurman, and acquired publishing house seconds to add to the collection.

Remodeling the house was also a community effort. Robert DesMarais, a State College architect, tested supports near the walls where shelves would be built and planned the interior of the building. O. W. Houts donated wood, and Porter Brothers gave paint. Roy Smeltz, a local carpenter, directed Penn State professors McComb, M. L. Odland, and Robert Bernreuter in building the shelves, and members of the Friends Meeting painted the rooms. Other groups contributed money and furniture.

Then, with the library scheduled to open in late November 1956, its meager collection enhanced by five hundred books borrowed from the Centre County Library, eighth-grader Carol Kountz, daughter of Rupert and Alice Kountz, suggested a book drive as a class project on community action. She and her teacher, Margaret Ferree, organized two hundred eighth-graders from the entire Centre Region, who, on November 14, enlisted their parents to drive them door-to-door collecting books and magazines.

"We thought they might get a few hundred," Charlie Schlow said. "But those youngsters collected 11,500 books!" By 11 p.m., his son Frank, a member of the library board, was persuading the manager of the neighboring Sears, Roebuck store to open his doors so the board could buy six large house jacks to brace the center of the basement ceiling, which was visibly sagging under the weight of all those books! The next day 2,000 more books were delivered, and the loan from the Centre County Library was canceled.

In 1957, Charlie Schlow's wife died of cancer, and in her memory he donated money to expand the library building, which in 1958 was dedicated as the Bella S. Schlow Memorial Library. But he alone was unable to keep the library solvent, so in 1960 the League of Women Voters, AAUW, and the Woman's Club led a massive "Save the Library" campaign, which resulted in voters' approving to allocate one-half mill of Borough real estate taxes to the library each year.

By 1965, the year Frank Schlow died of Hodgkins disease, both the library and the State College Post Office at the corner of Beaver and Allen were bursting at their seams. So when the post office moved into its new building on the site of the old Frazier Street School, its former home was sold for one dollar to the library's trustees. After extensive remodeling, the building opened in 1967 and was rededicated, in honor of both Bella and Frank, as Schlow Memorial Library. And the fireplace from the old building was moved to the new one, with a favorite Charlie Schlow adage inscribed on the mantel: "He ever liveth who giveth life to knowledge."

Industries sprouted, too, in the post-war years, many spinoffs from the College. The first major one was Haller, Raymond & Brown, founded in 1947 by three physicists who met during the war and coincidentally wound up at Penn State. George Haller grew up in State College, son of Frank Haller, a Penn State horticulturist and his wife, Barbara, an active suffragette, for whom the women's dorm, Haller Hall, is named. After earning a Ph.D. in physics from State and the rank of colonel from the air force, he returned to his alma mater as dean of the School of Chemistry and Physics (now the Eberly College of Science), where Richard Raymond was an associate professor and Walter Brown was a graduate student.

POLICE PROTECTION for State College stacks up this way, now that the second cruiser has been added. Seated: Robert Witmer, George Miley, Chief John R. Juba, W. W. Lucas. Standing: R. Q. Jones, O. F. Brown, Ralph M. Farmer, M. A. Seckinger, Donald Benner.

—Centre Daily Times, 5-3-55

Pennsylvania Financial Group, Inc.

ennsylvania Financial Group, Inc. (PFG), led by Managing Directors Robert A. Szeyller and Robert E. McNichol, Jr., is Central Pennsylvania's largest independent financial services firm. The organization's commitment to providing clients with excellent service, creative planning, and innovative financial product design, and a commitment to the community, is the backbone of PFG's success.

Group, Inc. in 1981, and continued to expand to other communities within Pennsylvania and several states. More services were added to the family of PFG companies — United States Casualty Company (property-casualty firm), PFG Capital Corporation (real estate investment firm), and PFG Leasing, Inc.

In the early '80s, as the country began to focus on comprehensive financial planning, PFG formed a registered investment advisory service (RIA) and began offering fee-for-service investment consulting. The RIA and NRPS served as the nucleus for what is now known as Aris Corporation. In 1990, Keith L. Weir, also a Penn State graduate, joined the PFG family as president and CEO of the future Aris Corporation, bringing Fortune 500 financial and operational management expertise.

Spectrum Financial Network, a new Aris division, is a third-party mark-

The PFG Building is located on Walker Drive in State College.

PFG's genesis was in 1960 when Bob Szeyller, an Altoona native and recent Penn State graduate, believed that the State College area contained all the ingredients for business success. With modest beginnings as an extended office of a Harrisburg firm, the future Szeyller Associates began offering insurance products and, later, mutual funds, stocks, and bonds. The company soon developed into a dynamic financial planning firm.

In 1972, the first spin-off company was formed. National Retirement Plan Services (NRPS) continues to function as PFG's retirement-plan administration, design, and actuarial consulting firm. In 1974, Bob McNichol, Jr., a State College native and Penn State graduate, joined PFG and was later promoted to partner and managing director. This team approach to the company's management enhanced the continued development of this success story.

The firm became known as Pennsylvania Financial

eter dis- tributing investment products to other financial institutions, primarily banks. Perhaps the most significant service to be developed was initiated by Aris in 1991. Asset & Wealth Services (AWS) presently manages capital in excess of $500 million for individual clients, corporations, and retirement plan trusts. AWS provides ongoing evaluation of money managers at the national level; this analysis is then used to provide independent evaluation, recommendation, monitoring, and reporting of financial results to clients.

PFG and its affiliates presently employ more than 100 people at its corporate headquarters in the PFG Building on Walker Drive in State College. In addition to offices throughout Pennsylvania, branch offices are located in Delaware, Florida, and Maryland. Under the joint guidance of Chairman Robert A. Szeyller and President Robert E. McNichol, Jr., Pennsylvania Financial Group, Inc., is uniquely positioned to lead its diverse client group into the next century.

Working part-time at first, the trio started an infrared-reconnaissance-equipment business in Brown's Windcrest trailer, expanded to Raymond's basement and garage, and then moved to a house at 401 Clay Alley (now Clay Lane). Phil Freed, who began his forty-plus-year career with them in 1948, remembered the three as "unorthodox idea men with a seriousness-to-humor ratio of one to two [Brown was the serious one] who could prove their scientific theories with bent metal, cardboard, and glue."

By 1954, HRB had annual sales of $1 million and 190 employees in the four-story Smithfield apartment building at 127 North Atherton Street. Four years later, the Singer sewing machine company, looking to diversify, bought the company and changed its name to HRB-Singer. By then Brown had died in a drowning accident, Haller and Raymond were executives at General Electric, and another product of Penn State's physics department, John McLucas, was in charge. In 1960, with more than 700 employees and $7.2 million in sales, the company built the first of its seven buildings on Science Park Road.

An early spinoff of HRB was Community Engineering (now C-COR Electronics), which was started as a sideline television business by Haller, Brown, and McLucas. "We filed for a station license in State College, but lost to the Altoona station [now WTAJ]," said John, who was the new company's first president, 1953-58, and was on C-COR's board of directors for many years. "So for a couple of years we sold people TV sets and also antennas so they'd have something to watch."

After spending most of their time and money installing and repairing antennas, especially after snowstorms, the men decided to put up a master antenna on the roof of Walt Brown's house, amplify the signal, and run wires to other people's television sets. That was the birth of cable TV in State College.

"In 1953," John continued, "we said, 'Let's concentrate on making the amplifier.' I became president on weekends and at midnight and often used my HRB paycheck to meet Community Engineering's payroll. Walt was chief engineer, and George was just an investor."

In 1958, ex-HRB engineer and part-time general man-

Sunday Movies Win In 3 County Areas

State College, College Township, and Philipsburg theatres will be showing movies on Sundays after 2 p.m. in about three weeks.

State College voters approved the question by 221 votes. The count was 2,006 in favor and 1,785 against, unofficial tabulations of ballots indicated. College Township's approval was by a scant 20 votes, 384-364 . . . .

—Centre Daily Times, 11-9-55

Open House
Town's Growth Marked With Increasing Problems

with KATEY and ROSS LEHMAN

The job of unpaid public servants, like those of the borough council and other committee assignments, is no easy one. This fast growing community poses many problems and many changes, and just the routine tasks sometimes push the question of the future into the reluctant back seat of progress.

This community has grown faster than its "britches." Before the war we were a sedate town of 6,000 people, but now we have an estimated 12,500 population . . . .

There are 34 miles of streets, 12 miles of sewer lines, . . . seven miles of water lines, and two large playgrounds with some smaller ones.

We have the best volunteer fire company in Pennsylvania, with seven pieces of equipment: four pumpers, an 85 foot aerial ladder, a squad truck, a water tank, and an extra water tank for out-of-town fires. Two ambulances service the community.

There's the traffic headache, one which aspirins won't cure. We have the traffic problems of a town of 50,000 because of the additional cars of thousands of students and the steady stream of visitors. A traffic commission has been formed.

Traffic, sewerage, fire protection, the general well-being of our town is getting more difficult to manage, but our "public servants" are keeping pace. — Ross.

—Centre Daily Times, 1-13-56

ager of C-COR James R. Palmer took over as president and led it quickly to the forefront of the cable TV business. C-COR manufactured successive generations of CATV electronics and built, owned, and operated cable systems in Pennsylvania, Ohio, and West Virginia, including the local system. Once located in a second-floor room at 418 East College Avenue, C-COR moved to its present headquarters at 60 Decibel Road, across from the Nittany Mall, in 1965.

To get operating capital for the fledgling company, Jim Palmer and his wife, Barbara, sold shares of stock at cocktail parties and even door-to-door. In 1986, they converted the shares they themselves had bought into a $3.5 million gift to Penn State for a cable television museum and an addition to the art museum now named in their honor.

Other major area employers started in the 1950s and '60s, most as spinoffs from Penn State. Applied Science Laboratory, founded in 1951 by chemical engineering professor Arthur Rose and his wife, Elizabeth (Gates), had offices in several buildings on North Barnard and Gill Streets by the late 1950s. It sparked several spinoffs of its own, including Supelco, Inc., founded in Bellefonte by Walter Supina and Nicholas Pelick. Centre Circuits (now Atotech USA but for most of its life Chemcut Corporation), under the leadership of Rufus Benton, pioneered in equipment for making printed circuit boards in 1956 in a small two-story building in Pine Grove Mills before moving to a thirty-four-acre complex on Science Park Road. Nease Chemical (now Ruetgers-Nease), founded in 1950 by C. Aubrey Nease to produce organic chemical additives, later moved to its present location near the Nittany Mall. Nuclide Analysis, under MIT professors Leonard Herzog and Dean Edmonds Jr., built their first mass spectrometer in the Smithfield Building in 1959. Erie Technological Products (now MuRata Electronics), not a Penn State spinoff, was instead inspired by the growing industrial base around State College. It moved here from Erie in 1957 and began building ceramic capacitors and other electronics components at its present but then much smaller Ferguson Township facility.

Increased population again brought the need for more medical care. In 1947, State College native Jack Light

Meyers BaRestaurant at 210 West College Ave. was almost the birthplace of the Little German Band. In 1964, on floor: Bob Skipper, Bill Manges, Charles Ryan. On chairs and kneeling: vocalist Margaret Hayes, Adele Haugh, Vonnie Henninger, Carolyn Brogdon, Loretta Greene, Ruby Venturato, Nancy Taylor, John Showalter, Alex Giedroe, director Guy Rachau, Thomas Burtnett. Next row: Sam Hayes, Hubert Haugh, Doris Rachau, Dick Greene, Olin Butt, Miriam Smith, Christine Butt, James Taylor, Charles Ammerman, Warner Eliot, Rollin Hosterman, Eugene DeMark. Back row: Dan Venturato, John Henninger, Chuck Smith, Al Brogdon, and Jack Meyers.

State College Woman's Club officers in 1959 were, front: Kathleen Dietz, Annette McHugh holding the clubhouse deed, Florence Graham, Lorraine Tietz, Madeline Campbell, and Helen Platt. In back: Anne Margolf, Rosemary Raleigh, Mary Miller, Shirley Hudson, Helen Hays, Jane Frey, and Lillian Raycroft.

American Philatelic Society staff members at the 1962 convention in State College were Col. James T. DeVoss, H. Clay Musser, executive secretary, and James M. Chemi, editor. Colonel DeVoss succeeded Clay as executive secretary, and Bill Welch later became editor of The American Philatelist.

Once "one of the residential boasts of the town," "Frenchy" Foster's eighty-year-old home on Beaver at Pugh housed "Peanuts" Morrell's peanuts-candy-and-popcorn emporium which had moved up from its hole-in-the-wall location just off College Avenue on Pugh Street. In the '40s and '50s, this home (now site of the Pugh Street Parking Garage) had headquartered Dean Probst's Sally's Sandwich Shop, which delivered sandwiches every evening to fraternities, sororities, and campus dorms.

In 1965, the State High 2-mile relay team and Coach Jackson Horner gained national prominence by breaking a 1962 national high school record time of 7:49.9. In front: Jack Walmer and Steve Gentry. Standing: Jerry Miller, Coach Horner, and Jim Dixon. This team's time: 7:47.8.

came back from World War II and opened his general practice at 426 South Allen Street. Dr. William L. Welch followed suit by taking over the private practice of the new College Health Service director, Dr. Herbert Glenn, son of postmaster George Glenn. Bill also moved into Glenn's former offices at 322 West College Avenue, next door to Hoy Brothers General Merchandise, where son Bill, now mayor of State College, whiled away many after-school and Saturday hours. Then in the late '40s and early '50s came the first of many specialists who would eventually outnumber the G.P.'s — William McFarland, first internist; Tom Mebane, first certified pediatrician; Walter Schuyler, first obstetrician-gynecologist; and George Lott, first psychiatrist.

Another first — regularly scheduled airline passenger service — occurred June 20, 1949, when All-American Airways (predecessor to USAir) landed a twenty-four-passenger DC-3 at the State College Air Depot just west of town. The depot's owner was veteran pilot Sherm Lutz, who, with financial backing from Aikens, Kennard, and Mateer, Inc., had opened the area's first airport in 1929 at the Old Indian Pine in Boalsburg, just north of the present elementary school. An early airmail depot was established, airport services (instead of farm fields) were offered for pilots of the day, and the first of an eventual 476 students were taught to fly. First woman to win her wings was Ellen Roberts Druckman, who received her pilot's license while a Penn State student and soloed at the Boalsburg Depot in December 1936.

In 1945, Sherm moved his operations closer to town after he and bookstore owner and Commerce Club president William Keeler bought two hundred acres of farm land off Route 45 in Pine Hall. Engineer Robert Minshall, another early advocate of better airport facilities, engineered the project, dominated by a 4,000-foot grass runway. Officials said, "When the new field is completed, State College residents will have a modern-design airport to keep them in close touch with the coming air age."

The inaugural flight from

Pedestrians Miss Injury From Bricks

Two State College residents narrowly escaped serious injury in the downtown business district yesterday afternoon when some 50 bricks broke loose and fell from the roof cornice of the Leitzell Bldg. at Allen St. and College Ave.

Mrs. Kenneth Hunter of 1012 Old Boalsburg Rd. and Susan Eberly, 256 S. Burrowes St., were both walking on the College Ave. side of the building when the bricks fell from the cornice some 30 feet above them.

. . . Mrs. Hunter was hit on the shoulder and Miss Eberly was hit on the arm.

—Centre Daily Times, 3-18-60

Students Riot in Cathaum Theatre

Police, Alphas, Officials Quell Nearly 1,000; Trio Injured, 3 Pay Big Fines

University students, protesting when their own antics caused interruption of a motion picture, turned the inside of the Cathaum Theatre in State College into chaos and then swelled into a riotous mob in the street outside early yesterday morning.

Flaunting attempts at order by Borough police and Alpha firemen, the mob of nearly 1,000 stone-throwing and jeering students was finally dispersed by the added appearance of University officials and State Police. Firemen were called to the scene to assist police in quieting the mob. Injuries in the fracas were limited to those caused by flying rocks and stones. Two firemen, Matthew Hayes and Eugene Sellers, were hit by the stones, and at least two students were reported struck by flying objects. . . .

The large plate glass window of the Ethel Meserve store, in the next block, was shattered by a stray bullet.

One Alpha fireman, roused from sleep and responding to what he thought was a fire at 1:15 a.m., went home again with his 1957 car battered by stones. The fireman, Richard Hoffman, said the rear window of the car was smashed and the paint scarred by rocks.

An estimate of damages to the theater has not been completed. . . .

Patrolman D. E. Benner described the audience upon his entrance as an "uncontrollable mob that was tearing the place apart."

Finally herded outside the theatre, the audience was reinforced by dormitory and fraternity students alike.

After nearly two hours of attempting to restore order, police finally cleared the street to permit traffic.

Leaders where identifiable were scurried off to the lockup.

—Centre Daily Times, 5-31-58

Pittsburgh was greeted by more than seven hundred people, including the State College American Legion Junior Drum and Bugle Corps; Burgess Yougel, who presented a gold key; and Commerce Club executive secretary Louetta Neusbaum who, with Addie Keeler, cut a gold mesh ribbon especially made for the ceremony by a Williamsport firm. Arriving passengers included Diana Huffman Storch, Fred Spannuth and son Freddie, and *CDT* staff writer Paul Houck, all of State College, and former *CDT* city editor George Scott, then editor of the *Progress* in Clearfield, where the plane had stopped before landing at the air depot. Later, at a breakfast for 125 people in the Hotel State College, an official of the airline congratulated the community on its work and said All-American was delighted to have the State College stop on its system. Sherm Lutz said, "It is the biggest day of my life," and George Haller, another proponent of air service, said, "In the future, I am sure we'll find the State College Air Depot one of the busiest on All-American lines."

But by December of that year, muddy and snow-covered runways forced All-American to discontinue flights into State College for the winter months. Earlier that year Borough councilman Eric Walker had introduced a proposal to build, at Borough expense, a hard-surface runway in exchange for a non-exclusive license to operate the airport, but the idea was rejected. All-American resumed flights the next summer and continued until 1951, when it moved service to Albert Airport in Clearfield and then to Black Moshannon Airport in Philipsburg. The next year, Borough Council proposed to expand Sherm Lutz's airfield into a municipal airport, but west-end residents protested that it would be a potential hazard to the community and to Corl Street Elementary School.

By 1957, after Walker was president of Penn State, the new State College Airport Authority, believing that an

Dante's Restaurants, Inc.

ndy Zangrilli has had his finger in the State College pie, so to speak, for more than thirty years. And ever since he opened the first Hi Way Pizza shop on Hiester Street in 1963 at age twenty-one, his piece of that pie has grown steadily. Now, with three Hi Way pizzerias, two Mario & Luigi's Italian restaurants, The Deli Restaurant, Crowbar, and The Saloon, Andy has plenty to keep him busy these days.

The first Hi Way Pizza in State College, in the present location of the Deli Restaurant on Hiester Street, opened in 1963.

The restaurateur got his start in the pizza business at age fourteen while working at an Altoona shop owned by Alfred Sicola. After managing one of Sicola's pizzerias in Philipsburg, Andy, with help from Al and Connie Sicola, struck out on his own in State College, opening his first Hi Way pizzeria and in the process introducing Sicilian pizza to the area. Prepared with fresh dough, his great-tasting pizza soon proved a hit with students and residents alike. It wasn't long before he opened another Hi Way on Garner Street at the present site of Mario & Luigi's. Nicknamed the "square pie shop," it became an instant success as an inexpensive student hangout. Hi Way restaurants on Westerly Parkway and at Village Square Plaza opened in the ensuing years, and Andy took advantage of his cooking training and

travels to Italy to add new specialties such as pesto pizza, foccacia bread, stuffed pizza, and spinoccoli.

Pizzerias proved to be just the beginning for Andy as he set about cornering the local Italian-dining market by opening his first Mario & Luigi's. The success of this downtown restaurant, with fresh pasta and brick-oven specialties, led to the debut of another location on North Atherton Street in 1992.

Meanwhile, The Deli Restaurant on Hiester Street built a loyal

Cathy Zangrilli is responsible for Hi Way Pizza's unique decor; Andy is the one to thank for the pizza's great taste.

clientele by offering something for everyone, including delicious sandwiches, specialty salads, and a "lite" menu. Next door, The Saloon marked Andy's entry into the local bar scene, while his most recent project, the popular Crowbar on East College, has live music six nights a week.

For Andy Zangrilli, hard work and innovation have paid off over the years. Now with a small empire that includes Gullifty's American Bistro in Harrisburg, he can fondly reminisce about a time, years ago, when it all got started with a small take-out-pizza shop.

C.C. Peppers now occupies the site of Hi Way Pizza's first Westerly Parkway location, shown here circa 1970.

all-weather airport would "generate a traffic potential to justify its existence," recommended a site north of the Borough, on University-owned property near Boogersburg. The next year, flight service began from University Park Airport, operated by the State College Flying Service, a corporation of private businessmen headed by J. Alvin Hawbaker. In 1960, HRB-Singer also leased property adjoining the airport, lengthened the runway to 3,200 feet, and built a hangar and taxiway for their company planes. Two years later the University took over operation of the airport and two years after that did a study revealing that 84 percent of passengers at Mid-State Airport, as Black Moshannon had been renamed, came from the State College-Bellefonte area. In 1965, the L. B. Smith Flying Service initiated commuter service from University Park to Harrisburg, Baltimore, and Washington, DC.

"University Park" was a name that resulted from what is still considered to be the biggest town-and-gown controversy in local history. It all started in 1950, when Dr. Milton S. Eisenhower came from Kansas State to be president of Penn State, then the twelfth largest college in the country. The most famous prexy Penn State had had, his tenure, 1950-56, coincided with brother Dwight's first term in the White House. As Ike's closest adviser, Milton brought international recognition to the school. He also had the ability to win as many friends among trustees, legislators, and alumni as he did among students, faculty, and townspeople. Soon money flowed in, buildings went up, new programs were developed, and, most important of all, the College officially became The Pennsylvania State University.

Wilmer Kenworthy, Milton's director for student affairs, said that students found him outgoing and open to their problems, and faculty members admired the way he handled meetings. "I enjoyed working for him very much. He was energetic, decisive, and didn't shoot from the hip." Milton's secretary, Jo Groesbeck, said, "From the moment Dr. Eisenhower literally bounced into the office of the president, I knew here was the man I had always hoped to work for. I learned, soon after, that one worked not only *for* but *with* this man who was a friend as well as a boss."

Sam Blazer, who later became Penn State's director of fleet operations, was Eisenhower's chauffeur for frequent, almost weekly trips to Harrisburg, Philadelphia, Pittsburgh, and, of course, Washington, D.C. "He always rode in the front seat with me so we could talk,

and he never missed a baseball game on the radio," said Sam. "One time in winter we got stuck on ice coming over Pine Grove Mountain, and Dr. Eisenhower got out and pushed while I drove on the berm!"

On November 14, 1953, in what Eisenhower considered to be the greatest accomplishment of his administration, Penn State became a university by decree of the Centre County Court of Common Pleas. But the fact that every press release issued by the University carried the dateline *State College* caused Milton to write to Chamber of Commerce President Herbert R. Imbt, saying, "The town has always honored the institution by bearing its name. Now, unfortunately, the name State College constantly misstates the situation to the world." He pointed out that people unfamiliar with the area often asked, "I know it is *the* state college, but what is the name of the town?" He then suggested that the Borough adopt an entirely different name, not to honor the University, but to avoid a possible new difficulty fifty years later, although he said he would not presume to suggest what the new name should be.

Changing the name of a town requires only a petition signed by 10 percent of the voters and delivered to the county court, which directs the election board to put the question on the ballot as a referendum. If a majority votes for the new name, the court issues a formal decree and the change is complete.

The chamber directors unanimously endorsed the idea in June 1954 and formed a "Committee of 50," headed by John Henry Frizzell, to come up with the best name to put on the petition. They chose "Mt. Nittany" over all others nominated because, they said, it "is descriptive of the location, provides historical and folklore significance, will wear well over the years, and will fit in with any future growth of the town."

Some thought the name had a solid yet picturesque flavor, like "Mt. Vernon," and would help to attract vacationers and newcomers. Others thought it sounded "hickish," lacked dignity, or connoted, as Helen Atherton Govier put it, "a small insignificant village comparable to Gum Stump or Bear Hollow."

The *CDT* quickly became a forum for both groups, and every evening there were letters to read. Some reasoned that it was not fair to the University to retain the present name. Others proposed alternate names such as State Centre, Centre City, University Centre, University City, Keystone, and Atherton (again).

In 1949, fifty-three years after opening State College's longest-running store, George Graham was photographed in front of Graham & Sons at 103 South Allen by Jack Kirkpatrick, who had recently opened Centre Film Lab.

The men who brought the Borough its first public swimming pool (and two who had just taken the first 60-degree plunge) are: architect Ed Burgener, fund-drive chairman Herb Imbt, contractor "Jack" Frost, building-committee chairman Hal Byers, and swimming-pool association president Dr. Bill Welch.

J. T. Sullivan proposed "Starling" as a pleasant word, musical, easy to pronounce and spell, and with some air of distinction. "Following the example of some European cities," he wrote, "we might go further and give it an aristocratic name, as for example, Starling-on-Pugh." Other tongue-in-cheek suggestions were: Dead Centre, Dry Gulch (since we had no wine or liquor stores), Sanctimony Dell (since we had no Sunday movies), and State 53 College (so that each time we uttered the name we could recall the year this all began).

A serious contender was Centre Hills, but its supporters never filed a petition because they learned that a majority vote would be required on *any* name submitted before a change could be made. Therefore, Centre Hills proponents Edwin Dill, Bill Keeler, and Clarence Bauchspies wrote in the *CDT*, if the choices on the ballot were "(A) Do you want to change the name of State College?" and "(B) If yes, (1) Do you want to change it to Mt. Nittany? or (2) Do you want to change it to Centre Hills?" a *majority* of the voters might be prohibited from deciding the issue if another name was added to the ballot.

Keeler and others who opposed the name change to Mt. Nittany then formed the Friends of State College, saying they saw no reason to change a name that had served a town so well for so many years. George Graham admitted that sentiment was connected with his opposition to change, saying, "When sentiment goes out the window, then greed, jealousy, egotism, and vanity creep in the door."

Eighty-year-old Mickey McDowell Sr., who had favored a change to Atherton in 1906 but didn't consider Mt. Nittany a suitable name, stood before a crowd just before election day and bellowed:

"It was State College when I was born.

It was State College when I was in middle age.

It is State College now in my old age.

Liquor Store To Open Soon in State College

A State Liquor store will open in State College in an estimated two months.

An unoccupied store at 216 W. Hamilton Ave., in the University Park Plaza Shopping Center complex, is being readied for occupancy . . . .

The question of a Liquor Control Board store in State College has been intermittently under discussion since 1959.

In recent months, the volume of mail received by the Liquor Control Board in favor of locating a store in State College Borough far outnumbered that against it.

—*Centre Daily Times, 12-31-64*

IT WILL BE STATE COLLEGE FOREVER!"

Tuesday, November 2, 1954, dawned cold, wet, and snowy, but 71 percent of the voters made it to the polls. They were surprised, however, to see not the variety of questions that Dill, Keeler, and Bauchspies had theorized, but only one: "Do you favor changing the name of State College to Mt. Nittany?" After months of debating change *per se*, they found a ballot permitting them to choose only between two names. Many people wanted to vote against Mt. Nittany, not against change, but the ballot lumped them together. The vote was 2,434 to 1,475 in favor of State College.

Eisenhower, who had given his official backing to Mt. Nittany, immediately moved to obtain a post office for Penn State. By early December the trustees had authorized the sending of an application to the Post Office Department in Washington, and though the procedure usually took many months or even years, Penn State's request was approved within two months, helped, everyone knew, by Milton's friend in the White House.

Choosing a name for the new post office — a substation of the State College Post Office — also was done by ballot mailed to all faculty, staff, and alumni council members and reprinted in the *Daily Collegian* and *Centre Daily Times*. The easy winner was "University Park." On February 22, 1955, the hundredth anniversary of Penn State's chartering, the substation opened in the new $3 million Hetzel Union Building, and "University Park" began to be used as a place name by the University.

ince Alex Woskob opened his first apartment building in State College thirty-three years ago, his company has served close to 100,000 residents, most of whom have been students. His four high-rise apartment complexes, dubbed "The Downtown Group," have earned a reputation for their convenience,

followed. These included Park Hill, Fairmount Hills, Penn Tower, Beaver Hill, Cedarbrook, Garner Court, and Alexander Court. In 1986, the couple built Woskob Industrial Park on Clyde Avenue near the Nittany Mall. The following year they designed and built The Graduate at 138 South Atherton Street, now owned and managed by their son George's company, GN Associates. Their son, Victor, is in charge of the day-to-day operations of A.W. & Sons. He also owns and operates a large farm in Ferguson Township on which he raises prime beef cattle.

A.W. & Sons owns and manages four apartment buildings in a one-block area downtown: Alexander Court, Beaver Hill, Cedarbrook, and Garner Court. The Woskobs' other properties have since been sold, although they still maintain control of the industrial park. Their four remaining apartment complexes encompass 449 studio, one-, two-, and three-bedroom units. On-site amenities include laundry facilities, fitness and game rooms, study lounges, and three computer labs with connections to the Penn State mainframe.

In addition to its all-inclusive rental policy and convenient location, The Downtown Group earns kudos for the appearance and upkeep of its apartments. The company won the 1994 State College Focus on Appearance award given by the borough's design review board. Services like its twenty-four-hour "we care" maintenance policy ensure that A. W. & Sons will remain a leader in the competitive downtown rental marketplace.

The A.W. & Sons properties on Beaver Avenue are popular with students.

high level of appearance, and comprehensive facilities. All are one block from campus, come fully furnished, and include cable and utilities. Considering their features, it's not surprising that A.W. & Sons properties traditionally remain at 100 percent occupancy.

Alex and Helen Woskob arrived in State College in 1963 after having founded a successful building business in Philadelphia in 1956. The couple, who immigrated from the Ukraine, were married in Germany in 1950, then moved to Canada before coming to America. After visiting State College and falling in love with the area, the Woskobs decided to make it their permanent home. Shortly after their arrival here, they began plans to build some of the first high-rise apartments in town.

The Woskobs' first project, Parkway Plaza, was built on Westerly Parkway with families in mind. Other apartment complexes, mostly for students, soon

State College was sixty-seven years old when Helen and Alex Woskob started building apartments in and around town.

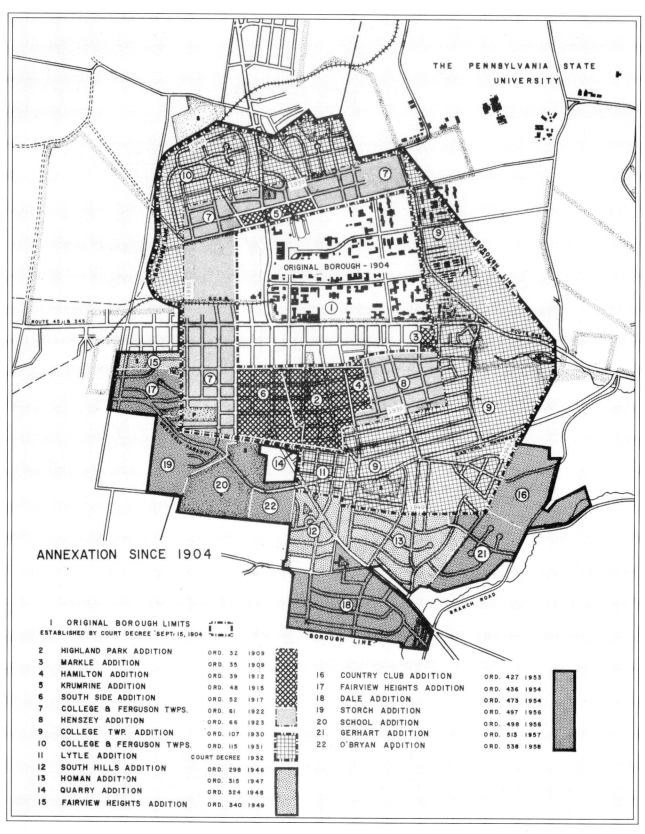

ANNEXATION SINCE 1904

1	ORIGINAL BOROUGH LIMITS ESTABLISHED BY COURT DECREE SEPT. 15, 1904		
2	HIGHLAND PARK ADDITION	ORD. 32	1909
3	MARKLE ADDITION	ORD. 35	1909
4	HAMILTON ADDITION	ORD. 39	1912
5	KRUMRINE ADDITION	ORD. 48	1915
6	SOUTH SIDE ADDITION	ORD. 52	1917
7	COLLEGE & FERGUSON TWPS.	ORD. 61	1922
8	HENSZEY ADDITION	ORD. 66	1923
9	COLLEGE TWP. ADDITION	ORD. 107	1930
10	COLLEGE & FERGUSON TWPS.	ORD. 115	1931
11	LYTLE ADDITION	COURT DECREE	1932
12	SOUTH HILLS ADDITION	ORD. 298	1946
13	HOMAN ADDITION	ORD. 315	1947
14	QUARRY ADDITION	ORD. 324	1948
15	FAIRVIEW HEIGHTS ADDITION	ORD. 340	1949
16	COUNTRY CLUB ADDITION	ORD. 427	1953
17	FAIRVIEW HEIGHTS ADDITION	ORD. 436	1954
18	DALE ADDITION	ORD. 473	1954
19	STORCH ADDITION	ORD. 497	1956
20	SCHOOL ADDITION	ORD. 498	1956
21	GERHART ADDITION	ORD. 513	1957
22	O'BRYAN ADDITION	ORD. 538	1958

The above map shows the many Borough annexations that took place between 1904 and 1958. Eight more annexations occurred, the last one being a part of Centre Hills Country Club in 1969. This is a prime example of the piece-by-piece accreation of a growing community. This piecemeal assembly of land, mostly determined by the established boundaries of separate private land holdings, points up the importance of planning and zoning in the abutting areas regardless of whether further annexation takes place.

158

BestEvent Rental

Party & Wedding Corner

For over three decades, Central Pennsylvania residents have turned to BestEvent Rental or its predecessors, Unlimited Rent-Alls and United Rent-Alls, for their rental needs.

Since 1964, the company has continually adapted to its market and now concentrates on special-event rentals and services plus sales of related merchandise in its companion department, Party & Wedding Corner.

The company opened in 1964 as the only rental center within sixty miles with mostly small contractor and do-it-yourself tools and only a few special-event related items. In 1966, the name Unlimited Rent-Alls was chosen to reflect the goal of offering a broad selection of rental items. Party & Wedding Corner was opened in 1985 to sell disposable food-service items, candles, balloons, decorations, etc.

In 1994, the tool inventory was eliminated and BestEvent Rental was created. Its services now include

BestEvent Rental supplies the needs of celebrations, fund raisers, trade shows, art festivals, and business functions.

production of custom-designed decorations and theme props along with consultation, planning, coordination, on-site installation, and equipment operation.

With a large inventory of party and banquet needs, tents, tables, chairs, beds, costumes, audio-visual equipment, stage and other rental needs, plus a complete stock of special-event merchandise, it's clear that BestEvent Rental and Party & Wedding Corner will continue as Central Pennsylvania's one-stop shop for planners and organizers of any special event.

Commonwealth Bank

a division of
Meridian

Commonwealth Bank's approach to banking is anything but commonplace. For more than thirty years, its employees have served customers with a personal touch more often associated with small community banks. Commonwealth traces its roots to north-central Pennsylvania. Four banks — from Wellsboro, Galeton, Lawrenceville, and Westfield — merged in 1965 and formed Commonwealth Bank and Trust Company. Assets then totaled $18 million.

Throughout the 1970s into the mid-1980s, Commonwealth expanded its service area to ten counties, making it the largest nationally chartered bank to be headquartered in north-central Pennsylvania. By the end of 1992, Commonwealth Bancshares Corporation, the bank's holding company, had fifty-nine offices in thirteen counties. With assets of $2.1 billion, it was the twelfth-largest bank holding company in Pennsylvania.

Commonwealth's entry into Centre County began in

1986 with the opening of an office in State College on North Atherton Street. Three years later, a second office was built on South Atherton Street. This growth phase was further enhanced by the opening of our Calder Square office which provides convenient banking to our downtown State College customers. Along with this period of intense growth, Commonwealth Bank expanded its commercial lending operations to better serve the business market.

The 1993 purchase of Commonwealth Banchares Corporation by Meridian Bancorp, Inc. brought many new products and services to Commonwealth customers. A diversified financial services holding company with $15 billion in assets, Meridian is headquartered in Reading, PA, and has 320 branches in Pennsylvania, New Jersey, and Delaware. Since the merger, Commonwealth Bank, a division of Meridian Bank, has been able to offer customers the technological advantages and convenience of a larger institution while maintaining its character as a community bank.

Edward L. Keller
Burgess 1947 and 1949

Tom Sauers
Fire Chief 1948-58

William S. Hoffman
Burgess 1950

David Mackey
Burgess 1954-57

Judge R. Paul Campbell administers oath of office to councilmen Philip
Freed, D. R. L. Robison, and Lawrence Perez, and Burgess-then-Mayor
Roy D. Anthony (1958-61).

State College
Burgesses, Fire
and Police Chiefs
1 9 4 7 to 1 9 6 7

Burgess Edward K. Hibshman, 1950-53,
with Larry Perez, Burgess 1967, and Hazel Fall.

Claude H. Decker
Burgess 1957-58

George Miley
Fire Chief 1959-60

Bower Moore
Fire Chief 1961-65

Student Book Store

t the "Big Blue on the Corner," a phrase coined by general manager Norm Brown, Penn State pride shines year-round, but never more brightly than on home football weekends. That's when the Student Book Store (SBS) pulls out all stops for Nittany Lions fans, organizing pep rallies, hosting vocal groups, and providing shuttle service to the game. But then, you'd expect nothing less from the only local bookstore owned and operated by Penn Staters.

The Student Book Store is especially full on a day when the Penn State football team has a home game.

The Student Book Store has been a fixture on East College Avenue since 1966

When it opened in 1966 on East College Avenue, SBS helped meet a need for a store with a complete selection of college textbooks and general titles. Barrett Morris, president of a Lexington, Kentucky-based bookstore company, had recognized that need while visiting the area, and set about searching for a suitable downtown building. He found it at 330 East College, a prime location SBS has enjoyed for three decades. Originally only about 6,000 square feet, the store has since grown to encompass 13,000 square feet on three levels. As it grew, SBS occupied two adjacent buildings, the most recent at 326 East College.

Now decorated in a classic blue-and-white motif, SBS is a full-service college book store carrying all titles for university classes plus general books and a line of gift items. With Penn State's admission into the Big Ten, it has branched out more heavily into Penn State-related clothing and accessories. Norm Brown, the first alumnus to manage the store, came aboard in 1989 and oversees a staff of up to thirty-five student employees. For them and thousands of other students and alumni, Penn State pride is alive and well at the Big Blue on the Corner.

The Penn State Pep Band entertains folks outside the Student Book Store on home football Saturdays.

CHAPTER SEVEN
1966 to 1976

Protests
&
Progress

everal noteworthy events in 1966 would have an enormous impact on State College Borough for years to come. And the decade itself was an activist period of social consciousness filled with a host of firsts and lasts that presaged the end of the small town and the beginning of the city-to-be.

First came an announcement that the University would stop building residence halls at University Park, even though enrollment was projected to increase well into the 1970s — it already had jumped from 13,000 to 22,000 since 1956. But projections showed that the baby boom was receding and that University Park enrollment should be capped at 25,000. By 1971, the nation's schools also were showing a downward trend when, for the first time, the first-grade class had fewer members than the previous year's class had. So, after finishing East Halls and bringing the total of students housed and fed on campus to only about half of those enrolled, Penn State concentrated on adding new academic and administrative buildings.

Next, and related to University housing, was the "Heels and Hose" demonstration by women students in March 1966 in front of Old Main. They were unhappy with outdated regulations prohibiting women from visiting men in off-campus apartments or living off campus themselves. This was the first protest march at Penn State during a time of student unrest at most college campuses, and it would be followed by others over the next four years.

In this year, too, Joe Paterno was named head coach of the Nittany Lion football team. He would rack up back-to-back 11-0 seasons in 1968 and 1969 and make

post-season bowl games a Penn State tradition for the next three decades. This also brought national prominence to the University, prosperity to area merchants, and traffic congestion six or seven weekends a year to Borough streets, not to mention the highways leading to State College.

In addition to all this, a years-long controversy was raging among area residents over the soon-to-be constructed State College Bypass. Later named the Mount Nittany Expressway, it would take longer to complete — more than twenty years — than any previous road in the county.

The no-new-dorms announcement of 1966 was supposed to be a cue for private developers to construct more apartments and other dwellings for students, but planning and construction took time. Meanwhile, the University gave in to student demands and agreed to treat women and men alike, first lifting the ban prohibiting women's visits to men's apartments and then, in 1971, allowing all women except freshmen to live off-campus, a privilege once extended only to second-semester seniors and "townies," both male and female students whose families lived in the State College area. At the same time, Penn State stepped up its admission of women, since it was no longer restricted by the number that would fit into campus dorms; thus, even more housing was needed in town.

One of the first to fill that need was Alex Woskob, a native of the Ukraine who had arrived in State College in 1963 by way of Philadelphia and would eventually do more to urbanize the town than did any other developer. The mid- to high-rise apartment complexes he and sons

162

Part of the first Arts Festival was set up from Allen to Pugh Streets on the sidewalk on the University side of College Avenue. Artwork hung on a snow fence. There was no charge for space. "The first day only about fifty to seventy feet was used," Wally Lloyd reported. "A few people looked at them and bought some. When people saw that, they all rushed home, got stuff, and displayed it. After the first couple days, the entire fence was filled!"

Claiming "The Loudest Sound This Side of Sherwood Forest," the local rock group Robin and the Hoods — Robin Breon, Geoff de Lissovoy, Mike Gilligan, Greg House, and Hugh Ridge Riley III — were a top act at the first Arts Festival.

George and Victor constructed during the '60s and '70s, mostly on East Beaver Avenue between Locust Lane and Hetzel Street, replaced dozens of private homes and rooming houses. The twelve-story Penn Tower, at 255 East Beaver Avenue, now part of what critics call "Beaver Canyon," is the tallest building in downtown State College. More recently, A W & Sons built The Graduate at Beaver and Atherton, bringing the company's total apartment units to twelve hundred.

Another pioneer in building student apartments was Henry Sahakian, an Iranian who came to Penn State in 1956 to study electrical engineering and ended up founding Unico Corporation, a division of which now owns 414 Uni-Mart convenience stores in six East Coast states, 300 of them in Pennsylvania. As for apartment buildings in the mid-'60s, Sahakian added two high-rises — Armenara Plaza and the Ambassador Building — to what had been "Pickle Hill" on East Beaver Avenue, across from Grace Lutheran Church. His most recent project, in 1989, was Gateway Center, four student high-rises on East College Avenue at the University Drive cloverleaf.

Also in the mid-'60s, three developers known for constructing single-family homes — Leonard Grove, J. Alvin Hawbaker, and Philip Sieg — turned their resources to apartment-building.

Phil Sieg and Alex Gregory, partners in Federated Home and Mortgage Company until 1985, had started building single-family houses in the Westerly Parkway/Sparks Street/Saxton Drive area in 1960. They also built the Holiday Inn on South Atherton Street and then, in 1965, their first multi-family building, the forty-unit Foster Avenue Apartments at the corner of Foster and University Drive. Six existing duplexes on that site were trucked to new lots on Lester Street in Lemont.

"Apartments then were primarily aimed at graduate students, married undergrads, and veterans who were students," Phil said in 1992. "The typical nineteen- or twenty-year-old undergraduate was not being accommodated — he was living in fraternity houses or rooming houses. As the student population grew and the University decided not to build additional dormitories, the responsibility shifted to private enterprise."

The partners shifted gears and built the ninety-unit University Towers on East College Avenue in 1966 and the 100-foot-high Beaver Terrace on East Beaver Avenue, in 1970, both aimed specifically at "young, single, undergraduate students," Phil said. Their next and most ambitious undertaking, for which ground was broken in 1966, was Toftrees, Pennsylvania's first planned community, designed along the lines of Reston, Virginia, and Columbia, Maryland. North of State College in Patton Township's Barrens, Toftrees was, as Phil said, "decidedly *not* student-oriented. It was designed to serve busy professionals and active families."

Leonard Grove, a former home builder and native of Bellefonte, in 1966 built his first rental units, Mt. Nittany Apartments on South Pugh Street, with forty one- and two-bedroom units. His partner on the project was Bellefonte/State College excavating contractor Benjamin F. Kofman. "We aimed at the student market from the beginning," said Leonard. "That building practically rented itself; all we had to do was get out of the way!" Grove went on to put up other new apartment buildings on South Sparks Street, South Allen Street, and West College Avenue.

Once his Park Forest Village development was well under way, J. Alvin Hawbaker went shopping for land, bought the 80-acre McCoy farm and the 120-acre Shoemaker farm in the area south of the present high school, put in streets, and then sold tracts to various out-of-town developers. That land, now part of the Borough, is the site of Lions Gate Apartments, Nittany Gardens, Executive House, and Imperial Towers.

In 1966, Hawbaker's company built Park Forest Villas I and II, each with fifty-six garden units on West Aaron Drive. He then completed Georgetown, the area's first condominium complex, consisting of thirty-eight townhouses off Valley Vista Drive.

As the apartment boom continued, out-of-town developers saw State College as the place to build. Large complexes such as Southgate and Briarwood, where Waupelani Drive meets Whitehall Road, Laurel Glen (now Heritage Oaks) on Vairo Boulevard, and Bluebell (now University Terrace) on Bellaire Avenue, quickly sprang up.

This era also saw the building of Vallamont, the first truly upscale development of all architect-designed homes in the Borough. Located east of University Drive on East McCormick Avenue and its side streets, the area was developed by H. O. Smith & Sons construction company on the last farm purchased from the Moses Thompson Estate and the Centre Furnace Lands. It was bought in 1955 from Hilda Thompson, Moses and Mary's granddaughter.

Before the plethora of apartment buildings in State College, Penn State students had put up a tent village on Old Main lawn along the Wall on College Avenue to protest a lack of student housing and dubbed it "Walkertown" in "honor" of University president

Corning Asahi Video Products

n 1947, Corning invented a glass-composition process that made possible the mass production of video-display glass used to manufacture television panels and funnels. The technology was licensed to Asahi Glass of Japan in 1953, beginning an alliance between the two companies that was solidified in 1988 with the formation of a U.S. partnership in which Corning owns the majority interest. Today Corning Asahi is one of only ten companies worldwide that produce video-display glass. The company sells primarily to customers in the United States. It's estimated that one of every four large-screen color television picture tubes manufactured in North America contains a glass panel and/or funnel made by Corning Asahi.

Work on Corning's State College plant began in 1966, with production commencing the following year. The company chose to locate here because of the quality of the available workforce, proximity to Penn State, and access to the arts, entertainment, and recreation. The installation in 1987 of a third tank, a large glass-melting unit, signaled the start of a major plant expansion project. Since 1986, the company has invested more than $150 million in technology and capacity upgrades at its State College plant, adding state-of-the-art robotics and advanced control systems, among other features. The 495,000-square-foot plant employs about 1,200 workers.

Corning Asahi products are manufactured to precision tolerances that require the rejection of a fifty-pound glass panel with a blister as small as one thirty-thousandth of an inch. To achieve such close tolerances, the company adheres to a system of total quality reflected in all aspects of operation, from production to administration. Efforts to meet high standards for air, water, and solid-waste disposal are part of that total-quality approach.

Corning Asahi's drive to achieve total quality has led to the development of improved equipment and processes that set the benchmark for the video-products industry. Glass-melting tanks, designed by Corning, offer unexcelled yield and purity. New production lines emphasize speed and accuracy, and computer-aided design enables the company to launch new shapes and products faster than ever. In recognition of its efforts, Corning Asahi received the 1990 LEAD Award for its integration of computers into manufacturing and processing.

A quality assurance employee inspects a panel produced at Corning Asahi Video Products, a joint venture between Corning Incorporated and Asahi Glass America, Inc.

As one of the largest private-sector employers in the Centre Region, Corning Asahi plays a vital role in the local economy. The company makes significant contributions to community organizations and Penn State through the Corning Foundation, as evidenced by its support of the Center for the Performing Arts, Bryce Jordan Center, Center for Total Quality Schools, and Central Pennsylvania Festival of the Arts. For Corning Asahi Video Products, it's all part of doing business in a community that relies on the help of neighbors — both corporate and individual.

Eric Walker, who began his fourteen-year tenure in 1956, following the departure of Milton Eisenhower. The last two Walker years also witnessed a sit-in by four hundred students in Old Main lobby who presented a list of "non-negotiable demands" to the administration, and an angry march by nearly five hundred anti-war protestors, mostly students, on the Ordnance Research Laboratory and its Garfield Thomas Water Tunnel, which, though not supplying Vietnam War materiel, was engaged in naval-weapons research at the time. The protest, which included a traffic-stopping sit-down on North Atherton Street, led to the lab dropping Ordnance and adding Applied to its name to better describe its research function.

A kinder demonstration — and the first one *for* State College — occurred in the spring of 1968 when word came that Atherton Street was to be widened and all trees lining it between College and Foster Avenues would be removed. Penn State theatre arts instructor Steve Schlow, who had grown up on West Fairmount Avenue, and his longtime friend Mike Bell led students, family, and friends — nearly a thousand people altogether — to the 100 block of South Atherton and staged a "tree-in." They sat in the trees and stopped the chain saws for several hours.

Steve said in a *Town & Gown* article that he first became aware of the trees on Atherton as a ten-year-old paper boy for the *CDT*. He called the tree-in a shout of "No!" to the automobile, government, and people who work with "traffic flow" and "economics," "progress" and "increased efficiency." "Stop looking at your figures and start looking at the trees," he wrote. "There are countless paper boys, young lovers, old lovers, truck drivers, men and women, children and adults who find the well laid-out, tree-shaded street a greater affirmation of human progress than all your 'efficiency' and chrome could ever promise."

Harold Zipser, Steve's uncle, who was on Borough Council at the time, said, "I received a phone call about six in the morning from [police chief] Juba asking me to disperse my nephew and his group from the trees."

"He never stopped us," Steve said. "Larry Perez [council president] could not stop us, but finally there was the approach of chain saws." Coincidentally, the small movie theatre Steve founded, Twelvetrees Cinema, where the Atherton Hotel is today, wasn't named for the trees, but for actress Helen Twelvetrees.

Also in that period's tree activism, citizens' groups attempted to preserve the neighborhood character of Beaver Avenue by saving its trees from being uprooted by the one-way system. A 1968 proposal, for which more

than six hundred residents signed petitions, would have eliminated parking and had the cartway reduced from thirty-three to twenty-four feet. The preservation plan — offered by such central figures as Wallis Lloyd, Peirce Lewis, Steve Schlow, Catherine Bell and daughter Cathy, Carol and Jim McClure, and Rick and Cynthia Schein — failed for the most part, but did succeed in keeping the western end of Beaver Avenue tree-lined and residential. Trees don't come down easily in State College.

All the tree savers should be happy to know that in 1994 the Borough celebrated its tenth consecutive year as a National Arbor Day Foundation "Tree City USA," and is now home to six thousand street trees and between three thousand and four thousand park trees, each with a serial number. "Across the state they look to us for a lot of advice," says Borough arborist Alan Sam. "We're right up there in the number of things we do in urban forestry."

Although no student protests here approached the turmoil that occurred at Berkeley, Harvard, and Columbia, about one hundred Penn Staters did descend on the president's house the night of April 20, 1970, breaking several windows and forcing the Walkers to leave by the back door. The last to live in that oldest building on campus, Dr. Walker retired from the presidency that summer. He was succeeded by John W. Oswald, who immediately initiated rap sessions with students and earned the nickname "Jack the Rapper." He also was the first to live in the new president's residence near Boalsburg, modeled after the Connecticut farmhouse in the 1938 film "Bringing up Baby."

Campus unrest would continue until the Vietnam War was over, but this era also gave birth to one of the most productive student traditions at Penn State — raising large sums of money for community organizations and charities — beginning in 1969 with the Phi Psi 500. Sponsored by Phi Kappa Psi fraternity, this springtime mini-combination of Boston Marathon and New Orleans Mardi Gras featured as many as eighteen hundred runners on a 1.1-mile course from the fraternity house through downtown State College, stopping for a beer or soda at each of six taverns. Winner of the first "Phi Psi," as it came to be known, traveled the route in 6 minutes, 35 seconds! Non-runners could enter the event's "Almost Anything Goes" costume parade that became a replacement for the then-defunct Spring Week carnival and parade, and a favorite spectator event for local residents as well as students. The first Phi Psi netted $340 for the

At left, professor of art education Yar Chomicky, with Sid Friedman, and the first of three Calder Way murals with happy Penn State art-class members who designed and painted the work on the former CDT plant on Fraser Street.

On the parade float marking the "Happy 75th" anniversary of the Borough's incorporation in 1971 are Charles Schlow, Lawrence Perez, Jo Hays, and John Madore.

The '69 J.V. basketball "dream team" was undefeated in 20 games. 1st row: D. Finlon, M. Archer, Coach Ron Faris, S. Brackbill, L. Baughman. 2nd row: D. Axelson, T. Szeliga, B. Bollinger, D. Martin, J. Rabinowitz, E. Bengtson. 3rd row: R. Allshouse, R. Hirsch, C. Ameringer, K. Kline, T. Gianetti, J. Lux.

State High's 1969 basketball team went 20-2 in winning the Central State League championship, in a season seeing Barry Parkhill scoring 1,000 points and becoming the Little Lions' highest scoring player. 1st row: A. Sperber, T. Shaner, B. Parkhill, S. McAlexander, D. Knode, D. DeFluri. 2nd row: Coach Ted Kemmerer Jr., D. West, S. Walker, D. Harrington, J. Martin, S. Mitchell. 3rd row: Mgr. D. Baker, M. Kennett, M. Curley, S. Gemberling, M. Koehler, S. Auker, R. Bitner.

Centre County (now Centre Community) Hospital building fund; others raised as much as $25,000 for a different local cause each year. But the throngs of spectators it attracted created so many problems for State College police — traffic congestion and public drunkenness, to name two — that it was discontinued after 1992.

The IFC Dance Marathon, now the largest student philanthropic event on any college campus, was first held in 1973. Proceeds went to various charities until 1977, when its sole beneficiary became the newly created Four Diamonds Fund for children with cancer at Penn State's Milton S. Hershey Medical Center. This annual forty-eight-hour endurance contest was praised in 1983 for raising a "record" $105,000. Ten years later, the 1993 event raised more than ten times that much — $1.35 million — still a record, although the '94 and '95 marathons also broke $1 million!

Ben Resnick, who was diagnosed with cancer two months after graduating from State High in 1989, benefitted from the Four Diamonds Fund while undergoing years of treatment. In gratitude, he and his actress-mother Nan became two of the Marathon's biggest promoters, on television and in newspapers.

Another still-ongoing student philanthropy, the Sy Barash Regatta, began in April 1975, just two months after the State College advertising executive and well-liked fund-raiser it is named for died of cancer at age forty-eight. As many as 15,000 students have participated some years in raising what has amounted to nearly $400,000 for the American Cancer Society.

The 1960s marked the debuts of two local publications — the free, advertiser-supported *Town & Gown* magazine, in January 1966, and the *Pennsylvania Mirror* newspaper, in January 1968, offering some morning rivalry to the afternoon stalwart *Centre Daily Times*. *T&G* has its thirtieth anniversary in 1996, and *State College Magazine*, published by Dan and Kay Barker, celebrates its tenth anniversary. But the *Mirror*, a subsidiary of the long-running *Altoona Mirror* and first to publish a local Sunday paper in Centre County, gave up its unprofitable enterprise after ten years. One *Mirror* staffer said at the end, "We were the best-read low-circulation daily in town," referring to the penchant of office workers to buy only one copy and circulate it. The *CDT* was bought by the Knight-Ridder chain in 1979, and in 1987 became a morning newspaper published every day, including Sundays and holidays, as is now the norm for successful dailies.

Another event of the '60s that reflects the growth that was beginning to push at the seams of State College was the opening of the Elks Country Club east of Boalsburg. State College Lodge No. 1600 Benevolent and Protective Order of Elks had owned a building at 119 South Burrowes Street since 1937, but members saw a community need for the 150-acre country club, built at a cost of more than $1 million. At the time, it was one of a kind locally, a showplace with banquet and ballroom facilities, an eighteen-hole golf course, and a swimming pool.

Club president Ray Ellenberger led the ambitious project, and officers John Glatz, Vincent Fudrow, Robert McCormick, and George Lucas administered the country club for many years. Membership soared from a 1935 charter group of 61 to 1,225 on April 1, 1966, as the club neared completion. Membership in 1995 is nearly 1,900.

Now the largest contributing lodge in Pennsylvania to the Elks' Cerebral Palsy Home Care Program, the State College group has been aided since the late 1970s by State High students who annually raise money for the Elks' charity with a twenty-six-hour dance marathon that involves about 150 students.

During the frantic construction of new buildings on both sides of College Avenue in the '60s and '70s, some landmarks bit the dust. One was the Allencrest Tea Room building at Allen and Beaver, occupied for many years and on many levels by Danks department store. In 1965, Danks demolished the old building, including the Blair Shop of Gifts, and put up a new store on the same site. That building, too, was vacated in 1995 when the seventy-four-year-old Lewistown-based department store chain closed all of its stores. Danks had been a fixture in downtown State College since 1942.

A campus casualty that brought protests and tears from both students and townspeople — and still brings grumbles from long-time residents — was an even older landmark, the Armory. Built along the Mall in the 1880s, the fortress-like structure had served as gymnasium, ballroom, and military drill hall, and featured unique semicircular windows, devised by President Atherton, that were opened and closed by rotating. Unused since 1958, the Armory was razed in 1964 to add a wing of classrooms to Willard Building.

The next year, Penn State's trustees voted to raze the three English Tudor-style barns — dairy, sheep, and beef — on Shortlidge Road that had served as playgrounds and sanctuaries for many College Heights children. "Traffic congestion in that section of the campus makes it difficult to handle livestock efficiently," said a University news release.

Rae Dickson Chambers, who grew up on Hartswick Avenue, spent ten years of her childhood as a "barn kid," running barefoot through fresh straw, sliding down big sawdust piles, and befriending the animals and the herdsmen, such as Johnny "Shorty" Houser and Walter Storch, who tended them. "There was always something pleasant, fascinating, or interesting to do," Rae said, including trips across the street to the Creamery for ice cream or cottage cheese when hunger pangs struck.

Kalin Wins Beard Contest

William Kalin of State College was adjudged the owner of the most attractive beard in the contest conducted during State College Borough's Diamond Jubilee . . . by the proverbial whisker, he edged out Mayor Chauncy P. Lang.

—Centre Daily Times, 8-30-71

Mid-State Bank

n the belief that financial advice is best shared among friends, Mid-State Bank has made community involvement the cornerstone of its service-oriented banking philosophy. Mid-State employees proudly participate in major civic, charitable, and cultural organizations in the bank's market area. In so doing, they help the communities they serve, and in the process gain a better understanding of customers' needs through one-on-one interaction in informal settings.

Mid-State's dedication to community service spans three decades in Centre County, and stretches back to the turn of the century in Central Pennsylvania. Today the bank and trust company boasts twenty-nine offices in five counties, including four locations in State College (one on the Penn State campus), two in Bellefonte, and one in Pleasant Gap and Milesburg.

During its history, Mid-State Bank has continued to offer customers innovative services. The bank introduced the ATM (automated teller machine) to Centre County in 1982, and pioneered biweekly mortgages as a solution to customer needs. Recent innovations such as the KeyCheck Card, a debit card that replaces checks, have maintained Mid-State's position at the forefront of the local financial services industry.

Mid-State Bank has an on-campus branch to serve Penn State students, faculty, and staff.

One of Mid-State's buildings is along South Atherton Street.

Now affiliated with Keystone Financial, Inc., a bank holding company with assets in excess of $5 billion, Mid-State Bank is in a position to provide a full range of financial services to both individuals and businesses. Through the combined lending authority of its parent corporation, the bank serves a large commercial customer pool. Yet despite its considerable growth, Mid-State remains first and foremost a community bank. Decisions are still made on a local level to ensure that the bank remains responsive to customer needs. As it has for three decades in State College, Mid-State Bank intends not only to serve the local community, but also to be an integral part of it.

Allen Crabtree, who as a boy lived on North Burrowes Street, recalls at the age of nine joining two other youngsters for a jaunt to the barns in 1930 and happening onto veterinarian James Shigley and Dr. Samuel I. Bechdel, professor of dairy production, repeating their famous operation of 1927 — putting a "window" in the side of a cow's stomach. "The two kids I was with ran away, but I stayed," Al said. "Doc Shigley told me if I was quiet, I could come in and watch. It was an interesting, fascinating thing seeing the inside of the second Penn State Jessie."

Built in 1913 where the Ag Administration Building now stands, the dairy barn, with stucco walls, red-tile roof, and cone-topped silos, was the last of the three barns to go. Once home to prize-winning cows that supplied milk for half the town's residents, the charming structure was being used as a mail room and an apiary by the late '60s. It was standing vacant on November 14, 1969, when a devastating fire caused $75,000 damage. When second-generation "barn kid" Cathy Crabtree Wirick came to visit her parents and saw what the fire and the wrecking ball had done to the barns in that block between Curtin Road and Park Avenue, she wept and wailed, "There goes my childhood!"

One of the biggest events of any State College kid's — and grown-up's — summer began in the early 1900s, when the Alpha Fire Company held food festivals on the vacant lot at the northeast corner of Allen and Beaver. Then, in 1923, they began their annual Fourth of July carnivals, complete with rides and games, on a campus lot west of the Armory. In 1934, the firemen moved back to Allen Street, closed the 100 block to traffic, and two years later constructed a canvas canopy on steel supports custom-fitted to the contour of the street. This protected participants in the Alphas' most popular games — bingo and the horse race — and patrons of their largest food stand against unpredictable downpours that typify midsummer weather in State College. Under the canopy, all could enjoy themselves, rain or shine.

Perennial bingo-callers included banker Gene Lee, Penn State scheduling officer Ray Watkins, and speech professor and chaplain John Henry Frizzell, whose amplified voices could be heard three blocks away: "Under B . . . eight! Under O . . . seventy-three!"

The carnival generally lasted three days and was highlighted by a colorful parade featuring fire companies, bands, and drum-and-bugle corps from several counties. Alpha firemen, in uniform in the early days, manned all the games and food booths, and people strolled the block visiting with friends, listening to band concerts, buying homemade bread and pie, and, in later years, riding Garbrick's Ferris wheel and merry-go-round at the top of the street close to Beaver Avenue. Perennially popular

Against Student Vote:

Injunction Sought

Five County residents yesterday asked Centre County court to issue an injunction against the County commissioners to halt registration of out-of-County students and to nullify those registrations already taken.

The plaintiffs are Thomas G. Starkey, Margaret Y. Meyer, M. I. Claster, Max E. Hartswick and J. Daniel Getz.

They ask the court to enter a decree permanently enjoining Commissioners George C. Smith, J. Doyle Corman and Grover A. Spearly from:

— Registering any University student without ascertaining that such person meets the election code and the State Constitution.

—Centre Daily Times, 9-24-71

were the penny-pitch and fishpond games, the baseball throw ("Knock the silver dollar off the tenpin and the barrel!"), the pet show, the doll show, and the talent show.

A new era in summertime entertainment began in July 1967, when the first Central Pennsylvania Festival of the Arts opened on the closed-off 100 block of Allen Street just two weeks after the last Alpha Fire Company carnival on Allen Street had ended.

The Alphas had many reasons for moving their annual fund-raiser to the Westerly Parkway Shopping Center in 1968, with more and more professional "carnies" and less and less participation by Alpha members. Fire company president Harold Albright said that Allen Street offered them no room for expansion to accommodate the growing crowds, parking was a problem, and many younger firemen had neither the time nor the inclination to get involved with the carnival. Former fire chief Tom Sauers also cited the potential obstacle of the curb-to-curb canopy, which would have sorely hampered firemen in the event of a fire in that block. Eventually the carnival was discontinued altogether, but the firemen's contribution of a summer tradition for seventy years was appreciated by generations of area residents.

By 1974, their seventy-fifth anniversary year, the Alphas were providing fire protection for some sixty thousand people in a 132-square-mile area comprising the Borough, the University, and the townships of College, Ferguson, and Patton. Long hailed as one of the most progressive — and least expensive to maintain — fire companies in the nation, the totally volunteer unit also prided itself on the training received by members, which for many years had exceeded state requirements. This training was enhanced in 1973 with the opening of a fire-training site north of Beaver Stadium, on land donated by Penn State. That was the same year the Alphas furnished pocket beepers to their members, replacing a phone hook-up to their homes.

"When a fire call came from the dispatcher during the day, a wife who stayed home all the time would call her husband at work," said former chief Ron Ross. "Some of the firemen weren't married, so one fireman's wife would have four or five to call." Before that system there had been wailing fire sirens in neighborhoods and before that a special code on the campus power plant whistle that indicated where the fire was located.

In September 1974, the Alphas and their fire trucks moved into the new 15,400-square-foot Public Safety Building on the southwest corner of Beaver and Atherton. The structure displaced a rooming and apartment house owned by Octavio Berardis and occupied on the first floor by Les's Sub and Pizza Palace, run by his son-in-law, Les

Maroon and Gray

The Little Lion soccer team won the District
6 title in 1973. 1st row: P. Lloyd, A. Shenk,
J. Patrilak, R. Semple, M. Warner,
P. Heasley, 2nd row: M. Hopkins,
J. Langton, D. Nelson, R. Schein, S. Adams,
G. Gramley, Co-captain A. Dreibelbis,
G. Searles, M. Hess. 3rd row: L. Clewett,
All-American D. Schmidt, C. Murphy,
Co-captain J. Heimer, J. Sallade,
J. Nordbloom, R. Allshouse, C. Neff,
E. Bengtson, D. Kressen, M. Woika.
K. Fogleman was head coach.

Pennsylvania Mirror, from Scott Yocum & Ted Kemmerer, Jr.

The No. 1 high school football team in Pennsylvania, 1973— 1st row: J. Sefter, D . Harris, C. Singletary, G. Smith, C. Coder, B. Curley,
S. Rider, S. Yocum, E. Boal, D. DeLong, mgr. G. Jackson. 2nd row: asst. coach T. Kemmerer, M. Suhey, J. Rainelli, T. Fox, K. Homan,
H. Hoffman, B. Ellis, N. Frye, T. Kerr, T. Basler, N. Eldridge, T. Sallade, mgr. B. Shuey. 3rd row: tnr. M. Williams, coach J. Williams,
P. Snyder, Jr., P. Kanagy, L. Campolongo, C. Sefter, D Haffner, J. Desmond, T. Magner, B. Shafer, D. Hopkins, D. Wise, J. Wilson, P. Gill.
4th row: R. Swanger, T. Kistler, T. Gambocurta, T. Bernitt, R. Agostinelli, A. Kesler, C. Stewart, B. Henderson, B. Lopez, B. Moir, A.
Bingaman, P. Suhey, asst. coach P. Snyder. 5th row: mgr. R. Swartz, C. Hoover, R. Hochberg, A. Reethof, R. Baughman, M. Toretti,
B. Scannell, D. Coder, E. Glantz, J. Pighetti, J. Simpson, G. Ellis, asst. coaches R. Pavlechko and T. Mills.

SCCentennial Collection, from the Rotary Club

The State
College Rot-
arians again
furnished
uniforms for
the high
school
marching and
concert
bands, this
time in 1972.

Shaw. In the basement was the Bo-Mar Tavern, owned and operated by Maria Capparelli. Used originally by the fire company and the Alpha Community Ambulance Service, which has since moved to 1012 West College Avenue, the new building was constructed for a total cost of $941,535, and partially paid for by a Borough bond issue. With the Alphas now gone from the Fraser Street municipal building, the old fire hall was remodeled into Borough offices.

In 1995, again using municipal funding, the Alphas and their first (since 1992) full-time paid administrator, Walter Wise, plan to renovate the space vacated by the ambulance service and to expand their building to include: a sprinkler system throughout the structure; bunking, shower, and kitchen facilities for overnight stand-by crews to reduce response time by eliminating the need for people to drive to the station; and an exercise room to improve their physical condition and attract more volunteers.

The neighborliness of the old Alpha carnivals was recaptured in many ways by the fledgling arts festival, which ran for nine days, July 22-30, 1967. Originally sponsored by the State College Area Chamber of Commerce and Penn State's College of Arts and Architecture and called the "State College Area Arts Festival," it was — and still is — a true town-and-gown effort.

It all started in 1966, when Wallis Lloyd, then Chamber of Commerce chairman, observed the excitement created by Penn State football in the fall and wondered if another event in another season could generate similar enthusiasm. A winter carnival and a music festival were suggested. "Then we thought, 'Why restrict it to music?' " Wally said. He wrote to Gary Moyer, chairman of the Downtown Merchants Association, and Jules Heller, dean of Arts and Architecture, suggesting that there be special emphasis on art, drama, and music with exhibitions of painting and sculpture, outdoor displays, and sidewalk cafes. "One thing is certain," Wally concluded, "the University could hold an arts festival without any help from the town; I don't believe the reverse is very likely. However, I do feel that the best possible festival would result from a cooperative effort." Other pioneers in that effort were: Ruth Aikens, Bill Allison, Sy Barash, Dee Blumenthal, Yar Chomicky, Jim DeTuerk, Marie Doll, Reed Ferguson, Guy Kresge, Wirth McCoy, E. Lynn Miller, Polly Rallis, and Margot Semple.

Part of the festival that first year was set up from Allen to Pugh Streets on the sidewalk on the University side of College Avenue, with a snow fence atop the wall on which to hang artwork. There was no charge for space. "The first day only about fifty to seventy feet was used," Wally Lloyd remembers. "A few people came and hung some paint-

ings. A lot of people looked at them and bought some. When people saw that, they all rushed home, got stuff, and displayed it. After the first couple days the entire fence was filled."

Banners were hung in town and on campus; artists in action showed their skills on Allen Street; the Little German Band, the Alard String Quartet, and Robin and the Hoods rock band performed. Despite a few mix-ups, the first festival was deemed a success, and it was easier to recruit volunteers the second year.

Bill Allison and Wally Lloyd co-chaired the 1968 Festival, then Joe Curilla Jr. took on the managing-director duties for 1969 and 1970, followed by Judy Hobbs (1971, the first year the CPFA was held the first full week of July after the Fourth, as now); Gloria Newton and Toni Coleman (1972); Pat Thomas (1973-75); Marilyn Keat (1976-77); Lurene Frantz, who was managing director the longest (1978-87) and is also executive director of the Borough's centennial celebration; and David Hatfield (1988-90).

A full-time executive director, Phil Walz, arrived in 1991 to manage both the summer event and First Night®, a family-oriented New Year's Eve observance with a parade, ice sculptures, performances, and fireworks, first held December 31, 1994.

The first year of the Arts Festival also was the last for the area's first indoor pool, in the Glennland building. Built in 1934, it was well patronized by the public and was rented to Penn State for men's swimming classes and team meets each September to May and, beginning in 1947, to State College Parks and Recreation for children's and adults' swimming classes during June, July, and August.

Longtime (1945-80) *CDT* editor Jerry Weinstein, a student lifeguard at the Glennland in its inaugural year, was responsible for forming Penn State's first swim team and urging English professor Bob Galbraith to coach, which he did for many years. But after State College Borough built its first community pool in 1959 and the University built the Natatorium in 1967, the Glennland pool was no longer profitable and was replaced by offices whose mosaic tile walls of marine life are the last vestiges of the old pool.

The Chamber of Commerce first proposed an outdoor pool in the early 1950s, realizing how crowded the Glennland was becoming — seventeen hundred people were taking lessons there each summer — and how local people wanted somewhere to swim other than Whipple Dam, twelve miles south of State College. From the late 1920s until its closing in 1949, David Garver's twenty-five-foot by thirty-foot pool, The Evergreens, in front of his Centre Furnace mansion, now owned by the Centre County Historical Society, had provided the closest cool

Pediatrician To Practice In County

Dr. Richard M. Stevko . . . will establish a medical practice in pediatrics in State College early in July, occupying the offices formerly used by Dr. Tom S. Mebane.

Dr. Mebane, who has given up his practice in order to direct out-patient services at Centre Community Hospital, will, after Dr. Stevko arrives, assume his new duties with offices at the new Mountainview Unit . . .

—Centre Daily Times, 4-18-72

McDonald's

State College food service shifted into the fast lane in the late 1960s. One of the very first fast-food eateries — and the only one to last from that decade — was McDonald's, opening on November 19, 1969. In the last twenty-five years, McDonald's, now with four locations in the Centre Region, has never stopped growing in a business that always has its share of quality competition.

The person most responsible for McDonald's State College success story, Paul Rittenhouse, started his career with the company in Delaware more than three decades ago. A Brockway native, Paul had visited State College as early as 1949. When the time came for him to open his own McDonald's franchise closer to home, the borough seemed a likely place to start. Penn State's presence meant there was no shortage of burger lovers here. In partnership with his then-boss Leo Chirtel, Paul opened a McDonald's — the chain's 1,352nd — on East College across from campus.

Building up the business was difficult during the first few years, mainly because of the student exodus each summer. Hard work and perseverance paid off, however, and Paul was able to open a second McDonald's restaurant at Hills Plaza in August 1976. A third franchise location followed in 1978 at the Nittany Mall, and a fourth at North Atherton Place in 1990.

As McDonald's grew in tandem with State College, it helped many local organizations raise much-needed funds through its dollar coupon program.

Nonprofit groups such as local high school sports clubs are issued coupons good toward purchases at area McDonald's restaurants. For every dollar coupon sold, the organization receives 40 cents, with the rest covering McDonald's cost. Through this program, and such additional services as providing food for firefighters and beverages for American Red Cross blood drives, the company has shown its concern for the community it serves.

Paul Rittenhouse

Today Paul presides over his successful McDonald's franchises as owner and operator. His sons — Paul Jr., Bruce, and Eric — all serve as supervisors and plan to follow in their father's footsteps as franchisees. The four Centre Region restaurants employ nearly 300 workers, and sell about two-and-a-half million sandwiches each year — a significant contribution to the "billions sold" by McDonald's. With continued growth forecast for State College into the next century, residents can expect the same from one of the area's very first fast-food restaurants.

The first State College McDonald's at 442 East College Avenue.

173

dip for locals. Fed by the spring that made the Duck Pond, it was, as Ilene Peters Glenn of Lemont said, "always, I mean *always* cold, because by the time the sun heated the water, it wasn't safe to swim in anymore. We didn't have any of the fancy purification systems and chlorination that we do today."

In 1953, Dr. William Welch, then head of the school board, with a strong interest in building an outdoor swimming facility for the community, was appointed by Chamber president Herbert Imbt to head a study committee for the pool project. With the help of John Dittmar, director of parks and recreation, Dr. Welch set up committees to plan the construction and financing of the pool and formed the State College Area Swimming Pool Association in 1957. Herb Imbt headed the first fund drive that by the end of 1958 brought in $87,000, mainly from business and professional people. John McLucas, president of HRB-Singer, headed a second fund drive that raised $100,000, enough to give State College a swimming pool.

Builder Edwin D. "Jack" Frost, who served on Borough Council for sixteen years, was low bidder (and the only one from State College) and, as Dittmar said, "He really gave the community a break." Working feverishly, Frost's workmen completed the pool in time for its scheduled opening, July 17, 1959, on three acres of land that the Swimming Pool Association had bought from the school board. Dr. Welch was the first to swim in the pool he had worked so hard to make a reality, and which, following his death in 1967, was named in his honor.

In 1969, the pool's upkeep was taken over by Centre Region Parks and Recreation, which built a second community pool in 1970, on School Drive in Park Forest Village. The school board then began discussing an indoor pool for the high school in 1973, but it did not become a reality for almost twenty years, until 1992, and is also used by the State College YMCA. Today private and club pools abound in the area, but none was built with more community involvement than Welch Pool.

In 1967, another long-time tradition — "milk runs" to the State Store in Bellefonte — came to an end when State College got its first liquor store, in the Hamilton Avenue Shopping Center. One of its first employees was Jim Shuey, now store manager. Until Borough residents voted in the May primaries to "go wet" and allow the sale of wine and liquor within Borough limits, as they had with beer in 1934, '35 and '39, it was necessary to drive to the county seat for these supplies. A second Wine & Spirits Shoppe opened in 1974, in Patton Township's Village Square Shopping Center on North Atherton Street, and a third in

1994 in Hills Plaza on South Atherton.

The availability of liquor licenses affected numerous Borough restaurants, including The Tavern, whose founding owners, Ralph Yeager and John C. "Jace" O'Connor, called on former waiter and Penn State alumnus Walter Conti, by then a noted Bucks County restaurateur, to help them with their wine list. Because it took the Pennsylvania Liquor Control Board six weeks or more to approve a liquor-license application, the Allen Room (now the Allen Street Grill) did not sell its first liquor drink until July. One frequenter recalls the exact time: "It was the first day of the first Arts Festival!" (July 22, 1967).

New bars sprang up and, with a few refurbished ones that formerly sold only beer, did a lively business in downtown State College. In 1969, at least one contingent of thirtysomethings made the rounds every Friday night of such establishments as the Shandygaff Saloon at the rear of 212 East College Avenue; the My-O-My with its go-go girls in the basement of 128 East College Avenue; Rita's Pub in the alley next to G. C. Murphy's rear entrance; the Phyrst in the basement at 111-1/2 East Beaver Avenue; Herlocher's at 418 East College Avenue, and Teddi's, later called the Scorpion, in the rear of the downtown Elks Club.

The Phyrst, which celebrated its first countdown to St. Patrick's Day in 1968, was purchased by ex-HRB engineer Ernie Oelbermann, who started the still-popular Phyrst Phamly sing-along group in 1969 with banjo-player Terry Countermine, Terry's wife Sherry, Ben Amato, and George "Chip" Ward. There have been thirty-eight other Phamly members since then.

So interested was Don Meyer of the Autoport in acquiring one of the coveted liquor licenses that he appealed to have his family's 12.2-acre wedge of land, then in College Township, annexed by the Borough. He succeeded in 1968.

Today, according to a PLCB spokeswoman, there are twenty-two bar/restaurant liquor licenses in State College Borough plus seven hotel, one club, and two catering-club licenses. "With the 1939 quota regulation of one license per 3,000 people, those twenty-two licenses are ten more than State College should have," she says, "so you probably won't be getting any more!"

In 1969, the Borough made its last annexation of land when it took in nearly seventy-six acres belonging to Centre Hills Country Club, including the new nine holes on the south side of Branch Road.

That same year in Patton Township, the northern section of the State College bypass, now christened the Mount Nittany Expressway, was completed and work

In 1968 the Alpha Fire Company carnival moved from Allen Street to Westerly Parkway, but it never seemed to have the spark of tradition that had made the downtown carnival an annual "town reunion."

Mike Shapiro's 1974 Central Counties tennis champions are one team in 15 consecutive years that helped to earn a mention in USA Today as one of the twelve longest high school sport winning streaks. From 1968 through '79, State high boys' tennis teams won 176 matches without a loss. 1st row: Todd Lundy, Nate Levine, Art Shenk, Chris Hoover, Mark Martsolf, John Gorlow. 2nd row: Coach Shapiro, Rich Heimer, Paul Lloyd, Rich Schein, John Cox, Tom Pratt, and Assistant Coach Ron Jochen. Paul Riexner is absent.

Before this half-block became an attractive bricked walkway, pedestrians , motor vehicles, and Tavern Restaurant customers shared McAllister Alley.

175

began on the southern section in College and Harris Townships. The latter was completed by the end of 1972 but stopped just short of Centre Hills Country Club; the northern section ended in a field. Little did anyone know that it would be well into the 1980s before the 4.3-mile middle section of this four-lane, divided, interstate-type highway would be finished and the ends finally connected.

By that time, two major additions had been made to the area between State College and Bellefonte, both predicated on accessibility to the new highway. The first, which had opened at the Dale Summit "Y" in 1967, was the Nittany Mall, the area's first enclosed shopping center. By 1972, the mall housed twenty-four stores and was anchored by the W. T. Grant and Penn Traffic department stores and by new arrival Sears, which had moved from its long-time location downtown at 232 West College Avenue.

In July 1972, another traffic-generator — the Mountainview Unit of Bellefonte-based Centre County Hospital — opened just east of Beaver Stadium, and "Centre County" was changed in the hospital's name to Centre Community. The original Bellefonte hospital became the Willowbank Unit. But like the bypass, this, too, would generate arguments and hard feelings among county residents, especially later when the unpopular but financially imperative decision was made to close the Willowbank facility in Bellefonte by the end of 1978 and consolidate operations at Mountainview. State College had now "stolen" their hospital, Bellefontians charged; what would come next, the courthouse?

To gain easier access to the hospital — which at first could be reached only via Orchard Road from Puddintown or a winding farm lane from the old apple-orchard buildings past the University's sheep barns — a cloverleaf interchange and a four-lane extension of Park Avenue were drawn into plans for the middle section of the bypass. Part of the delay in finishing it was caused by the Centre Citizens Council, a three-hundred-member organization headed by Dick Garner, which opposed completion for several reasons, mostly involving the midsection's "over-design," as some people called it.

"The massive hospital interchange would dump substantial traffic onto Park Avenue," argued the council, "and is justified only by a relocated Benner Pike which may never be built." The group, whose most vocal members were Joe Carroll, Dick Kummer, Jim McClure, Vince Norris, and Susan F. Smith, also objected to a "trumpet" interchange with East College Avenue, which would have wiped out Millbrook as well as Centre Furnace Mansion and deposited "a Chinese Wall" of fill carrying the new road over Elmwood Street and East College Avenue. The council also pushed for the bike paths which were eventually incorporated into the

JOE'S DON'T GO ARMY GETS A LITTLE LARGER

Yesterday's mail brought another 91 postcards to his Recreation Building office, sending the total to 272.

In addition, more than 100 letters – some of them lengthy – dwelt on the same theme, as did scores of Christmas cards.

—Centre Daily Times, 12-30-72

bypass right-of-way. Other people wanted the midsection redesigned to less than interstate standards, with only two lanes.

At a public meeting in 1973 with the Centre Citizens Council and the Centre Region Council of Governments (COG) bypass committee, a PennDOT official remarked, "We've never had more trouble with a road than with the State College bypass! We've been unusually patient and cooperative with you, trying to come up with an acceptable design. But we will not back down on the median width or the need for four lanes. Projected traffic volume dictates four lanes; the sixty-foot grass medial strip is for safety reasons."

PennDOT was opposed to any change that would significantly delay Section 2 construction, scheduled to begin in the fall of 1973. "The highway would be out there now if it were on schedule!" the PennDOT man declared.

The Citizens Council called for an environmental impact study, which did cause a delay, but PennDOT ordered an extension of Section 1 built, for emergency vehicles only, as far as the hospital parking lot. This surprised some out-of-town football fans who drove around barriers at the north end of the bypass only to wind up at the hospital and not the stadium!

In response to a letter soliciting local officials' opinions for a 1972 *T&G* article on the bypass, Chauncey P. Lang, then mayor of State College, wrote, "When I was a boy, most people were in favor of a good road, provided the road went past their place. Now many people are opposed to good roads even if they do not go past their place and more so if they *do* go past their place."

A Penn State professor emeritus of agricultural extension, Lang had declined at first to run for mayor when the Democrats, needing a candidate, asked if they could nominate him. But he consented at the urging of his wife, Catherine, and was elected in 1966. During his eight-year tenure, COG was created to combine some municipal services for the Borough and its five neighboring townships (College, Ferguson, Halfmoon, Harris, and Patton), in 1969; the one-way system was instituted on Beaver and College Avenues, in 1972; the Borough's first public parking garage, at Pugh and Beaver, was built, also in 1972; and the Borough police force was enlarged from nineteen to thirty-three officers — one for every thousand residents. In 1994, with fifty-three officers and about 38,000 Borough residents and 20,000 people in College and Harris Townships, which contract for police services, the ratio was still the same, about 1:1,000.

To obtain reactions from younger people on various issues as they were considered, such as whether or not to build the Pugh Street parking garage, Lang created the Mayor's Regional Youth Council. "He really liked young people and was active in getting them involved in

Centre Community Hospital

ealth care in the Nittany Valley has come a long way since the six-bed Bellefonte Hospital opened in 1903 in a large frame house on Willowbank Street. During its first full year of operation, the hospital treated 101 patients at an average cost of $1.88 per day. Nearly a century later, the 200-bed Centre Community Hospital near Beaver Stadium serves a growing community in Central Pennsylvania and beyond. Now in the midst of a five-year master facilities plan, Centre Community Hospital is taking steps to ensure it remains at the forefront of health-care technology well into the twenty-first century.

Between 1906 and 1958, Bellefonte Hospital grew in concert with the communities it served. In 1927, by then known as Centre County Hospital, a new fireproof wing was added and the old building renovated, increasing capacity to forty-eight beds. Bed size was increased to seventy-nine with a $1.2 million construction project completed in 1952, and doubled to 160 beds after the 1958 addition.

An artist's drawing of the Centre County Hospital in the late '50s.

The Mountainview Unit admitted its first patient on July 26, 1972.

As the hospital grew, so, too, did the variety of services it offered. Physical therapy and intensive-care departments were added, and specialists in radiology, pathology, anesthesiology, and other fields were on staff full-time.

By the early '60s, the Centre County Hospital was unable to accommodate additional expansions. After much debate, a thirty-acre site off Orchard Road in College Township was selected for the construction of

The hospital's ambulance circa 1930.

a new facility. Ground-breaking for the Mountainview Unit of Centre County Hospital took place in July 1969, and the new five-story, 200-bed facility accepted its first patient three years later.

Renamed Centre Community Hospital, the Mountainview Unit and the Bellefonte Willowbank Unit operated as one. The financial constraints of operating two hospitals, however, suggested consolidation of the two units at Mountainview, which took place by the end of 1978.

The next few years saw further additions and enhancements to Centre Community Hospital, including the South Wing in 1981 and Health Services Wing in 1984. Paramedic services debuted in 1987, and the Jack E. Branigan Wing opened in 1989 with a new emergency facility. Meanwhile, cardiac care and cancer-treatment services expanded, diagnostic imaging and computerized laboratory equipment were added, and a sleep lab and special birthing rooms were introduced.

As part of its current $16-million master-facilities plan, the hospital will add more private rooms, a new labor-delivery-recovery unit, plus other patient-care improvements. At the nearby Centre Medical Sciences Building, the new Centre Community Surgical Center, Inc. (a separate nonprofit corporation), specializes in same-day surgical procedures. The building also houses the hospital's Breast Care Center, X-ray and lab facilities, and the Cardiopulmonary Rehab and Wellness Center. With continued growth forecast for the region, it seems only a matter of time before Centre Community Hospital expands again.

politics," said Dan Chaffee, who had been chairman of the youth council as a State High student and served as an elected Borough councilman from 1980 to 1988. "That youth council is how I got involved in politics," Dan continued. "He also was the first mayor to recognize that State College was a changing community and that it needed more professionals in local government," citing the mayor's decision to give control of the police department to the full-time Borough manager.

Borough Council had created the borough-manager form of administrative government in 1945, passing an ordinance on March 5 over the veto of Burgess Albert Yougel. First to hold the job was Hugh B. Rice, followed by Robert Y. Edwards in 1948; Frederick Fisher in 1965; Carl Fairbanks in 1969; and Peter Marshall in 1986.

In 1970, John Juba retired after thirty-one years as chief of police and was succeeded briefly by Herbert Straley Jr., who proclaimed, "Any police department can fight crime for crime's sake, but the real problem today is to fill our responsibility to *prevent* crime." Sometimes the zealous chief went overboard in trying to fulfill his pledge. After one Penn State football victory, students began tossing water balloons from apartment balconies along East Beaver Avenue. Chief Straley tried to stop them by turning on his car's public-address system and announcing, "I'm coming in to arrest the next person who throws a water balloon!" At that moment a huge water-filled garbage bag, not a balloon, fell from the sky and landed on his patrol car, knocking off its emergency lights and soaking the chief. Straley resigned shortly thereafter and Elwood G. Williams Jr., who had been with the force since 1961, was promoted to chief in 1974. But post-game celebrations, some reaching riot proportions, continued to plague Borough police into the mid-'90s. The stresses of increased student population also led to stricter Borough ordinances on noise, housing, and trash removal. And environmental concerns led to the current effective Borough sign ordinance, developed at Borough Council request after considerable public discussion and preceding creation of the Borough's Community Appearance and Design Review Board.

Meanwhile, at State College High, Jim Williams, former Little Lion (and later Nittany Lion) center under Coach Bill Leonard in the 1950s, took over the football coaching reins from Hal Wausat in 1969. Over the next eight seasons, until he joined Paterno's staff in 1977, Jim's teams compiled a 65-13 record, including a 36-game winning streak beginning with the final game of 1970 and running into the middle of the 1974 season. Under his

direction, State College won the mythical Pennsylvania state title in 1973 and became recognized as one of the top programs in the Keystone State, with many Williams-coached players earning collegiate grants-in-aid. Many played at Penn State, including Larry, Paul, and Matt Suhey, sons of Penn State All-American Steve Suhey and Virginia "Ginger" Higgins, daughter of former Penn State coach Bob Higgins. Matt also played professional football with the Chicago Bears, becoming well-known as *the* blocker for record-setting Walter Payton.

Also during Williams's tenure, in 1973, '74, and '75, Bellefonte was dropped from State College's schedule for the first time since the rivalry had begun in 1920. The Red Raiders came back on the 1976 schedule but were dropped again, in 1986, this time by Williams's successor, Ron Pavlechko who, in 1991, decided to resume the Iron Kettle contest. In 1992, under Coach Pavlechko, the Little Lions went undefeated and made it to the semifinals of the PIAA state championships before losing to Upper St. Clair. The following year, they lost to Bellefonte, too, sending the Kettle up the Benner Pike for the first time since 1968. But in 1994, it made its way back to the State High trophy case.

Jo Hays, former school superintendent and state senator, succeeded Chauncey Lang as mayor for one term (1974-78), winning over long-time State College Borough Council President Lawrence Perez. A civil engineering professor, Larry is known as "the father of Stone Valley Recreation Area." Jo, for whom a vista atop Tussey Mountain on the way to Stone Valley is named, was State College's first mayor to serve under the home-rule charter, which changed the mayor's responsibilities. He remained as ceremonial head of government but became presiding officer of council without a vote, yet with the power to veto ordinances. During his tenure, he also banned smoking in the council chambers of the municipal building, putting him in the vanguard of a trend that would gain momentum over the next two decades.

Although Philadelphia was the first city in Pennsylvania to adopt home rule (with a strong mayor), in 1952, State College became the first borough to operate under a mayor-council home-rule charter (with a weak mayor charged with a leadership role), beginning January 1, 1976. Eighty-four percent of the voters said "yes" to that form of government which, according to its charter, "will be the most responsive to the needs and desires of this Borough, both now and in the future." Heading the State College Government Study Commission which prepared

*Whitehall Road was extended to meet University Drive at South Atherton Street in 1975. The erstwhile
A&W Drive-In, foreground, was one of the few commercial buildings close to the intersection.*

the charter were Elizabeth Smedley, chairman; Jo Hays, vice chairman; and James M. Rayback, secretary.

Since 1894, when the State College Woman's Club did its first good deed for the village that was not yet a borough, volunteerism has been a zealous avocation for most people in State College — some say it may even be the heart of our town. The Central Pennsylvania Festival of the Arts would never happen without volunteers and annually attracts the most, more than 1,000, while charities, clubs, service organizations, and support groups for nearly any illness or disease known to man also benefit from the time and talents of countless residents every year.

In 1974, Ann Cook and others from the American Association of University Women (AAUW), founded the matchmaking service that now recruits and places volunteers with about seventy-five to eighty agencies — the Voluntary Action Center, renamed Volunteer Center of Centre County (VCCC) in 1994. Since opening its doors in Mary Foster's former home at 409 South Allen Street (its present location is 1524 West College Avenue), VCCC has referred nearly 11,000 people who have given more than 163,000 hours in service to the community.

One of the emerging social services of the time was the Centre County Women's Resource Center, founded in 1975. Three years later it merged with the Task Force on Domestic Violence and the Rape Crisis Center. In 1982, the State College-based center opened a shelter for battered women and their children at its new headquarters, 140 West Nittany Avenue.

Penn State professor emerita Rose Cologne, known to many as "the queen of volunteers" and "the founding mother," moved to State College in 1941 and for more than fifty years devoted her life to finding gaps in human services, filling them, funding them, getting other people fired up about them, and then moving on to fill another gap. Saying in 1992 that she did not "found most area agencies because nobody does it alone," she nevertheless was instrumental in starting VCCC, Habitat for Humanity, Centre County Council for Human Services, Meals on Wheels, Keystone Legal Services, International Hospitality Council, Community Alternatives in Criminal Justice, Counseling Service, Home Health Services, Child Development Council, Adult Education Association, Interfaith Mission, Center for Independent Living, Penn State's Volunteer Service Center, and the Penn State chapter of Delta Delta Delta sorority, to name a few!

In 1971, the year State College observed its seventy-fifth anniversary as a borough, Sidney Friedman, who in 1942 had proposed to his wife, Helen, in a booth at the Corner Room, bought the booth — for sentimental

reasons, he said. He, along with Russell Adamitz and William Ulerich, whose interests now belong to Sidney's sons Ron and Ed Friedman, also bought the Corner Room, the Hotel State College, and the buildings on either side of it.

This most significant of State College landmarks was not the first piece of downtown real estate Sidney had owned. He had bought the first in 1953, but his career as downtown developer began in earnest in 1959, when he replaced about a dozen old houses in the east end of town with the Campus Shopping Center. He and his sons now hold title to sizable chunks of an area stretching from Garner Street on the east to Burrowes Street on the west, between College Avenue and Calder Alley, which was renamed Calder Way at his request in 1977, following his award-winning beautification projects. Friedman properties house more than one hundred commercial tenants in such places as the Metzger Building on South Allen Street; the Fye Building at 200 West College Avenue; the former *Centre Daily Times* offices and printing plant on South Fraser Street, which Sidney turned into the Fraser Street Mini-Mall; the Cathaum Theatre building; and Calder Square I and II, in the alley behind The Tavern.

Born in Altoona, Sidney Friedman came to State College in 1938, when he enrolled as a freshman at Penn State and to earn money opened a bicycle rental agency and managed a sandwich shop, the Blue and White Restaurant, in part of what is now The Tavern. He later sold advertising for the *Centre Daily Times*, and in 1945 was the first commercial manager of radio station WMAJ.

He also started Commercial Printing in 1948 and five years later founded a sign business, Nittany Advertiser, for which he recruited Sy Barash as a partner in 1953. In 1959, Sy and wife Mimi bought it from him and merged it with Morgan Signs a year later.

Sidney also accomplished something unprecedented in State College history when he convinced Borough Council to relocate a street, and talked a homeowner, Sarah Kauffman, into moving her house from what is now the intersection of Garner Street and East College Avenue. That was back in 1959, when he had bought a number of properties in the vicinity of his printing plant to build the Campus Shopping Center. "In those days Garner Street stopped at Beaver Avenue and from there an alley angled down to College Avenue and came out next to what was then the Nittany Dell restaurant," he said. "By putting Garner through to College, a real traffic bottleneck was eliminated."

State College Council Asks Bypass Delay

An otherwise routine meeting of State College Borough Council last night was enlivened in its closing minutes when Councilman James McClure asked for a clarification of the stand of the present council on the question of the State College bypass and introduced a motion asking for delay of the completion of the bypass . . .

In a straight party vote, the motion passed 5-2, with Democrats Ingrid Holtzman, Dean Phillips, Alan Patterson and Richard Kummer voting with Democrat McClure, while Council President Arnold Addison and E. D. Frost, both Republicans, voted against the motion.

Councilman Frost moved to table the motion, but no Democrat offered a second. The 5-2 vote was then cast.

—*Centre Daily Times, 7-2-74*

Lions Gate Apartments

With an optimistic feeling about State College's future and the potential of the local university market, New York native Stephen Barkin came to town in the 1970s searching for real-estate investment opportunities. He found what he was looking for in the 239-unit Whitehall Plaza complex off Waupelani Drive, since renamed Lions Gate Apartments. Though neglected by its former owners and in need of repair, the complex, with its spacious grounds and unusually large apartments, possessed great potential. Stephen bought the property and set about replacing and renovating everything. Today the success of his efforts is measured in Lions Gate's occupancy rate, which has been at or near 100 percent for twenty-five years.

Comprising seventeen three-story buildings on thirteen attractively landscaped acres, Lions Gate is one of the biggest apartment complexes in State College. Its residents, about three quarters of whom are Penn State people, enjoy on-site tennis and basketball, and are permitted to keep pets. Lions Gate offers tenants a level of roominess and privacy difficult to find downtown, yet is near Westerly Parkway Plaza shopping and within easy reach of the university.

Aside from its first-rate facilities, much of Lions Gate's success can be attributed to its owner's fair and honest approach toward renters. Security deposits are promptly returned, and a concerned resident manager is always on hand to deal with any problems that may arise. Redecoration and maintenance continues on a daily basis to ensure that apartments remain in top condition. For Stephen Barkin, it's all part of doing business in a town where quality, affordable housing is always in high demand.

Lions Gate Apartments feature beautifully landscaped, spacious grounds and large apartments.

Jo Hays got "a few laughs" when he told a group of retirement-age citizens that "State College is a good place to retire, but if you don't like young people, don't come here!"

The acquisition of Co-op Corner in 1971 marked the revitalization of the central business district, which had begun to deteriorate. "About that time," Sidney said, "this downtown was dying a fast death. More and more stores were moving or going out of business — Metzger's, the Athletic Store, Keeler's, Woolworth's, Schlow's, Rea and Derick, Western Union. Movie theatres were barely operating, and the Nittany Theatre, which students had dubbed 'The Armpit,' was closed during every University vacation. The Corner Room was closing earlier and earlier, and there was even talk of tearing down the hotel."

Symbolic of the old that was fading away with the downtown slump was the closing in 1973 of Hoy Brothers general merchandise store at 324-28 West College Avenue, after forty years in business. The town/gown hangout had sold at one time or another everything from canned soup and handmade soft drinks to propane gas and overalls.

The downtown's first "mall" occurred in this era as a result of the demolishing in 1969 and subsequent rebuilding in 1970 of the main office of Peoples National Bank (now Omega Bank) at 117 South Allen Street. While its new building was under construction, Peoples operated out of the Metzger Building's vacant first floor and basement across Calder Alley. The space was then rented to a group of "hippie"-run businesses that formed a rabbit warren/mini-mall they called Peoples Nation, deriving the name from scratching off "al" and "Bank" from the gilt window sign. Peoples Nation merchants carried such items as Frank Zappa posters, beads, Indian fabric, and art supplies, the latter sold by "Uncle Eli." Douglas Albert, the sole survivor of Peoples Nation still in business today in downtown State College, says, "I opened Uncle Eli's in July 1970 and moved three times in five years until settling in at my present location, 129 East Beaver Avenue." Doug, who also has an art gallery at 107 McAllister Alley, across from the Tavern Restaurant, adds, "Peoples Nation lasted about three years, but I moved out after six months."

While the downtown was changing to keep up with changing times and population, so were other parts of the State College area. The school district built a second junior high school, in Park Forest Village, in 1971, after which

the *CDT* remarked, "Over half the district's present 14 schools were built in the last 20 years to accommodate the remarkable growth of both the University population and the school district." A school teacher's starting salary then was $6,700.

The opening of Interstate 80 in 1970, with its closest exits at Milesburg and Bellefonte, brought more of the outside word to what people were beginning to call "Happy Valley." Then, in 1973, Allegheny Airlines, soon to be renamed USAir, established commuter service at University Park Airport, connecting State College with Pittsburgh, Harrisburg, and Washington, D.C., several times a day.

In October 1973, The *Centre Daily Times* moved from 119 South Fraser Street, across from the State College Municipal Building, where it had been since 1940, to its present site in College Township next to Corning Asahi. It also converted from hot-metal letterpress to offset printing. "Today's edition," wrote Editor Jerome Weinstein in the "Good Evening!" column for Saturday, October 13, "is the last to be published by the letterpress method, which hasn't really changed a great deal since Gutenberg's time."

In 1974, mass transit arrived once again with the birth of the Centre Area Transportation Authority (CATA), thanks to the efforts of Penn State transportation specialists Joe Carroll and Jim Miller and Borough councilman Jim McClure. Soon, orange and white buses were connecting students, workers, and shoppers from the suburbs with the classrooms, offices, and businesses of the campus and downtown, and Miller served on the CATA board of directors and was its chairman from 1982 until 1995.

By the nation's bicentennial, when Penn State commissioned the writing of an opera entitled "Be Glad Then, America," some residents of this area were ready to sing "Be Glad Then, State College." Others, wistfully remembering the small town that had been, were not so ready to move into the future.

Chauncey Lang
Mayor 1966-1973

Jo Hays
Mayor 1974-77

William Lower
Fire Chief 1966-71

State College
Mayors, Fire
and Police Chiefs
1966 to 1976

Ronald Ross
Fire Chief 1972-78

Herbert Straley Jr., Police Chief 1970-74,
is flanked by the Police Department.

Sgt. Thomas Hart with
Elwood G. Williams Jr., Chief of Police 1974-93

Coming of Age
&
Heading for
the Future

*C*oming up on its centennial year in 1996, the Borough is showing signs of age but is still a youngster at heart, full of pep and enthusiasm and wide-eyed hope for the future. Its growth has stabilized, but the townships that surround it are burgeoning with former Borough residents, Penn State alumni, and newcomers attracted by publicity State College received in the 1980s and '90s: Rand McNally's *Places-Rated Retirement Guide* — twelfth-best place in the U.S. for retirees (1983); *Psychology Today* — number-one stress-free city (1988); *Changing Times* — one of the top ten "supersafe" communities to live (1992); *New Choices* — an ideal place to retire, "an attractive climate, excellent health care, lots of cultural and sports activities, access to an airport, and a thriving community inhabited by people of all ages" (1993); *Money* — one of the "300 Best Places to Live" (1987-94) and NBC's "Today"— one of the best places to retire (1995). In addition, *Expansion Management* magazine, aimed at helping managers make decisions about where to relocate their companies, rated the State College Area School District third in the nation for 1993, based on high-school graduation rates, average college-board scores, student-teacher ratio, and other factors. And a national arts magazine, *Sunshine Artist*, ranked the Central Pennsylvania Festival of the Arts as one of the U.S.'s twenty most prestigious arts-and-crafts shows.

In the mid-1990s, many observers feel that Penn State has become one of the top ten public research universities in the nation, just as Bryce Jordan vowed it would be when he assumed the presidency in 1983. *U.S. News and World Report* continually ranks it as one of "America's Best National Universities." Its Nittany Lion sports teams, which had been powerhouses as far back as the 1920s, were attracting more and more national attention and winning more and more national championships, even before joining the Big Ten in 1990. The most highly touted successes were the football team's national titles in 1982 and 1986 and its Big Ten championship for 1994, when the Rose Bowl hosted the Lions for the first time since 1923. Lady Lion sports, especially basketball, field hockey, and gymnastics, and State High girls' teams, particularly cross-country, were winning national and state titles of their own as well as legions of fans.

In the late 1970s, the ambiance of State College, that "sleepy little college town" remembered from youthful student days, was attracting hundreds of alumni looking for an ideal retirement setting. In recognition of this, two new continuing-care facilities were built — Brookline Village, north of Hills Plaza in College Township in 1985, and Foxdale Village, at 500 Marylyn Avenue, on the south edge of the Borough, in 1987, each with apartments, rooms, and a nursing-home facility. These complexes added to the services for the elderly already available in the Borough, including University Park Nursing Center, which was started by Philadelphia developers as Parkwest Manor Nursing Home in 1966, and Renaissance, a residential care facility within Parkway Plaza Apartments since 1982.

Heading the University in 1976 was John Oswald, about halfway through his thirteen-year tenure as Penn State's thirteenth president, while presiding over the town was Mayor Jo Hays. Since graduating from Penn State in 1923, Jo had been State High principal, supervising

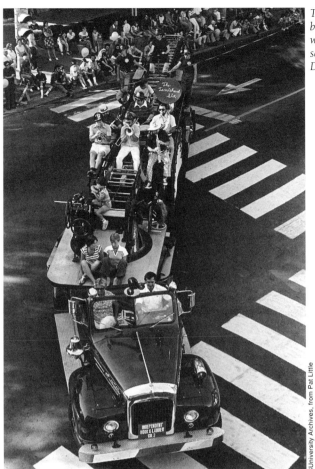

The Tarnished Six had already climbed the ladder of Dixieland band success when they were featured in this 1977 parade. They were cornetist Jim Ressler, trombonist Roger Munnell, saxophonist Johnnie Thomas, banjoist Phil Cartwright, drummer Dick Greene, and sousaphonist John Kovalchik.

State High's first state soccer championship came in 1976. The yearbook reports that "A lucky penny, found by Coach Fogleman, sparked the team to a stupendous win over arch-rival Middleburg, 3-2," assuring it a place in the PIAA play-offs, where it defeated North Allegheny and Bethlehem-Freedom for the title.
Seated: Co-captains M. Cunningham, D. Rung. 1st row: K. Huntley, C. Johnson, D. Brewer, D. Shelow, B. Langton, J. Infield, C. Gill, S. Muthersbaugh. 2nd row: Coach K. Fogleman, mgr. B. Bloom, W. Gotshalk, J. Harpster. T. Frey, J. Guthrie, D. Pearce, D. Beik, C. Schein, asst. coach D. Wagner. 3rd row: mgr. S. Harding, S. Ergler, E. Diethorn, D. DeMartino, R. Moore, T. Brush, J. Harper, J. Hettema, mgr. C. Marro.

Organist Ken Pahel played banjo with Ernie Coleman's piano accompaniment, entertaining an early meeting, in 1976, of the Senior Center at the Christian Church on Easterly Parkway.

A home at 141 East Fairmount Avenue that had given long service to a succession of State College residents was carefully refurbished and preserved by Brian White in 1980, becoming a dental office for him and his associates.

principal (now called superintendent) of State College schools, and state senator, before being elected mayor for the 1974-78 term. Following him, from 1978 to 1994, was Arnold Addison, who has the longest mayoral tenure in State College history and was active in local government for nearly thirty-five years. He began in 1957 as chairman of the police civil service commission, then served eighteen years on Borough Council (1960-78), and was council president in 1974 and '75. His "real" job for most of that time was as personnel director of Applied Research Lab and Penn State professor of industrial engineering.

Among Arnold's accomplishments as mayor were creating the Student Leadership Task Force, whereby he met monthly with student leaders to discuss issues and problems, and the Municipal Intern Program, in which Penn State undergraduates earned college credit for participating in and working with local government. "I think the biggest thing I've done as mayor has been in the public relations area," he said nearing the end of his tenure. "I've concentrated a great deal of effort on town-and-gown relations."

Home Rule Charters Take Effect

It's a whole new world in State College today. On this, its second day of existence under the new home rule charter, it's no longer a Borough — it's a Municipality.

The voice that answered the "city hall" telephone today said "State College Municipal Building" rather than "State College Borough."

—Centre Daily Times, 1-2-76

Well, the Incredible Finally Happened

No news is good news to some people, but certainly not to people in the newspaper business.

Every day The Times holds space open on several pages of the paper for traffic accidents, thefts, criminal mischief, etc., from the State College bureau of police services.

Well, it finally happened — absolutely nothing happened in State College last night.

So how is a newspaper supposed to fill that news hole when there is no news?

We just did. — **brian weakland**

—Centre Daily Times, 3-13-76

He also wrote a how-to guide on being mayor that he dedicated to Jo Hays; annually updated a booklet called *ABCs of Local Government*; and, for the Borough's centennial, wrote a book entitled *In the Service of This Borough*. Like his predecessors, Mayor Addison handled citizens' appeals of parking tickets and fines for failure to remove snow and weeds — nearly six hundred annually — issued proclamations such as that in support of the American Cancer Society's Smoke Out, cut ribbons, and spoke as the Borough's representative at events like the Arts Festival.

The current mayor, Bill Welch, refers parking ticket supplicants to the proper people and has not yet vetoed any legislation, the only real power the largely ceremonial job has. Arnold's use of that authority may be the one way he upset the most people. In 1989, he vetoed a fair-housing ordinance that would have banned discrimination only in cases involving traditional factors, such as race, religion, and sex. He said it was not broad-based enough to protect against discrimination in housing for *all* citizens, such as gays, lesbians, and

Uni-Marts, Inc.

ou don't have to look far in State College for signs of a local success story. Since Uni-Marts opened its first convenience store in the Ambassador Building on Garner Street in 1972, it has enjoyed phenomenal growth. Now with thirty-five stores in Centre County and a total of almost 420 stores in six mid-Atlantic states, Uni-Marts shows no signs of letting up.

Uni-Marts' accomplishments have been due in no small part to the efforts of company founder Henry D. Sahakian, who came to State College in 1956 to pursue a mechanical engineering degree at Penn State and today is company CEO and chairman of the board. In 1962, he established Unico Corporation, a local real estate development and management company that later became the parent corporation for Uni-Marts. After the first store opened, others followed under a franchise arrangement with a major convenience-store chain. By 1976, there were thirty stores in the Centre County area, and in 1977 thirty-two additional locations were acquired, expanding operations into Southern New Jersey, Delaware, and Eastern Pennsylvania. In 1981, with eighty-nine stores, the chain terminated its franchise agreement and began operating independently, under the name of Uni-Marts.

Ensuing years saw continued growth as the company expanded into Western Pennsylvania, New York,

From gasoline to food products, Uni-Marts provides fast and convenient services.

Virginia, and Maryland. In 1986, with 208 stores, Uni-Marts spun off from Unico and sold an initial public offering of two million shares of common stock, raising capital for further growth into the '90s. In 1994, Uni-Marts was featured on the CNBC series *Profiles of America*, a fine feather in its cap. The company recently reported two successive years of record growth, with net earnings of more than $3.6 million for the fiscal year ending September 30, 1994.

Today Uni-Marts still maintains its corporate headquarters in downtown State College, and employs approximately 350 people at its Centre County general office and convenience stores. A portion of its mission statement, which reads in part, "We will build good public relations, be responsible 'citizens,' and maintain a positive image in the communities we serve," is nowhere more true than where Uni-Marts began. Through its stores, employees, and corporate benevolence, Uni-Marts supports a number of worthy causes: volunteer, health, and emergency-care organizations, youth and disabled services, athletics and educational scholarship funds, public safety, the arts, and public broadcasting services.

Uni-Marts is in the midst of a three-year, $25-million capital expenditures program that encompasses constructing new stores, remodeling existing locations, and upgrading gasoline-dispensing facilities. It has also formed alliances with Burger King, Blimpie Subs, and other fast-food giants to provide customers with the convenience of fast-food service at several locations. With recent record earnings and ambitious plans for the coming years, the little convenience store chain that started in downtown State College has unquestionably made it big.

Henry D. Sahakian, Chairman of the Board and Chief Executive Officer of Uni-Marts, Inc.

The Nittany Valley Symphony rehearsed works from Eastern Europe in Eisenhower Auditorium in September 1990 under then-conductor Barbara Yahr. Michael Jinbo now conducts.

unmarried couples. In 1993, council passed a more definitive housing ordinance surpassing federal requirements, thus avoiding an Addison veto.

Prior to that event, in January 1993, Arnold announced his decision not to seek a fifth term, but he wanted to continue actively as chairman for the Borough's upcoming centennial celebration "if the borough council and the new mayor will let me." They did. He also was honored in the naming of Arnold Addison Court, a new eighty-nine unit high-rise at 120 East Beaver Avenue, in the heart of downtown. In-

WOMEN'S RIGHTS: About 400 persons marched through State College Saturday to celebrate "Equal Rights for Women Day" and to express support for the Equal Rights Amendment.

—Centre Daily Times, 3-15-76

tended for low- and medium-income residents age fifty-five and older and the disabled, the building was planned and begun during his tenure and opened in 1994. It was the first public-private housing partnership in the Borough.

Bill Welch, former executive editor and general manager of the *Centre Daily Times* and son of the doctor for whom Welch Swimming Pool was named, was elected mayor in 1993. Although born in Philadelphia while his dad was in medical school, he is a true mix of Bellefonte

(his mother, Betty Woomer Welch Bice, was born there) and State College (his grandfather came to work in Dairy Extension at Penn State in 1917), and has lived here since age two, mostly in College Heights. He now is editor of the American Philatelic Society's monthly magazine but also keeps office hours as mayor two afternoons a week. In keeping with the leadership role defined under the Home Rule Charter, Bill, like his predecesssors, convenes meetings with citizen groups, is a frequent speaker, performs weddings, and acts as "mayor" wherever asked in the Centre Region.

When announcing his decision to run during the midst of a three-year study and discussion about the Borough's consolidating with the surrounding townships, Bill suggested that the new municipality created by that move be named Atherton, since the street runs through all but one of the Centre Region member territories. That name-change is a throwback to a suggestion made in 1906, and he is not its only supporter.

An area native was chief of police from 1974 to 1993. Elwood Williams Jr., it was said, "took the State College Police from Mayberry to Metropolis." Hired as a patrolman in 1961, he professionalized the department as chief

Jostens Printing & Publishing

nyone who's ever bought a class ring or yearbook is familiar with the Jostens name, but few people realize the true extent of the multifaceted company's operations. For nearly a century, Jostens has been synonymous with quality school products. The company began manufacturing class rings in 1906 and later branched out into graduation announcements, diplomas, yearbooks, sports rings, caps and gowns, educational resources, and school photography. Today Jostens is a Fortune 500 corporation encompassing six major operating divisions with thirty-six plant and office facilities in the United States, Canada, and England. From its State College printing plant at 401 Science Park Road, the company produces yearbooks for schools from Ohio to Maine. And with a growing commercial-printing business and recent expansion into short-run book manufacturing, it continues to expand its publishing expertise.

Jostens traces its history to a small jewelry and watch-repair shop opened in Owatonna, Minnesota, by Otto Josten in 1897. After years of gradual growth as a supplier of class rings to Midwest schools, the company built its first manufacturing plant in 1930. Jostens expanded into the yearbook field in 1950, by which time annual sales had reached $5 million. By the mid-'60s, the company became the industry leader in class rings, and by the late '60s was the leader in yearbooks.

Now with annual sales in excess of $825 million, Jostens employs more than 8,000 workers and 1,200 independent sales representatives. Besides class rings, yearbooks, and other school products, the company manufactures technology-based educational software, customized business-performance and service awards, sports awards, and customized affinity products. It has produced most of the rings for the Super Bowl since 1966 as well as for NFL conference championship, Stanley Cup, World Series, and other championship teams.

Known primarily for yearbooks, Jostens also prints a variety of history books for clubs, churches, and towns.

Jostens' presence in State College dates to fall 1972, when it opened its Science Park Road printing plant. The bulk of the facility's work — some 90 percent — involves printing yearbooks for schools, colleges, and universities in the Northeast. Jostens' local plant produces about 2,300 different yearbooks, half of which are distributed in Pennsylvania, including those for most of Centre County's high schools. The remainder of Jostens' State College products focus on commercial printing plus short-run trade and textbook manufacturing. Commercial products include *State College the Magazine*, the *Beaver Stadium Pictorial*, magazines, brochures, and town histories. Book products include scientific/technical publications, monographs, scholarly journals, children's books, and collectibles.

With approximately 550 workers at its State College plant, Jostens is an important Centre Region employer. Through programs such as its Total Quality Involvement Process, an employee-training and evaluation program, the company improves its printing processes and overall product quality. As its local operation continues to grow and prosper, Jostens builds on its century-old reputation for excellence.

Jostens has been a fixture along Science Park Road since 1972.

to meet the needs of our growing community, creating, among other things, the centralized record-keeping and communications systems now used by Centre Region departments. He also came up with the idea of having the townships contract with the Borough for police services and disband their own municipal forces. College Township adopted the plan in 1975 and Harris in 1981.

"Junior," as Elwood has been called most of his life, attributed his success to his education (an associate degree in community service from Penn State) and his training at the hands of his early mentor, Sergeant Oakey F. Brown, a thirty-three-year veteran of the force who died of cancer in 1981. When Chief Williams started, most officers had no more than high school diplomas. Today the average officer has three years of college, and some have advanced degrees.

Chief Williams retired in 1993 to head the Centre County Office of Emergency Communications (911), and his successor, Chief Thomas R. King, a twelve-year veteran of the force, took command of fifty-four officers and eighteen civilians. Shortly after being sworn in as chief, Tom instituted patrolling on bicycles for some officers, citing easier movement in traffic and closer, friendlier involvement with the public than is possible with officers in cars.

For about thirteen years police headquarters had been a house at 134 South Fraser Street, but since 1979, it has occupied half of the municipal building's first floor. There are seventeen police cars, marked and unmarked. The department is computerized and has access to the latest cast-making, fingerprinting, and photographic equipment, a far cry from Albert Yougel's days, when they had little more than a desk, a filing cabinet, a typing table, and a fingerprint kit in one small room in the old fire hall.

Borough ordinance enforcement officers now do many of the tasks once the responsibility of the police — checking sidewalks, weeds, parking meters, and complaints about stray dogs — while the State College Borough Police Department responds to some 18,000 calls annually. One of their busiest weekends was during the 1987 Arts Festival, when they received 287 complaints and issued more than 400 tickets for illegal parking.

Another memorable moment was during an Iron Kettle football game between State College and Bellefonte when police rounded up about twenty high school students, boys and girls alike, for throwing eggs, locked them all up, and started calling parents. Chief Williams recalled, "I can remember one parent giving us all kinds of hell, saying, 'How could you *think* of locking up boys and girls together?' It wasn't what they had been *doing*, it was just how terrible it was that *we locked them up together!*

"We have a quiet community here with a very low crime rate," he went on. "In my thirty-two years on the force there was only one time a gun was fired in the line of duty by an officer." That was about twenty-five years ago, when burglars were fleeing the area's first modern-day discount store, the Town & Country, in what was then called the University Shopping Center on Westerly Parkway. An officer fired at the escape vehicle, shooting out one of the tires.

First woman to join the force was Barbara May, in 1973, after which time the police*man* designation was changed to police officer. Five years later, Ingrid Holtzman became the first woman president of Borough Council, although she was the fourth woman to serve on that body. First had been Gladys Tanner (1952-60), followed by Helen Albrecht (1960-62) and Hanna Lattman (1962-63). In 1995, four of the seven Borough Council members were women: Janet Knauer, Felicia Lewis (who previously served 1981-85), former Council president Ruth Lavin (1990-92), and current president Jean McManis.

Only one Penn State president ever served on Borough Council — Eric Walker, who was elected twice, 1948-50 while he was director of Applied Research Lab, and 1956-60, while heading the University. His close friend, civil engineering professor Larry Perez, was elected in 1958 and served until 1974, fourteen of those years as president — a record. Larry was also acting mayor for four months in 1967 and '68 during Chauncey Lang's tenure. Other long-time Councilmen were prominent general contrac-

Scholastic baseball state
champions in 1979 were these
State College team players:
1st row: Mgr. Robin Stump,
Pete Zucco, Chris Palazzari,
Randy Gibbs, Vince Brush,
Mgr. Linda Burgess. 2nd row:
Bill Ferrara, Bob Zonts,
Dave Weakland, Doug Fasik,
Bob Perks, Tim Sweitzer,
Doug Wagner, Darryl Scrudders.
3rd row: Coach Pat Snyder,
Mike Sullivan, Mike Weakland,
C. J. Sichler, Perry Wilson,
Mark Bernlohr, Dave Hall,
Coach Ken Barto.

Girls' track and field at
State College High School brought
home the 1978 PIAA trophy.
1st row: Kelly Jo Homan,
Tina Gardiner, Cindy Sterling,
Kathy Hettmansperger,
Martha White, Lisa Dignazio.
2nd row: Paula Froke,
Terry Sweitzer, Laurie Upshaw,
Hope Shaw, Beth Heinsohn,
Kelly Myers. 3rd row:
Coaches Hubie White and
Steve Gentry, Denise Games,
Stacy Barber, Sally Bingaman,
Bev Pazur, Carolyn Allison,
Cindy Wambold, Ann Infield.

Another State High team — this softball aggregation — brought back a PIAA title, in 1978.
Kneeling: Cari MacElwee, Beth Hoss, Nan Barash, B. J. Pennabaker, Janet Adams,
Mary Langton, Karen Moyes, Suzy Simmet, Audrey Horner. Standing: Coach Barry Rossman,
Daphne Robb, Dee Jaye Brown, Jenny Gladfelter, Leslie Hoy, Carolyn Sarson, Elaine Gebhard,
Dee Marrara, Cindy Webb, Lorrie Campbell.

A row of motorcycles in spaces for motorcycles on East College Avenue made a statement of the times in 1983.

tor Edwin D. "Jack" Frost, 1960-76, and long-time HRB vice president Philip J. Freed, 1958-69.

Schools had changed a lot by the mid-1970s. There were two junior high schools, one on Westerly Parkway, the other in Park Forest Village, and students were assigned to the one closest to home. But in 1980, the 2-2-2 system went into operation, whereby all students in grades seven and eight attended Park Forest Junior High, all ninth and tenth graders attended Westerly Parkway "Intermediate" High School (now the high school's South Building), and only juniors and seniors attended the Senior High School (now North Building). Another change comes with the centennial — a new middle school, accommodating grades six through eight, adjacent to Panorama Village Elementary School in College Township, and conver-

Good Evening!

1890s Calder Alley Horse Identified

The Times recently published a photo of a horse standing in Calder Alley, State College, taken in the 1890s. The photo was of particular interest to Russell L. Foster of Mahanoy City, who reveals that the horse was one of a half dozen owned by his father.

William L. Foster had a business on E. College Ave. at the corner of S. Pugh St.

"The horse is standing near the stable, which is not in the picture and to the left of the pole and is now occupied by the Alley Cat," Mr. Foster writes.

He says that when he looked at the building several years ago the exterior was very much as it was in the early 1900s, when his father had a livery business which always included a couple of riding horses.

"In fact," Mr. Foster writes, "to the western end of the building on the second floor is still what was once a door leading into an ice storage room which was for the ice being kept in the sawdust."

—*Centre Daily Times, 9-13-77*

sion of Park Forest Junior High to a middle school as well.

Teachers' salaries began at $28 a month in 1889 (less than $200 for the school year) and averaged about $1,500 a year by 1928. During the Depression, single teachers, especially women, sometimes went a month without pay, preference being given to married male teachers who had families to support. To balance the 1933 budget, the school board *reduced* all teachers' pay by as much as ten percent. In 1948, teachers were making a little less than $2,000; by the early 1950s, that number had risen only slightly, to just over $2,800 a year; but by 1970, starting salaries averaged $7,200. For the 1995-96 school year, minimum salary for a teacher in the State College district is $25,716 and maximum is $52,666. (In 1989, they were $21,691 and $38,606.)

Renovation and expansion of the high school's physical

Internal Medicine Associates

of State College, P.C.

ore than two decades ago, Internal Medicine Associates was among the first to provide Centre Region residents with specialized medical services at the local level. While the group remains committed to covering all major subspecialties of internal medicine, it recently expanded its primary care services in response to the nationwide trend toward managed health care. By emphasizing primary care as an adjunct to its specialties

Building near Centre Community Hospital. The move tripled the amount of space available for serving patients, and permitted the addition of new, state-of-the-art equipment.

In addition to its State College facility, Internal Medicine Associates maintains a primary care office in Bellefonte. The office moved from its former site in the Bush House to a new medical park complex at 1217 Zion Road in March 1993.

Now with two locations offering primary care, the physicians' group is better able to address the Centre

Internal Medicine Associates has spacious modern offices in the Centre Medical Sciences Building.

and participating in most major health-insurance programs, Internal Medicine Associates intends to remain at the forefront of the constantly changing field of health-care delivery.

Founded in 1974 by nephrologist Dr. Jonathan Dranov, the practice was originally located in downtown State College's Glennland Building. With the addition of Dr. Dranov's first associate the following year, oncologist and hematologist Dr. Richard Dixon, the practice began gradually adding physicians in the major subspecialties of internal medicine. Today the group has a medical staff of seventeen physicians specializing in allergy and immunology, cardiology, dermatology, endocrinology, gastroenterology, geriatrics, hematology, nephrology, neurology, oncology, pulmonary medicine, and rheumatology.

As Internal Medicine Associates grew, so, too, did its need for expanded and enhanced facilities. In 1980, IMA relocated to the Boalsburg Medical Office Building. By the end of 1994, with space once again at a premium, the group opened offices at the new Centre Medical Sciences

Region's growing need for quality medical care. As it has in the past, Internal Medicine Associates is poised to meet the changing needs of the communities it serves, building on its reputation for high-quality primary and specialized medical care.

Patients benefit from IMA's seventeen expert physicians.

education and guidance facilities were accomplished in 1989 under then-superintendent of schools Seldon V. Whitaker Jr. Costing approximately $6.7 million, the 51,000-square-foot addition features a large gymnasium more than twice the size of the old gym, with two full-size basketball courts, bleachers seating eighteen hundred spectators, and a six-lane swimming pool, 75 feet 1 inch by 45 feet, with a one-meter diving board.

Erik Kopp, a 1983 graduate who was a member of State High's swimming team in the pre-pool days, remembered practicing in Penn State's Natatorium. "The coach would pick us up at 5:30 a.m. to go to the Nat," he recalled, adding, "I wish we had had that addition when I was in school." However, he regrets the passing of two soccer fields in front of the school that made way then for parking lots. "The fields were so pretty, but I guess they have to have some place for the kids to park their cars."

The old oak tree, where for thirty-two years State High teams, graduates, and families had posed for pictures, was also lost to make room for the addition. Between the pool and gym today are shelves to display hundreds of State High trophies and medals from twenty-two different sports as well as a preserved cross-section of the tree believed to be two centuries old. The class of '88 contributed $1,000 for its preservation.

Lewis Rodrick, director of administrative services and former principal of Park Forest Junior High and State College Senior High, said of the school population in 1989, "The growth rate, which had been something like ten to fifteen percent a year, stopped dead in its tracks. We went from about eight thousand students to fewer than six thousand." Growth has begun to show up again, what with the baby boomers who had brought on the original school population expansion in the '60s and '70s now sending their own children to school. Two elementary schools were closed for a number of years (Matternville and Boalsburg) but were reopened in 1989 to accommodate the spurt in growth.

For years, the entire school district had been housed in three buildings surrounding The Hollow — the Frazier Street School served the entire school population of State College until 1914, when a high school was built a block away on Frazier Street between Fairmount and Nittany Avenues, followed, in 1924, by the Nittany Avenue Grammar School to accommodate increased enrollment in fifth and sixth grades. Today, the post office sits on the site of the Frazier Street School, the Nittany Avenue building houses school administrative offices, and the old junior and senior high school building — probably the first split-level school in the state, with its "Northwest Passage" — contains both Fairmount Elementary School and the Delta Program alternative secondary school, originally called the Alternative Program.

Another alternative means of education for a large number of residents, the South Hills Business School, was opened in 1970 by attorney S. Paul Mazza and celebrated its twenty-fifth anniversary in January 1995. School director Maralyn Davis Mazza said, "The idea for the school came from Paul's secretary, Eva Burke, who had gone to a secretarial school and thought State College should have an alternative to a four-year college education."

The school started with seven students in the South Hills Office Center at 1315 South Allen Street, moved to the vacant Boalsburg Elementary School in 1982, then, in 1989, moved back to the Borough into its own new, well-equipped building at 480 Waupelani Drive where its faculty now trains more than three hundred students a year.

Although apartment houses had fueled the building boom of the 1960s and '70s in downtown State College, office buildings became the focus in the 1980s. This was especially true in the 100 block of South Burrowes Street.

Open House:

A Zest, Freshness And Innocence Then

(Editor's Note: Today's guest columnist is a teacher of creative writing at Southern Connecticut College, New Haven, and the sister of Anne Folwell and Wayland Dunaway of State College.)

+   +   +

By MAY DUNAWAY HARDING

The Penn State campus was to us children our special park and playground.

It was mostly green rolling campus, then, though it had its own railroad, the Bellefonte Central, running right by the violet-covered banks in front of the engineering buildings.

I remember its small station particularly for its penny machines. The station was on my way to Sunday School, which was held in the engineering building because the Baptist Church had not yet built its church, and some of my collection pennies found their way into the coin slots of those irresistible machines, which rustily dispensed chewing gum. For years this was my most guilty secret.

The college golf course was there for us to take walks on, we thought, the horticulture woods were fine for our picnics, the cow barns and sheep barns were our zoo, the dairy building our ice cream parlor. The college orchards supplied us with barrels of flawless apples, the college dairy delivered certified milk thick-topped with golden cream to our doors, and on Christmas left us a gift pint of whipping cream. The college was all taken for granted; it served us; we owned it.

We had Easter egg hunts in the campus woods. The Ghost Walk, a dark, miraculously preserved forest, the rich loam of its path lined with ferns, ladyslippers, and other wildflowers, was then part of the campus, a spooky sidetrip. So was a natural amphitheatre sloping down to a grassy stage embowered by leafy tree branches and lighted at night by paper lanterns when the evening May Day festival took place, or the college plays. Its enchantment lingers in my mind like a fragment of a midsummer night's dream.

How possessive we children felt about everything, the tree-lined walks and the front wall on College Ave. so perfect to sit on. It was a grand playground; that's what we loved it for, and when our parents took us for Sunday walks through it, or when we played and rolled on the grass and down the hills on our own, the campus was always gloriously ours, though we knew that our fathers did something there, they went every day during the week, and the library had a lot to do with it, being mysteriously adult, not for children, like all those other buildings except Old Main, which had a great tower to climb.

Lovely times in a small town where everybody knew everybody else and the faculty knew uncompetitive security and owned houses with vegetable gardens and fruit trees in back. A town spreading out on all sides into country, still very much country. A wholesome zest, a freshness and innocence filled the days then. I could not be wrong about that.

—Centre Daily Times, 6-19-79,
from Peg Fletcher Pierson

The 1988 Sidewalk Days in downtown State College filled the 100 and 200 blocks of South Allen Street with buyers and sellers.

Kristin Meister, 7, Holly Callahan, 6, and Karl Larson, 9, practice their peanut toss for a Peanut Carnival.

AAUW's annual used book sale is greatly anticipated by thousands each spring. Its benefits to the community had become legend by this 1984 edition.

There, after moving his auto dealership (the last to leave the downtown) out West College Avenue to Pine Hall, Charles Rider refurbished his former sales and repair spaces in Peck Snyder's building into offices leased by The Barash Group, *The Daily Collegian*, Penn State's School of Communications, Paul & Tony's Stereo, and C-NET, the local government/education access TV channel. Charlie also built two office buildings, one in mid-block at 120 South Burrowes and one on the northeast corner of Burrowes and Beaver. Both filled almost immediately and almost entirely with Penn State offices, picking up the overflow from an overcrowded campus. Penn State also was leasing space in Calder Way, Greenwich Court, The Towers, CATO Industrial Park, and other locations around the Centre Region.

However, at the beginning of 1993, with another Rider office building on the drawing board, at the northwest corner of Burrowes and Beaver, then-University Vice President for Business and Operations James Wagner announced, "We hope to get out of most or all of our space in downtown State College and surrounding townships within the next five to ten years."

What caused him to say that was a sudden building boom on campus, much of it financed by private funds from vigorous development campaigns and by a state-funded brick-and-mortar program called "Operation Jump Start." Included in the new additions were: the largest building in Centre County, the 16,000-seat Bryce Jordan Center, scheduled to open in January 1996, providing space (seven-and-a-half acres) for Big Ten indoor athletic events, commencements, and concerts; a new wing on the Museum of Art that doubled its size, thanks mainly to a large contribution of C-COR Electronics stock from Jim and Barbara Palmer, for whom the museum is now named; the Mateer Building, new home of the school of hotel, restaurant, and recreation management and named for its largest donors, Corner Room co-founder Marlin C. "Matty" Mateer and his widow, Laura; major renovations to the former Mechanical Engineering Building, renamed Reber Building in 1991 in honor of the founder of Penn State's College of Engineering; and the Penn State Scanticon conference center hotel and two office buildings in the 130-acre Penn State Research Park, near the Park Avenue interchange of the Mount Nittany Expressway.

In 1992 and '95, the Nittany Lion Inn was renovated and enlarged from 130 to 262 guest rooms plus an alumni ballroom, lounge, courtyard, health-and-fitness rooms, a new lobby, and an entrance on the Park Avenue side that is nearly a mirror image of the original entrance facing Rec Hall. Parking decks at Keller Building, Eisenhower Auditorium, and Hetzel Union Building are alleviating parking problems on campus. An-

other parking deck is to be built across University Drive from the Bryce Jordan Center.

Along with the first downtown public parking garage, on Pugh Street, additions in the mid-1980s to early '90s of the Fraser Street parking garage and the McAllister Street parking deck have helped to solve the downtown dilemma of where to park for the day or the hour by bringing the number of public parking spaces to 1,600 — 1,200 of them within one block of Schlow Library. To discourage commuters from parking in Borough neighborhoods, a successful rollback parking ordinance, passed by Borough Council in 1991, requires on-street time limits and purchased parking passes.

On November 9, 1983, a downtown landmark, the All-American Rathskeller, celebrated its fiftieth birthday and set a Guinness record by selling 843 cases of Rolling Rock beer at a party attended by then-owner John O'Connell, "The Dean" (former owner Dean Smith), ex-bartenders, cooks, and hundreds of "Rock" fans.

Also in 1983, Millie and George Bubash moved out of their home of thirty-one years, at 142 McAllister Street, and into the Way townhouses on Kemmerer Road. "We were the last of the Mohicans," Millie said about being the last private residents of a house in "center-city" State College. "It was a farmhouse built in 1855, nothing fancy, and it had an outside kitchen. We bought it in 1952, and three of our four children were born there." The Bubashes also took in as many as nine student roomers, and from 1958 to 1968 operated a lady's hat shop on the first floor.

Friday the thirteenth in November 1987 marked the destruction of a newly renovated landmark, also bordering McAllister Street — St. Paul's United Methodist Church — whose congregation was preparing to celebrate its one hundredth birthday in 1988. The fire, attributed to an electrical problem associated with the renovations, gutted the stone building but did not discourage the group from rebuilding on the site.

Another fire, devastating an Allen Street landmark, occurred in May 1989 — Neil Foster, pharmacist and co-owner of McLanahan's Drug Store at 134-136 South Allen Street, was awakened by a phone call from a former employee who lived downtown. "There are fire trucks around your store," she said, "and smoke is coming out of the second floor."

For the next six hours, Neil, store manager Mike Webb, and Bob Neiderer, owner of Kelly's Shoes next door, watched their businesses go up in smoke. "It was a nightmare," Mike remembered. It took three more days to locate Neil's partner, Phil McIntyre, who had just left on a vacation to South Carolina and had pinned his vacation phone number to the pharmacy bulletin board. "Don't

Bus Parking Plan Sparks Protest

Moves to expand the Centre Line bus fleet and its garage facility drew fire last night from Corl St. residents . . .

Backed by a petition signed by 140 residents who live near the bus garage off Osmond St., John Dombroski, 232 Corl St., told council that the "bus facility in itself creates a heck of a noise problem and is a cesspool of noise and odors.

"We're not opposed to the expansion of CATA," Mr. Dombroski said. "We are opposed to sinking money into an area that won't allow future expansion."

—Centre Daily Times, 9-9-80

The Victorian Manor

When residents and visitors to the area celebrate a special occasion — a birthday, holiday, anniversary, or class reunion — one restaurant consistently tops the list of fine dining choices. Since it opened on September 13, 1977, The Victorian Manor in Lemont has earned a deserved reputation for superb cuisine and attentive service. Add to those key ingredients the elegant ambiance of a century-old Victorian mansion, and it's easy to see why the restaurant has gained such a loyal following.

Diane and Chris Exarchos first discovered the three-story gabled house that was to become their home and business while auction hunting in 1975. A year later, they purchased the 901 Pike Street residence with the idea of renovating it and living there. At the suggestion of friends, and with their favorite restaurant, Mill Hall's Dutch Inn, as inspiration, the couple soon decided to open a fine-dining establishment.

After extensive renovations that saw the addition of new plumbing, heating, and wiring, plus a restaurant kitchen and dish room, The Victorian Manor opened for business. The Exarchoses did much of the restoration work themselves, carefully preserving the historic home's beautiful stained-glass windows and original woodwork. Neighbors like current kitchen manager Linda Narehood lent a hand.

The Exarchoses have preserved most of the original house and have renovated the garage and train station behind it.

In the beginning, Diane served as hostess, laundress, bookkeeper, and personnel manager. Today she has turned over many of those duties to dining-room manager Mike Gerber, who joined the Manor as a waiter in 1979 during his senior year at Penn State. Chris has maintained a low profile in the restaurant while he pursues postdoctoral studies and other career interests. The Exarchos family, including sons Nicholas and Alexander, lives on the house's second and third floors, and maintains a 300-acre farm on Sandy Ridge near Jacksonville.

Over the course of nearly two decades, The Victorian Manor has clearly found its recipe for success. Enticing entrees such as chateaubriand and rack of lamb continue to draw patrons, and the restaurant's delicious Caesar salad, prepared tableside, is reason enough for a visit. Lily's Piano Lounge, added in 1984, provides the perfect setting for casual cocktails. Now with about thirty-five employees, the restaurant continues to emphasize attentive service, as evidenced by its waiters who commit all orders to memory. For a special occasion or an elegant night out, The Victorian Manor is the perfect setting.

Unpaved streets ran by the future Victorian Manor at the turn of the century.

A good thing got better in 1985 as Schlow Memorial Library got a facelift and more usable space.

Council May Open
All Municipal Meetings

State College Municipal Council will throw open its doors to the public for all authority, board and committee meetings if it approves a proposed open meeting resolution.

Initiated by council member Joseph Wakeley Jr., the three-page resolution will be discussed by council at a private work session Monday evening.

A public discussion on the resolution was promised by council president Mary Ann Haas at council's Oct. 6 meeting.

"It seems ludicrous to discuss in public whether we should discuss things in public," Mrs. Haas said today.

—Centre Daily Times, 9-18-80

New Cab Owners Will
Be Asked To Take Over
Paratransit Service

The Centre Area Transportation Authority approved the idea of developing paratransit service through the new owners of the Centre Cab Co.

Although no final plans were adopted Friday, CATA Managing Director Paul Oversier was authorized to negotiate an operational plan with Jim and Noreen Byers, who will take over the cab company from the borough this week.

. . . CATA has a van equipped with a wheelchair lift to use for paratransit. It also has a legal mandate by the state Department of Transportation to provide such a service.

If Mr. and Mrs. Byers take on the operation, they can dispatch cabs as well as the van for paratransit use.

—Centre Daily Times, 10-31-82

GOING, GOING, GONE: The State College YMCA auction yesterday raised at least $16,000 for a community center, . . . Chairman Marie E. Fedon said. A llama was a big hit . . . . About 235 people attended the bidding, held on the proposed site of the center at the corner of Waupelani Drive and Whitehall Road.

—Centre Daily Times, 5-7-84

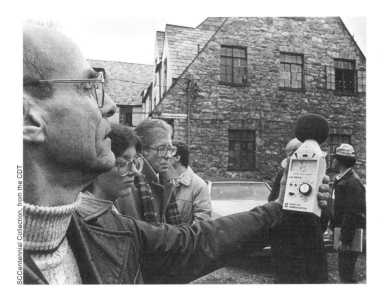

Acoustics Professor Jim Prout checked noise levels in the fraternity section. In 1984, the State College Planning Commission recommended changing the law to control noise in the Borough — "in a split 3-2 vote," reported the CDT, the commission "suggested that the allowable noise level stay at 55 decibels Sundays through Thursdays, but be raised to 62 decibels on Fridays and Saturdays, from 7 p.m. to midnight."

Officers and active volunteers at the dedication of the Second Mile House near University Park Airport, June 26, 1982, were Jill Kissinger, Dave Wilson, John Vidmar, Earl Strong, Second Mile founder Jerry Sandusky, Ron Coder, Virginia Eisenstein, Fred Vondracek, and Cal Zimmerman. Begun in 1977 for highly motivated but educationally deprived inner-city youth, Second Mile by 1995 had eight programs touching 100,000 children.

Presidential Award Goes To Student

A student at State College Area Senior High School has been chosen as one of the state's two outstanding graduating seniors. Senior Thomas Liu will receive a 1984 Presidential Scholar award at the White House early next month.

Presidential Scholars are chosen partly on the basis of performance on Scholastic Aptitude Tests.

Thomas has also been named Pennsylvania's outstanding math student and is a National Merit Scholar.

—Centre Daily Times, 5-7-84

State College Will Let High-Tech Firm Move In

State College Borough Council will not appeal a decision to let a high-technology business into an area zoned for homes and offices.

Six council members reached that conclusion in a work session last night. Zoning Hearing Board chairman Sylvia Stein explained to them why the zoning board decided to let Interactive Microware operate at the former American Philatelic Building, 336 S. Fraser St.

Mrs. Stein stressed that the board viewed Interactive primarily as "an engineering office for design of (computer) software" with the assembly of computer circuit boards "an incidental and subordinate use" allowable in places zoned for homes and offices (R-O districts).

—Centre Daily Times, 11-1-83

List sent on to borough council

Forty-four recommendations on how to improve State College neighborhoods are on their way to borough council.

The top concern of residents is inadequate street lighting in residential areas.

Background noise from neighboring properties ranked second on the list. It was followed by lack of parking near residences, vandalism, poor communication in the neighborhood and changes that affect neighborhood quality.

—Centre Daily Times, 5-13-86

State High girls were 1986 Central Counties Tennis League champions. 1st row: Carolyn Pickering, Captain Cathy Kissell, Kirsten Willey, Stephanie Hulina, Paige Willey. 2nd row: Coach Mike Shapiro, Meg Padden, Lisa Stine, Adrienne Mason, Judy Lee, Kim Kramer, Assistant Coach Sandy Lex.

Under Coach Shapiro, State High boys were 410-46 in dual meets from 1958 through 1994; the girls from 1982 through 1995 were 143-24, bringing Mike Shapiro's coaching record here to 553 wins, 70 losses. He had coached four PIAA singles titleists, 25 Central Counties League champions, and, since its inception, three of three District 6 tournament champions.

State High's girls' cross-country team reached state-championship heights in 1994. Kneeling: Lou Hohnka, Lauren McGrath, Gretchen Lindner, Liz Messersmith, Chris Shea; standing: Coach Sue Brindle, Bethany Baumbach, Caitlin Fitz, Chris Crowe, Coach Steve Gentry.

call me unless the place burns down," he had quipped, and everyone had laughed. Touted at its 1948 grand opening as "one of the nation's most modern stores," McLanahan's, by then in its third Allen Street location, was actually in a remodeled building. It, like many in downtown State College, had grown from a house built near the turn of the century into a maze of cubicles with false ceilings, all topped off with a thick tarpaper roof. This made it impossible for Alpha firemen to save it. But they *did* keep the blaze from spreading by resorting to "surrounding and drowning," from aerial ladders, that caused water damage but little else to other stores in the block.

According to its co-owners, Chuck and Bob Noel, the building had started out as a house where their grandparents, Ernest and Carrie Sproul Gernerd, lived and operated a tailor shop beginning in 1910. The Noel boys' mother, Alice Kathryn Gernerd, was ten at the time. The Gernerds built an apartment house around the old house, living in one and renting the others to students. Grandfather Gernerd, whom students nicknamed "Pappy," also put up a storefront for his expanded tailoring, tux rental, and retail clothing shop and added two storerooms for rent beside it. In 1938, he put second stories on the shops and faced them with brick.

State College, meet Warwick Stone

The second in what is expected to be a long line of sculptures was lifted into place in downtown State College yesterday.

Called The Warwick Stone, the work was installed on a special plaza next to the Pugh Street Parking Garage yesterday by the Arts in Public Place Committee and the borough.

"We think it's a real nice addition. It works well with the new facade of the garage," said Bob Potter, who co-chairs the 30-member committee with Pat Farrell.

—*Centre Daily Times, 1-7-88*

"Our family rented to Ward's Restaurant and the A&P," Bob Noel said. "Then when Ward moved out, Fred Spannuth Sr. moved in with Fred's Restaurant." After Pappy died in 1940, the tailor shop space was taken over by Centre Hardware, then Persia's (later Bottorf's) Shoes, and finally Kelly's Shoes.

One of State College's oldest still-operating businesses, McLanahan's first opened in 1933 at the northeast corner of Beaver Avenue and Allen Street, when Bob McLanahan and his mother, Ivaloo, decided to introduce the "cut-rate drugstore" idea to this small college town. They priced soap at five cents a bar, shaving cream at twenty-one cents a tube, cigarettes at eleven cents a pack, and a bottle of one hundred aspirins at thirty-nine cents. With two registered pharmacists who exercised "extreme care and accuracy in compounding prescriptions, using only the purest of drugs and chemicals," and a soda fountain where a hot-fudge sundae cost fifteen cents and a club sandwich cost a quarter, the store was a success.

In 1948, McLanahan's took over the 4,000-square-foot space vacated by the A&P in the Gernerd/Noel building and spent six months remodeling it, adding an eighty-foot-long soda fountain that seated thirty-one people, and installing the newest in customer comfort — air conditioning. The store's grand opening on December 8 attracted more than ten thousand shoppers from town,

Lions Pride

hile attending a football game at the University of Tennessee, Gary and Judy Moyer were amazed by the "sea" of orange created by the sportswear worn by Volunteer fans. Sporting more than your typical orange T-shirts and orange sweatshirts, they were wearing orange blazers, orange skirts, orange shirts, and orange polos — all emblazoned with Tennessee team logos.

Gary and Judy believed there was a market for more upscale Penn State sportswear beyond the basic T-shirts and sweats being offered by local shops and bookstores. They formulated a concept, and in June 1976 opened Lions Pride at 105 South Allen Street. The store slogan, "Everything Penn State for Every Penn Stater," appropriately described the store's expanded lines of Penn State sportswear and memorabilia, with Penn State apparel and gifts for all ages — from newborn infants to adults. Items ranged from basic T-shirts and sweats and buttons and bumper stickers to the more upscale Oxford button-downs, polos, slacks, ties, and executive

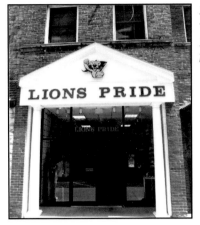

If it says "Penn State," Lions Pride has it.

gifts all bearing Penn State logos.

Business grew steadily, and Lions Pride moved twice to larger locations, the latest at 112 East College Avenue. Through the years Lions Pride became part of the proud Penn State tradition, offering alumni and fans the very best in traditional and contemporary Penn State sportswear. Lions Pride truly is "Everything Penn State for Every Penn Stater."

Merrill Lynch

errill Lynch is bullish on State College, if recent activity in the region by the financial power-house is any indication. The nation's leading financial-services company first opened a branch here in 1979 with a half-dozen brokers in an office on the 100 block of East College Avenue. The new office functioned as an associate of the company's Williamsport branch. Ed Blackburn, a retired Merrill Lynch veteran living in State College, managed the Williamsport office at the time and oversaw the opening.

The company's success in Central Pennsylvania has been due in no small part to its association with William A. Schreyer, chairman of Penn State's board of trustees and president, CEO, and chairman emeritus of Merrill Lynch. Schreyer's father managed the Williamsport office for thirty years, and Bill got his first taste of finance there minding the stock tote board and handling other duties. He attended Penn State, where, not coincidentally, he was a Sigma Phi Epsilon fraternity brother of Ed Blackburn.

As Merrill Lynch grew in the State College market, so, too, did its need for more office space. In the mid-'80s, the firm moved to Calder Square, dramatically increasing its

space and visibility in the marketplace. The new office employed eight to nine brokers, including Phil Sieg, who later became resident manager.

By September 1993, the State College Merrill Lynch office had once again outgrown its quarters, prompting another move, this time to 120 Regent Court in Scenery Park. Twice the size of the Calder Square location, the 5,700-square-foot facility employs more than a dozen financial consultants. In recognition of the importance of this branch, it was made the hub of Merrill Lynch's newly created Northcentral Pennsylvania complex, which also includes the Williamsport, Johnstown, and Altoona offices. Phil Sieg was named senior manager of the regional complex.

What began as a brokerage dealing solely in stocks and bonds has grown to encompass practically every kind of financial product on the market. Although stocks and bonds are still a big part of Merrill Lynch's business, it now offers more than 200 types of products and services. Among other things, the company handles financial and estate planning, commodities, mutual funds, options, home mortgages, IRA and cash-management accounts, and lines of credit. As a trusted financial advisor for thousands of clients, Merrill Lynch works hard to remain at the top of the industry.

Before The Graduate apartment high-rise went in, Boots Dairyette was the focal point on the northwest corner of Atherton Street and Beaver Avenue in the fall of 1986.

campus, and county — about eight hundred every hour!

In 1969, Ray Agostinelli, McLanahan's controller, and Hubie Shirk, who started working at McLanahan's at age fourteen in 1946 and was later manager of the Self Service Store that Bob opened in 1959, bought two stores from Bob McLanahan. Within four months, the two new owners had opened the Village Square drugstore on North Atherton Street and, in 1974, a store and pharmacy at 611 University Drive. Four months after the fire, Phil McIntyre and Neil Foster, who had bought a franchise for the Allen Street store in 1986, reopened in smaller quarters at 116-118 West College Avenue. Kelly's Shoes relocated to 126 East College Avenue. Both say their customer base has changed entirely, from seventy-percent resident to seventy-percent student, just by moving around the corner. The fire site has been vacant ever since, hidden by a board fence facing Allen Street that has been painted and repainted several times by young people under the direction of HUB Arts and Crafts Center director Isabel Farrell — the first time by her son Benjamin.

In 1993, three long-time businesses in downtown State College passed from the scene — the Weis-owned Big Top Market at Beaver Avenue and Pugh Street, marking the first time in

Final shift for 'legendary' Nurse Light

By BARBARA BRUEGGEBORS
Times County Editor

Juliet Light, R.N., swoops along the mint green corridor and through the door into the third-floor nurse's station. Wordlessly accepting a telephone receiver from an outstretched arm, she flips open a patient chart and picks up a pen.

"Uh-huh. Yes. All right. Good-bye." No ands, ifs, buts. End of conversation.

Notations made, chart refiled, Nurse Light is up and moving again, barking instructions over her right shoulder, resuming her rounds through the staid sanctity of Centre Community Hospital's medical-surgical floor.

At 73, silver-haired and dressed in white down to her toes, Juliet Light — "Julie" to close friends, "Sarge" to doctors — is a blizzard of energy on the final day of a 52-year nursing career.

"I hate to quit, but this is my choice," said the Houserville resident, shrugging. "I want to retire before I burn out or become inefficient. These days, 5:30 comes awfully early in the morning."

Now that she has retired, Light plans to travel more, fish more, see more of her children.

"And I'll probably sign up to volunteer at the hospital," she said, fingering the small gold Jefferson nurse's pin she's worn on her uniform every working day since 1938. "I always said I wouldn't, but I think I will."

—*Centre Daily Times, 5-1-90*

Borough history that downtown residents were left with no comprehensive food market; fifty-year-old Centre Hardware, at 221 South Allen, where it had moved in 1948; and G. C. Murphy variety store, at 131 South Allen since its opening in 1927. But not all long-time businesses are gone — the State College Floral Shoppe, operated by the Shirk family (Harold and son Bob), has been a downtown fixture since 1929; Kaye's Korner, founded by Kaye Vinson in 1940 and owned since 1977 by Nguyen Binh; Mr. Charles women's clothing store, opened originally as a men's store on South Allen Street by Charles and Mary Louise Petnick in 1940; and the first Hi-Way Pizza Pub, opened in 1963 by restaurateur Andy Zangrilli, who has since added the Deli, the Saloon, and Mario and Luigi's to the list of downtown places to eat and drink. Among the changes occurring in 1994 were the closing of the Carriage House, founded in 1965 at 111 South Pugh Street, site of the Spudnut Shop in the 1950s and Harvey's Restaurant for years before that, and the closing of Crabtrees Jewelers after seventy years in the same building. But taking their places have been new businesses, such as CVS health and beauty aids in the former Weis location, Eddie Bauer clothing and Chili's restaurant where Murphy's used to be, and Aurum Goldsmiths continuing the

As in decades past, downtown State College, here on East College Avenue near Pugh Street, bustles with Penn State student traffic.

Ethel Meserve was one of State College's first women retailers when she opened her gift shop in 1946, first on College Avenue for 33 years then here, at 127 South Allen Street. It closed in mid-1995 when 95-year-old Ethel decided to retire!

Sunset Road in west College Heights is one of many tree-lined neighborhood streets that retains its quiet beauty. The corner home at 363 Ridge Avenue, originally owned by Mary L. Willard, is a mail-order house.

jewelry tradition in the "little pink-granite-fronted building at 123 South Allen Street."

Today, restaurants, coffee houses, clothing stores, and specialty shops characterize the downtown in a revitalization aided by the merchant-, government-, and University-supported Downtown State College, Inc., headed by Bob Price. Aurum's John Mason and Tinderbox Gifts' Steve Artz, who together own four other businesses, have played an active role in the growth of specialty shops in the downtown.

Gary Moyer, owner of Moyer Jewelers, said in 1993, when chairing a Downtown Improvement task force, "It's worth it to keep downtown exciting for everyone to work and shop. We don't want it to become another town adjacent to a college — all beer and pizza places."

Gary, whose father B. P. Moyer founded the business in 1949 and whose daughter Lori is now a registered gemologist and store manager, has two other successful downtown shops — the Animal Kingdom, run by his wife Judy, and Lions Pride — near his headquarters store at 100 East College Avenue. He also has an advertising specialties business, Collegiate Pride, in CATO Industrial Park.

Two internationally famous groups are headquartered in State College — the American Philatelic Society and Accu-Weather Inc. In 1995, the 109-year-old APS, largest organization of stamp collectors in the nation, celebrated its first half-century here. Originally headquartered wherever each new APS elected secretary lived, it found a permanent home in State College with the 1945 appointment of its first executive secretary, H. Clay Musser, who lived here. Starting in modest quarters above Kaye's Korner, the APS built its own building at 336 South Fraser Street in 1971, but had outgrown that by 1982 when the present headquarters and research library were constructed at 100 Oakwood Avenue in Patton Township.

Accu-Weather, the world's largest private weather-forecasting service, was founded in 1962 by Penn State meteorology graduate Joel Myers. Its forecasts, heard on radio and seen on television and newspapers in all parts of the world, emanate from three old houses and a former church in the 600 block of West College Avenue and from another house on North Gill Street.

The State College Community Theatre and the Nittany Valley Symphony, two cultural groups made up of local residents, almost all of them amateurs in the truest sense — doing it for love — also have had a long history in this area. SCCT, founded in 1955, provides laughs and tears every summer at the Boal Barn Playhouse in Boalsburg,

while NVS, begun in 1967, gives six concerts a year in Eisenhower Auditorium.

As the downtown has changed from full-service to specialty shops, full-service providers have sprung up in the townships — Hills Plaza (1973) and Hills Plaza South (1992), on South Atherton Street in College Township; Northland Center (1989) off North Atherton Street in Ferguson Township; North Atherton Place (1991), with its flagship Wal-Mart store, and Lowe's mammoth lumber and home-improvement center (1994) in Patton Township. Another Wal-Mart and its affiliate Sam's Club are set to open across Benner Pike from the Nittany Mall in 1995.

Bookstores are having a major renaissance in the State College area, crowned by an Encore Books "superstore," which opened in Hills Plaza South in August 1994. State College mainstays — University Book Centre (formerly Keeler's) and the Student Book Store downtown, and the Penn State Bookstore on campus — saw the arrival of the first big book store chain, B. Dalton, in 1980 both downtown and at the Nittany Mall, followed by scholarly Svoboda's Books downtown in 1983 and the Little Professor Book Center in Patton Township in 1992. There also are shops specializing in religious, comic, and used books, including Horner's Book Store, where the CDT press room used to be.

The University has redesigned some holes on its Blue and White Golf Courses in preparation for building its new "West Campus," stretching from Atherton Street to Corl Street on part of the old White Course. In response, Borough Council has rezoned the area north of Calder Way and West of Atherton Street from residential multi-family, office, and industrial to the newly designated Urban Village District. This will allow property owners to develop motels, bed and breakfasts, and restaurants, and still preserve their neighborhood atmosphere.

Other concerns of burgeoning growth that government officials are grappling with are water service — a new filtration system is planned — a newly expanded sewage-disposal plant that may need to be expanded again in a few years, a sharp increase in truck traffic on some Centre Region roads, and the relocation of two major arteries, U.S. 220 and PA 26.

Churches, too, are changing to meet modern demands. A second church was added to Our Lady of Victory Parish in 1989 by the Roman Catholic Diocese of Altoona-Johnstown, which felt that the size of the first church (built in 1969 at 820 Westerly Parkway and serving 2,600 families) was becoming unmanageable. The 515-family Church of the Good Shepherd congregation met in

Omega World Travel

For D. Brent Pasquinelli, executive vice president of Omega World Travel and manager of the company's regional headquarters in State College, business success goes hand in hand with community involvement. He feels that without a vibrant, growing, caring community, the climate for operating a successful business simply doesn't exist. That's one reason he has been chairman of Downtown State College, Inc., for two years, and why he chaired the 1994 Centre County United Way campaign, which raised more than $1 million for the first time in the county's history. Another reason is a desire to give something back to his adopted hometown by helping provide opportunities for less-fortunate members of the community. Currently he serves as chairman of the board of the local United Way.

A native of the Saint Marys area, Brent came to State College in 1980 to establish a branch agency of DuBois-based Airlandsea Travel & Tour, Inc. A specialist in senior-citizen tours while working in north-central Pennsylvania, he saw in the Centre Region an opportunity to branch out into the business-travel arena. After ten years of independent operation, his company joined Virginia-based Omega World Travel in 1990. With 225 offices across the country and approximately $400 million in annual sales, Omega is the nation's seventh largest travel company.

Today the State College-based Omega World Travel, at 216 West College Avenue, acts as a regional headquarters, overseeing seven branch offices in Pennsylvania and Ohio.

Brent manages fifty-three employees, who account for $23 million in annual sales. A business-travel specialist, Omega serves most major corporations in the Centre Region and many smaller companies. Besides all facets of domestic and international business travel, the company handles vacation and leisure travel.

The agency is soon moving to larger quarters, where it will include Rocky Mountain Adventures, a new outdoor-travel division. For area residents, the expansion will make Omega the last word in travel.

Leonard S. Fiore, Inc.

What began as a series of odd jobs nearly fifty years ago is now Leonard S. Fiore, Inc., one of the most successful general-contracting firms in Central Pennsylvania.

In 1948, Leonard Fiore, Sr., a pipe fitter in the Altoona car shops of the Pennsylvania Railroad, began doing small

Seated: Leonard S. Fiore Sr. and his wife Mary E. Fiore. Standing: Richard F. Fiore, Leonard S. Fiore, Jr., and Michael A. Fiore.

construction and repair jobs to supplement his income. Six years later he became a full-time builder, and in 1957, expanded into commercial work. To date, the Altoona-based firm has completed more than 300 major projects — including apartment houses, supermarkets, schools, hospitals, churches, shopping malls, and office complexes — in Pennsylvania and Maryland, and over thirty projects for Penn State University.

Fiore's is very much a family enterprise. Leonard's wife, Mary, joined the company as secretary/treasurer in 1966, and, like her husband, had a successful career in real-estate ventures. Leonard Fiore, Jr., is now president of the firm; his brother, Richard, serves as executive vice president and secretary; and a third sibling, Michael, serves as vice president and treasurer. Leonard, Sr., remains active as chairman of the board.

In addition to their thriving business, which provides hundreds of area jobs each year, the Fiores are active in Little League, AAABA baseball, and Special Olympics, and fund scholarships in architecture at Penn State's University Park campus and in engineering at Penn State's Altoona campus — just a few of the many causes they've helped with their time and resources.

While State College's first three movie houses had closed long before 1989, the movie business was still rolling along. This line told the story here, at The Movies, which now has the largest screen in town.

temporary quarters until 1993, when its permanent building was completed in Patton Township at 867 Gray's Woods Boulevard, off Scotia Road. St. John's United Methodist Church at West Beaver Avenue and South Burrowes Street, whose membership was decreasing, combined with African-American and Chinese congregations who now share the same building and sometimes the same worship service in the renamed Jacob Albright and Mary Bethune United Methodist Church. Meanwhile, the State College Presbyterian Church at the corner of West Beaver Avenue and Fraser Street has greatly enlarged both its sanctuary and education building; the Jewish Community Center at 620 East Hamilton Avenue has expanded and gotten a new facelift; and the Islamic Center of Central Pennsylvania, at 709 West Ridge Avenue, now occupies a former site of the Unitarian Universalist Fellowship, which put up a new building in 1991 at 780 Waupelani Drive Extension.

As a new century approaches, change may even transform State College's form of government. A referendum question to consolidate College and Patton Townships with the Borough into one city made the primary election ballot in 1995, but was soundly defeated. Nonetheless, the long-studied issue will likely fuel an argument between supporters and opponents for years to come, just as most suggestions for change have always been greeted in State College.

Statistics from the 1990 census

25 more school employees to retire

April is emerging as another banner month for retirements in the State College Area School District thanks to a new law giving public school employees a retirement bonus.

Monday night the district accepted the retirements of 25 employees. They included elementary principals Peter Carpenter and William Keenan, English coordinator Callie Kingsbury, two guidance counselors and 18 teachers.

High school physical education teacher Jackson Horner topped Monday's list of retirees with 38 years in the district.

Horner, who began work in 1955 when the high school was on Fairmount Avenue and housed grades 7-12, said the most remarkable thing for him was seeing the district grow.

Retiring elementary teachers are June Barnard, with 24 years' experience in State College; Elinor Burns, 27 years; Marguerite Carpenter, 18 years; Suzanne Conklin, 33 years; Nancy Faris, 18.5 years; Jean Gotolski, 25.5 years; Elisabeth Herzog, 23 years; Nancy Klaban, 28 years; Margaret Long, 32 years; Emily McCormick, 32 years.

Retiring secondary teachers are Gary Deivert, 28 years; Jackson Horner, 38 years; Ronald Jochen, 33 years; Callie Kingsbury, 27.5 years; Norman Lampman, 35 years; Thomas Mills, 35 years; Michael Patrilak, 36 years; Dorothy Simons, 24 years; Ronald Strapel, 32 years.

Also retiring are guidance counselors Thomas Fonda, 27 years and Sherdell Snyder, 30 years; school psychologist Robert Noll, 26 years; and school nurse Ernestine Snyder, 26.5 years.

—Centre Daily Times, 4-13-93

reflect the college-town demographics of State College, with a population of 38,981, a 7.8 percent increase over 1980, but only 3,559 families, a 4.7 decrease from 1980. People over age 18, including Penn State student residents, accounted for 93.8 percent of the Borough's total, while married couples with and without children accounted for just 27.8 percent of the number of households. The bedroom community of Harris Township, on the other hand, where 74.1 percent of the residents are over age 18 and married couples account for 69.4 percent of the households, showed a 22 percent increase in population and a 31.4 percent increase in the number of families.

State College is by far the largest municipality in Centre County, but the area around it that makes up "Greater State College" has a population nearly equal to it, bringing total population of the Centre Region, as it is officially called, to more than 72,000.

In 1996, new housing options in the Borough are varied. A Galen Dreibelbis development of seven building lots bordering West College Heights on the cul de sac of Hillcrest Avenue and the Ralph Way Subdivision of thirty-one lots along University Drive Extension next to Foxdale Village are offering some of the last single-family residential land in the Borough. Luxury condominiums, such as The Towers at 403 South Allen Street and the Summit and Ridgeway overlooking Hills Plaza in College Township, have come on the scene. Luxury

Members of the State College Area Senior Citizens' Club, which meets weekly at St. Andrew's Episcopal Church, enjoyed this 1990 meeting. 1st row: club advisor Robert Ayer, Nell Duda, Alice Brumbaugh, Amos Neyhart, Catherine McCloskey, club president Ethel Gauthier. 2nd row: Almeda Lucas,Olive Williams, Beatrice Woodcock, Robert Woodcock, Edna Titus, Mildred Moser, Kathryn Eppihimer, Agnes Robinson. 3rd row: Ernest Gackenbach, Jane Gackenbach, Marian Jones, Mary McQueary, club coordinator Sara Krumrine, Mary Whitesell, Bertha Parks, Walter Storch, Sharon Glossner. 4th row: Leila Washko, Peg Noel, Sue Miller, Mary Kline, Mary Foster, Elda Wiser, Elizabeth Jodon. 5th row: Ken Pahel, Ida Dunne, Robert Foster, Joe Intorre. 6th row: Anne Sunday, Ernest Everett, Gladys Chesworth, Richard Truscott, Erma Boone, Gladys Oaks, Ferne Stebbins, Charles Noel, Earl Hosterman, Myrtle Wasson.

Among the first fruits of the State College Centennial celebration was this 32-foot photographic montage laboriously reproduced in 1988-89 by Ed Leos from negatives preserved from a photojournalism course he had taught. Separate photos were pieced together from frames shot in late 1972 by Penn State students D. Ryan Hixenbaugh and Ed Joella of College Avenue, from McAllister Street to Fraser Street.

In June 1989, Gatsby's last dance signaled another sad closing for a proud place of business. Few of the last dancers remembered this room with its ornate ceiling on College Avenue as the Cathaum Theatre, whose opening sixty-three years earlier had been a "major event" in town.

Rachele Dini and Dylan Fitz watered tiny oak trees growing from acorns planted by students at Corl Street Elementary School.

207

Tom Shade Jr. and his wife came from Alabama in 1969 when Tom III was an honor exchange student at State High. Nearly every morning Tom Jr. waves to passersby near his West Beaver Avenue home.

People come and go, automobiles come and go, trees come and go and are now back again. The one constant in the past 75 years has been the bank clock at 117 South Allen Street — and in 1995 the name of the bank changed!

homes costing as much as $700,000 are being built in the rural areas around State College by such developers as Fred Kissinger, Gary McShea, Bob Poole, and Mike Taylor. More than thirty larger-than-usual (3,500 to 6,500 square feet) homes have sprouted up since 1990 in neighborhoods like Chestnut Ridge in Ferguson Township, Gray's Woods in Patton and Halfmoon Townships, and Aspen Heights in Harris Township.

In a *Centre Daily Times* article, Sam Hawbaker, president of Home Builders Association of Central Pennsylvania, said, "As long as we have continued growth in the economy, I think there will continue to be homes built and sold in that range. There is a demand for quality housing in this community."

The homes are being purchased by retired and working Centre County attorneys, bankers, doctors, investment and real estate brokers, local business owners and Penn State professors, developers say. Also moving in are former university students and professionals from other towns

McLanahan's site sought by borough

The Borough of State College may try to buy the former McLanahan's site on South Allen Street, in hopes of later selling or leasing the now-vacant lot to someone who could develop it.

"I think, and many people think and say to me, that the most discouraging thing about our downtown is that vacant lot," borough council president Jean McManis said Tuesday. "We're going on five years of having a vacant lot there and it's sending out a message I don't think is true: that the downtown is not worth investing in."

— *Centre Daily Times, 6-1-94*

coming to Happy Valley to spend their retirement years. Stable employment in the area and Penn State's Research Park are expected to bring in more new buyers.

But a salesman for Bob Poole's S&A Custom Homes said that most Centre Region new-home construction is more modest. The average cost of $118,420 was below the national average of $149,800 and accounted for more than ninety-four percent of houses built in the first nine months of 1993.

In addition to devising the new Urban Village zoning, State College is preserving its older neighborhoods. Holmes-Foster, College Heights, and the Highlands with its Fraternity District all went on the National Register of Historic Places in 1995 "for their excellent representation of early twentieth-century architecture." The homes that fill these neighborhoods range from those designed by respected architects and by residents making personal statements to mail-order houses, all dating from the early 1900s to the late 1930s.

"Everything that was avail-

Geisinger Health System

*G*eisinger, recognized as a leader in developing an integrated health system, has demonstrated that a private institution can effectively improve the *accessibility* of health care in a large rural region. Since 1981, when it acquired the Moshannon Valley Medical Group in Philipsburg, Geisinger has established 28 rural medical practices and expanded additional practices in Northeast and Central Pennsylvania.

At the organization's heart is the Geisinger Health Plan (GHP), noted for low premiums and quality services. By 1995, over 25,000 GHP members were enrolled at Geisinger's five Centre County locations. With more than 170,000 members in all, GHP had become a model for health-maintenance organizations (HMOs) across the country and had grown into the nation's largest rural HMO.

Geisinger's history spans more than three generations. With the founding of the George F. Geisinger Memorial Hospital at Danville in 1915, nearly all Pennsylvanians had access to specialized health services for the first time. Known since 1981 as Geisinger Medical Center, the hospital has grown from 70 to 548 beds and still emphasizes emergency medicine, cardiovascular surgery, and newborn intensive care. Geisinger's more than 500 physicians, working with hundreds of GHP impaneled physicians, represent 75 medical specialties and subspecialties. They also practice at Centre Community Hospital, Geisinger Wyoming Valley Hospital, Philipsburg Area Hospital, Tyrone Hospital, and others.

Geisinger established its State College and Bellefonte group practices in 1987 and opened its Snow Shoe location in 1989.

State College is the hub of Geisinger's western region, and 31 salaried physicians work at Scenery Park and Patton Forest Corporate Park, and Bellefonte. There are specialists in allergy/immunology, cardiology, dermatology, family practice, gastroenterology, general surgery, hematology/oncology, internal medicine, neurology, pediatrics, plastic surgery, pulmonology, rheumatology, and pediatric cardiology, pediatric endocrinology, and pediatric neurology. Locally hospitalized patients use Centre Community Hospital; more specialized cases are referred to Danville's tertiary-care medical center.

Polestar Plastics

*F*ounded in 1982 by James W. Powers Sr. and Howard L. "Pete" Jeffries, Polestar Plastics has grown in concert with the medical, electronics, and business-machine industries it serves. The custom-injection molding company produces precision plastic parts used in various industrial applications. By making quality its number-one priority and constantly striving to maintain state-of-the-art equipment, Polestar Plastics has become the supplier of choice for major companies across the country.

After canvassing the north-central United States for a suitable site, Jim and Pete decided to locate their business at CATO Industrial Park in State College primarily because of financial assistance offered by various state and local agencies and conventional financing from Peoples National Bank. With the help of family members and a handful of employees, they opened for business with eight injection-molding machines in a 26,000-square-foot building, which has since been expanded to 32,000 square feet. Today the company employs more than 200 people and operates thirty-six injection-molding machines at two sites, including a 21,000-square-foot facility opened in 1993 at Philipsburg's Moshannon Valley Enterprise Center.

In the fall of 1993, Polestar was acquired by Tredegar Molded Products, a division of Tredegar Industries of Richmond. Still under the direction of its founding partners, the company remains committed to total quality in all aspects of its operations. Polestar Plastics also remains dedicated to supporting the community that helped it succeed. As its mission statement points out, "We contribute to our community with our time, talent, and financial support in exercising our responsibility as corporate citizens."

Polestar Plastics has seen tremendous growth at its facility in CATO Industrial Park.

able, from Cape Cod to international, got used by State College residents as they created their community," said Jacqueline Melander, head of both the Centre County Historical Society and the Borough's Historic Resources Commission. "Inclusion in the national collection says that compared with all the cities and towns across America, this is something worthy, and worth preserving."

An historical echo was heard from Penn State at about the same time — a decision to house its presidents on campus once again, not in the old President's House but at the former Mitchell estate, "Lisnaward," bordering College Heights. With the coming of a new president, Graham Spanier, in September 1995, the 1928 English-Tudor manor house, designed by Pittsburgh Judge H. Walton Mitchell, a Penn State alumnus and president of the board of trustees, is being enlarged, refurbished, and renamed in honor of the current trustee president, William Schreyer and his wife Joan, who gave the one million dollars necessary for the project. The architect in charge is Robert Hoffman, a State College native.

Eric Walker (1956-70) was the last president to live on campus; Presidents Oswald (1970-83), Jordan (1983-90), and Thomas (1990-95) lived in the President's Residence on Kennard Road near Boalsburg. But for two months in the fall of 1990, Joab and Marly Thomas did live in "Schreyer House" and found it pleasant and peaceful — except for one Sunday afternoon when five Penn State steers strolled into the yard and begun munching on the landscaping!

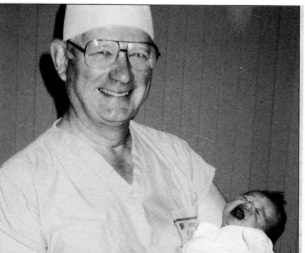

An obstetrician/gynecolgist who delivered, on average, two babies every three days for nearly thirty years became more than just a good doctor. Charles Rohrbeck, M.D., is a local legend, and will be remembered fondly by 7,000 couples and their children delivered by him, children who could guide the future of our town well into the next hundred years. His last delivery, for Teresa Benninghoff, was daughter Kelley, photographed by her daddy.

Both the past and the future of State College are reflected in two events of the 1990s, each occurring, coincidentally, in Patton Township. The first, in 1991, was the coming of the first Wal-Mart, the giant discount chain that prides itself on locating its stores in population centers of isolated large towns. Way back in 1959, however, Penn State students hinted at the northward growth when they revived *The Lemon*, the underground magazine from the turn of the century, and wrote a parody of columnist Drew Pearson's "Predictions of Things to Come." Using the pen name "Drew Fearsome," some farsighted undergraduate wrote that by the year 2000, the center of State College's population would be the J&L Barbecue on North Atherton Street. Although out of the barbecue business since the 1960s, the former J&L building, which more recently housed Stan Belinda Sr.'s pharmacy, and then a used car dealership, is across the street and within view of Wal-Mart.

The second event is the proposed rerouting of U.S. 220/322 west of the Matternville School, which has brought many residents of the pastoral Sellers Lane area to township and COG General Forum meetings with both plaintive and angry appeals to not disrupt their neighborhood for the benefit of trucks traveling between the Pennsylvania Turnpike and I-80. It's all reminiscent of the bypass meetings of the 1960s and '70s.

With respect to the bypass, Borough Councilwoman Felicia Lewis recalls her husband Peirce's words: "We're at the crossroads of the Lakes-to-Sea Highway and Interstate 80. All roads are leading to a twenty-first-century city." In the process, the geographic borders of incorporated State College become perceptibly fainter and fainter.

Mayor Welch believes that despite its growth State College is still a small town at heart. "Its charm is its vitality and energy and all the young people on the streets. And if you go to Borough Council Chambers and look at the montage of College Avenue taken by Ed Leos's photojournalism students nearly twenty-five years ago, you'll see that though some of the businesses have changed, only one building is gone — the house with Dr. Dale's office at the corner of Fraser and College. The heart of our downtown is virtually unchanged in twenty-five years, which I think makes us unique among Pennsylvania towns."

On the other hand, State College has come a long way since 1896. Medical and financial services are state-of-the-art. Restaurants run the gamut from fast food to home-style to gourmet with many ethnic cuisines. And the media include a public television station, four AM and six FM radio stations, two daily newspapers, a regional office of The Associated Press, two monthly magazines, a monthly business journal, and fifty-plus channel cable television. Yet we're still secluded in our Nittany Valley; still enjoying the fresh, dry, pure air; and still "far from the temptations and annoyances peculiar to railroads."

State College has always been unique. That's why so many of us live here, stay here, and love it here. Happy One Hundred and more to follow!

RE/MAX Centre Realty

A few years ago, REALTORS Richard Porter, Linda Lowe, Lassie Martsolf, Scott Yocum, Jacki Hunt, and Mary Lou Bennett decided they needed a challenge. Together they bought the RE/MAX International franchise for State College, opening an office at 1454 Martin Street on December 10, 1992. Since then, the business has grown to employ twenty sales associates. RE/MAX Centre Realty offers complete real estate services, including residential, commercial, farm, and land sales, as well as property management.

RE/MAX was established in Denver in 1973. By providing professional full-time real estate agents with attractive business opportunities, the company's franchise system expanded across the country. Today there are over 40,000 RE/MAX agents in more than 3,000 offices in the United States, Canada, Europe, and the Pacific Rim. Short for Real Estate Maximums, the company's name illustrates its goal of providing maximum service and expertise to the public as well as maximum benefits to member agents.

With a successful first few years, RE/MAX Centre Realty is intent on continuing to answer every real estate need. The firm's success has been largely due to its emphasis on a team approach within an office environment that promotes good interpersonal relationships. By providing an upbeat experience for employees and clients, RE/MAX expects to maximize its influence in State College.

The RE/MAX staff in 1995: (first row) Tom Cali, Lorraine Spock, Lassie Martsolf, Mary Lou Bennett, and Richard Porter. Second row: Charlene Wallace, Jacki Hunt, Pam Calkins, Carolyn Lowry, and JoAnn Lew. Third row: Ellen Kline, Linda Lowe, and Eileen Weglarz. Fourth row: Ron Rumbaugh, Andree Keebaugh, Bonnie Avillion, and Karen Zwigart. Fifth row: Greg Elliott, Scott Yocum, and Gene Farrell.

Chamber of Business and Industry of Centre County

With all the talk of consolidation in Centre County during the 1990s, it's not surprising that two of the region's most important economic-development organizations have joined forces to better address county-wide concerns. The 1993 merger of the State College Area Chamber of Commerce and the Centre County Industrial Development Corporation (CCIDC) gave birth to the Chamber of Business and Industry of Centre County, dedicated to promoting economic progress in the county.

The chamber has come a long way since its formative years in 1920-21, when a committee was organized to investigate the "rat nuisance" and the Clean Town Committee first secured a place to dump the borough's trash. At the time, the total assessed value of State College property was just over $1 million, and all borough services were operated under an annual budget of less than $20,000. In the following years, a number of local organizations sprang from the chamber, including the Bellefonte/State College Industrial Development Corporation, which later became the CCIDC. After twenty-five years of independent operation, the CCIDC came full circle and returned to its affiliation with the chamber.

Now headquartered at Penn State Research Park's Technology Center, the Chamber of Business and Industry continues its economic development efforts. Ten fledgling companies occupy the chamber's Advanced Technology Business Incubator, and the second phase of development has commenced at Penn Eagle Industrial Park near Bellefonte. The organization is actively involved in local issues, including highway and air-transportation development, sewage treatment, water quality, educational advancement, and areas of concern to Centre Region businesses. By working in concert with local entities such as Penn State University and Downtown State College, Inc., the chamber strives to encourage steady economic growth while maintaining a high quality of life for all Centre County residents.

Arnold Addison
Mayor 1978-93

Ernest Sauers
Fire Chief 1979

Marvin Robinson
Fire Chief 1980-88

State College Mayors, Fire and Police Chiefs
1 9 7 6 to 1 9 9 6

Robert Kauffman
Fire Chief 1988-91

Steven Triebold
Fire Chief 1992-

William L. Welch Jr.
Mayor 1994-

Thomas R. King
Chief of Police 1993-

The Allenway

A unique blend of lush contemporary living with distinctive office suites, the Allenway was developed in 1969 by John E. Sroka. The award-winning design features an atrium with skylights, sculptured fountain, and exotic plants.

American Philatelic Society

Founded in 1886, the American Philatelic Society came to State College in 1945. Today we serve 57,000 stamp collectors in more than 100 countries from the American Philatelic Building, 100 Oakwood Avenue.

Associated Realty Property Management

Rents State College!

Founded in 1978
456 East Beaver Avenue

Founded in 1973, Filmspace, Inc., has been located at 615 Clay Lane since 1975. Principals Marilyn Mitchell and Tom Keiter produce award-winning visual communications for corporate image, education, and fund raising. National clientele includes Schering Plough, Penn State, Rensselaer, Merck, and SmithKline.

Auman's Key Shop

"Key" may be the store's middle name, but Auman's is much more than that. Since 1975, the shop's professional locksmiths have been installing locks and hardware, card access systems, high security systems, and much more. Serving industries, businesses, and residences, Bob Auman and his staff provide fast while-you-wait key service at the shop in the Westerly Parkway Plaza.

Balfurd Cleaners

State College was only thirty-one years old in 1927 when Nathan Balfurd opened a clothing-pressing shop in what is now Zeno's. Today located along West Beaver Avenue, Balfurd Cleaners is run by Scott and Bob Fogelsanger, and provides dry-cleaning services, shirt laundry, and mat and industrial-uniform rentals.

Central Penn Printing Co.

Central Penn Printing Co. has been making businesses look better on paper since 1974, when Dean Dreibelbis started the company on North Atherton Street. Today, located at 1470 Martin Street, the business employs six and specializes in precision single and multiple color printing — from letterhead and invitations to brochures and business forms.

Centre Area Transportation Authority

CATA has helped people get around the area for more than twenty years. Today carrying some 1.9 million passengers a year, CATA offers eleven regional routes along with a variety of special shuttle services for events like the Central Pennsylvania Festival of the Arts and all Penn State home football games.

Centre County Memorial Park

A cemetery is a history of people — a perpetual record of yesterday and a sanctuary of peace and quiet today. Since 1942, Centre County Memorial Park has provided area families with the finest interment facilities, services, and merchandise.

The area's largest and oldest independently owned and operated travel agency has been serving Central Pennsylvania since 1966. In 1970, Kay Rogers became owner/manager of the company. Our qualified and experienced travel consultants provide a complete range of domestic and international travel services.

Claster's Building Materials

From humble beginnings as a coal-delivery business in 1901, Claster's has grown to include eleven retail stores in Central Pennsylvania. Our State College store opened on Sparks Street in 1935, then moved to the present Benner Pike location in 1961. The Claster's wagon symbolizes our commitment to old-fashioned quality service.

Dix Honda

In 1955, George Dix came to State College to sell Cadillacs. Today his son David, along with twenty other employees, including David's son Jason, operates Dix Honda at 1400 North Atherton Street. Dix Honda is proud to offer quality automobiles, courteous salespeople, and professional service to the community.

Dunaway, Weyandt, McCormick, Gerace & McGlaughlin
Attorneys at Law

In 1945, Wayland F. Dunaway III entered law practice in State College. The present partnership began in 1969 and includes attorneys Charles J. Weyandt, Reed McCormick, Anthony Gerace, Ronald McGlaughlin, and Michael Eggert. The firm provides individual, commercial, and municipal clients a variety of services from its office at 919 University Drive.

Eisenstein & Bower
Attorneys and Counsellors at Law

Founded in 1979 by Jeffrey M. Bower and Virginia B. Eisenstein, the firm has a general civil practice emphasizing business law, real estate, media law, wills and estates, family law, and municipal law.

403 South Allen Street, Suite 210 • 234-2626

John C. Haas Associates Inc.
Architects Engineers Planners

The firm of John C. Haas, AIA, Architect, was first organized in 1972. Eight years later, the company relocated into its own office building at 1301 North Atherton Street. A 1986 merger with the firm of Robert DePuy Davis, Structural Engineer, created the current organization of John C. Haas Associates Inc., Architects Engineers Planners.

Eloise B. Kyper Funeral Home, Inc.

Established in 1991, Eloise B. Kyper Funeral Home is a full-service funeral home where you can pre-plan your needs. We are building a tradition of trust, comfort, and understanding. Our goal is perfection in every detail.

Lee, Martin, Green & Reiter, Inc.

Our law firm has been serving the community since 1937. Originally located in Bellefonte's Heverly Building, the firm now has offices on High Street and in State College on Walker Drive, where attorneys Donald Lee, Robert Martin, Joseph Green, Dennis Reiter, Robert Mix, and William Fleming provide expert legal services.

Lush Brothers

In 1893, Henry W. Lush started a home-furnishings store in Galeton. Ninety years later, in 1983, his great-grandson Sam came to State College and opened a furniture store in the historic Klinger Farms barn. Lush Brothers is proud to have offered quality home furnishings to Central Pennsylvania for over 102 years.

Microdata Systems, Inc., has been assisting companies nationwide with business administrative services since 1970. From business consulting, general ledger/profit and loss statements, and billings to payroll check processing/employee reports, W-2s and benefits tracking, we help businesses operate more efficiently and profitably.

The Nittany Quill

Joy and Keith Rodgers-Mernin founded the Nittany Quill in 1984 in the basement of 100 South Fraser Street. Today the elegant shop at 111-115 South Fraser Street offers a wonderful selection of stationery, fine pens, calligraphic quotes and poems, and many unique gifts.

Rest & Repast   (814) 238-1484
Bed & Breakfast Reservations

On April 1, 1985, State College Borough Council passed an ordinance permitting bed and breakfast lodging as a home occupation for borough residents. Rest & Repast was responsible for initiating that proposal, and today is proud to offer more than fifty inspected properties in the borough and across Central Pennsylvania.

John F. Robison, D.M.D.

A third-generation dentist, John Robison is following in the footsteps of his father, D. Ronald L. Robison, and grandfather, Fred A. Robison, one of State College's first dentists and the town's fifth burgess. Dr. John Robison provides general dentistry from his office at 237 South Allen Street.

Shinham, Leoniak, Bair & Company
Certified Public Accountants

Founded in 1981, our firm advises privately owned and emerging businesses, and nonprofit and governmental entities utilizing the CFO Source, our rental CFO/Controller program. Our clients' business and personal financial success is our primary focus.

Taricani Associates

Taricani Associates is a certified public accounting firm founded in 1964 by Joseph F. Taricani. Located on Beaver Avenue, the firm is now managed by Tom Taricani and specializes in tax, financial, and estate planning for individuals and small businesses.

Known before 1974 as Keelers, the University Book Centre offers textbooks, general reading books, supplies, and Penn State imprinted items to students, faculty, townspeople, and visitors. Providing quality products at competitive prices is a tradition at UBC.

King Printing

Providing quality printing and copying to the State College community since 1978.

1305 West College Avenue • State College
238-2536

For more than thirty years, State College residents have turned to WRSC each day for news, sports, weather, and information. 97-QWK Rock, launched in 1969, has provided rock music for a generation of baby-boomers.

Since its opening in 1988, Heritage Realty has helped individuals and families find the perfect residence. The business has departments in Sales, Leasing, Farm and Land, Property Management, and Appraisals.

RITCHEY COX & ASSOCIATES

Certified Public Accountants
315 South Allen Street
Suite 416
State College, PA 16801
814-238-5555

Ethel Meserve GIFTS

Ethel Meserve and her employees were proud to offer exclusive gifts from locations on West College Avenue, then Allen Street, for forty-eight years.

RINALDO'S BARBER SHOP

Founded by George Smith in 1924, purchased by Dick Di Rinaldo in 1953, and owned by Wayne Britten since 1987, Rinaldo's is proud to be State College's oldest barber shop.

PORTER BROTHERS

Porter & Weber was founded in 1913 on South Fraser Street by Leroy Porter and Fred Weber, and renamed Porter Brothers in 1952. In 1977, the paint and wallpaper business was re-established by P. David Porter and John Porter at Corl Street and College Avenue. It is the headquarters for Pratt and Lambert paints.

O.W. HOUTS & SON, INC.

Founded in 1920 as Houts Lumber Company, O.W. Houts & Son remains a State College landmark — the largest locally owned retail store in Centre County, with everything to "build, furnish, and maintain" your home.

RICHARD M. MADORE, D.D.S.

Charles Morgan established a dental practice on College Avenue in 1927, and moved to the current location on Beaver and Allen five years later. Dr. Morgan's nephews, Dr. Dick Barrickman and Dr. Bill Barrickman, entered the practice in 1955 and 1958, respectively. In 1986, Dr. Morgan's grandson, Dr. Richard Morgan Madore, acquired the practice and today provides general dentistry services.

Pennsylvania
BUSINESS
CENTRAL
Central Pennsylvania's BUSINESS newspaper

Serving the community with the best in business news and information.

2011-201 Cato Avenue • State College • 867-2222

DISTRICT OFFICE,
STATE REPRESENTATIVE
LYNN HERMAN

Opened in 1983, Representative Herman's office provides state-related constituent and legislative services to area residents. These include obtaining copies of birth certificates and state publications, solving vehicle-registration and driver's license problems, and more.

PAID FOR BY CITIZENS FOR LYNN HERMAN COMMITTEE

215

Acknowledgements

BIBLIOGRAPHY:

Bellefonte Republican, The

Bezilla, Michael, *Penn State: an illustrated history*, The Pennsylvania State University Press, University Park and London, 1985.

Centre Daily Times and its predecessor, *State College Times*

Centre Democrat, The

Collegian, The Daily

Democratic Watchman, The

Dunaway, Wayland F., *History of The Pennsylvania State College*, Lancaster, PA, 1946.

EXTRA! The War Years, As recorded in the pages of the Centre Daily Times, 1939-1945, Historical Briefs, Inc., 1992.

Ferree, Walter Lincoln, Penn State master's thesis, "An Introduction to the History of State College, Pennsylvania," 1932.

Froth magazine

Gruver, Robert, *A Field Trip to Visit and Recount the Significance of the Iron Industries to Centre County Development*, Centre County Historical Society, 1991.

Hays, Jo, and Margaret Riley, *The Public Schools of the State College Area: A History, The First Forty-Four Years, 1896-1940*, 1983.

Hench, Vivian Doty, *The History of State College, 1896-1946*, Centre Daily Times, State College, PA, 1948.

Keystone Weekly Gazette

La Vie

Lean, Garth, *On the Tail of a Comet: The Life of Frank Buchman*, Colorado Springs, CO, 1988.

Lemon, The, 1906-08 and 1959.

Linn, John Blair, *History of Centre and Clinton Counties, Pennsylvania*, 1883, Centre County Historical Society, Bicentennial Edition, Reprinted 1975.

Maroon and Gray

Mitchell, J. Thomas, *Centre County, from its earliest settlement to the year 1915*, 1915.

Penn State Alumni News and *The Penn Stater* magazine, Penn State Alumni Association, University Park, PA.

Penn State Source Book, University Park, PA, 1990.

Reber, Louis E., *Recollections of The Pennsylvania State College, 1876-1907*, c. 1944.

State College Borough Council minutes and scrapbooks

State College Chamber of Commerce, *Our Town*, 1925.

State College Pennsylvania ConSurvey Directory, Mullin-Kille Company and Centre Daily Times, 1943.

Stevens, Sylvester K., and Philip S. Klein, *The Centre Furnace Story, A Return to Our Roots*, Centre County Historical Society, State College, PA, 1985.

Stevens, Sylvester K., Penn State master's thesis, "Centre Furnace, a Chapter in the History of Juniata Iron," 1927.

Town & Gown magazines, The Barash Group, State College, PA, 1966-1995

Excerpts and information from articles by:

Mike Aquilina

Elizabeth Ball

Betty Bechtel

Jo Chesworth

Terry Dunkle

Nancy Folkenroth

Horton "Budd" Knoll

Erik Kopp

C.O. Williams and Jo Hays, "Towne Talkies," edited transcripts of interviews about life in the State College area before 1920, from the Schlow Memorial Library's Oral History Project, 1970s.

PERSONAL INTERVIEWS, 1992-95:

Milton "Mickey" Bergstein

Mr. and Mrs. Hal Byers Sr.

Madeline Campbell

Hope Jeffries Coder

Allen Crabtree

Phyllis Watkins Crabtree

George Fleming

Margaret Hoy Hoenstine

Louise Homan Horner

Charles L. Hosler

Bob Houts

H. Richard Ishler, M.D.

Mary Jane Ishler

Sara Stringer Jeffries

Jack Light, M.D.

Betty Light

Helen McCord

Milton S. "Mickey" McDowell Jr.

Don Meyer

Jim Meyer

Justus (Jut) Neidigh

Elmer Queer

Virginia Dale Ricker

D. Ronald L. Robison, DDS

Patricia Lamade Robison

Steve Schlow

Robert Y. Sigworth

Grace Antes Strong

Norman Taylor

Ruth Balthaser Torrance

Carl Volz Jr.

Helen Breon Volz

Don Watkins

Bill Welch

OTHERS WHO HELPED:

Arnold Addison, *Centennial Commission Chair*
Doug Albert
Paul Bender
Michael Bezilla
Phyllis Deal Bierly
Millie Bubash
Maria Capparelli
Centre Region Code Administration (Harry Burd)
Centre Region COG Office (Jim Steff, D. J. Liggett,
    Kathy Prosek)
Centre Regional Planning Office (Bob Bini, Cliff Warner)
Centre Region Parks and Recreation Office (Bob Ayer)
Tom Chesworth
Michael Chesworth
Joanne Holben Chuckran
John Dittmar
Don Dorneman
Frances Gibbons Farrell
Patricia Farrell
Sidney Friedman
Lurene Frantz, *Centennial Commission Director*
Dick Fye
Susan Godje
Don Heebner
Frances Harpster Homan
Sally Horn
Ken Hosterman
Marnie Forbes Hoy
Emilie Westgard Jansma
Ted Kemmerer Jr.
Fred Kissinger
Sara Krumrine
Jim Langton
Ethel Leach
Gene Lederer
Don Lee
Jackie Melander
Fred Metzger Jr. & Fred Metzger Sr.
Gary Moyer
Bernadette Myers
Penn State Student Interns
    Stephanie Ambro
    Cynthia Bent
    Debbie McDougall
    Angela Pomponio
    Jennifer Ryan
    Valerie Sciotto
    Amy Terrill
    Courtnie Willard
Penn State University Archives staff
    Leon Stout, *Archivist*
    Jackie Esposito
    Alston Turchetta
    Michelle Dzyak
Nick Petnick
Sue Reighard, *indexer*
Eugene Reilly
Rufus "Boots" Ripka
Jean Taylor Ritenour
Ron Ross
Les Shaw

Betty Berardis Shaw
John & Lew Sheckler & Sheckler Photographics
Jim Shigley
Jim Shuey
Hilda Lonberger Snyder
State College Area School District Personnel Office
State College Borough Administrative Offices
    Barbara Natalie
    Ernie Dabiero
    Ron Davis
State College Borough Finance Office (Mike Groff)
State College Borough Planning Office (Carl Hess)
State College Borough Public Works/Engineers' Office
    (Lee Lowry, et al)
State College Centennial Collection Donors
Dan Stearns
Bob Struble
John Thomchick
George Van Sant
Virginia Keeler Smith
Donn Wagner
Tom Wallace
John Weber
Barbara Struck West
Edward West
Elwood Williams Jr.
James N. Williams
Walter Wise
Scott Yocum
Harold Zipser

THE BARASH GROUP:

Mimi U. Coppersmith Fredman, *president*
Ron Shroyer, *creative director*
Chip Mock, *art director*
Whit Yeagley, *editor*
Michael Poorman, *managing editor*
Erik Kopp, *editorial/advertising coordinator*
Liz Ball, *editorial consultant*
Anne Angelelli
Jim Colbert
Amy J. Dawson
Edna Dombrowsky
Robynn Duck
Nancy Folkenroth
Ginny Gilbert
Dick Hall
Robert W. Henninger
Michelle Jordan
Lynne Mannino
David Miller
Tony Moscatello
Brian Ray
Gary Reid
Joanne Steranko
Ted Swanson
Carl Von Wodtke
Lois Wolfe

CENTENNIAL BOOK COMMITTEE:

John A. Brutzman
Anita Genger
Nadine Kofman
Carolyn Clinefelter Smith

Index

221